The Official RED BOOK®

A GUIDE BOOK OF
BUFFALO AND
JEFFERSON
NICKELS

Complete Source for History, Grading, and Values

Q. David Bowers

Foreword by
Bill Fivaz

Valuations editor
Lawrence Stack

Whitman
Publishing, LLC
PUBLISHING SINCE 1934

www.whitman**books**.com

© 2007 by Whitman Publishing, LLC
3101 Clairmont Road, Suite C, Atlanta, GA 30329

The WCG™ pricing grid used throughout this publication is patent pending. THE OFFICIAL RED BOOK is a trademark of Whitman Publishing, LLC.

Correspondence concerning this book may be directed to the publisher, at the address above.

ISBN: 079482008-5

Printed in China

Disclaimer: Expert opinion should be sought in any significant numismatic purchase. This book is presented as a guide only. No warranty or representation of any kind is made concerning the completeness of the information presented. The author, a professional numismatist, regularly buys, sells, conducts auctions, and sometimes holds certain of the items discussed in this book.

Caveat: The price estimates given are subject to variation and differences of opinion. Before making decisions to buy or sell, consult the latest information. For certain issues that are normally found with areas of light striking, well-struck coins may command significantly higher prices. Past performance of the rare coin market or any coin or series within that market is not necessarily an indication of future performance, as the future is unknown. Such factors as changing demand, popularity, grading interpretations, strength of the overall coin market, and economic conditions will continue to be influences.

Advertisements within this book: Whitman Publishing, LLC, does not endorse, warrant, or guarantee any of the products or services of its advertisers. All warranties and guarantees are the sole responsibility of the advertiser.

The Official RED BOOK® Series includes:

- *A Guide Book of Morgan Silver Dollars*
- *A Guide Book of Double Eagle Gold Coins*
- *A Guide Book of United States Type Coins*
- *A Guide Book of Modern United States Proof Coin Sets*
- *A Guide Book of Shield and Liberty Head Nickels*
- *A Guide Book of Flying Eagle and Indian Head Cents*
- *A Guide Book of Washington and State Quarters*
- *A Guide Book of United States Commemorative Coins*
- *A Guide Book of United States Barber Silver Coins*
- *A Guide Book of United States Liberty Seated Silver Coins*

ABOUT THE AUTHOR

Q. David Bowers, of American Numismatic Rarities, LLC (Wolfeboro, New Hampshire), has been in the rare coin business since he was a teenager in 1953. He also serves as writer and numismatic director for Whitman Publishing, LLC.

Bowers is a recipient of the Pennsylvania State University College of Business Administration's Alumni Achievement Award (1976); he has served as president of the American Numismatic Association (1983–1985) and president of the Professional Numismatists Guild (1977–1979); he is a recipient of the highest honor bestowed by the ANA (the Farran Zerbe Award); he was the first ANA member to be named Numismatist of the Year (1995); and in 2005 he was given the Lifetime Achievement Award. He has been inducted into the ANA Numismatic Hall of Fame, today being one of just 12 living recipients with that distinction. Bowers was given the highest honor awarded by the Professional Numismatists Guild (The Founders' Award) and has received more "Book of the Year Award" and "Best Columnist" honors given by the Numismatic Literary Guild than has any other writer. In 2000 he was the first annual recipient of the Burnett Anderson Memorial Award for writing. In July 1999, Bowers, along with just 17 other numismatists, was recognized in the "Numismatists of the Century" poll by Ed Reiter (*COINage*). He has written more than 50 books, hundreds of auction and other catalogs, and several thousand articles, including columns in *Coin World* (now the longest-running by any author in numismatic history), *Paper Money*, and, in past years, *The Numismatist*.

The writer of the foreword, William F. Fivaz, was born in 1934, discovered numismatics in 1950, and has been a collector ever since. He joined the ANA in 1959, and in time became a popular instructor at the Summer Seminar. A two-time recipient of the Medal of Merit, he also served on the board of governors. A familiar figure at shows and conventions, Bill has presented many programs and educational forums. Over the years he has discovered or verified a number of overdates and major varieties that are now listed in standard references. He is often consulted about minting procedures, authenticity, and technical aspects of numismatics. The author of many numismatic articles, he is best known today for his book the essential *Cherrypickers' Guide to Rare Die Varieties* (written with J.T. Stanton), which has sold tens of thousands of copies through several editions. His most recent book is the *United States Gold Counterfeit Detection Guide*.

About Values, Population Reports, and Estimates

Values and population reports: Valuations editor Lawrence Stack has provided the estimated market prices at the time of compilation (summer 2005), using information available from multiple sources. Actual transactions may take place at higher or lower figures. The population reports are the combined figures from ANACS, the Numismatic Guaranty Corporation of America (NGC), and the Professional Coin Grading Service (PCGS). Many figures are apt to increase as new coins are presented and previously certified examples are resubmitted. A population-report figure may or may not reflect the actual rarity of a coin and should be used very carefully as an aid to determining value. Only a tiny fraction of existing common, modern, and low-value coins have ever been—or are likely ever to be—certified. Well-worn Buffalo and Jefferson nickels of common dates exist in large numbers, but few have ever been certified!

Field populations: The author has provided estimates—very broad estimates in some cases—for the number of coins surviving today in circulated grades, Mint State, and Proof, as appropriate, for various issues. Actual information is difficult or impossible to find in most instances. Estimates are most reliable for Proofs of known mintage, as these were sold at a premium to buyers who, for the most part, kept them. Descriptors such as *very common, in the millions,* and so on are used for modern issues and certain others that exist in huge quantities, either from original production numbers or from their ongoing production today.

CREDITS AND ACKNOWLEDGMENTS

The author expresses appreciation to the following for help in the ways indicated. Included are some of the finest people and institutions active in numismatics today.

ANACS population data have been studied and cited. **Wynn Bowers** reviewed the text. **Roger W. Burdette** read the manuscript and furnished ideas and historical information. *Coin World* (Beth Deisher, editor) granted permission to use information, including a transcript of a presentation by Jefferson nickel designer Felix O. Schlag. **Darrell Crane,** president of the Full Step Nickel Club and publisher of the *Portico,* made information available for use. **Charles Daughtrey** provided the portrait of James Earle Fraser. **Gloria Eskridge** provided sketches of proposed nickel designs. **Dr. Michael S. Fey** and **Danny Fey** provided illustrations of certain die varieties. **Bill Fivaz** helped in many ways, including writing the foreword and sharing his thoughts concerning die varieties across the denomination and points to observe on Buffalo nickels. **Krystal Fontaine** assisted with research in 19th- and 20th-century numismatic publications. **Full Step Nickel Club** provided useful information from its publications and web site. **Mark Hooten** read the manuscript and offered advice, valuations, and suggestions. **Katherine Jaeger** read the manuscript and made valuable suggestions. **Jenna King** sorted thousands of photographs and arranged them for study. **David Lange,** numismatic expert and author at NGC, shared comments and research and has been frequently cited in the present text. **Tom Mulvaney** provided many of the photographs. **Bernard Nagengast** shared extensive information concerning Jefferson nickels, details of sharpness by variety, and more. The 5 Full Steps (5FS) and 6 Full Steps (6FS) information is largely from his authoritative study, *The Jefferson Nickel Analyst.* *Numismatic News* has been a valuable source of current and historical information. *The Numismatist,* in recent times simply called *Numismatist,* has been a valuable source of current and historical information. **Donn Pearlman** provided photographs of a U.S. Mint ceremony for new nickel designs, 2005. **Ron Pope** studied tens of thousands of photographs of Buffalo nickels to determine degrees of sharpness in design details, and shared his findings for this study. **PCGS** (Professional Coin Grading Service) population data have been studied and cited. **Scott Schechter** of the Numismatic Guaranty Corporation of America provided many images of nickels for study for sharpness and other characteristics. **The Smithsonian Institution,** Dr. Richard Doty and James Hughes, provided access to pattern coins and helped in other ways. **David Sundman** provided information on field populations. **Saul Teichman** provided information on pattern nickels. **The United States Mint** generously provided information, original artists' sketches, and other data relating to five-cent pieces, with emphasis on the new designs that commenced in 2004. **Robert Van Ryzin** provided information concerning the background of the portrait and bison on the Indian Head / Buffalo nickel. **Frank Van Valen** reviewed the text and helped with research. **Fred Weinberg** provided Mint errors for study and photography and contributed much to appendix B. **Robin Wells** reviewed the text. **Gordon Yoder** loaned information and memorabilia relating to Jefferson nickel designer Felix O. Schlag. The selected bibliography gives other valuable sources, as do the notes. All photographs are of actual coins (not composites made by using the obverses and reverses of different specimens). This is especially important for appendix A, a study of patterns. Certain historical, numismatic, and archival information and illustrations are used on a nonexclusive basis by special arrangement with the author.

Contents

FOREWORD

B uffalo nickels and Jefferson nickels—what a duo! The Buffalo nickel is the classic All-American Coin, with the effigy of an impressive American Indian filling the entire obverse and a representation of a plains buffalo or bison across the reverse. Sculptor-designer James Earle Fraser had both a profound interest in western themes, having grown up on the northern plains of the Midwest, and a special concern for the plight of the dwindling herds of American bison. The bold obverse and reverse designs still draw a dramatic collector following for this series, and specimens in all grades are eagerly sought.

Dave Bowers presents us with the complete Buffalo nickel story, from Fraser's initial concept, through the difficult teens and twenties when strike was a serious problem for branch-mint issues, right up to the final Denver strikings in 1938.

This series has two major rarities, the 1916-P Doubled Die Obverse and the 1918/7-D Overdate, each of which is covered in detail by the author. Both are prohibitively rare in Mint state, the 1916 Doubled Die exceptionally so. Worn dies and dies that had become eroded because of extended use permeate most mintmarked coins from 1918 through 1928, making these issues a challenge to locate in choice, well-struck condition. The following pages will lead the reader through all of these complexities and will provide comprehensive insight into this very popular series.

Felix Schlag's Jefferson nickel, first minted in 1938, is a fascinating series for many reasons. There are no "stoppers" (dates that are extraordinarily expensive), making it a very affordable set, even in Mint State. It is, in my opinion, the perfect set for young numismatists, beginning collectors, or even advanced variety enthusiasts to collect. For the collector concerned with the strike factor in the grading equation, the Jefferson nickel is a classic coin. The six steps on the Monticello building on the reverse are the last portion of the design to strike up, and few dates with six complete steps are known. Because of this, for a long time a 5FS nickel was considered by some to be a "full step" coin. Today, 6FS is becoming the goal for many. Bowers explains why this is a problem and indicates in his date-by-date analysis those that are particularly difficult to locate.

Varieties run rampant through the Jefferson issues, with an overdate (1943/2-P), several overmintmarks (1949-D/S, 1954-S/D, 1955-D/S), and a host of major doubled dies. The two most valuable varieties in Mint state are the 1942-D / Horizontal D and the 1946-D / Inverted D.

This is a series in which a collector can "name his poison," choosing any of the following: collecting strictly by date and mintmark in either circulated or Mint State condition; assembling a set whose specimens are all in Mint State with Full Steps; or collecting all the major varieties. Whichever road you take, I guarantee you'll have fun with this series!

If you have even the slightest interest in Buffalo or Jefferson nickels, this book by Dave Bowers is an absolute MUST!

Bill Fivaz

INTRODUCTION

I t seems like only yesterday, but it was the early 1950s when, as a teenager, I collected a complete set of dates and mintmarks of Buffalo nickels from circulation. Most of the early ones had the dates worn nearly smooth. This was the time when low-mintage dates that were hard to find in pocket change were considered key issues, while no one paid much attention to varieties that were rare in high grade, but otherwise plentiful. Nearly all dates and mintmarks from 1927 onward were available in Mint State in bank-wrapped rolls. Most of the 1930s were also plentiful in this form, especially the 1938-D. In the marketplace, the rarest single coin among the regular issues was the 1913-S Type II Buffalo. I should say at the outset that what collectors everywhere call *Buffalo* nickels actually depict a *bison*, a different zoological species. The proper name might be Indian Head nickel, but few know the coins by that term. Perhaps Indian Head / Buffalo nickel, as used frequently in the present text, is a good compromise, otherwise Buffalo nickel it is.

In the early 1950s, everyone talked about the recently minted low-mintage 1950-D Jefferson nickels, certainly one of the greatest sensations of the rare coin market. Rolls and bags of 1950-D nickels were common, but they were hard to pry loose from their owners because it seemed that every time a new issue of the *Numismatic Scrapbook Magazine* came out, the price reached a new high level. Having a little stash of these was like owning an oil well; the situation was positively *electric*, and is somewhat difficult to translate into words today. You had to be there!

When I entered the rare coin profession in 1953, about a year after becoming a collector, Jefferson nickels were commonly traded in rolls, beginning with the first year, 1938. The rarest roll was 1939-D. To me, 1942-D seemed to be rare in bank-wrapped roll form, but no one else ever said much about it. Five-cent pieces were being cranked out each year at the Philadelphia, Denver, and San Francisco Mints, and it was a popular pastime to keep sets updated by adding three coins each year to a Whitman folder, "National" page, or "Popular" album, the last having attached green covers. Most advanced numismatists used National pages for Buffalo nickels. These came in two sizes and fit into ring binders. Because Jeffersons were not considered valuable, it was popular to keep them in the aforementioned Whitman folders, which seemed to be available just about anywhere hobby supplies were sold.

I was fascinated with a particular variety known as the 1939 Doubled MONTI-CELLO nickel and recall interviewing its primary advocate, Malcolm O. E. Chell-Frost, about its importance—this was in the late 1950s, and I was in the company of my friend Ken Rendell. I found Chell-Frost in a small and rather sparsely stocked office in a high-rise building in downtown Boston. This sort of face-to-face research came about for several coins after I read about them in old issues of the *Numismatic Scrapbook Magazine* or the *Numismatist* and endeavored to learn more.

This was an era before the existence of *Coin World*, with its focal-point "Collectors' Clearinghouse" column treating unusual varieties. Frank Spadone, a New Jersey dealer, had not yet published his *Major Variety and Oddity Guide* (1963); Bill Fivaz, who would become brilliant in the field of unusual die varieties, would not be heard from until the 1970s and *Walter Breen's Complete Encyclopedia of U.S. and Colonial Coins*, so essential today, was not published until 1988. It is amazing to contemplate the many specialists who have become prominent in the past quarter century studying doubled dies, repunched mint-marks, mint errors, and other items of interest. In recent years, the availability of inexpensive cameras capable of taking close-ups and the increasing use of the Internet as a communications tool have put the appreciation of such things in the fast lane. It is remarkable how quickly and effectively information and illustrations can be shared today.

I have studied Buffalo nickels throughout my business career and have consistently found the differences in striking sharpness to be extraordinary. I have often wondered why so few people are interested in this aspect. The 1926-D in particular nearly always has mushy details and is as flat as a pancake. This was the only mintmarked Buffalo nickel of the 1920s (before 1927) to appear by the roll, although rolls of 1921 nickels would also occasionally show up—and would be especially brilliant and lustrous. Today it would be unusual to see two or three single Mint State 1926-D nickels in the same place. For reasons I do not understand, 1926-D nickels with decent sharpness are now frequently available on the market. I wonder where they all came from. Similarly, in the 1950s at least virtually all of the 1937-D 3 Legs nickels on the market showed evidence of circulation. I might see an Uncirculated (the term *Mint State* was not used) once a year, if indeed that often. Now, such high-grade coins seem to exist in fair numbers. Again, this remains a minor mystery.

What I thought was a sensational discovery, the first overmintmark in American numismatics, came my way in 1962. Two numismatists from upstate New York, Robert Kerr and C.G. Langworthy, had found an oddity—a 1938-D Buffalo nickel that, under magnification, seemed to have an S mintmark as well. They contacted *Coin World*, then in its second year of publication and without an in-house expert. The editor got in touch with me and asked if I would view this most curious specimen and, if authentic, write about it, which I did. Then the floodgates opened and other overmintmarks surfaced, including several in the Jefferson nickel series. Later, while leafing through the November 1928 issue of the *Numismatist*, I came across an item submitted by Kansas collector Will W. Neil, who had in his possession a strange 1900-O dollar, and whose commentary included this: "Upon closer examination of the mintmark it has the appearance of the O having been punched in over the letters CC." I realized then that credit for the first overmintmark belonged to Neil, not to Kerr and Langworthy.

Then came a deluge of newly discovered varieties, ranging from trivial to remarkable, as more and more numismatists took out their magnifying glasses and microscopes and checked the dates and mintmarks of pieces in their collections. Today we have several different overmintmarks in the Jefferson nickel series, each obvious even under low magnification. It is amazing that these were completely unknown to earlier generations of numismatists. Since the 1960s, the "Collector's Clearinghouse" column in *Coin World* has served as the focal point for announcing new discoveries.

Jefferson nickels were popular years ago, probably even more than they are today. Most were acquired matter-of-factly as Uncirculated coins taken from rolls. Few collectors paid much attention to the sharpness of the striking. In fact, I listened to or participated in many 1950-D nickel discussions in the 1950s and early 1960s and never heard anyone mention how sharply the coins were struck, or whether one was "choice" and another a "gem." An Uncirculated 1950-D nickel was an Uncirculated 1950-D nickel, nothing more, nothing less.

Slowly, the aspect of sharp strike began to be considered. Someone discerned that the strike quality of a Jefferson nickel could be determined simply by counting the steps on the portico of the Monticello building on the reverse. If all six steps were visible, or even just five, the coin was of special quality. This finding sent interest soaring in the 1970s, especially after several specialists organized the PAK Full Step Nickel Club in 1977. From that point interest climbed onward and upward, culminating in the dynamic Full Step Nickel Club and its *Portico* newsletter enjoyed by so many today.

Today, the leading grading services are certifying Jefferson nickels by their step counts. It is rather curious, though, that scarcely anyone cares whether Buffalo nickels are sharply struck. I suspect this will change, but for now that is how it is. I see it as a great advantage for anyone seeking to build a collection of Buffaloes: acres of numismatic diamonds are at your feet, waiting to be picked up! I devote quite a bit of space to comments about this fact that you can use to profit in the marketplace.

Writing this book has been a great pleasure. It has stirred many fine memories and has brought me up to date on current market activity. The project has also given me the opportunity to review and study the great wealth of information—old and new—now available on nickel characteristics and die varieties.

The story of nickels continues. It is said that someone in the early 19th century suggested the United States Patent Office be closed because everything useful had already been invented. Similarly, when *Coin World* was launched in April 1960, most writers and researchers of my acquaintance generally agreed that most of the important varieties had already been discovered, and that anything new would only be minor items. Wrong! Probably 90% of the coins illustrated in the Fivaz-Stanton *Cherrypickers' Guide to Rare Die Varieties* were not known in 1960.

The denomination is in the news more today than ever before, especially now that the Mint is putting out the Westward Journey series. This book is your passport to the five-cent pieces of the past, a denomination that at first glance seems to be a simple string of dates and mintmarks, but which upon close inspection yields as many interesting varieties and collecting challenges as any coins of the past century. Capture the nuances of this series, and you will find a new dimension of numismatic fun.

Q. David Bowers
Wolfeboro, NH

JAMES EARLE FRASER

James Earle Fraser
Designer of the Indian Head / Buffalo Nickel

Portrait by Charles Daughtrey

CHAPTER ONE

THE STORY OF THE NICKEL—
BEFORE THE BUFFALOES

A NEW DENOMINATION

The Act of May 16, 1866, created the nickel five-cent piece, providing in Section 1:

> That, so soon as practicable after the passage of this act, there shall be coined at the Mint of the United States a five-cent piece composed of copper and nickel, in such proportions, not exceeding twenty-five per centum of nickel, as shall be determined by the Director of the Mint, the standard weight of which shall be seventy-seven and sixteen hundredths grains, with no greater deviation than two grains to each piece; and the shape, mottoes and devices of said coin shall be determined by the Director of the Mint, with the approval of the Secretary of the Treasury; and the laws now in force relating to the coinage of cents, and providing for the purchase of material, and prescribing the appropriate duties of the officers of the Mint and the Secretary of the Treasury, be, and the same are hereby, extended to the coinage herein provided for.

The American monetary system was chaotic at the time. Silver and gold coins, which had been hoarded by the public since 1862, had not yet returned to circulation, and the highest denomination in use was the new (as of 1865) nickel three-cent piece. Larger transactions were typically conducted with Fractional Currency notes, in denominations up to 50¢, and larger paper money, including Legal Tender and National Bank notes. Silver coins did not appear in quantity in the channels of commerce until after April 20, 1876, and gold coins did not return until late December 1878. In the meantime, the nickel five-cent piece was the dominant coin of the realm—as curious as this seems today.

While there were no silver and gold coins in the East and Midwest, California and other West Coast areas had a different monetary system. In reaction to the unpleasant memories held by Forty-Niners and others of failed banks in the East, the California State Legislature had made paper money *illegal* under the Constitution of 1850. While the rest of the country used Demand Notes, first issued by the federal government in 1861 and followed by Legal Tender and other issues, silver and gold coins were used in California. Anyone wanting to exchange paper money for a $20 gold double eagle had to pay a stiff premium to do so. The discount on federal paper money in California was equal to the premium citizens in the East had to pay for gold coins available from exchange brokers and banks.

Nomenclature: In text, quoted and original, *denticle*, for toothlike projection on the inside rim of a coin adjacent to the field, has been changed to *dentil*. Instead of *business strike*, referring to a coin made for circulation, *circulation strike* is used.

Proof is capitalized in numismatic usage, as are grades such as *Mint State*, *Very Fine*, etc. The term *Full Details* is capitalized, as is *Full Steps*, similar to Full Head, Full Bands, etc., being capitalized in other series.

Minor typographical errors in quoted text have been corrected, thus avoiding the repeated use of [*sic*]. Minor editing has also been done for clarity. Generally, spelled-out numbers in government reports, such as "fifty-seven thousand and six hundred dollars," are given here as $57,600.

SHIELD NICKELS

Chief Engraver James B. Longacre, who had been at the Philadelphia Mint since 1844, designed the first nickel five-cent pieces. Longacre had already created many new coins, including the 1857 Flying Eagle cent, 1859 Indian Head cent, 1864 bronze two-cent piece (the first circulating coin to bear the motto IN GOD WE TRUST), the 1865 nickel three-cent piece, the gold dollar types of 1849, 1854, and 1856, the $3 gold of 1854, and many patterns.

For the obverse of the new nickel, Longacre used the Union shield, similar to that recently introduced on the two-cent piece, but with different ornamentation. The reverse consisted of the large numeral 5 surrounded by 13 stars. Between each two stars, a ray was inserted, creating what is known today as the *Shield Nickel With Rays* type.

The Shield nickel went into circulation in the summer of 1866 and was an instant success. True to form, both numismatists and the general public offered many criticisms of its appearance. In early 1867 the rays were dropped from the reverse to permit better metal flow during the striking process, but the overall design endured and was used until 1883.

The hardness of the alloy created many difficulties in coining Shield nickels in the early years. Dies often cracked and broke. Punching the dates in the dies was a major challenge for Mint engravers, who often created doubled impressions and other oddities—to the extreme pleasure of numismatists today. More than for any other coinage of its era, Shield nickels offer a playground of collecting delights—a kaleidoscope of intricate and often illogical details.

A basic set of Shield nickels includes the 1866, 1867 With Rays, 1867 Without Rays, one of each later date through 1883, and the 1883/2 overdate. The two rarities

The Shield nickel of 1866 features a Union shield on the obverse, adapted from a motif used on the bronze two-cent piece of 1864. The reverse has the large numeral 5 surrounded with 13 stars and a like number of rays, with inscription around the border.

are the 1877 and 1878, which were made only in Proof format. The estimated mintage for the 1877 is 1,000 to 1,250; the 1878 has a known mintage of 2,350. Because collectors and investors have been focusing on later coins in "ultra" grades, such as MS-68 or higher, and on building Registry Sets (where numbers are all-important, but quality is often overlooked), I believe Shield nickels offer a wonderful opportunity for numismatic challenge and exploration. The current prices of choice and gem Mint State and Proof coins are, for most issues, fractions of what similar pieces sold for in 1990!

High-grade sets are often formed by mixing Mint State coins with Proofs. Each format has its own challenges. Among Mint State nickels, the 1867 With Rays, 1879, 1880, 1881, and 1883/2 are particularly scarce and gems are rare. The 1880 nickel is the Holy Grail of Mint State coins because of confusion generated that year by the Mint's use of Proof dies to make some circulation strikes. This development resulted in many Proofs being sold as gem Mint State, a popular caper that has been going on for a long time.

Among Proof coins, the only major rarity is the 1867 With Rays, of which only several dozen exist. John Dannreuther has discovered that at least three different obverse dies were used to make these coins, most of which are restrikes produced through the 1870s. Interestingly, the 1879 and 1881, which are scarce in Mint State, and the 1880—super-rare if *really* Mint State—are all quite common as Proofs!

Early in 1867 the rays were dropped from the reverse of the Shield nickel, creating the **Without Rays type** that was made continuously until early 1883.

High-quality Shield nickels offer excellent eye appeal, but can be hard to find if you insist on a sharp strike on a good planchet. The nice part is that 90% of buyers only look at the grade label on holders and don't know to inspect for quality. Points to check for sharpness include the horizontal lines and the frame of the shield on the obverse, and the center parts of the stars on the reverse.

I invite you to acquire a copy of my *Guide Book of Shield and Liberty Head Nickels* to learn more. I believe you will be fascinated with both of these designs.

LIBERTY HEAD NICKELS

A new nickel design, the Liberty Head by Chief Engraver Charles E. Barber, made its debut in February 1883. The obverse depicted Miss Liberty as a goddess wearing a tiara, with stars around and the date below. The reverse showed a wreath with inscriptions around. The denomination was marked simply by the Roman number V—logical enough, since the three-cent pieces of the day were identified by III.

However, the Liberty Head nickel was close in size to the $5 gold coins in circulation. Unscrupulous sharpers had gold-plated the new nickels and added reeding to their edges, creating what seemed to be a new design of a five-dollar gold piece. A common ploy was to give one of these coins to a salesperson in payment for a cigar, a piece of candy, or something else costing five cents or less. Often, the sales person would return $4.95 in change. The Treasury Department sent Secret Service operatives (as agents were called) to stop the deception. Some miscreants, when arrested, defended themselves by saying that they had never claimed the golden nickel to be a five-dollar gold coin; the salesperson had just assumed it was and had proffered the change. Nevertheless, the government viewed the gold nickel swindle to be a serious crime, and one San Francisco passer of such coins spent a year in prison for his trouble.

The Mint soon revised the reverse design, eliminating the V and adding the word CENTS. Newspaper reporters, coin dealers, and others spread the word that the Mint had made a terrible mistake, and would be calling in all of the original nickels, after which the coins were certain to be high-priced rarities. Naturally, the public scrambled to find as many as possible. So many were saved that today this is the most common of all Liberty Head nickels in Mint State!

The first Liberty Head nickels of 1883 had the denomination on the reverse expressed simply as the letter V. Unscrupulous people gilded the coins and passed them off as $5 gold pieces. The reverse was soon changed. In the meantime, the public scrambled to save these coins, believing they would become rare and valuable.

The Mint continued to make Liberty Head nickels showing CENTS through 1912. In that year, the Denver and San Francisco Mints each struck this denomination for the first time. After that the curtain came down on

The second type of Liberty Head nickel, with CENTS on the reverse, was minted from spring 1883 onward. Shown here is an 1886, one of the rarest dates, but readily collectible today.

the Liberty Head nickel, and in 1913 the Indian Head/Buffalo nickel took its place.

However, someone at the Mint—possibly numismatist Samuel W. Brown, who was employed there as storekeeper—secretly struck a few Liberty Head nickels with the date 1913. In the autumn of that year, Brown moved to North Tonawanda, New York, where in time he became prominent in the chocolate business, and even served as mayor for a time in the 1930s. In 1920 Brown revealed that he had five 1913 Liberty Head nickels available for sale. There was no numismatic interest at the time, and no buyers came forward. All five were eventually sold to Colonel E. H. R. Green, whose estate later sold them to Eric P. Newman. Finally they were dispersed into the marketplace. Today each is a highly prized rarity.

Except for the unofficial 1913, all Liberty Head nickels are readily collectible today. A complete set includes the 1883 Without CENTS, 1883 With CENTS, one of each date from 1884 through 1911, and three varieties of the last year: 1912, 1912-D, and 1912-S. There are some minor date doublings in this series, but they don't receive much attention—a very different scenario from the die error free-for-all surrounding Shield nickels.

In gem Mint State the rarest is 1886, with 1885 nipping at its heels. The 1912-D and 1912-S are only available as circulation strikes. The 1912-S has the lowest mintage in the series, but it was produced late in the game and enough were saved by numismatists that they are readily available today. In contrast, it could take many months, or even a year or two, to find a gem 1886.

Proofs are available in proportion to their mintage quantities, which for the issues in the 1880s were substantial—averaging several thousand each year. The 1885 and 1886, rare in circulated grades, are among the most plentiful of the Proofs. The lowest-mintage Proof is the 1907, but enough are in floating supply that they are easily found in dealers' stocks or auction offerings.

As with Shield nickels, finding *high-quality* Liberty Head coins can be a challenge. Also like the Shield series, Liberty Head nickels are usually collected as a mix of Mint State and Proof coins. Availability can vary depending on the format. Nevertheless, because most buyers concentrate only on the grading number, insiders who look for quality can usually find it. The points to check first for sharpness on Liberty Head nickels are the star centers and the hair above Miss Liberty's forehead on the obverse, and the kernels in the tiny ear of corn to the left of the ribbon bow on the reverse. Many Liberty Head nickels were made in haste, including Proofs sold to collectors! Liberty Head nickels are fairly plentiful in the marketplace. The 1912-S is the only issue that cannot be found with Full Details (i.e. needle-sharp definition of all design features). If you know what to look for, you can build a sharply struck, beautiful set.

Nickels on the American Scene
Automatic Merchandising

In the 1890s, coin-operated machines began popping up in public places by the tens of thousands. The coin of choice was the nickel, with the Indian Head cent as the runner-up. Aside from gambling devices, few machines used dimes, quarters, or larger coins.

The advantages of vending machines were enormous. Early machines dispensed many kinds of goods, perhaps hitting their stride at the turn of the century with the *automat*, a device pioneered in Germany but popularized in America by Childs, Horn & Hardart, and other restaurateurs.

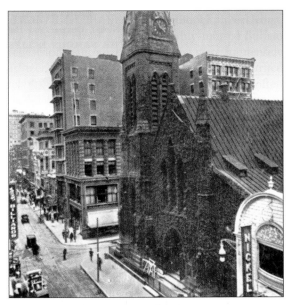

Patrons would put a nickel into a slot, turn a handle, and receive a sandwich or a slice of pie. In the 1950s, a Horn & Hardart located across 57th Street from Stack's, the well-known New York City coin dealer, was a popular place to get a quick lunch. By that time, though, prices had risen, and quarters were more useful than nickels. At the automats, attendants worked continuously behind the scenes, but devices in railroad stations, hotel lobbies, and elsewhere functioned completely automatically, at any hour, without the need for a staff of workers. The owner would come around occasionally to empty the coin box of its nickels and restock the machine.

In Providence, Rhode Island, **the Nickel Theatre** offered entertainment to anyone with a coin in hand.

GOODS AND SERVICES

Until the 1940s, a nickel had a lot of purchasing power. This era included both the Shield and Liberty Head years and the entire lifetime of the Indian Head / Buffalo nickels studied and appreciated in this book. A nickel would buy a glass or bottle of Hires root beer, Coca-Cola, Moxie, or Vin Fiz. Many magazines cost a nickel, and every newsstand, hotel lobby, and saloon had a wide selection of five-cent cigars. Beer cost a nickel a glass in many places. Anyone with a pocketful of nickels could eat and drink for a week.

AMUSEMENTS

Early in the 20th century, and continuing into the dawn of the Buffalo nickel era, the nickelodeon theater was ubiquitous in America. These movie houses, sometimes called "electric theaters" because of the myriad of light bulbs illuminating their elaborately carved facades, were usually set up in a storefront on a busy street. At a ticket booth in a front alcove, a nickel bought admission to a non-stop series of one-reel motion pictures, each about 12 minutes in

In 1918, **the Fourth Street Elevator** connecting uphill to Fenelon Place, Dubuque, Iowa, charged a nickel for "a magnificent view of the business district, Mississippi River, and three states," according to an advertisement. Billed as the world's shortest scenic railway, it used 296 feet of track to ascend 189 feet.

CHAPTER TWO

THE MINTING OF NICKEL FIVE-CENT PIECES

MAKING OBVERSE AND REVERSE DIES

CREATING WORKING DIES

Nickel five-cent pieces are created by two dies fitted to a coining press, which will be described in a later section of this chapter. In earlier times, the nickel five-cent series dies were made by a fairly complex process that involved hand-punching the date into each working die and then heat tempering, cooling, and finishing it to be suitable for use. However, the dates for the Buffalo and Jefferson series were added earlier in the process and the master die, complete with date, stamped it into the working die. Consequently, there are no differences in date placement, numeral size, or spacing within a given year in these series.

On the other hand, there are overdates in these series including the 1918/7-D Buffalo and 1943/2 Jefferson issues, each of which was created when a working die was given a blow by two different master hubs, each with a later date. Taking the 1918/7-D as an example, a perfectly serviceable 1917 obverse might have been on hand early in 1918, but would have been useless for coinage. It was probably softened by heating and impressed with a new 1918-dated master hub, but not so much that the earlier date was entirely destroyed. Because both overdates were created in war years—times of sharply increased minting activity—it is easy to imagine an inexperienced employee making such an error.

THE DIE-MAKING PROCESS IN 1896

For inclusion in the 1896 *Report of the Director of the Mint,* Chief Engraver Charles E. Barber contributed the following overview of the process in use at that time. During the later era of Buffalo and Jefferson nickels, the steps were about the same.

Coinage and medal dies are prepared in the following manner: When a coin or a medal is required, the first thing to be obtained is the design. . . . After the design for the coin or medal is settled upon, the engraver prepares a model in wax, or any material he may prefer to use, of the design selected, or as much of it as he may think most desirable for the production of the medal or coin. The model is generally made three, four, or five times as large as the finished work is intended to be. When the model is finished an electrotype is made. This electrotype when sufficiently strong is prepared for the reducing lathe, and a reduced copy is made the size required for the coin or medal, as the case may be.

The reducing lathe is a machine, working somewhat upon the principle of the pantograph, only in this case the one point traces or follows the form of the model, while another and much smaller point made in the form of a drill cuts away the material, and thus produces a reduction of the model. This process of reducing the design from the model is necessarily a very slow operation, as accuracy of the reduction depends entirely upon the slow motion of the machine and delicate handling of the operator. While it is not in the power of the operator or machine to improve the model, it is quite an easy matter, if not properly managed, for the machine to distort or the operator to lose the delicacy of the model. The reducing machine can work either from a model in relief or intaglio, though the relief is more often used, and is considered the better way.

In describing this process, I have said the engraver makes a model of the design he wishes to produce, or as much as he thinks desirable. To explain more fully, I would say some designs or parts of a design are not calculated for reducing by machine, and therefore the engraver only reduces so much of the design as he knows from experience will give the desired effect; the rest he cuts in . . . with gravers and chisels. When the reduction is made by the machine from the model it is then taken by the engraver and worked over and finished in all the detail and delicate parts, as the machine does not produce an entirely finished work. When finished by the engraver it is hardened and tempered. If the reduction has been made intaglio, when hardened it is completed and is called a die, and coins or medals can be struck from it; but if in relief, it is called a hub, and the process of making a die from it commences, which is done as follows:

The hub or relief being made hard, a piece of steel is prepared in the following manner to receive the impression of the hard hub:

Take a block of steel sufficiently large to make your die, and carefully anneal it until it is quite soft. This is done by heating the steel to a bright red and allowing it to cool very gradually, being careful to exclude the air by packing the steel in carbon. The steel being soft, turn off the surface of the block of steel and smooth it before you commence the process called hubbing, which is as follows: Place the block of soft steel under the plunger of a strong screw press; then put the hard relief or hub on top of the soft steel, and bring down your plunger with a good sharp blow. This will give you an impression upon the soft steel. In order to make a proper impression, the process of annealing the steel and the one just described, called hubbing, must be repeated many times, until you have a perfect impression of the hub. This being obtained, you have a die which only requires being hardened and tempered to be ready for use. This process of making dies is followed for coinage and medal dies of the most artistic character.

To harden the steel dies, they are packed in cast-iron boxes filled with carbon to exclude the air, and when heated to a bright red are cooled suddenly with water. As this would leave them too hard, and liable to crack and break on the edges, the temper is what is technically called drawn, which is done by gently heating until you notice a color appearing upon the surface of the steel. A light straw color is a good color for cutting tools, but dies are generally brought to a deeper color, and in some cases to a blue.

In 1896, a four-digit date logotype was punched into each working die. This practice ended with the advent of the Buffalo nickel in 1913, since which time the date has been incorporated into the hub, master die, and working dies.

CHANGES

From time to time in the chain of die-making processes, changes were made to the hubs used to make the master and working dies. These have included the strengthening of certain features, such as the obverse of the Buffalo nickel in 1916, and several adjustments to the reverse of the Jefferson nickel.

While obverse dies were always discarded soon after the end of a calendar year, reverse dies, sometimes with older hub variations, were kept in service until they wore out. Accordingly, among early Jefferson nickels, two reverse hub variations can be found for certain years. At the time this was done at the Mint, there was no thought that numismatists would ever take notice of such things!

MINTMARKS

Mintmarks first appeared on nickel five-cent pieces with the 1912-D and 1912-S Liberty Head issues. Subsequently, Buffalo and Jefferson nickels carried the D and S mintmarks. Although the date was included in the master die for these later series, mintmarks were not—at least not until the 1990s. Therefore, the Engraving Department at the Philadelphia Mint (where all dies were made) used small punches to impress a D or an S into the reverse die of a Buffalo or Jefferson nickel. Because this was done by hand a number of variations occurred, including doubling if a mint letter was punched twice and a few instances in which the letter was first punched at a tilt and then corrected. Some were even punched horizontally by mistake. Beginning with 1938-D/S in the Buffalo series, several of these "overmintmarks" represent dies originally destined for one mint that were overpunched with a letter signifying another.

The reverse was the standard place for mintmarks until 1968, when the position was relocated to the obverse on Jefferson nickels. Philadelphia coins carried no mintmark until the large P was added to the wartime silver issues of 1942 through 1945. A small P was introduced in 1980 and has been standard ever since.

Today P, D, or S mintmarks are included in the master die, which is then used to make multiple working dies. As a result, doubled, tilted, and other position variations of mintmarks no longer occur. Beginning in the 1990s, some dies are made at the Denver Mint, but models, reductions, hubs, and other early processes are still done at the Philadelphia Mint.

THE COINING PROCESS

PREPARING THE PLANCHET

Nickels as well as other coins are struck on planchets—circular discs the approximate diameter of the finished coin.[1] For nickels, blanks were cut out of long strips of copper-nickel alloy, much as cookies are punched out of dough by a cookie cutter. Sometimes this was done at the Mint, first by using narrow strips and punching out one planchet at a time, and later by using gang punches that make a tremendous noise and stamped out multiple blanks in one blow. At other times it was the practice simply to order finished blanks from suppliers, removing the planchet-cutting process from Mint supervision. Each blank had to be of a specified diameter and with a weight of 77.16 grains, with two grains' variation (about 2.5% up or down, or about 5% overall) allowed.

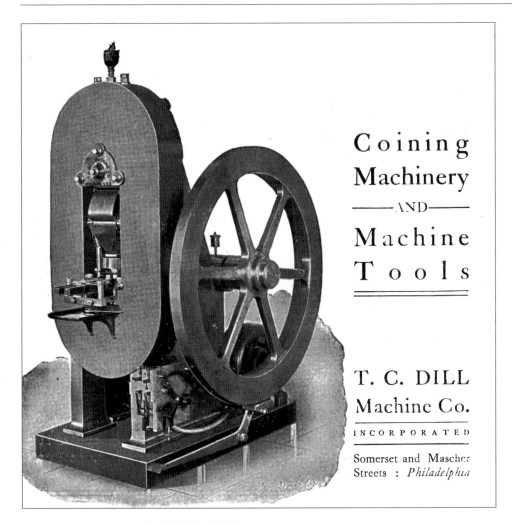

Coining
Machinery
——AND——
Machine
Tools

T. C. DILL
Machine Co.

INCORPORATED

Somerset and Mascher
Streets : *Philadelphia*

New coining press made in Philadelphia by the T.C. Dill Co. and installed in the third Philadelphia Mint in 1901. Over the years several different firms built similar presses to Mint specifications.

After the circular disk or blank is ready, it would be put into a milling or upsetting machine and run at high speed between a roller and an edge, in an area in which the diameter decreased slightly, forcing the metal up on ridges on both sides of the coin. This process created what is called a *planchet.* The resultant planchet was blank on both sides but had a raised rim.

Although processes varied over a period of years, it was customary to soften the planchets by annealing them (heating, then cooling slowly). Next, the planchets were cleaned in a soapy or acidic mixture, rinsed, and then dried by tumbling in sawdust or exposing them to currents of air.

At the end of this, the dry planchets would be ready for coining. Tumbling around in a cleaning machine imparted countless nicks and marks to both sides. It was hoped that the squeezing and compression of the planchets in the coining press would obliterate these marks. In practice, as discussed below, for many coins the dies did not come completely together in the coining press, and the deepest areas of the dies, representing the highest areas on the finished coins, were not completely struck—with the result that marks from the original planchets were still visible.

STRIKING THE COINS

The working dies were fitted to a coining press, at first driven by a system of steam-powered shafts and pulleys, then in the 1880s converted to electrical operation. The typical press was vertical with more or less an elliptical frame, with an area at the center to hold the dies. The anvil, or bottom, die (sometimes the obverse and sometimes the reverse in the nickel series) was firmly fixed in position. The anvil, or hammer, die was fixed to a matrix that moved up and down as the flywheel on the press rotated and actuated a cam. Either die could be removed when it became worn or damaged. This general type of press was called a *knuckle press*, from the mechanism's resemblance to a finger knuckle. The collar—a flat piece of steel with a smooth-sided circular hole the diameter of the finished coin—lies on top of the anvil die and defines the dimension of the coin as it is squeezed outward. Modern presses run at high speeds and sometimes have dies grouped together into "gangs," that strike several coins in a single blow. Coin presses are very noisy and necessitating ear protection for those spending extended time near them.

In the days of the Buffalo nickel, blank planchets were fed by an attendant into a tall tube mounted at the left front of the press, not far from the die. Each planchet would be grasped by mechanical fingers, taken to position and dropped into the collar. The fingers then retracted automatically; the hammer die came down and stamped the coins, which were then forced from the collar; and mechanical fingers then ejected the finished product. At that point each coin went down a slide at the back of the press which fed into a little hopper or bin. Modern mints also use a *riddler* machine—essentially a sieve with openings slightly larger than a nickel—to check the finished coins. Because oversized pieces will not fall through the holes, the riddler catches many double-struck coins and certain other types of mint errors.

WHY "FULL DETAILS" COINS ARE SCARCE

It was the intention of the Philadelphia, Denver, and San Francisco mints, to produce the largest number of nickel five-cent pieces possible in the shortest amount of time and with the least amount of effort. In fact, minor coins were held in generally low regard at the mints, and less attention was paid to them than to denominations struck in precious metals. There was no consideration whatsoever to pleasing numismatists who might later collect such coins.

The sharpness of a finished nickel five-cent piece depended on the technician who adjusted the press as well as the weight and preparation of the planchet. If the dies were fit precisely the right distance apart, and a planchet was of precisely the correct weight and annealed to ideal softness, the result would be a coin with every detail needle sharp. However, the authorization for the nickel five-cent piece permitted a 5% latitude in weight, as noted previously. If a pair of dies was adjusted perfectly in the manner just mentioned, for a planchet weighing the authorized 77.16 grains, this would result in the striking of a perfectly detailed coin.

If a slightly overweight, but still legal, planchet is fed into the press, the metal will have nowhere to go into the dies and will be forced out the edge, creating a wire rim (called a *fin* in mint jargon) and wearing the die in the process, or, worse, cracking the die.

The obvious answer is to space the dies slightly farther apart than optimum, so that slightly overweight planchets can be accommodated and coined at high speed without attention. Under this arrangement, only overweight planchets produced perfectly struck coins, while correct-weight and underweight planchets created coins with areas of weakness.

This is precisely what has happened ever since nickel five-cent pieces were first made for circulation way back at the beginning of the Shield series in 1866. In addition, the hardness of the planchets (resulting from poor annealing processes, poor metal flow, and design peculiarities) contributed to strike weakness in some cases.

WHY QUALITY IS ELUSIVE

With this information, you now know that whether coins with Full Details (FD) exist for a given variety depends on two factors: first, the weight and preparation of the planchet, and second, the spacing of the dies. Numismatists have found that in certain runs, such as for nearly all 1926-D Buffalo nickels, the dies were spaced significantly too far apart, and the resulting coins were very poorly struck.

Adding insult to injury, coins with shallow or light details often have areas of the original planchet that are not flattened out, or nicks, scratches, and other marks on the planchet remain visible on the completed coins! On Buffalo nickels these marks are common at the center of the obverse and on the front left leg of the bison. On Jefferson nickels they are often seen on Jefferson's shoulder.

Recently a reader of *Coin World* wrote to complain that new Westward Journey nickels had nicks and marks, even though they had been purchased from the U.S. Mint at a premium. The answer was that old bugbear: the dies were spaced too widely, and original nicks and marks on the planchet were still visible on the finished coin, although for coins sold to collectors, the Mint had taken care to handle the coins carefully after they were struck.

While it has been a general rule that planchets were bright and clean, although nicked and marked, in some instances the quality of the nickel was poor—discolored, stained, or irregular. This is particularly apparent with certain of the Jefferson nickels, especially many struck at the Philadelphia Mint in 1958, which were almost *black* at the moment of coining!

After the box receiving newly minted nickels at the back of the coining press was filled, it was taken by an attendant and dumped into a hopper with other nickels. Afterward the coins, still mixed together, were run through a mechanical counting machine, then put into cloth bags and tossed into a vault, to be shipped away. As mentioned, in modern times a riddler machine has been added to the process, before counting, to prevent certain mint errors escaping into the hands of eager numismatists! Such machines add even more abrasions to the coins. At no time, past or present, has any care been taken to prevent nicks, marks, or other damage, including during the bagging, shipping, and delivery process.

The result of this is that very few production-run nickel five-cent pieces survived in high Mint State (MS) grades such as MS-65, 66, or 67 after such handling. As illogical as it might seem now, decades ago few people cared about the sharpness of nickels, or whether they had planchet marks. (Recall my earlier comment that 1950-D nickels were simply traded as Uncirculated coins, with no division into grade categories and no attention to sharpness of details.) A banker viewing a bag of nickels might find few coins any nicer than MS-63 or so.

PRODUCING PROOF NICKELS

Proof coins were made in a different manner. The die production steps are essentially the same, except that, beginning in 1936, the face of each Proof was given a high degree of polish to create brilliant or mirror Proofs. For the special Matte Proof Buffalo nickels from 1913 through 1916, the die face was etched. A pair of dies was fitted into a hand-fed press located in the Medal Department of the Philadelphia Mint. A planchet was placed into the collar, the press actuated, and a coin struck. In most years, including in recent times, the press struck each coin twice in quick succession to bring up all details sharply. The finished coin was then removed by hand, and a new planchet inserted. The presses, which are of the old knuckle-action style and were once used at high speed for regular coinage, are operated slowly when Proofs are struck.

The planchets for Proof coins were always inspected (although sometimes not carefully) to be sure they did not have chips, flakes, discoloration, or damage. They also went through a special cleaning process, after which they were dried.

After striking, the Matte Proof Buffalo nickels of the 1913-to-1936 period were wrapped in thin tissue paper, then placed on sale. Later on, Proofs were packaged in cellophane, and still later in hard plastic. Sometimes Proofs were carelessly handled before packaging. Occasionally, a Proof still in its original wrapper will be found to have a few surface marks.

All Proof nickels were made at the Philadelphia Mint through 1964, then at the San Francisco Mint. The S mintmark was added in 1968. In addition, Special Mint Sets (SMS), carefully struck and sometimes with mirrored surfaces, were made at the San Francisco Mint from 1965 through 1967, but bore no mintmark. When I took a tour of the San Francisco Mint in the 1970s, the finished Proof nickels were carefully stacked on top of each other in small piles in a tray.

Some special Matte Finish 1994-P and 1997-P nickels were made, called Proofs by some numismatists.

MINTS AND THE DISTRIBUTION OF NICKELS
QUANTITIES MINTED

Nickels cost less than five cents to produce, and, accordingly, they were continually a source of profit for the Mint, as were coins in nickel alloy or bronze. The profit, called *seignorage*, contributed heavily to the operating profits of the various mints and, accordingly, the production of such pieces was highly encouraged. This was quite unlike the situation for silver and gold coins in the early days, when gold was of full intrinsic value, and for a long time silver was likewise, resulting in little if any profit to the mints.

The aspect of seignorage profits has been largely overlooked in numismatic accounts, but it is a major factor affecting the mintage quantities of minor coins. Over the years, demand varied for new nickels. In robust economic times, new coins would be needed in quantity. Typically, during recessions or slow times, supplies on hand would fill all needs.

By the time the Buffalo nickel made its debut in 1913, the nickel was highly important in commerce—in vending machines, amusement devices, Woolworth's new 5- and 10-cent stores, and elsewhere. Some nickelodeon theaters were still around, but admission to see a movie was increasingly being hiked to 10¢ or 15¢. All went well with the production of nickels until 1921, when the boom economy engendered by World War I paused to catch its breath and nickel production dropped. For the first time, no nickels were made in Denver; in 1922 none were made anywhere. After that, mintages increased through the so-called Roaring Twenties, although the purchasing power of the coins was not what it had been a decade earlier.

Then came the depression of the 1930s, and nickel production was cut sharply. In 1930 only the Philadelphia and San Francisco mints made this denomination. In 1931, nickels were made only in San Francisco. The mintage if the 1931-S might have been minuscule had not a Mint official realized that a numismatic rarity was in the process of being created, and production was hiked at the end of the year. Even so, the quantity was just 1,200,000, which is low for a five-cent piece.

No nickels at all were made in 1932 or 1933, but in 1934 the presses started up again, and from then through the end of the Buffalo type in 1938, large quantities were struck. This period also saw a dynamic spurt of interest in coin collecting. Many of the 1931-S nickels, as yet undistributed, were retrieved by coin collectors circa 1934 or 1935, and all current date and mintmark issues were saved in roll quantities. In his *Complete Guide to Buffalo Nickels*, David W. Lange notes that certain earlier varieties dating back to the 1926-D were still being distributed in the early 1930s, resulting in the inordinate number of Mint State coins that still survive today.

Jefferson nickels were made in large quantities during the heady economic era of World War II, but suffered smaller mintages in the postwar economic slump.

If some graduate student in economics needs a subject for a term paper, a good one would be the relationship of the health of the American economy in relation to the mintage quantities of the most-used coins, these being the minor denominations. The correlation is very direct. However, to be really accurate, the degree candidate should also know about special situations that tweaked the mintage figures from time to time—in history such things including why in the Shield series no nickels were made for circulation in 1877 and 1878, how coin-operated devices spurred nickel mintages from the 1890s onward, and the effect of sales taxes in recent generations.

THE PHILADELPHIA MINT

From 1866 through 1911, nickel five-cent pieces were made only at the Philadelphia Mint. From the 1860s through the 1880s, there was not much demand for nickel five-cent pieces in the Midwest or West. Silver coins, which had been hoarded in the East and Midwest since spring 1862, were not hoarded in the West, and half dimes, dimes, and other denominations continued to circulate freely. More important, westerners simply did not like "small change." Indian Head cents were not popular there either, as reflected in many Mint reports. In the early 1880s, there was a great deal of interest in the new Liberty Head nickels. Supplies were sent to the Pacific states and, beginning in the 1890s, coin-operated machines and, later, theaters and amusement devices became as popular there as anywhere else.

All 19th-century nickels were coined at the second Philadelphia Mint, the cornerstone of which had been laid in 1829. By 1866, when the nickel five-cent piece became a reality, many improvements had been made in the processes used to create dies and in the use of steam power to drive presses and other machines.

The third Philadelphia Mint, first occupied in October 1901, produced Buffalo nickels from 1913 through 1937 and Jefferson nickels from 1938 through the mid-1960s. The Engraving Department and die-making facilities for all mints were located here.

When Buffalo nickels came on the scene in 1913, the Philadelphia Mint had been located in its third facility since the autumn of 1901. Much new machinery had been installed, and all operations were electrified. This structure remained in use until the fourth Philadelphia Mint was inaugurated in 1967.

During these transitions the Philadelphia Mint remained the center for creating designs and making dies, although later, in the 1990s, some die-making was assigned to the Denver Mint. The Engraving Department, however, was and is headquartered in Philadelphia. The Mint Collection was on view there until the spring of 1923, when it was transferred to the "Castle" building of Smithsonian Institution. Today the collection is known as the National Numismatic Collection and is housed in the Smithsonian's Museum of American History. An expert curatorial staff cares for the treasures and the facility is a magnet for researchers.

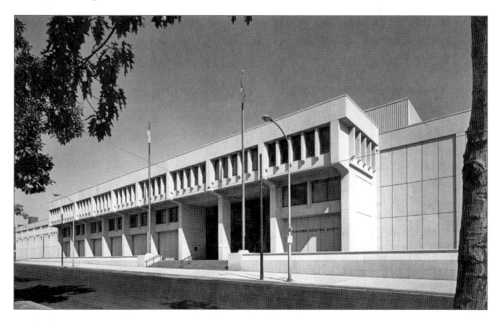

The fourth Philadelphia Mint, in use today, was inaugurated in 1967. (Library of Congress)

The Denver Mint as it appeared early in the 20th century. The facility opened in 1906.

THE DENVER MINT

Construction began on the Denver Mint in 1904 and its first coins were struck—all in silver and gold—in 1906. It was not until 1911 that the first cents were made there and not until 1912 that nickels were first struck. When Buffalo nickels went into production in 1913, the Denver Mint coined its share, as it has ever since. The facility was enlarged in 1937 and is still in use today, although with many improvements in technology. In recent years, limited die-making operations have been set up there as well.

Throughout the annals of the five-cent piece, the Denver Mint has earned the lowest marks for the quality of its coins. This is especially true for the period from 1914 through much of the 1920s (details will be found in the appropriate listings). As a class, the Denver Mint coins present the greatest numismatic challenge for anyone seeking coins with Full Details (FD).

THE SAN FRANCISCO MINT

The San Francisco Mint went into operation in its second location— an impressive structure nicknamed The Granite Lady—in 1874, and struck its first nickels in the waning days of 1912. In 1937, it moved into a new building on Duboce Street, a modern fortress-like structure that still looks more like a penitentiary than a center of coining and numismatic activity.

In 1955 the Treasury Department announced that the San Francisco Mint would close its coining operations forever. In that particular year, Roosevelt dimes and 1955-S Lincoln cents had been made there, but the last Jefferson nickel to be coined in San Francisco was the 1954-S. However, the Mint did resume coinage later and produced a limited number of nickel five-cent

The San Francisco Mint in the second decade of the 20th century. The added automobile is an artist's conception, to bring the picture up to date.

The third San Francisco Mint on Duboce Street has been in use since 1937.

pieces for circulation, as well as, beginning in 1968, Proofs of all denominations. Special Mint Sets (SMSs) were made there from 1965 to 1967, but those coins had no mintmarks.

PRODUCTION OUTLOOK FOR THE FUTURE

Today the 5¢ cigar, glass of Coca-Cola, candy bar, and theater ticket have all been relegated to the history books. In fact, a five-cent piece, on its own, isn't good for very much—it takes a handful of them just to buy a stamp or occupy a city parking space for half an hour.

In spite of all this, though, nickels are more popular than ever. Nearly every state has its pesky sales tax, and a nickel or two can come in handy when tendering payment. In addition, the denomination has enjoyed an artistic renaissance with the inception of the Westward Journey series in 2004. Today, nickels are very much in the news and will doubtless be with us for many years to come.

CHAPTER THREE

How to Be a Smart Buyer
AS I SEE IT

REMARKS AND OPINIONS

For your Buffalo nickel collection, you will have to *buy* everything and pay a premium for each issue. Gone are the days of finding them in your pocket change. You can pluck Jefferson nickels of recent decades out of circulation or order them from the U.S. Mint, but you will have to turn to a coin dealer to buy earlier varieties.

This chapter gives general ideas on what I would do if I were building nice collections in the Buffalo and Jefferson series and wanted to obtain excellent value for my money. As a rare coin dealer, I have always been a careful buyer. I study each example closely for good eye appeal. Market fads and passions come and go, and I've sought to avoid these. I am a contrarian and prefer, as they say, to think outside the box. Although I am not from Missouri, I am a "show me" person, skeptical in the marketplace until I find proof of real value.

Much of what you read here is not available in any other handy reference—especially my comments on planchet marks (see above), evaluating the sharpness of Buffalo nickels, and detecting detail in Jefferson nickels beyond the counting of steps.

In my opinion, many buyers of nickels and other coins are simply lazy. They look at the grade marked on a holder, check the market price, and write a check. Such people are the darlings of the rare coin business, for they eagerly buy things that real connoisseurs would not even consider. (You will read a lot about this among the listings for Denver and San Francisco Mint nickels of the 1920s.) A poorly struck nickel with artificial iridescent toning, a wretched coin from my point of view, will sell instantly if it is certified at, say, MS-65, and offered at a price slightly below the market rate.

If you take the time to read the descriptions I give under each Buffalo and Jefferson nickel, you will see these coins from the perspective of an insider. You will know as much, or nearly as much, as specialists and connoisseurs who have been pursuing and enjoying nickels for many years.

SEEKING VALUE

I suggest that you seek good value in every coin you buy regardless of how much money you have available. Even if I won the lottery, I would not be eager to pay $5,000 or more for a condition rarity—say, certified in MS-69, or perhaps with the very rare 6 Full Steps—when a beautiful MS-66 of the same date and with 5 Full Steps can be bought for $5. There is a lot of this sort of activity, though, and every dealer in rare coins is grateful for the flood of business created when people build registry sets—a concept created by David Hall, who was a marketing genius and the linchpin in the 1986 founding of the Professional Coin Grading Service (PCGS). At present, most registry set builders chase *numbers*, but not quality. This is just the opposite of my practice of chasing *quality*, and letting the numbers take care of themselves. To my mind, a superb quality, sharply struck MS-65 nickel with good eye appeal, will always trump a spotted or weakly struck MS-67.

Certified coins and registry sets breed excitement without requiring deep numismatic knowledge. Anyone with an adequate bank balance can be king of the hill—sort of the numismatic equivalent of a high-stakes gambler in Las Vegas. While it may not make much economic sense, being known as a big spender will always get you a royal welcome and, from what I've heard, a great deal of pleasure. A long-time client, the late Armand Champa, told me proudly that he had papered a small room in his Louisville home with credit slips from Las Vegas casinos, some four million dollars' worth. I am digressing, but the point is that the way I spend my money might be different from the way that brings the greatest enjoyment to you. In the end, it is your choice.

IT IS YOUR CHOICE

Because you are reading this book, it is probably safe to assume that you want to be a serious, knowledgeable—in a word, *savvy*—collector or investor, that you want to learn before you invest, and that you would like to *enjoy* your coins. If this is not the case, you can easily build a high-grade (which is not the same as high *quality*) collection of nickels simply by buying coins in certified holders.

Surprisingly, there is a large market for nickels and other things aimed at investors and dealers who buy coins sight unseen. A dedicated collector of Buffalo or Jefferson nickels would never buy coins this way without good reason and careful consideration. To tell the truth, I did so once myself several years ago when I first contemplated writing this book. I wanted a good reference group of coins to look at, so I asked David Sundman, a close personal friend, to have his Littleton Coin Company staffers pick out a set of choice and gem Jefferson nickels with good eye appeal, mount them in an album, and send them to me with a bill. He did this, and the coins were and still are great. However, this commission would not have been given to just anyone, and, because expediency won out over pleasure, I missed the fun of building the set coin by coin.

KNOWLEDGE AS THE KEY TO SUCCESS

As you will see in the following chapters, Buffalo and Jefferson nickels are among the most complex of all American series. And yet this fact is unknown to many people who simply check price listings in a *Guide Book of United States Coins*, the *Certified Coin Dealer Newsletter*, *Coin World* (and its *Coin Values* supplement), or *Numismatic News*.

The complexity is in the area of *quality*. Internet listings are not much help in disseminating useful information beyond rarity and price. Quality is seldom discussed. Photographs can be altered to hide defects, and negative information about a Buffalo or Jefferson nickel simply won't be mentioned. So the more you know, the better in the better your chance to buy high-quality coins.

For example, if you want to buy a common 1934 Buffalo nickel, you need to know that only a very small number of coins in the marketplace have Full Details. Nearly all 1934s are weakly struck in one area or another. You can go to conventions, examine a hundred or so 1934 nickels graded MS-65 or MS-66, and for *no extra cost* pick up the one or two Full Details coins that might be available. Your competitors will be clueless and will be happy with a 1934 with no fur details on the head of the bison, or with some other shortcoming that they will not recognize. Eventually though, Full Details nickels will be appreciated—just as Full Bands (FB) Mercury dimes or Full Bell Lines (FBL) Franklin half dollars are today. At one time, these FB and FBL points were not known, and collectors could purchase sharp coins at ordinary prices. Then came the awakening—and huge jumps in cost. When this happens for Buffalo nickels, you will be sitting pretty with your Full Details 1934!

"Too soon old and too late smart," the old Pennsylvania Dutch saying goes. By being a smart buyer now, you will not suffer the disappointment of learning later that, indeed, some 1934 nickels are needle-sharp with Full Details, but you paid the same price for a doggy flat strike! The sooner you become smart, the happier you will be, the more fun you will have, and the greater value you will obtain for your money.

There is even a smart aspect to buying new coins directly from the Mint. Because some circulation issues are not fully struck, nicks and marks from the *original planchet* can still be seen on the portrait of Jefferson. By knowing what to look for, you can ask for a replacement, which will be cheerfully given. I hasten to add that such problems rarely occur, but it is still worthwhile to know what to look for. Further, the thrill of the hunt is a large part of the enjoyment of numismatics. It is fun to read about Buffalo nickels and then to go on a secret hunt for that rare Full Details 1934.

Ways to Collect Nickel Five-Cent Pieces

Different Types

Nickel five-cent pieces from day one (1866) to the present time, neatly break down into four major categories. These comprise the Shield (1866–1883), Liberty Head (1883–1913), Buffalo (1913–1938), and Jefferson (1938 to date) types.

Indian Head or, as most people call them, Buffalo nickels, include the Type I with the bison standing on a mound, and the revised Type II, with the animal on a level plain. The Jefferson nickel series is still in progress, creating new excitement with the 2004 Keelboat and Indian Peace Medal reverses, and the 2005 obverse with the Bison and Ocean in View reverses. In addition, we have the general copper-nickel alloy type made in the Jefferson series from 1938 to 1965, without the designer's initials, interrupted from 1942 to 1945 by a distinctive type in silver alloy. Then from 1966 to 2003 we have nickels bearing FS, for designer Felix O. Schlag, on the obverse.

For starters, I suggest that you build a type set. While there are only four type sets for Shield and Liberty Head nickels (included below in light font for comparison), there are no less than ten for Buffalo and Jefferson coins. Even a gem Mint State-65 type set from 1913 to date is affordable to just about anyone:

1866–1867 Shield With Rays

1867–1883 Shield Without Rays

1883 Liberty Head Without CENTS

1883–1913 Liberty Head With CENTS

1913 Buffalo Type I

1913–1938 Buffalo Type II

1938–1965 Jefferson, regular alloy, without initials

1942–1945 Jefferson, silver alloy

1966–2003 Jefferson, regular alloy, with designer's initials (FS)

2004 Keelboat

2004 Indian Peace Medal

2005 Bison

2005 Ocean in View

2006: New Jefferson portrait, slightly restyled Monticello

While I recommend connoisseurship when you buy, it is perfectly okay to have gotten your feet wet at a local coin shop or regional convention by buying one of each of the different types from 1913 to date, before you read this book. Not much money was involved—and you will get smarter, later!

Now contemplate your type set. Would one of the series be worth collecting in a more expanded form? Here are some considerations.

BECOMING A SPECIALIST

While the following chapters provide as much information as you probably want, and perhaps even more than that, here is an overview of collecting each of the two motifs covered in this book:

Buffalo nickels from 1913 to 1938 have been incredibly popular for a long time. There are no "impossible rarities" among dates and mintmarks, although several varieties can be elusive. The 1918/7-D, for instance, ranges from scarce to rare depending on the grade, and the 1916 Doubled Die, quite spectacular, but strictly in the category of specialized varieties, can also be a challenge to find, as can several others.

Jefferson nickels, at first glance, seem to be easy enough. Hundreds of pieces abound—a veritable string of dates and mints. However, taking this approach to collecting them would be like looking at the entry gate at Walt Disney World and never seeing what is inside! The world of Jefferson nickels is alluring, but there are dangers—such as tripping on those pesky steps. (It would have been easier for numismatists if Jefferson had designed Monticello with a *ramp* leading up to the portico!) There will be many decisions for you to make. It may surprise you to learn that there are certain Jefferson nickels coined in the 1960s that are worth less than a dollar in Mint State, but if one of them has 6 Full Steps (capitalized here because this is the formal notation) clearly visible on the Monticello building, that coin is worth thousands of dollars! This does not mean that you should mortgage the farm to buy nickels for thousands of dollars apiece. You may want to consider coins that are 90% as sharp and only cost a few dollars. Decisions . . . decisions!

There are pleasures galore awaiting you if you collect nickels, not the least of which is meeting or corresponding with other enthusiasts. At the American Numismatic Association convention in San Francisco in July 2005, I spent time chatting with members of the Full Step Nickel Club at their booth; attended the unveiling of new nickel designs on tap for 2006 conducted by Deputy Mint Director Gloria Eskridge and well-known Mint engraver John Mercanti; and enjoyed many conversations about nickels, old and new. (I also wandered around the bourse examining nickels on display for sale and discovered that, in many instances, coins offered as MS-66 were no nicer than some rated

MS-65 that were selling at half the price. I quickly realized that a reader of this book, forearmed with knowledge, could have spent $10,000 at this convention and landed better buys than a naïve investor who spent twice as much.)

Another delight of collecting Buffalo, especially Jefferson nickels, is that you do not need to be a big spender to form a nice set. This is in dynamic contrast to, for example, becoming a specialist in pattern coins, Proof gold, or early large copper cents. By cherrypicking for coins with Full Details and good eye appeal, you can build a set of nickels in the MS-63 to MS-65 range that is of better overall *quality* than a set rated at MS-66 or higher built by a well-financed buyer who is not aware of aesthetics.

The icing on the cake is that the Jefferson series is ongoing. We will have to stay tuned to see what new things arrive on the scene. As is the case with the State Reverse quarters, the panorama is ever changing, and delightfully so.

The Sheldon/ANA Grading System

In the marketplace most nickel five-cent pieces are offered with a notation based on the *Official American Numismatic Association Grading Standards for United States Coins*, adapted from the Sheldon scale, and using points from 1 to 70. Perhaps you are already familiar with this, but if not, here is a quick review.

Dr. William H. Sheldon's study, *Early American Cents*, was published in 1949. The text treated the limited field of large copper cents from 1793 to 1814 and described more than 200 die varieties. This volume was updated and revised in 1958. The new edition, titled *Penny Whimsy*, and includes contributions by Walter Breen and Dorothy Iselin Pascal.

When Sheldon died in 1977, he had been inactive in numismatics for some years. After his passing, pandemonium broke out when numismatists learned that, over a period of years, he had swapped many of his lesser-grade cents for superb coins in the collection of the American Numismatic Society, and, for good measure, had stolen coins from others who had trusted him, including leading collectors and dealers.

Dishonesty notwithstanding, Sheldon's name lives on with both his Rarity Scale and Grading Scale. The grading scheme he proposed in 1949 was essentially a *market formula* based on numbers. Each die variety described in his book was assigned a Basal Value, determined by its rarity and popularity. A very common large copper cent back then might have a Basal Value of 50 cents or $1, while a rare variety might have a Basal Value of $5 or so. Then, with current market values in mind in 1949, Sheldon came up with a scale of grading numbers, which, if multiplied by the Basal Value, would yield the current price of a coin.

The numbers were designed to fit the market, and that is how the scale of grades from 1 (Basal State, so worn as to be virtually unidentifiable) to MS-70 (Gem Mint State) came to be. The theory was that a particular coin with a basal value of $5, if in EF-40 grade, was worth $5 × 40 or $200. In Mint State-60 it was worth $5 × 60 or $300. While that might have worked in 1949, within a few years it was way out of kilter as collectors paid increasingly large premiums for coins in higher grades. The gap widened, and today a Mint State coin might sell for 10 or more times the price of an Extremely Fine.

In the late 1970s, the American Numismatic Association (ANA) took up the Sheldon Scale and adapted it to what is now known as *The Official American Numismatic Association Grading Standards for United States Coins*, as described in the book by that name (mentioned earlier). Definitions are given for various grading steps, all the way from well worn (such as Good-4, abbreviated G-4) to gem Mint State (MS-65) and continuing to perfect Mint State (MS-70). No effort is now made to use Basal Values or to employ the numbers as part of a mathematical formula to determine market price.

THE SEARCH FOR PRECISION

To many if not most casual observers, numbers are scientific, whereas adjectives are fuzzy. If, to a newcomer to the hobby, I say, "I offer you a Very Fine 1926-S Buffalo nickel," the normal reaction would be, "Dave Bowers has just offered me a *very nice* nickel of this date and Mint." As to how very fine, good, fair, extremely fine, very good, and fine sort themselves out can be hard to understand. To help matters, in numismatic circles the grades are capitalized, so that a Very Fine 1926-S nickel means one that is in the specific grade of Very Fine, not just *very fine*, as a drive through the countryside or the experience of eating a strawberry might be.

The ANA Grading System adds a number to each of the adjectives. Now we have— using the same example—VF-20, Good-4, Fair-2, EF-40, VG-8, and F-12. Now it is easy for a newcomer to arrange them in order: Fair-2, Good-4, VG-8, F-12, VF-20, and EF-40. Already, you suspect that an EF-40 coin is a heck of a lot nicer than a Good-4!

In the Mint State category Dr. Sheldon had just three separations in his 1949 book: MS-60, or basic Mint State; MS-65, or gem; and MS-70, equal to perfection—the last being a theoretical ideal. Not long after 1949, a few numismatists started using the numbers to describe series other than the 1793 to 1814 cents, particularly later large copper cents of 1816 to 1857 (none were coined in 1815), copper half cents from 1793 to 1857, and American colonial and state copper coins.

NUMBERS BECOME VERY POPULAR

Then, during the crazy, hectic days of the 1960s, the market became white hot. The fire was fueled by the launching of *Coin World* in 1960, the discovery of the 1960 Small Date Lincoln cent, and other factors including, of course, the Treasury release of silver dollars beginning in November 1962. Prices of nearly all coins rose. As pieces achieved high values and as hundreds of thousands of newcomers came into the field, there was an increasing demand for precision grading.

In 1977 *The Official ANA Grading Standards* put an end to at least some of the confusion. Kenneth E. Bressett, using information contributed by many collectors and dealers, gave definitions for each of the numbers, with the definitions being different for each series or type. Accordingly, a Liberty Head nickel in MS-65 was subject to a different set of rules than a Morgan silver dollar or Liberty Head double eagle with the same number. In the Mint State category, the divisions of MS-60, MS-65, and MS-70 were used. When Thomas K. DeLorey was hired by the American Numismatic Association Certification Service (ANACS) to start the commercial grading of coins for a fee, these were the divisions used. However, the market demanded additional levels, and DeLorey arbitrarily added MS-63 and MS-67. These levels were used for about six months, at which time John Jay Pittman, a member of the ANA board of directors, said that this could not be done, as the Board had not approved. "I told him that they had better do so, and retroactively, and they did," DeLorey recalled.[1]

For many coin buyers the Sheldon numbers, now with intermediate steps, fit the bill exactly, as they appeared to be scientific—a panacea for what appeared to be wild confusion in grading descriptions, including the use of numbers with no standard definition of what they meant.

ANA guidelines notwithstanding, many collectors and dealers added flowery adjectives, other intermediate steps, and more. In the early 1980s, it was not unusual to see coins graded as MS-61, MS-62, MS-63, MS-64, MS-65, MS-66, MS-67, MS-68, MS-69, and MS-70, sometimes with one or two pluses or minuses added, as MS-63++. If this seems improbable to present day readers, all you need to do is to secure a copy of *Coin World* or *Numismatic News* from the era and see for yourself. For the purposes of the present book however, I hasten to add that while Buffalo nickels were advertised this way, Jefferson nickels, not being of great value, were not. The latter were commonly traded as bank-wrapped rolls or as full date and Mint Sets in albums.

The ANA guidelines were hardly perfect then, nor are they today, because they are highly subject to interpretation. Consider the definition for this grade in the Buffalo nickel series:

> **MS-65:** No trace of wear; nearly as perfect as MS-67 except for some small weakness or blemish. Has full mint luster, but may be unevenly toned, or lightly fingermarked. A few barely noticeable nicks or marks may be present.

What if a coin has two small blemishes, but no "barely noticeable nicks or marks." What if it has no blemishes or marks, but the weakness is not "small"? How large is a "small weakness"? Can it be measured? What if the finger marks are light, but are obviously placed on the cheek of the Indian? How would that coin compare to one with finger marks that are more or less hidden in the fur of the bison?

If I found a little hoard of Uncirculated 1914-D Buffalo nickels, put away coin by coin many years ago, and asked leading experts to grade them, no two experts would come to the same conclusions. With the ANA guidelines, most would at least be in the same ballpark, within a point or two, but "a point or two" can mean a big difference in money, such as between MS-64 and MS-65 or 66. We all wish that such differences of opinion did not exist, but they do, because grading is not scientific.

THE RANGE OF NUMBERS

The ANA Grading System, explained in detail, with information as to what to look for, is given separately for the Buffalo and Jefferson series in the chapters to follow. Nonetheless, here is a quick view of the numbers used and their abbreviations. Not all of the intermediate grades are defined, but they are widely used in the marketplace, in descending order from perfection (more theoretical than actual) down to well worn—the steps a coin goes through from the time it is first minted until it has been in circulation for decades.

In the Mint State category, we have these degrees, from perfection downward: MS-70, MS-69, MS-68, MS-67, MS-66, MS-65, MS-64, MS-63, MS-62, MS-61, and MS-60.

Then, through various levels of light wear, we have the About Uncirculated grades: AU-58, AU-55, AU-53, and AU-50.

Then on to these categories:

- EF-45 and EF-40 (EF = Extremely Fine, sometimes slangily abbreviated as XF)

- VF-30 and VF-20 (Very Fine)

- Fine-10

- VG-8 (Very Good)

- Good-4

- AG-3 (About Good)

- Fair-2

- Poor-1

Commercial services sometimes use additional grades, such as Good-6, VG-10, Fine-15, VF-25, and VF-35. Except for a handful of rare varieties, however, most Buffalo nickels are desired in grades of Fine or better, and Jefferson nickels in, say, MS-60 or higher. Accordingly, the discussion of lower grades here is more academic than useful. I seriously doubt if you will ever seek any Buffalo or Jefferson nickel in AG-3 or Fair-2 grade or a Jefferson nickel in any grade below VF or EF.

WHAT NUMBERS ARE AND ARE NOT

A scientist looking at this list might wonder why the Very Fine (VF) category begins at VF-20 and extends to EF-40, a span of 20 numbers, while Mint State coins, so important in the marketplace, are shoehorned among 11 numbers from MS-60 to MS-70. This is an artifact of the old Sheldon market formula, of which you are now aware.

That said, we can dismiss the illogic of the numerical distribution and use the numbers simply for shorthand in arranging coins in order. A VF-20 coin is more worn than is an AU-53, and the latter has more marks and friction than does an MS-65 or MS-66.

The same numbers are also used to classify Proof coins, but usually only from Proof-60 through Proof-70. (In popular use, Proof is either spelled out, as Proof-65, or abbreviated as PR-65, PF-65, or Pr-65. Impaired (circulated or damaged) Proofs are seen now and then and are given lower numbers, such as Proof-53, Proof-55, or Proof-58. However, in the Buffalo and Jefferson series, Proofs in grades from about Proof-63 and below are apt to be rather unattractive; it has been my experience that few people seek them.

A newcomer discovering coins for the first time would by every right think, "How scientific, they have captured the essence of grading precisely." It requires little thinking to know that a coin listed as MS-64 is nicer than one listed as MS-63 but not as nice as one listed as MS-65. However, the emperor has no clothes—the system is flawed, and although everyone uses it, the foundation is not very strong. The explanation is simple: grading has always been, is presently, and probably always will be a matter of personal opinion. Remember my example of grading experts with a group of 100 1914-D Buffalo nickels? Elaborating on that, even if these 100 coins had been sent to a leading grading service, returned to their owner, cracked out of the holders, and resubmitted to the same service, many of them would have been given different grades than they had received the first time.

Grading numbers are a convenient shorthand; they are not based on science. If they were, then a collector in Keller, Texas, using *The Official ANA Grading Standards*, would be able to view a 1926-S Buffalo nickel, grade it as, say, MS-63, and then mail it (without the grade affixed) to a numismatist in Shamokin, Pennsylvania, who would unfailingly assign MS-63 to it—after which a long succession of viewers, using only the printed guidelines, would come to the same conclusions.

Under the present non-scientific system this cannot happen. In Keller it might be an MS-63, in Shamokin an MS-61, in Peoria an MS-64, and at a commercial grading service, a "no-grade due to environmental damage."

If it makes you feel better, the same situation exists in other fields of collectibles, no one considers those other systems to be precise. Book dealers and collectors use such terms as *mint, very fine,* and *reading copy,* among others, but experts can and do assign these terms differently. No two dog-show judges would grade the a field of a dozen canines the same, and Olympic Games judges do not unanimously agree on the ranking of ice skaters. Perhaps weather forecasting, which has been called an "inexact science" is similar.

What to do?

Basically, you have two choices:

1. Buy a coin that has been graded by someone else, such as a dealer, another collector, or a grading service, and put it in your collection, content that it is an MS-63, or an MS-65, or whatever it says on the holder.

2. Learn about grading so that on your own you can check that 1926-S nickel when it is offered to you and say to yourself, "It is an MS-63, lustrous, but showing metal flow lines from tired dies and the die spacing is too far apart. Details are missing on the obverse center, on the reverse the fur on the head of the bison is just a blob, and the mintmark is mushy. I think I'll wait for a nicer one to come along." This is what I hope *you* will do as a smart buyer.

Authenticity

In the marketplace, particularly on the Internet, in antique shops and shows, and at gun shows, there are many fakes, alterations, and other non-genuine coins. In some areas such as "Wild West" saloon tokens, "1804" dollars, and "1913" nickels, the phonies outnumber the real ones. Fortunately, fakes are in the minority in the Buffalo nickel series, and in the Jefferson series they are almost no problem at all. However, even buying a single phony coin can spoil your day.

Among Buffalo nickels, some rare mintmark varieties have been faked by drilling into the side of Philadelphia Mint coins at the bottom of the reverse, inserting a tool, and forcing metal in the mintmark position, up into an embossing die bearing a D or an S. Afterward, the hole is filled and smoothed over. Some 1937-D 3-Legged coins have been faked by grinding away the fourth leg.

The leading grading services often guarantee *authenticity* of what they encapsulate, but policies are subject to change, and I am not aware of any single source where you can keep tabs on changing grading policies. My advice is to contact your favorite service and ask for a written copy of any guarantees they provide. There have been more than 100 grading services in business since the 1980s, and some have sold fakes and/or vastly overgraded coins. Stick with your pick among the top several leaders, but ask around among dealers and collectors before making a choice.

With Jefferson nickels, unless you are forming a registry set or buying an ultra-grade coin on the long side of MS-67 or so, chances are that most of your coins will not be certified. There are a couple of reasons for this. For the vast majority of dates and mints, the cost of certification, usually running from about $10 to $20 per coin, is far greater than the market price of the coin, which might be less than a dollar to perhaps several dollars. In addition, because there are hundreds of varieties in the Jefferson series, unless you have a personal valet or porter, and few of us do, the sheer weight of so many "slabs," as holders are often called, is unmanageable. There are exceptions to this, though. Someone with an ultra-high grade coin, or one that is common if lightly struck, but is a rarity with 6 Full Steps, might want to have it certified.

Fakes and alterations will be no problem at all if you buy Buffalo nickels certified by one of the leading services and if you can resist buying "bargains." One exception, however, is the minefield of Matte Proof Buffalo nickels dated 1913 to 1916. In my opinion, more than just a few circulation strikes have been certified as Matte Proofs. Be careful. Although a few Jefferson nickels have been faked, notably the 1950-D, you should be safe if you buy uncertified or "raw" coins from a reliable dealer. I will say more about this later.

BEYOND THE NUMBERS

Another aspect of logical decision making that is important for you to know, but not discussed in the wide marketplace, is that for any Proof Buffalo or Jefferson nickel to be other than gem grade, say Proof-65 or better, it has to have been subject to some handling. If it has hairlines (tiny abrasions), this is because the coin has been cleaned. However, the grading services are inconsistent as to how they handle such situations. Generally, a Buffalo nickel with hairlines, for example, will be graded less than Proof-65—perhaps Proof-62 or Proof-63. If the cleaning is serious, it might be called Proof-60. A correct listing would be as follows: "Proof-62 due to hairlines from cleaning." Some services will return a coin ungraded if it has been *severely* cleaned, others may put a "net grade" on it, and the like. There is little consistency in this regard. However, most coins in the numerical ranges of 60 to 63 have not been submitted to the grading services, as the market values of these coins are not high for most varieties. Actually though, in the Buffalo and Jefferson series most Proofs are generally of high quality, quite unlike the situation with the earlier Shield and Liberty Head types of this denomination.

An early Buffalo nickel that has made it safely to the present day will always show some light toning, even if it has been held by only the most careful of numismatists. If it is as brilliant as it was when first minted and has a bright edge, it probably has been dipped. Coins kept in bank-wrapped rolls can have brilliant edges, but among Buffalo nickels, such rolls are generally found only from 1931-S onward.

Then there is the matter of strike sharpness. Some nickels have flat areas, while others show Full Details (FD). Most circulation-strike nickels are a compromise, especially among high-mintage dates. There are some Buffalo nickel varieties for which Full Details coins are relatively rare (comprising less than 5% of the population) or are unknown. There are even more Jefferson nickel varieties that are unknown with 6 Full Steps.

You can see that nomenclature such as MS-63, MS-66, or whatever, doesn't tell you much if you really want to be a connoisseur. Instead, you need to apply your own expertise and thinking. Suggestions are found in the chapters that follow.

Some time ago, for Whitman Publishing, LLC, I devised a process that I named "Four Steps to Success." The approach has caught on with a number of readers who have applied it to their own fields of interest. For Buffalo nickels, these steps are given in chapter 5; for Jeffersons you will find them in chapter 8.

CHAPTER FOUR

INDIAN HEAD/BUFFALO NICKELS
1913–1938
HISTORY AND BACKGROUND

THE DESIGN OF THE COIN

NEW MOTIFS WANTED

The Coinage Act of September 26, 1890 stated, in part, "No change in the design or die of any coin shall be made oftener than once in 25 years from and including the year of the first adoption of the design, model, die, or hub for the same coin." By the early 20th century, therefore, the general rule was that there were to be no major changes in coin designs until an existing motif had been in use for at least that length of time. The government, however, as governments often do, violated this law more than once—such as with the termination in 1930 of the Standing Liberty quarter series, begun in 1916, and again by ending the 1948 Franklin half dollar design in 1963.

The Liberty Head nickel had been in circulation since 1883, making this denomination an ideal candidate for revision. This was an era of awakened interest in artistry of coins. For many years, the coins of Charles E. Barber had been criticized by both citizens and the community of artists. Sculptor Augustus Saint-Gaudens went so far as to call Barber's silver coins "wretched." In all fairness, though, I have read countless newspaper and numismatic articles about coinage of this period and have never encountered complaints about Barber's Liberty Head nickel, which might well be considered his finest work.

The gold $10 and $20 designs had been changed in 1907 to make use of the talents of Saint-Gaudens, who had taken the commission at the personal request of President Theodore Roosevelt. Saint-Gaudens was also to have revised the $2.50 and $5 gold denominations, but after his death on August 3, 1907 sculptor Bela Lyon Pratt was commissioned for this task. Yet another sculptor, Victor David Brenner, designed the Lincoln cent, which made its debut in 1909. All of this was much to the consternation of Chief Engraver Barber. The creation of new coin designs had traditionally been the responsibility of the chief engraver or an assistant at the Mint. Outside artists were not supposed to be involved.

The idea of revising the appearance of the nickel five-cent coin had come up in 1896, when Barber created a shield and wreath design, which, in the view of numismatists, was rather uninspired. The Liberty Head remained in use until 1909 when, following the release of the Lincoln cent, interest again turned toward the nickel. An item in *The Numismatist* in December of that year notes:

> The daily press has contained numerous dispatches from Washington stating that a new type five-cent piece, to bear the head of Washington, would soon be issued. As our five-cent coin is the only one under existing laws that may now be changed, a new type of this denomination is evidently expected, but so far there has been no official announcement as to the general character of the coin or when it would be issued.

> The announcement that Washington's head is to appear on our coinage is welcomed, and should it prove a fact, it is not improbable we may have a complete series of portrait coins for circulation of which the Lincoln cent is the first.

By this time, Barber had created several varieties of Washington-head patterns, listed today as Judd-1933 through 1939. Viewers found these uninspired as well, and again the Liberty Head continued as the style in use. Perhaps as a last hurrah, Barber turned out another Washington-head coin in 1910 (Judd-1942), but this one, too, was insipid from an artistic viewpoint.

There the matter rested, but only for a short time. In 1911, Franklin MacVeagh was secretary of the treasury, the Cabinet position charged with overseeing, among other things, changes in coinage designs. His son Eames wrote to his father on May 4 of that year, noting in part:

> A little matter that seems to have been overlooked by all of you is the opportunity to beautify the design of the nickel or five-cent pieces during your administration, and it seems to me that it would be a permanent souvenir of most attractive sorts.
>
> As possibly you are aware, it is the only coin design of which you can change during your administration, as I believe there is a law to the effect that the designs must not be changed oftener than every 25 years. I should think also that it might be the coin of which the greatest number are in circulation. . . .[1]

JAMES EARLE FRASER

Although the idea was hardly new, Eames's suggestion did spur Secretary MacVeagh into action and Assistant Secretary Abram Piatt Andrew spread the word that a new design was being sought. When news of this reached him, James Earle Fraser, an accomplished artist and sculptor, became interested in the project. (Fraser had been a student of Saint-Gaudens and had worked on the *Sherman Victory* statuary group that had earned numismatic fame when its goddess inspired the famous MCMVII $20.) When the artist met with Mint officials, Mint Director George E. Roberts for some reason told him that a *Lincoln* head was desired. On June 13, 1911, Fraser wrote to Roberts:

> I think your idea of the Lincoln head is a splendid one, and I shall be very glad to make you some sketches as soon as possible and let you see them. I think they should be reduced to the actual size of the coin; otherwise we will not be really able to judge them, even in the sketch period. I will have that done here, where I can watch the process. I have numerous sketches underway, some of which I hope may be of value.

The Lincoln idea seemed to please no one, especially in light of the recent debut of the Lincoln one-cent piece. The Treasury Department then decided that a competition among artists might produce good results. This did not please Fraser, who wrote to MacVeagh on June 20:

> In reference to the competition, I think the great trouble is that you may have numbers of sketches in the competition one of which you choose and, if I'm not

mistaken, you will be forced to stick very closely to that design, even though it might not be quite up to what you would want. Whereas, working with a competent man, there would be no doubt that a great many designs would be made, in fact, you would go on working til something of real merit was produced.

You may say, if you like, that I would be perfectly willing to satisfy the Art Commission Mr. MacVeagh spoke of. I will send you a few photographs of my work provided you wish to use them for reference.

Fraser developed his own motifs, and on September 11, 1911, wrote to the Mint, "The idea of the Indian and the buffalo on the same coin is, without doubt, purely American and seems to be singularly appropriate to have on one of our national coins." On September 19, he sent this to Secretary MacVeagh:

Although I realize that no definite commission has been given me in regard to the designs for the new coins, I have become so much interested in the sketches that I have pushed them a little further and now they are in the shape of electrotypes which I should like to submit for your consideration. Of course, this means that they are still merely sketches and not finished products, but I have had them reduced and made into their present form for the purpose of showing exactly what I would wish done, provided I furnished them. At present, they are the size of the penny but they could easily be enlarged to any size desired.

The idea of the Indian and the buffalo on the same coin is without doubt, purely American and seems to be singularly appropriate to have on one of our national coins. You will see that the Indian is entirely different than any that has ever been used on a coin. Most of the heads have been Caucasians with an Indian head-dress; in this case I have avoided using the war-bonnet and have made a purely Indian type. Therefore, I should like to ask whether or not you would consider placing these designs on the new model. I have also carried the Lincoln head further, not only because I was personally interested in it, but because Mr. Roberts has rather encouraged the idea of my doing so. Possibly you will be interested in knowing that the Italian Government has purchased a collection of my models for its National Museum in Rome. The Belgian government obtained a somewhat similar collection of my work last year.

By this time, Indian and buffalo motifs had long been in use on money already in circulation. Indians, both realistic and imaginary, had been used on coins, an Indian chief was familiar on paper money, and a bison could be seen on currency as well. Neverthless, the idea found reception at the Mint, and several models made by Fraser earned favorable comments.

THE LIFE OF JAMES EARLE FRASER

James Earle Fraser was born to Thomas Alexander and Cora West Fraser in Winona, Minnesota, on November 4, 1876. Having developed an interest in art at an early age, Fraser began his formal studies at the Art Institute of Chicago, later going to Paris to enroll at the École des Beaux Arts, the Académie Julian, and the Académie Colarossi. In 1898, he won a sculpture prize given by the American Art Association in Paris.

From 1898 to 1902, Fraser studied with America's most famous sculptor, Augustus Saint-Gaudens, assisting with the *Sherman Victory Monument*, erected in New York in 1903. Later Fraser worked with Saint-Gaudens at the artist's studio on a verdant hillside in Cornish, New Hampshire, and became a member of the artists' colony there. Fraser's first widely acclaimed work, a medallion portrait of a child, Horatio Hathaway Brewster, was exhibited at the National Academy Exhibition in 1902. This accomplishment brought him several commissions and launched his eminently successful career. *The End of the Trail*, his equestrian sculpture of an Indian in despair, as well as a seated figure of Jefferson were among hundreds of art objects on display at the 1904 Louisiana Purchase Exposition in St. Louis.

From 1906 to 1908, Fraser was an instructor of sculpture at the Art Students League in New York City. In 1910 a group of his medals, on exhibit at the Brussels International Exposition, was purchased by the Belgian government for its museum in Ghent. The Italian government also bought a selection of his medals for display in Rome. Both of these acquisitions are mentioned in Fraser's September 19, 1911 letter to Treasury Secretary MacVeagh.

Possibly inspired by his experiences as a youth in the Indian district of South Dakota, *The End of the Trail* had a direct influence on Fraser's nickel motif. Completed while he was still in his twenties, the sculpture earned Fraser a $1,000 prize and would become his most famous work. *The End of the Trail* was eventually purchased by the town of Visalia, California.

The list of Fraser's artistic works extends over decades and includes such prominent sculptures as the Robert Todd Lincoln sarcophagus at Arlington National Cemetery, "The Arts of Peace" figures at the Washington, DC, end of the Arlington Memorial Bridge, and statues for the Cathedral of St. John the Divine in New York City. His equestrian grouping at the Lincoln Memorial Circle in Washington, D.C. was a gift from Italy to the United States in 1951.

Fraser also produced a bust of his mentor, Augustus Saint-Gaudens, for the Hall of Fame maintained by New York University. In 1925 he created the motifs for the octagonal Norse-American Centennial silver and gold medals (The Norse-American Centennial, Inc. had requested a coin, but Congress granted a medal). He was president of the National Sculpture Society from 1925 to 1927, and was vice-president of the American Institute of Arts and Letters from 1926 to 1927. Fraser also served for many years as a member of the Commission of Fine Arts, a position that enabled him to direct commissions to his friends.

On November 13, 1913, Fraser married Laura Gardin, a well-known sculptor in her own right who had learned the art under Fraser's guidance. Together they designed the 1926 Oregon Trail Memorial commemorative half dollar. (Laura Fraser also stands high in the annals of American commemorative coins as the designer of the 1921 Alabama Centennial half dollar, the 1922 Grant Memorial half dollar, the 1922 Grant Memorial gold dollar, and the revision of the Sidney Bell design for the 1925 Fort Vancouver Centennial half dollar.)

The couple maintained a studio in Westport, Connecticut, until James's death on October 11, 1953. They had no children. So excellent was their work that historian Don Taxay, wrote this dedication in his book *An Illustrated History of U.S. Commemorative Coinage*, "To the late James and Laura Fraser who did so much to elevate the art of American coinage."

OVERVIEW OF THE NICKEL DESIGN

Returning now to the chronology of the new nickel design, the following is an overview of the situation given in a memorandum from Mint Director George E. Roberts on March 18, 1913:

> The first step in the negotiations for the new nickel piece was taken by Assistant Secretary Andrew in 1911. As a result of his interest in the subject, Mr. J.E. Fraser of New York, upon his own initiation, prepared several small wax models showing the Indian head and the buffalo about as they now appear on the coin, although in somewhat higher relief.
>
> Mr. Fraser was a pupil of Augustus Saint-Gaudens and much interested in the latter's work upon our gold coins. He shared in Saint-Gaudens' feelings that our coins, besides being counters in trade, should be examples in art, exerting an influence upon the artistic taste of the people. It was also his desire to make the new coin characteristically American in its type.
>
> Assistant Secretary Andrew and myself were both pleased with his designs and submitted them and introduced him to Secretary MacVeagh. The latter was pleased with the piece but cautious about committing himself to a change in the coin. He inclined to the opinion that if changers were to be made other artists should be invited to compete.
>
> The matter rested at this stage for some time, and although there was more or less discussion over it, and interviews with artists and connoisseurs, it was nearly a year before the Secretary took up the subject seriously. By this time he had made up his mind that if any change was to be made he wanted the Fraser designs.
>
> Mr. Fraser was requested to lower the relief and, if practicable, increase the size of the lettering showing the denomination. It was now mid-summer 1912. The Secretary was satisfied with the design as modified, but wished them submitted to the Fine Arts Commission. The Commission was scattered and it was necessary to see members individually. All who saw the models gave cordial approval to them. . . . These letters were submitted to the President . . . and the President's approval obtained. . . . [2]

During the next year, Fraser made modifications to the relief and to certain other features. In the summer of 1912, George Reith, an inventor employed by the Hobbs Manufacturing Company in Worcester, Massachusetts (makers of a device claimed to reject counterfeits when installed in a coin-operated machine) protested that the new nickel would not work in his counterfeit-detection apparatus, which, apparently, had been tested using Liberty Head coins. The sticking point was that the American Stamp and Ticket Vending Machine Company, whose devices accepted coins, was a prime Hobbs customer. Reith and company president Clarence W. Hobbs disrupted matters for many months; nevertheless, they did influence a few changes—such as removing the stars from around the border.

In 1907, Frenchmen Henry and Felix Weil had formed a private New York City firm, the Medallic Art Company, which was commissioned to make the hubs from Fraser's models. The Weils owned a fine Janvier portrait lathe that could do better work than the related Hill lathe at the Mint. (The Mint had installed a Janvier lathe in 1906, but no one had been trained in its operation, and it had remained idle until John Sinnock—who later became chief engraver—used it in 1918 to make reductions for the Lincoln, Illinois, commemorative half dollar.[3]) The Weil brothers had created hubs for earlier coins, including the Saint-Gaudens MCMVII $20, as well as both the hubs and the *coining dies* for the 1903 Louisiana Purchase Exposition commemorative gold dollars. (This is believed to have been the first time since 1792 that dies had been made outside the Philadelphia Mint.)

The hubs and dies for the new nickel were delivered to Chief Engraver Charles E. Barber on December 26, 1912. On January 11, 1913, Philadelphia Mint Superintendent John Landis advised Director Roberts in Washington that hardening of the dies and hubs was to be done that day, and that coinage would begin the following Monday.

The first 17 coins were struck on January 13, bearing the pattern known today as Judd-1950. (These were similar to the design adopted later, but lacked the sculptor's initial F.) There then followed a small run of another pattern, now known as Judd-1951, which had the motifs set in farther from the rim and more space around. These were shown to Reith, who, somehow, was allowed to make further suggestions that resulted in additional small revisions. But Fraser was patient and waited until January 20, when he sent a telegram to Director Roberts saying, "Dies are finished and will be in Philadelphia tomorrow, delay caused by working with inventor until he was satisfied. The coin is practically the same."

Inventor Reith and a Mr. Henson from the Hobbs firm, followed the dies to the Mint, where they insisted on yet another minor change. This adjustment was accomplished in the machine shop, after which the two men "allowed" the coinage—apparently of test impressions—to commence on January 24. One of these impressions was sent to the Hobbs Manufacturing Co., generating a reaction from Hobbs that included a long list of changes that had to be made in order for their device to work. Further meetings took place, with a Hobbs device on hand for testing and Hobbs' attorney taking notes. Eventually patience ran out, and on February 15, Secretary MacVeagh stated that no further changes would be made for any reason.

It was soon learned that dozens of other companies—including 70 that had submitted proposals to the Post Office Department for stamp-vending devices—were not only making counterfeit coin detectors for vending and other machines, but that none had experienced any problems with the new nickel. It may be poetic justice that today, in the early 21st century, collectors of coin-operated devices do not even recognize Hobbs as an important name in the industry. Indeed, the firm may actually have failed, as evidenced by a poignant letter, unearthed in the National Archives by numismatic researcher David W. Lange, from Fraser's attorney Meredith Hare to Secretary MacVeagh. In response to the Hobbs claim (regarding the Liberty Head nickels already in use) that its machines were in extensive use throughout the Northeast, Hare writes:

> Today I have had an interview with Mr. Wilbur Fiske, the executive officer of the Hudson & Manhattan Rail Road Co., who has charge of such matters, and he showed me a copy of a letter he had sent to the agent of the Hobbs Manufacturing Co., telling him that the Hudson & Manhattan R.R. Co. was entirely dissatisfied with the coin-detecting machine and required to have them all removed from the railroad's premises.[4]

As a collector and historian of coin-operated devices, particularly musical instruments and gambling machines, I am quite familiar with the state of the art of detection devices of the era. None of those used in popular devices at that time were at all sophisticated. Although procedures varied, generally the dimensions of the coin slot prohibited slugs and counterfeits that were too thick or too wide from entering the machine. Slugs that were too narrow or that could be detected by a small magnet went to the floor of the machine, rather than to the cash box. Because the Liberty Head nickels, and some of the Shield nickels still in circulation, were often worn thin, the detectors were built with a degree of latitude so as not to reject legitimate coins and annoy patrons. (As a result, many slugs were taken in—a factor considered part of the cost of doing business.) I am not aware of any machine that would accept Liberty Head nickels that would not accept the new Buffalo type.

After the Hobbs brouhaha, much ado about nothing from a company whose devices did not work well even with the Liberty Head nickels, the new Buffalo nickel finally became a reality!

DESIGNS ILLUSTRATE THE WEST

It is customary to talk about the obverse of a coin before discussing the reverse, so the correct nomenclature for the Buffalo nickel should be Indian nickel or Indian Head nickel. However, in this case, the reverse of the coin has taken both numismatic and popular precedence, so we will begin there.

Technically, the Buffalo nickel does not depict a buffalo at all. Rather, it shows a *bison*, a slightly different variety of viviparous quadruped—as John Audubon called four-legged mammals. Bison (or *buffalo*—after all, it's "Buffalo Bill" Cody, not "Bison Bill") once ranged in immense numbers in the American West and were a defining icon during the age of exploration. Even the creator of the coin, James Earle Fraser, called it a buffalo. According to conventional, but incorrect, wisdom, the animal depicted on the nickel was modeled after Black Diamond, who hailed from the Central Park Zoo in New York City, not way out West where the buffalo—er, bison—roamed. Even in the artist's lifetime, this attribution was widely published in newspaper and numismatic accounts such as this one from the August 1915 issue of *The Numismatist:*

> Black Diamond, the famous bison of the Central Park Zoological Garden, New York City, whose image adorns one side of the nickel, will be slain within a few days, but his massive head will be preserved and mounted. The animal has been the model for many sculptors and painters.
>
> Despite his fame, there were no bidders when he was put up at auction, but recently the bison was sold to a dealer in poultry and game for about $700. Black Diamond was born 19 years ago in the Zoological Garden and weighs something more than a ton. He is docile and considered a splendid specimen of his kind, but has outlived his usefulness.

The buyer was allowed to leave the animal at the zoo for a time, which he did, but on December 17, 1915, the most numismatic of all viviparous quadrupeds was slaughtered. His carcass weighed 1,550 pounds and yielded about 750 pounds of dressed meat and a hide measuring 13 by 13 feet, the latter destined to become an automobile robe. Black Diamond's head was later mounted and has been exhibited throughout the country, including at the 94th annual ANA summer convention in Baltimore in 1985, the last year in my term as ANA president.

James Earle Fraser seems to have had multiple memory lapses when discussing his nickel, as did his wife Laura, who later added her opinions. Fraser is quoted as having later said that "He was not a plains buffalo, but none other than Black Diamond, the contrariest animal in the Bronx Park Zoo; I stood for hours watching and catching his form in plastic clay." This seems authoritative enough, until examined. Robert R. Van Ryzin in his masterful 1995 book, *Twisted Tales: Sifted Fact, Fantasy and Fiction from U.S. Coin History,* points out that the animal was never at that zoo, but according to official records, was indeed at Central Park, as stated in the above item from *The Numismatist.* Van Ryzin also mentions other locations that were said to have been the animal's home.

As living—er, dead—proof that Black Diamond was probably not the model for Fraser's design, the animal's extant mounted head has its horns set much higher and of different proportion than those depicted on the nickel. If Fraser did use him as a model, the sculptor was sloppy in his work—which seems unlikely. The scenario is very confused. In modern times, even the U.S. Mint has questioned the Black Diamond attribution.[5] For good measure, here is another claimant, as noted in an item from the August 1926 issue of *The Numismatist:*

> Bronx, the buffalo whose portrait adorns the Buffalo nickel, is no longer king of the Bronx Zoological Park herd, says a press dispatch. His 35-year reign ended recently when Cheyenne, a younger bull, challenged his leadership and, after a terrific battle, gored his right side and knocked off one of his horns. After the keepers separated the animals the deposed monarch was exiled to a separate pen and Cheyenne was left to lead the herd.

Another creature, an animal named Pablo, is said to have modeled the 1901 Legal Tender $10 "Bison Note" for which Marcus Baldwin engraved the vignette. However, Van Ryzin cites information stating that the $10 bill image was taken from a stuffed animal, on display since the 1880s at the Smithsonian Institution, not far from the Bureau of Engraving and Printing. The chief taxidermist was said to have removed the glass from the case so that the figure could be photographed for the engraver. On the other hand, as Van Ryzin points out, there are two sides to that story, too.[6] All of this folderol leaves this author wondering if anybody really cares.

THE INDIAN PORTRAIT

The obverse continues the American West theme, showing an authentic American Indian profile. Fraser created a composite portrait from sketches he had made earlier using three subjects as models. One of his models was the Sioux Chief Iron Tail (possibly Iron *Trail*), who had bested General George Custer in his "last stand" at the Battle of Little Big Horn. Another was a Cheyenne Chief named Two Moon,[7] who later toured the amusement circuit showcasing himself as the "Indian on the nickel." The third was a man whose name Fraser could not recall. Here are Fraser's words, including a slight misspelling of what should have been Two *Moon*, in a letter to Mint Director George Roberts in 1913:

> I have your letter asking whether or not the Indian head on the new nickel was a portrait or a type. It is a type rather than a portrait. Before the nickel was made I had done several portraits of Indians, among them Iron Tail (Custer's opponent at Little Big Horn), Two Moons, and one or two others,

and probably got characteristics from those men in the head on the coins, but my purposes was not to make a portrait but a type.

The Numismatist, August 1913, printed a photograph of Chief Iron Tail (or Trail) of the Cheyenne (Iron Tail was Sioux, as mentioned above). Two Moon, who is (was) Cheyenne and whose status seems secure (as a model), was not illustrated. Writing in *The Numismatist* in May 1913, W.H. De Shon took the view that the portrait was of one person, rather than a composite, and commented: "On the obverse is a most artistically executed head of a Comanche Indian." Until this point, Comanches had not entered into the equation. Misinformation was rife in the numismatic community.

Robert R. Van Ryzin published an article in *Numismatic News*, February 6, 1990, titled "Which Indian Really Modeled?" in which he debunked certain later impostors. Additional details are given in his aforementioned book, *Twisted Tales: Sifted Fact, Fantasy and Fiction from U.S. Coin History*, 1995.

One of the more vocal claimants was Two Guns White Calf, son of the last Blackfoot tribal chief, who capitalized on his made-up status. To end this, Fraser wrote on June 10, 1931, in a letter made public by the Bureau of Indian affairs:

> The Indian head on the buffalo nickel is not a direct portrait of any particular Indian, but was made from several portrait busts which I did of Indians. As a matter of fact, I used three different heads. I remember two of the men. One was Irontail, the best Indian head I can remember. The other one was Two Moons, the other I cannot recall.

The artist seems to have had a memory jog and in 1938 remembered the identity of the mystery Indian:

> In fact, the profile is a composite of three plains Indians—a Sioux, a Kiowa, and a Cheyenne. The three Indians were Iron Tail, a Sioux, Big Tree, a Kiowa, and Two Moons, a Cheyenne. The Indians had come to visit President Roosevelt and had stopped off in New York. During this time I was able to study and photograph them. The three had the combined features of the hardy, virile types of Great Plains Indian.[8]

With this as a clue, Van Ryzin did some checking, found records of two Indians named Big Tree, and learned that there was only one from the Kiowa tribe. This fellow, known as Chief Adoette, and a companion had attacked a freight wagon train in May 1871, and killed seven teamsters. The chief was sentenced to prison, but was released in 1873. By 1913, the year of the nickel, Big Tree was a Sunday school teacher at the Rainy Mountain Baptist Church. By the time the impostor Chief John Big Tree came into the limelight, the Big Tree of nickel fame (assuming that Fraser recalled the Big Tree name correctly) had long since departed this earth.

This did not stop Chief John Big Tree from playing the publicity for all it was worth, including in numismatic circles. One article, "Chief John Big Tree, the Man on the Buffalo Nickel, Highlights 1966 Texas Numismatic Association Convention," in *Numismatic News*, April 25, 1966, helped promote this fiction. I should mention that *Numismatic News* did not create the hoopla, they simply reported it:

> The limelight of the convention was shared by . . . Chief John Big Tree, one of the three Indians who posed for the Indian Head nickel. Clearly, the spry, witty,

old chief stole the show. Chief John Big Tree who posed as a model for the original buffalo nickel was commissioned by Falstaff Brewing Corporation of Galveston, Texas to appear at the convention of the Texas Numismatic Association.

Chief John Big Tree, who claims to be 104 years old, is a full-blooded Iroquois who now lives with his wife on the Onondaga Reservation near Syracuse, New York. He was one of three Indians selected to pose for design of the buffalo nickel in 1912. According to the Chief, he was used as the model for the nose and forehead of the Indian nickel while a Sioux modeled for the cheek and chin of the likeness and a Cheyenne for the hair and headdress. Chief Big Tree says he was working in a Coney Island show when he was chosen to pose, "because of his classic facial features."

MORE INDIANS

Indians, imaginary and real, had been used numismatically for a long time before Fraser's 1913 nickel. The 1854 gold dollar and $3 pieces each had an Indian Princess motif, with Miss Liberty as an Indian maiden wearing a headdress of ostrich plumes. This was slightly off the mark in realism, as few American Indians would have had access to the plumage of an African bird. There was also the Indian Head cent, minted from 1859 to 1909, with Miss Liberty dressed in an Indian war bonnet—in spite of the fact that, in actuality, only males wore war bonnets.

Reality emerged at last in 1899 with the $5 Silver Certificate, which featured an authentic Indian chief. The model is said to have been a man named Running Antelope, although a few other names have appeared in paper money texts over the years. In 1908, the gold $2.50 and $5 coins, both designed by Bela Lyon Pratt, depicted the head of a real chief. Meanwhile, in 1907, the Augustus Saint-Gaudens $10 coin appeared, showing a fanciful Indian, modeled by Saint-Gaudens's mistress, Hettie Anderson, who was also fitted out with a war bonnet.

DETAILS OF THE INDIAN HEAD/BUFFALO DESIGN

Unlike any preceding coin made for circulation, the Buffalo nickel had little in the way of open, smooth field surfaces. Instead, most areas on the obverse and reverse contained design elements or, especially on the reverse, an irregular background as on a bas-relief plaque. The entire ensemble was done in high relief on both sides—very artistic to be sure, but causing great problems to the proper striking of the design. (I will say more about this later.) A summary describing the motifs of the first issue (early 1913, before modification) reads:

Obverse

An Indian head, large in the context of the coin's surface, faces to the right. Three feathers are at the back of his head, and hair and a braid extend downward concealing the ear.

The word LIBERTY is in small letters at the border at the upper right. At the lower left the date 1913 is on the Indian's shoulder, and the designer's initial F is incused or recessed below. The border is plain (not dentiled), this being the style for all nickels of later designs as well.

Reverse

A bison stands on a mound of earth, facing to the left. In the field at the upper right is the motto in three lines, E / PLURIBUS / UNUM, in small letters. Curved at the top border is UNITED STATES OF AMERICA. Below the mound at the bottom of the coin is FIVE CENTS. Coins struck at the Denver and San Francisco mints had an appropriate mintmark, D or S, above the rim, more or less below the space separating FIVE and CENTS. The edge is plain (not reeded).

MORE ON NOMENCLATURE

As is seen in the quoted correspondence, this coin was called a *Buffalo* nickel from the outset, including by Mint officials and its creator, sculptor James Earle Fraser. The term is still overwhelmingly popular. However, over the years, many have disagreed with its use. Take as an example an article by Stuart Mosher in *The Numismatist*, August 1945.

Mosher was a person to be reckoned with. He had been curator of the coin collection at the Smithsonian Institution, a dealer with New Netherlands Coin Co., editor of *The Numismatist*, and the main researcher for the first *Guide Book of United States Coins* in 1946 (cover date 1947). He took the U.S. Mint to task for issuing a news release using the term "casting pennies," rather than "striking cents," stating that the penny had no

part in the United States monetary system. He further observed that the animal on the five-cent piece was a bison, not a buffalo, and that a "nickel" contains three times as much copper as it does nickel, to which he added, "We are uncertain why it is called a 'Buffalo nickel,' although the name is preferable to 'Bison copper,' which it might logically be called."

Today, in the early 21st century, *Coin World*, which has the largest circulation of any numismatic periodical, identifies the coin as an Indian Head nickel. The ever-popular Red Book takes an ambivalent view, calling it the "Indian Head or Buffalo type." Whatever you call them, these pieces are clearly numismatic favorites.

> At the Eagle Theatre, probably somewhere in the Midwest, it was announced that Chief Blue Sky, "a genuine Sioux Indian from the Rose Bud Reservation will speak to you all about Indian life. Also, he sings, dances, and imitates the church chimes, animals, etc." A look-alike (not quite) in a war bonnet stands in front. The time was Wednesday, June 24, 1914, and the nation just couldn't get enough of Indians, the Wild West, and other related lore. No doubt, the new Indian Head / Buffalo nickel fed the interest.

Producing the New Nickels
Getting Ready

In January 1913, there was much public and numismatic interest in the forthcoming new design. The old Liberty Head design was not lamented, and there was no mention in the popular press about this coin being made. Instead, efforts were put toward striking the new Indian Head/Buffalo coin.[9] Director of the Mint George E. Roberts, wrote this on January 10, 1913:

> Replying to your letter of the third I beg to say that the old type of five-cent piece will not be coined at all in 1913. The San Francisco Mint as well as the other mints will issue the new five-cent piece.

Acting Superintendent Albert A. Norris of the Philadelphia Mint wrote, also on January 10, 1913:

> We do not know when the Proof coins for the year will be ready, as we are delayed by experiments with the new five-cent piece. Our orders are that there will be none of the old design five-cent pieces struck this year.

Another source commented:

> The information comes from Washington that the issue of new nickels has been held up on account of protest of the slot machine manufacturers. The manufacturers complained that just as they had perfected chewing gum and other slot machines to refuse counterfeit nickels and "slugs" designed for fraud, the government was about to place in circulation a five-cent piece, the design of which would practically nullify their inventions.

PREPARING THE DIES

It fell to Chief Engraver Charles E. Barber and others at the Mint to prepare dies from the models created by James Earle Fraser, these supplanting the ones made by Medallic Art Company. Meanwhile, the Hobbs Manufacturing Co. representatives were an annoyance, as described earlier. On January 26, 1913, Fraser wrote to George E. Roberts, commenting on what had been done:

> I find the engraving which was necessary to make the two sides of the coin fit exactly, the reduction of the edge, and the simplifying of the background under the buffalo's head beautifully done, showing no difference between the surface which I put on the models and the one they have made. I am delighted with the work at the Mint.[10]

MINTING BEGINS

On March 4, 1913, Chief Engraver Charles E. Barber, then in Philadelphia, wrote this to Mint Director George E. Roberts, in Washington, D.C., commenting on problems already experienced with the new nickels:

Dear Mr. Roberts:

> I mentioned when in Washington that although we had made a few of the new nickel pieces that the real test would come when we commenced regular coinage. Well, that test is certainly upon us.
>
> We find that we are getting only about one third the number of pieces per pair of dies that were produced by the old design, consequently we are using three times the number of dies. This is taxing my department to the very limit, in fact I am only just able to supply the demand of the several mints without their working overtime. I have had to call a halt on overtime in the coining room as I had not dies to keep the presses running more than the regular working day. . . .
>
> I do not find any fault with the coiners of this Mint or other mints. The difficulty is in the design and shape of the die. In the first place the dies are so convex that if the feeders skip a feed the dies come together. This causes the loss of many dies. Next, the movement of the metal over the rough convex surface of the dies grinds small particles from the blank, which remain [in] the low places of the die and fairly grinds all detail from the design, leaving a very poor, worn, faded-out impression of both the Indian and the buffalo. . . . The dies are worn out, being smooth in some parts and in others too rough to be allowed to remain in the presses.
>
> If it was not the question of getting a large output in a short time I certainly would suggest that fewer pieces per pair of dies be made, and the dies changed still more frequently. I feel that a large portion of our present coinage is not calculated to bring us any credit. . . .
>
> One other cause for the destruction of dies is brought about by the automatic feed or hopper. If a blank becomes fixed in the tube there is no one to notice or remedy this condition. In consequence, the dies come together. Formerly, the attendant at the press saw the lodgment of a blank

in the tube and dislodged it, which allowed the blanks to fall in place, and no damage was done.[11]

Each of the three mints then in operation produced nickels of the new Indian Head/Buffalo design. The Philadelphia Mint would go on to issue them from 1913 to 1921, from 1923 to 1930, and from 1934 to 1937. The Denver Mint made them from 1913 to 1920, from 1924 to 1929, and from 1934 to 1938. (In 1934, Buffalo nickels were struck only at the Denver Mint. The output included the curious 1938-D/S variety.) At the San Francisco Mint, coinage of Buffalo nickels extended from 1913 to 1921, from 1923 to 1931, and from 1935 to 1937. In 1931 this would be the only mint to make coins of this denomination.

The first production at the Philadelphia Mint had commenced on February 17, 1913, on a single press that turned out 120 coins per minute. Some of the first pieces were sent to Secretary MacVeagh, who forwarded them to the Chicago Coin Club, where they were distributed to members before appearing in circulation.[12]

INTO CIRCULATION

In a special ceremony held on March 4, 1913, at Fort Wadsworth, Long Island, New York, President William Howard Taft, in one of the last acts of his administration, turned the first spade of earth for a memorial to the American Indian, a statue measuring 165 feet high. *The New York Times* covered the event the next day, including this commentary:

> The new five-cent piece made its first appearance in circulation yesterday afternoon at Fort Wadsworth, when, as the chief surprise of the ceremonies inaugurating the memorial to the North American Indian, Dr. George F. Kunz, on behalf of the American Scenic and Historical Preservation Society, produced a canvas bag and from its bulky depths drew forth a handful of shining new nickels fresh from the Mint. . . .
>
> Dr. Kunz fixed it up with Director Roberts . . . and a bag of the new coins was sent to New York in time for yesterday's gathering. . . . The first coin was given to President Taft, the second to Rodman Wanamaker (originator and backer of the memorial project), and the next to the Indian chiefs (33 of them) there present. Then everyone in the crowd was presented with one.[13]

George Frederick Kunz was a noted gemologist with Tiffany & Co., whose career flourished in the late 19th and early 20th centuries. He was primarily concerned with rocks and minerals, meteorites, medals, coins, and similar objects. Kunz joined the American Numismatic and Archaeological Society on January 16, 1893. In 1895, he was instrumental in a movement to replace the current designs of silver coins with those displaying better artistry—an effort that resulted in many newspaper and other accounts, but no coin changes. From 1907 to 1908, he headed the American Numismatic Society Committee on New Coinage Designs, during which time he advised President Roosevelt concerning production of the MCMVII double eagle.

The new nickels were distributed from each of the three mints and received enthusiastic public response. There was a strong demand from the public at banks all across the country. Large numbers of them were saved, at least for the time being, as evidenced by the availability of such coins today. It was not until November 1913 that the artist himself encountered such a coin in pocket change. Years later Laura Gardin Fraser, recalling her wedding day, recounted this:

> A little footnote for the archives! When we left the Little Church Around the Corner as Mr. and Mrs. Fraser, we took a bus to go up to our favorite haunt, the Metropolitan Art Museum. Mr. Fraser gave a quarter to the bus conductor, and in change we received the first buffalo nickel we had seen in circulation. . . .[14]

As often happens, though, the novelty of the pieces eventually faded, and many that had been set aside were placed into circulation.

A MODIFICATION TO THE DESIGN

PROBLEM FORESEEN

Early in the life of the Buffalo nickel, it was realized that the word FIVE CENTS on the reverse, being on a raised mound, was likely to wear away quickly. The same could have been said for the date, also on a raised background, but no thought was given to that—perhaps as the problem did not manifest itself until later.

In the spring, Chief Engraver Charles E. Barber made changes to the design that included placing FIVE CENTS in a recessed area, reducing the hair details on the obverse portrait, and eliminating some details of the bison. These alterations apparently met with the approval of designer James Earle Fraser, per his April 25, 1913 letter to Mint Director George E. Roberts:

> Your letter of April 22nd last, together with the enclosure, reached me in due course, and it seems to me that the nickel enclosed with the "Five Cents" made clearer is good and does not at all interfere with the general design. . . .[15]

At the same time, the fields of the coin were made more smooth than on the earlier version, somewhat reducing the artistic effect. Traditional numismatists were used to flat fields with slight curvature (basining) toward the rims, so the open areas gave the portrait and other devices a cameo effect. During this era, when outside artists created designs for the Mint, the nature of the fields was sometimes altered. This was especially true of the 1907 Saint-Gaudens double eagle and the later 1916 Standing Liberty quarter by Hermon A. MacNeil, both of which had little in the way of smooth open areas. Years later, in 1988, Walter Breen gave this opinion: "Actions by chief engraver Charles E. Barber "greatly diluted the vigor of Fraser's original design."[16]

The modified design is known today as the Type II, while the earlier design is the Type I. The first Type II nickels were struck on May 10, 1913. The change, however, seems to affected the die life. David W. Lange quotes National Archives data to the effect that the last 12 pairs of dies used to strike Type I nickels at Philadelphia averaged 150,168, while life of the Type II nickel dies, as evidenced by the first 12 pairs, plummeted to an average of 109,389.[17] It is likely that whatever Type I dies were still in the presses remained in use until they were worn enough to require replacement.

A SMALL REVISION

The chief engraver's implied request to lower the relief of the dies was not honored. However, in 1916 the portrait of the Indian is said to have been revised ever so slightly, particularly the nose, although the difference either does not exist or is difficult to discern. The word LIBERTY was made stronger and placed slightly more toward the center, allowing more distance between it and the rim. The striking of Buffalo nickels continued to be fraught with difficulty until the series ended in 1938.

Connoisseurs and specialists are very aware today that finding needle-sharp examples of certain issues is very difficult, if not nearly impossible. We will explore this subject in depth in the next chapter.

On most coins, the anvil (lower) die is the "tail" or reverse of the coin, but for the Buffalo nickel, the anvil die stuck the "head," or obverse side. As to Barber's assertion that planchet dust and residue were problems, it is true that this detritus would have accumulated in the anvil die, the "head" or obverse die for the Buffalo nickel. This could account in part for the obverses of coins often being very weak in their design detail. However, as a general rule, the reverse, struck by the hammer die is even weaker. I suggest that Barber's analysis is not correct, and that die spacing was the main factor, which we will discuss in the next chapter.

REVIEWS AND COMMENTS
REACTION TO THE DESIGN

The Numismatist, March 1913, carried this account by Edgar H. Adams, editor:

> Through the courtesy of the Hon. George E. Roberts, Director of the United States Mint, we are enabled to show in this number a reproduction of the new five-cent piece, which is now being coined at the mint. It was intended to issue this coin early in February, but it was not until Feb. 17 that regular coinage started, when one press produced them at the rate of 120 per minute.
>
> The design is radically different from that of any five-cent piece that has ever been issued at the mint, and is slightly concave on both sides, somewhat like the present $10 and $20 pieces. Directly under the figure 3 of the date 1913 on the obverse is the letter "F" for the designer of the piece, James Earle Fraser of New York City. It is said that Mr. Fraser took as a model an Indian of the Cheyenne tribe who recently visited New York City. The bison was modeled after a specimen in the New York Zoological Garden.[18]
>
> Mr. Fraser, the designer, is reported as saying that the capital "F" below the date has met with the approval of the Secretary of the Treasury, the Director of the Mint, and also the National Art Commission. Already, it is said, the presence of this tiny letter has aroused a certain amount of criticism, similar to that which greeted the appearance of the letters "V.D.B." on the Lincoln cent, which resulted in their removal, doing an injustice to Mr. Brenner, its designer, and violating all precedents.
>
> It is to be regretted that the new coin does not show much more finished die work, which could easily have been accomplished. We are inclined to think that the rough finish of the design will encourage counterfeiters, whose handicraft

need not now fear comparison which it has met in the past with the ordinarily delicate and finished mint issues.

The new piece certainly has radically changed the old-time tradition that Columbia is our best representation of "Liberty." In view of the rather restricted character of both of the Indian and the buffalo today, it is an open question whether either is a good symbol of "liberty." Saint-Gaudens, in an interview, once stated that his conception of a symbol of "Liberty" was that of 'a leaping boy.' We still prefer Miss Columbia as the proper representation of freedom, and regret that she does not appear on the new five-cent piece. We have no doubt that the original enlarged model of this design was of a handsome character, but that it would not allow for the great reduction to the size of a five-cent piece is quite apparent.

From an artistic point of view no doubt the design is all that it should be, but there is another element to be considered in the making of a coin design, and that is the one of practicability. For instance, the date and the motto are in such obscure figures and letters that the slightest wear will obliterate them beyond understanding.

Altogether the new design emphasizes the absolute necessity of the appointment of a proper committee to pass upon new coin designs. Such a committee should be composed of sculptors, numismatists, and die engravers. One of this committee should be the Chief Engraver of the Mint. It will not be until the appointment of such a committee that we may expect to see a coin that will embody all the proper requisites. . . .

There can be nothing, however, in the story going the rounds that the government will "recall" the coins already issued. The government cannot repudiate them, nor can it get possession of hundreds of thousands of them already in circulation to destroy them. It can only change the design and issue new coins of that design to circulate with the others, as was done in 1883, when the five-cent piece with the word "cents" was issued instead of the piece without "cents."

This lukewarm review by Adams, perhaps the leading numismatic writer of his day, probably influenced some readers not to collect the series. Modern coins were not particularly in favor anyway, largely because there was no convenient way to store or display them, so many dealers did not have them in their stocks.

The comment about complaints regarding the initial F must have been limited, for I have come across no other mention of it in the popular press.

Adams had further comments in the May 1913 issue of *The Numismatist*:

Satisfactory changes in the design might be as follows:

Retain the head of the Cheyenne Indian, which is really an artistic creation, but reduce the size so as to give more field surface to the obverse. Above the head place the word "Liberty" and, underneath, the date in figures as large as those of the old design. If the initial of the designer's name is retained, let it be incused in the bottom of the Indian's neck.

Eliminate the buffalo from the reverse entirely. Discard also the motto "E Pluribus Unum," as there seems to be no good reason why it should appear on any of our coins. Around the upper border place the legend

"United States of America," in the center the figure 5 as appeared on the old shield nickels, and on the lower border, the word "Cents." A design of this kind would be sufficiently artistic. . . .

T.L. Comparette, curator of the Mint Collection, included this in his description of the new nickel in the article "Coins and Medals in the United States in 1913," for the *American Journal of Numismatics:*

> It may not have been wise to place a type on each side of the small piece, a simpler reverse might have been better; the Indian head and the buffalo may be too softly modeled for coin types; perhaps inscriptions have been sacrificed to the types, so that the former are too small and the latter too large for the size of the field; but with all the faults that may be alleged against the new piece, one outstanding truth remains, that Mr. Fraser's designs are works of art, powerfully modeled, and strong.

In 1917, in *Mehl's Numismatic Monthly*, B. Max Mehl noted this in his feature article, "The Men Who Designed Our New Coins":

> The Buffalo nickel has been greatly admired and was a pleasing contrast to the five-cent piece which had been coined for so many years. Its designer, James Earle Fraser, is a native of Minnesota and has been prominent in the art world for many years.

The Numismatist, December 1927, included this tribute:

> Dr. Gustave Alexander, professor of the University of Vienna, is attending a joint session of the Interstate Post-Graduate Association and the Kansas City Southwest Clinical Society, in session at Kansas City. In an interview with him the *Kansas City Star* says:
>
> He says prettier things about Kansas City, and all America, too, for that matter, than almost any visitor we have had from foreign shores for a long time. He likes America's coinage, for instance. He keeps a ready supply of buffalo nickels in his pocket because he believes they are so beautiful. What? You never saw any beauty in a buffalo nickel yourself? Neither did the writer, but he got a fine calling down from Dr. Alexander for that lack of appreciation.
>
> "I believe sincerely the American 5-cent piece is the most beautiful coin in the world," Dr. Alexander says. "The head of the Indian is perfect and the head of the buffalo is, too. The dimensions are as good as they were on the old Greek coins, which were supposed to have been classics for all time."

Numismatic Art in America, Aesthetics of the United States Coinage, by Cornelius Vermeule, published by Harvard in 1971, stands today as the most valuable book on coin designs ever written by a numismatically knowledgeable author. The comments of Vermeule, long associated with the Boston Museum of Fine Arts, include these:

> The so-called "buffalo" nickel, designed in 1912 and placed in circulation in 1913, is the ultimate homage to our native or Indian-prairie tradition. The small coin is overwhelmed by the mighty plasticity of the Indian's rugged head and the majestic buffalo on his plot of prairie.

In the model dated 1912 and the first issue of 1913 the bit of earth was like a mound, but this feature was modified for some reason to emphasize the beast at the expense of flattened landscape. Despite the rough naturalness of modeling and the true flavor of the man and beast, it is an amusing commentary on Fraser's sources of photographic faithfulness that the three Indians used were probably all performers on the Wild West show or sideshow circuit, one having been snatched from performances at Coney Island, and the buffalo, or technically bison, was "captured" by the artist in the New York Zoological Gardens. . . .

Richard Doty, now numismatic curator at the Smithsonian Institution, had this to say in his 1998 book, *American's Money America's Story:*

The five-cent piece was modified [in 1913], and America's most artistic minor coin resulted. Struck until 1938, the "Indian head," or "buffalo," nickel showed what a gifted designer (in this case James Earle Fraser) could do with a humble coinage in base metal.

For more than a generation, Buffalo nickels were fresh in circulation. After the first year or two they did not attract much notice in the press, save perhaps in connection with Indians, many of whom were called "chiefs" in an honorary sense, who traveled with vaudeville troupes, Wild West shows, patent medicine caravans, and the like. Buffaloes also got their share of attention in such shows.

By 1938 the Indian Head / Buffalo nickel had been in circulation for 25 years and, under the terms of the Coinage Act of 1890, could be replaced. This was done and, without mourning the old design, the Jefferson nickel made its debut.

MINTAGES AND DISTRIBUTION OVER THE YEARS

Buffalo nickels were struck nearly every year from 1913 to 1938. Generally, the quantities coined reflected the American economy and the mood of the times. From 1916 through 1920, the Mints produced Buffalo nickels in large numbers, reflecting the boom times during World War I, when factories worked around the clock to furnish supplies to combatants in Europe. Then in 1921, a recession set in and production of copper, nickel, and silver coins—except for dollars, which were subject to special legislation—slowed as well.

The years from the mid-1920s through the end of the decade were prosperous, but the Depression followed, hitting its deepest point in 1933. In a time when money was scarce, the low-denomination nickel fared well. Beginning in 1934, mintages were generous, reaching a high for the denomination of 118,997,000 in 1936.

Production took place at each of the three active Mints—Philadelphia, Denver, and San Francisco. Quantities made at each mint depended on regional demand, which was measured by the Federal Reserve System and the needs of local and regional banks. In 1931, only the San Francisco Mint struck nickels. In 1938, nickels were coined only in Denver.

Typically, banks stored the coins in paper rolls of 40 nickels each. Until the 1930s, most coins were probably put into circulation as soon as banks received them. In the 1930s, however, many remained in vaults, resulting in bank patrons being paid in rolls dated a few years earlier.

PROOFS MADE FOR COLLECTORS

UNPOPULAR INNOVATIONS

For many years, dating back to 1821 or even a few years earlier, the Mint had been striking Proof coins for collectors. As with the Shield and Liberty Head coins, these coins had mirrorlike or *brilliant* finishes, made by using special, highly polished dies and striking the coins carefully on special planchets. Proofs of various denominations were widely sold beginning in 1858. By 1913, they were a firmly established tradition. In an era before collecting by mintmark varieties was popular with numismatists, a Proof served to represent a given date in a favorite series.

In 1908, Sand Blast Proofs of the new $2.50, $5, $10, and $20 coin designs were offered to collectors. These Proofs were made using regular dies, but the coins were struck slowly on a medal press to bring up all of the design details. Each coin was then "blasted" with a high-speed stream of air carrying minute sand particles, producing a matte finish.

The Paris Mint, considered by many to be the leading edge in artistry, had been using matte, rather than mirrored, finishes for some years. The Philadelphia Mint had used the process in the 1890s on Assay Commission medals and other products, but not on coins. Styles of matte finishes varied, but no detailed accounts were kept of the manufacturing processes. It is likely that several methods were used, including pickling or sandblasting the *dies* before making coins from them, or treating the coins themselves after striking, as with the Sand Blast Proofs.

Mint officials had thought the Sand Blast Proofs would be viewed as especially artistic, but Collectors detested the new style and its 1909 successor, the Satin Finish Proof. They voted with their pocketbooks and simply didn't order them. The American Numismatic Association even made a formal complaint to the Treasury Department, but to no avail. Proof gold coins continued to be made in these unpopular finishes, despite declining sales and mintages.

MATTE PROOF BUFFALO NICKELS

The last of the Liberty Head nickels were struck, in mirror Proof format, in early 1913. Following the process initiated in 1909 with the then new Lincoln cent, Proofs of the new Buffalo nickels were produced with the matte finish. This seems to have been done by lightly pickling the die faces, which gave a somewhat "beaded" or "orange peel" appearance to the field, and a satiny luster finish overall. In the May 1913 *Numismatist*, editor Edgar H. Adams wrote:

Matte Proof nickel, 1913 Buffalo Type I. Coins with the Matte Proof finish were virtually impossible to distinguish from circulation strikes, unless the edge (viewed edge-on) was examined and found to be completely mirrorlike.

> No five-cent pieces of the old type have been coined this year, Proofs of the new type are not yet ready to be delivered, although, as no money sent with orders for the coins has been returned, it is inferred that Proofs may be issued eventually. There is a possibility, however, that, because of the widespread objection to the new coin, no Proofs of it may be struck until changes are made in the design.

Heretofore Proof nickels have been struck by a hand press from specially prepared dies on burnished planchets. The result was that the field of the coin, which was of considerable area was given a mirror-like surface. The cents of the Indian head type were struck in the same way.

With the advent of the Lincoln cent, however, the brilliant polish of the field disappeared, with the result that, outside of perhaps a clearer impression, there was practically no difference between Proofs and the regular cent just issued for circulation. The area of the field of the new nickel is very small because of the size of the Indian head on the obverse and that of the full-length buffalo on the reverse, and what is most of the field has a roughly finished surface that is suggestive of lead rather than of nickel. Moreover, there is a concave surface, the striking of which appears to have forced up the metal along the edge, thus making the coin there so much thicker than that of the old type that it cannot be used in the slot machines now so common.

If the field surface of Proofs of the new nickels is to be as lacking in brilliancy as is that of the ones issued for circulation, there will be little difference between the two. Possibly, there may be a change in the design of the new coin.

Later, when Matte Proofs became available, Adams commented:

The Proof of the 5-cent piece is even more unsatisfactory than that of the Lincoln cent. While the lines of the design are finer and struck up more clearly—the wrinkles on the buffalo's skin, and parts of the Indian's head, for example—the appearance of the coin is practically the same as one struck for circulation. . . . Although a different die is supposed to have been used in striking these Proofs, there is no detectable difference in design between it and that used for the nickels distributed for circulation.

As Adams anticipated, the new Matte Proof nickels were confusing, as there was no quick and easy way to discern them from a sharply detailed circulation strike. In time, word got around that if, upon close examination, a nickel had a flat rim and, when viewed edge-on, a mirrored (not striated or unfinished) appearance, chances were good that it was a Matte Proof. Collectors, who paid premiums for such coins, were disappointed.

MINTING AND DISTRIBUTING THE MATTE PROOF NICKELS

For each year from 1913 to 1916, including both Type I and Type II in 1913, Buffalo nickels were made in Matte Proof format and were offered as minor-coin sets, along with Matte Proof Lincoln cents, at 15¢ each. Mintages were as follows: 1913 Type I, 1,520; 1913 Type II, 1,514; 1914, 1,275; 1915, 1,050; 1916, 600.

Unresponsive to collector requests, the Mint watched the demand drop, and then drop some more. Finally, in 1916, those in charge threw in the towel and stopped making the Proofs altogether. By that time, the Sand Blast Proof gold coins were already history—sales had declined nearly to the vanishing point, and production had stopped in 1915.

The Mint wholesaled large quantities of unsold Matte Proof cents and nickels (but not gold coins) to dealers. William Pukall, an old-time dealer in Union City, New Jersey, had hundreds of these in the 1950s, each wrapped in thin tissue paper as issued by the Mint. (I bought many from him during those years.) He started buying current coins in quantity around 1914, so he told me, including mintmarked Buffalo nickels, making him a pioneer in that market. By the 1950s, Pukall had large numbers of Proof Indian Head cents and nickel three-cent pieces from the high-mintage years of the 1880s, which had descended unsold through the dealer ranks until they reached him.

Satin and Mirror Proofs of 1936–1937

No Proof Buffalo nickels are known to have been struck between 1916 and 1936, when the Treasury Department resumed making them. As unusual as it might seem, there was not a great deal of collector interest, primarily because numismatists were occupied with the great boom in the market for commemorative half dollars.

Proof sets, priced at $1.81, contained five pieces: Lincoln cent, Buffalo nickel, Mercury dime, Washington quarter, and Liberty Walking half dollar. Individual coins could also be purchased. The 1936 mintage of Proofs nickels numbered 4,420 pieces.

Cents and nickels made early in that year have a satiny appearance, essentially a hybrid of the mirror Proof and the Matte Proof finishes. Perhaps half of the mintage was made with this finish before the dies were completely polished, and mirrorlike coins were issued. The Indian head and bison were neither frosty nor matte, but were also lightly polished. Today, Satin Proof, or Type I Proof (not to be confused with the design designation types I and II) nickels, are often collected as a separate Proof variety, but they command a lower market price. Mirror Proofs, or Type II, are in greater demand. In 1937 all Proofs—5,769 of them—were of the mirror finish.

Brilliant Proof Buffalo nickel of 1937. Coins of the mirror type were much more popular with collectors, although, on this design, there was not much open field to display the Proof surface.

Until the mid-1980s, demand was light for the 1936 Satin Finish Proofs, but heavy for the 1936 and 1937 Proofs with the mirror finish. Today, all are collected with enthusiasm.

CHAPTER FIVE

INDIAN HEAD/BUFFALO NICKELS 1913–1938
GUIDE TO COLLECTING

GRADING STANDARDS AND INTERPRETATIONS

An important part of collecting Buffalo nickels, as we fondly call this design, is learning the standards by which they are graded. While all grading standards are subject to interpretation, those propounded by the American Numismatic Association are the most widely used by the leading grading services. The information reproduced here is (with slight edits) from *The Official American Numismatic Association Grading Standards for United States Coins*, sixth ed. (pp. 115–118).

OFFICIAL ANA GRADING STANDARDS:

INDIAN HEAD/BUFFALO NICKELS 1913–1938

Often Buffalo nickels were weakly struck, and lack details even on Uncirculated examples. The following dates are usually unevenly struck, with weak spots in the details: 1913-S (varieties I and II), 1917-D, 1917-S, 1918-D, 1918-S, 1919-D, 1919-S, 1920-D, 1920-S, 1921-S, 1923-S, 1924-D, 1924-S, 1925-D, 1925-S, 1926-D, 1926-S, 1927-D, 1927-S, 1928-D, 1928-S, 1929-D, 1931-S, 1934-D, 1935-D, and 1935-S. Nickels dated 1919-S, 1920-S, 1923-S, 1925-S, and especially 1926-D are seldom found with Full Details. Matte Proof coins from 1913 through 1916 are sometimes spotted or stained. In the 1937-D three-legged Buffalo nickel, the entire design is always weak because of excessive die polishing. Coins will not always have the exact stated amount of mint luster, strike, or absence of marks. Overall eye appeal and appearance may also influence the stated grade.[1]

Mint State (MS)
Coin is Uncirculated and shows absolutely no trace of wear.

MS-70 • A flawless coin exactly as it was minted, with no trace of wear or injury. Must have full mint luster.

MS-67 • Virtually flawless but with minor imperfections.

MS-65 • No trace of wear; nearly as perfect as MS-67 except for some small weakness or blemish. Has full mint luster, but may be unevenly toned, or lightly fingermarked. A few barely noticeable nicks or marks may be present.

MS-63 • A Mint State coin with attractive mint luster, but noticeable detracting contact marks or minor blemishes.

MS-60 • A strictly Uncirculated coin with no trace of wear, but with blemishes more obvious than for MS-63. May lack full mint luster, and surface may be dull or spotted.

About Uncirculated (AU)

Coin shows small traces of wear on highest points.

> **AU-58 *(Very Choice)* •** Has some signs of abrasion: high points of Indian's cheek; bison's hip bone and flank. Shallow or weak spots in the relief (especially the horn) are usually caused by improper striking, and not wear.

> **AU-55 *(Choice)* •** OBVERSE: Only a trace of wear shows on high point of cheek. REVERSE: A trace of wear shows on the hip and flank. SURFACE: Some of the mint luster is still present.

> **AU-50 *(Typical)* •** OBVERSE: Traces of wear show on hair above and to left of forehead, and at cheekbone. REVERSE: Traces of wear show on tail, hip, and hair above and around the horn. SURFACE: Traces of mint luster still show.

Extremely Fine (EF)

Coin shows very light wear on only the highest points.

> **EF-45 *(Choice)* •** OBVERSE: Slight wear shows on the hair above the braid. There is a trace of wear on the temple and hair near the cheekbone. REVERSE: High points of hip and thigh are lightly worn. The horn and tail are sharp and nearly complete, although often weakly struck.

> **EF-40 *(Typical)* •** OBVERSE: Hair and face are lightly worn but well defined and bold. Slight wear shows on lines of hair braid. REVERSE: Horn, hair, and flank are lightly worn.

Very Fine (VF)

Coin shows light to moderate even wear. All major features are sharp.

> **VF-30 *(Choice)* •** OBVERSE: Hair shows nearly Full Details. Feathers and braid are worn but sharp. REVERSE: Head, front leg, and hip are worn. Tail shows plainly. Horn is worn but distinct on coins that are well struck.

VF-20 *(Typical)* • OBVERSE: Hair and cheek show considerable flatness, but all details are clear. Feathers still show partial detail. REVERSE: Hair on head is worn. Tail and point of horn are not always visible.

Fine

Coin shows moderate to heavy even wear. Entire design is clear and bold.

F-12 • OBVERSE: Three-quarters of details show in hair and braid. LIBERTY is plain. REVERSE: Major details are visible along the back. Horn and tail are smooth, but partially visible. Rim is complete but flat in spots.

Very Good (VG)

Coin is well worn. Design is clear but flat and lacking details.

VG-8 • OBVERSE: Outline of hair is visible at temple and near cheekbone. LIBERTY merges with rim. Date is clear. REVERSE: Some detail shows in head. Lettering is all clear. Horn is worn nearly flat. Rim is flat.

Good

Coin is heavily worn. Design and legend are visible, but faint in spots.

G-4 • OBVERSE: Entire design is well worn with very little detail remaining in central part. LIBERTY is weak and merged with rim. Date is partially visible. REVERSE: Bison is nearly flat but is well outlined. Horn does not show. Legend is weak but readable. Rim is worn to tops of letters.

About Good (AG)

Coin shows outlined design. Parts of date and legend are worn smooth.

AG-3 • OBVERSE: Design is outlined, with nearly all details worn away. Date and motto are partially readable but very weak and merging into rim. REVERSE: Entire design is partially worn away. Rim is merged with letters.

Most numismatists seek Buffalo nickels in the higher grades. Except for some of the rarer issues, most market activity is concentrated on pieces in AU preservation or higher.

Grading in Transition

Grading interpretations have changed over time. In the 1950s and 1960s it was mandatory that in order to be classified as Fine, a Buffalo nickel had to show the animal's *full horn*, including the tip. Such a coin would eventually rise to VF-20, and today would be graded VF-30.

A reader of my *Coin World* column who wrote to me in 2005 has graciously granted permission to share this excerpt:

Dear Mr. Bowers,

I'm a long time CW subscriber and always look forward to your column every week. I am a true collector, and it is apparent that collectors are your target audience.

When my brother and I were about seven and eight, our dad gave us a roll of Abt. Good Barber dimes to split, a couple Whitman albums, and a Red Book. We had to utilize the book to make sure one of us wouldn't let the other get the best of him as we alternated picks—a nice early study on the hobby. We are now 42 and 43 years old and we are both coin collector nuts—with bigger budgets of course. We've both grown to love no-problem, mid-grade (VF to AU) coins of most series.' You know . . . "real" collector coins.

I've been waiting for someone to comment on the effects that gradeflation has had with respect to an actual "percentage gain boost" to coin values. Your article mainly studies the higher grades, but the mid-grades are seeing this same "inflation" as well.

Over the years, I've become very good at grading, but have needed to keep abreast of how the slabbers' standards are slipping—so I could slip with them, I guess. I've commented to my brother that "I'm sure glad I finished my Buffalo nickels in the 1990s- all my VFs are now EFs!" A full horn, right to the tip, gets a slabbed EF-40+ these days every time. With just the "tippy-tip" missing, you get a VF-35. Far less horn than that often secures you a VF-20. . . .

In my book, this is great news for every collector that owns a coin.

Even a new purchase made at today's inflated grade is okay as long as all the grading firms stick to the new reality they've created, and market acceptance of this downward process continues. Could you ever imagine a mass retreat to alter what has become today's lucrative reality? There is no incentive for anyone, on any end of the business, to go back.

Yesterday's VF has not only doubled in value as of late, but has gone up a grade, thus doubling (or more) again! Same old coin? Yup!

Love your column!

Bart H.

The comments may be a bit tongue-in-cheek, but they do reflect reality.

David W. Lange also addressed this "horn problem" in his study, "Grading Buffalo Nickels," in *The Numismatist*, September 1996:

The traditional criteria for grading a Buffalo nickel Very Fine include the presence of a fully visible horn. This would be okay if it were not for the fact that many *Mint State* coins of this type lack a fully visible horn! How do you grade a Buffalo nickel that is only lightly worn yet has little or no detail evident in the bison's head? . . . The market-oriented approach employed by grading services such as Numismatic Guaranty Corporation (NGC) seeks to establish a coin's relative worth when assigning a grade. In so doing, the coin's overall wear and surface quality play an important role.

A Buffalo nickel that has only a touch of wear and retains most of its luster normally would be graded About Uncirculated (AU). Yet if it's so poorly struck that it displays the detail of a coin grading only Fine, it should not be called AU. Graders may compromise by assigning a "net" grade of Extremely Fine or Very Fine that reflects its relative market value.

Collectors often have a difficult time rationalizing this practice and seldom understand how it works. If you're uncomfortable with these "compromise coins," hold out for a well-struck coin for each date, one that began its existence with reasonably Full Details and is thus graded solely on the basis of wear. This will require enduring patience. . . .

Both of these comments reflect changes, uncertainties, and differences of opinion. Since my purpose here is to help you understand the situation, let me ask you this: Which would you prefer—a 1920-D nickel graded MS-64 by NGC *solely on the basis of wear* because it is well struck, or one with the bison's head weak and horn flat, but graded MS-65 because of its *relative worth?*

I am not sure there is a clear answer. Personally, I would rather have the sharp one. The point here is that the listed grade only tells part of the story about a coin's appearance—or its worth.

LEARNING THE TECHNIQUES OF GRADING

Even though the ANA Grading Standards and other guides are useful, and many Buffalo nickels are already graded and in holders, the ability to grade coins yourself is always beneficial. The best way to learn grading is to spend time looking at nickels. Visit coin shows and shops and look through as many Buffalo nickels as you can. Inventories will range from a dozen or so, to perhaps 100 or more, although few dealers will have in-depth holdings across the board—unlike with Jefferson nickels, for which you may well find more coins than you have time to inspect. It is considered good form to advise the dealer that you are seeking education—and to make a courtesy purchase of a coin or a book or two.

You will gain knowledge very quickly—faster than you ever imagined!

BEING A SMART BUYER OF BUFFALO NICKELS
REALITIES OF THE MARKETPLACE

As this chapter will show, Buffalo nickels are very complex. Because there are so many variation in sharpness, die wear, planchet quality, luster, and eye appeal, there is no way a single number can truly represent the *market value* of a Buffalo nickel. One coin graded MS-64 may be a real dog, while another may be sparkling and beautiful, beckoning even the most seasoned specialist.

In my opinion, one of the greatest factors in being a smart buyer of Buffalo nickels is the ability to find coins with excellent design details. Information on this important subject is extensive, but studying it can pay dramatic dividends.

On the other hand, sharpness may not concern you. After all, in the current marketplace, collectors, dealers, and commercial grading services assign only a single grade to any given coin. Similarly, numismatic newspapers, market guides, and reference books usually list grades and prices for those grades, but say nothing about sharpness!

DETERMINING STRIKING SHARPNESS

It is perhaps curious that three coins from the golden age of artistic coin designs—the 1913 to 1938 Buffalo nickel, the 1916 to 1930 Standing Liberty quarter dollar, and the 1916 to 1947 Liberty Walking half dollar—all have prominent striking problems. Among Buffalo nickels, the sharpness of detail, or lack thereof, creates fantastic potential for you.

Both the obverse and reverse of the Buffalo nickel are sculpted in high relief with exceptional and intricate details. In order to achieve full striking of these details, the metal from a full-weight planchet had to flow into the deepest recesses of both dies, and the dies themselves had to be spaced precisely the correct distance apart. The resulting coin would be described as having Full Details (FD).

While this technique produced ideal coins, it also created problems. The Mint Act of May 16, 1866, mandated that the weight of the planchet for the nickel five-cent piece be 77.16 grains, "with no greater deviation than two grains to each piece." This allowed for a fluctuation in planchet weight of about 2.5% in either direction, or about 5% variation overall. A planchet weighing more than prescribed would cause problems because the excess metal, having filled the deepest recesses of the dies, would have nowhere to go and would be squeezed out at the rim, creating a wire rim (called a *fin* in mint jargon). Further, the added strain on the dies would cause them to wear more quickly, or even to crack.

The obvious solution was to space the dies ever so slightly too far apart, so that the occasional overweight planchet would completely fill the deepest depressions, but would not spill over the rim. Now however, a correct-weight planchet would behave as if it were too light, and would produce coins with areas of weakness. Incidentally, the striking pressure of the coining press is typically 50 to 55 tons (generally 55 tons today) and does not vary, so weak details cannot be caused by less than standard pressure. Rather, weakness results from a combination of die spacing and planchet weight.

Bill Fivaz suggests that, if you are looking for a Buffalo nickel with Full Details, you should start by checking two specific areas that reflect the deepest features on the dies and are, therefore, the last to strike up. His recommendations are as follows:

Obverse: Look for a groove, or indentation, in the hair extending upward and slightly to the left, immediately above the top of the horizontal tie on the braid. If this groove is visible, is the coin will almost always be a strong or full strike in the other obverse features as well.

Reverse: Check the line, or edge, of the raised fur above the bison's left front leg. If this is sharply detailed, then the other features on the reverse are usually also well struck.

Remember, these two features are only the *starting point.* If either is weak, then the coin cannot be a Full Details specimen. However, if both features are well defined, the chances are excellent that the coin is a Full Details Buffalo nickel. Don't reach for your wallet quite yet, though; you must still check all other features of the nickel—the hair and feather details of the Indian, the word LIBERTY, the fur on the head of the bison, and everything else. Only if *all* of the details are fully delineated do you have a Full Details coin.

ELEMENTS OF THE "DETAILS SYSTEM"

Drawing extensively on the research of Ron Pope[2] (who has taken notes on tens of thousands of coins across the series), the photographs of Scott Schechter (NGC), the archives of American Numismatic Rarities, and my own notes, I have developed a system for evaluating sharpness in Buffalo nickels. The system delineates four levels of sharpness, and while it is not foolproof and is certainly subject to modification, I believe it is useful. I call the four categories Weak Details, Typical Details, Sharp Details, and Full Details. Although the classifications may not be entirely precise (reminiscent of grading numbers!), they serve nicely as a basis for discussing or writing about striking quality. If anyone wants to use these designations, be my guest!

Weak Details: The coin appears flat at the centers with little detail, and is mushy in other areas. There is little or no fur on the head of the bison. The fields may be grainy and irregular. The mintmark may be weak or mushy. Some Weak Details coins have been struck from worn or "tired" dies, resulting in rough-textured "flow lines" perpendicular to the rim. If the planchet was not squeezed deeply into the dies, nicks and marks *from the original planchet* may be visible, most often at the center of the obverse above the braid, but possibly also on the high points of the bison.

Typical Details: Center details will be weak or non-existent; the fur on the head of the bison will be incomplete; the fur above the left front leg will have no sharp delineation where it meets the leg; and other details will be missing. The coin will seem to be rather "flat" at the center of one or both sides. The field areas, especially below the bison, may be grainy or slightly mushy. The mintmark may be slightly weak. Some Typical Details coins have been struck from worn or "tired" dies, resulting in rough-textured "flow lines" perpendicular to the rim. If the planchet was not squeezed deeply into the dies, nicks and marks *from the original planchet* may be visible, most often at the center of the obverse above the braid, but possibly also on the high points of the bison. (These marks are not widely understood in numismatic circles, and most collectors believe them to be abrasions from poor handling or wear.)

Sharp Details: On the obverse, much of the "groove" in the hair immediately above the tie on the braid is visible. On the reverse, the line at the bottom edge of raised fur above the bison's left front leg is visible. All other features are fairly well delineated. There is no mushiness, although some of the hair and feather details on the obverse, or fur details on the bison on the reverse, may not be sharp. If it is a branch mint coin, the mintmark will be crisp and sharp, not mushy. A Sharp Details specimen should be worth a strong premium if it is of a date and mint that rarely produced coins of this quality.

Full Details: All features are needle-sharp. This designation is more of an ideal than a reality. In the real world of Buffalo nickels, FD coins are exceedingly rare and are even unknown for some dates and mintmarks. Many of the known FD Buffalo nickels may have been struck on slightly overweight planchets that allowed extra metal to fill the die recesses—however, I have not conducted a weighing program to verify this possibility. Complicating the matter further is the fact that, as the Buffalo nickel series progressed, the hub dies and master dies tended to become worn, with the result that many working dies *never* had Full Details at all. This would account for certain later varieties being very common with Sharp Details, but quite rare or unknown with Full Details.

Usefulness and Limits of the System

Naturally, each of these definitions—Weak Details, Typical Details, Sharp Details, and Full Details—reflects an element of personal opinion. Because there is some overlap in the descriptions, there will be instances in which one expert considers a coin to be a Sharp Details while another rates it as a Full Details. Despite its subjectivity, I believe that this system works at least as well as some of those now in use for other series. Consider, for instance, that with Mercury ("Winged Liberty Head") dimes from 1916 to 1945, Full Bands (FB) is used to describe the sharpness of the horizontal bands on the reverse, but there is no descriptor for the obverse. Thus, it is not unusual to find certain dates—1921 is an example—that are described as FB, but have other parts quite weak, such as the bottom of the date numerals and/or the rim. Another case in point is the even less satisfactory descriptor Full Head (FH) for 1916 to 1930 Standing Liberty quarters. A designation of FH is supposed to indicate that the head details of Miss Liberty are full (complete?). In practice, however, most coins in the marketplace that are certified FH are actually only *almost* FH, which of course is not *really* FH! Moreover, it is very common for a Standing Liberty quarter to be described as FH and have two rivets at the lower left of the shield be weak or even missing!

As I see it, Weak Details, Typical Details, Sharp Details, and Full Details are effective terms for describing the sharpness of Buffalo nickels. Clearly, any coin that meets the Full Details criteria—if it is really a full strike, not almost a full strike—is potentially important. Although opinions may differ slightly regarding a given coin, these descriptors, if used on certified holders, would tell buyers the relative sharpness of a specimen. It is unlikely that a Typical Details would ever be confused with a Full Details. Unfortunately, they are *not* on holders—at least not yet. Until they are, you can gain a powerful inside advantage by knowing what is possible to find by cherrypicking and what is not.

The System in Use

Your next step is to understand how I have put the Details System to work, so it is time to look at an actual entry from the next chapter.

The first listing in the Buffalo series, the 1913 Type I, includes this notation:

> **Sharpness of Design Details:** *Weak, <1% • Typical, 9% • Sharp, 71% • Full, 20%.*
> Sharply detailed coins are the rule for this issue. When weakness is seen, it is usually minor and is on the fur on the bison's head and/or the center of the obverse. On a few specimens the date numerals are not sharp, and on some there is lightness at LIBERTY and the obverse rim.

The notation "<1%" (read "less than 1%") means that some pieces, but not as many as 1/2 of 1% of all the coins studied for this variety, have been classified Weak Details. On the other hand, an estimated 71% of all the 1913 Type I Buffalo nickels studied are considered Sharp Details, making them much more prevalent and, therefore, easier to find. Full Details, at 20%, are scarcer, but since this is a common date, are also readily available. Following the statistical notations, the *Notes* section gives descriptive information about the coin.

In contrast, consider this description for the 1925-S:

> **Sharpness of Design Details:** *Weak, 27% • Typical, 47% • Sharp, 25% • Full, 1%.* Sharpness varies, but is usually weak in one or more areas, sometimes flat on numerals and lettering. On some, the mintmark is just a blob. Sharp coins are elusive.

If you are seeking a 1925-D in MS-65 grade and are confronted with offerings of certified coins, the above information will help you pick out a coin that is superb, rather than one that is run-of-the-mill. *Someday*, when the general market wakes up, you will be in the catbird seat as the owner of a Sharp Details coin or even—lucky you—a Full Details specimen!

To me it is rather silly that in 2005, as I write these words, listings in the popular registry sets do not yet reflect consideration of sharpness of details. A coin with Weak Details and a high grading number will trump one with Sharp Details and a grading number one notch lower! What do you think? Would you rather have a 1925-D ranked MS-63 with Full Details, or one ranked MS-65 with Weak Details?

COMPARATIVE RARITY OF BUFFALO NICKELS SEEN WITH FULL DETAILS

As might be expected, coins with Full Details are more plentiful for some dates and Mints than for others. The following lists show the relative difficulty of finding Buffalo nickels with Full Details for each issue. Each list gives the percentage of Full Details specimens known to exist among all the coins seen of a given variety. In other words, the likelihood of finding a 1920-S Buffalo nickel with Full Details is extremely small based on the fact that, to date, no 1920-S coin of that quality has been seen. By comparison, 55% of all the 1921 specimens seen so far have Full Details, indicating that examples are much easier to locate. The lists are ranked from most rare to most common.

The Ultimate Degree of Rarity
No coins with Full Details are known for these dates:

None at all: 1920-S • 1924-D • 1924-S • 1926-D • 1926-S • 1927 • 1927-D • 1928-D • 1929 • 1929-D • 1930 • 1930-S • 1931-S • 1934-D

Home Runs for the Cherrypicker
This group lists varieties for which a very small number of Full Details coins are known. Despite this, in the "Less than 1%" category, all except the 1919-S are considered to be common in Mint State—affording an ample hunting ground. While the other categories include some dates that are scarce and expensive in Mint State, they also contain several common varieties such 1924 and 1925 in the 1% category, and 1936, 1936-D, and 1937 in the 2% group.

Less than 1%—1919-S • 1926 • 1928 • 1929-S • 1935 • 1935-D • 1935-S

1%—1914/3 • 1924 • 1925 • 1925-S • 1927-S • 1934

2%—1913-S Type II • 1914 • 1918/7-D • 1918-S • 1936 • 1936-D • 1937

3%—1915-D • 1916-D • 1917-D • 1917-S • 1918 • 1918-D • 1920 • 1920-D • 1923-S • 1925-D • 1928-S

4%—1919-D

Expanded Opportunities

Most of the coins in these categories range from common to very plentiful in Mint State, affording even greater opportunities to find coins with Full Details.

5%—1913 Type II • 1913-D Type II • 1916-S • 1917 • 1919 • 1923

7%—1914-S • 1938-D/S

8%—1916 • 1938-D

9%—1913-S Type I

Still a Challenge

Finding coins with Full Details for most of the categories in this group is still a challenge. Only the 1921 variety gives you a free ride!

10%—1914-D • 1936-S • 1937-D • 1937-S

12%—1915-S

15%—1921-S

20%—1913 Type I • 1915

22%—1913-D Type I

55%—1921

If you find a coin with Full Details that is listed under "None" you will know you have a first-class rarity! However, the figures given here may change. New discoveries are always being made and the idea of evaluating Full Details is a new one, so you should expect to see adjustments as countless Buffalo nickels are examined for their sharpness.

COMPARATIVE RARITIES OF VARIETIES REPORTED WITH SHARP OR FULL DETAILS

Mounting a collection of Full Details Buffalo nickels would be a daunting, if not impossible, task. There have been many choice and gem sets (of basic dates and mintmarks, not necessarily with overdates and other varieties) formed over the years, but I have never seen one in which all the coins are sharp! (In fact, I can say the same for sets of Mercury dimes of 1916 to 1945, Standing Liberty quarters of 1916 to 1930, and Liberty Walking half dollars of 1916 to 1947.) A more realistic approach to building a truly memorable collection of Buffalo nickels would be to search for varieties with *either* Sharp Details or Full Details. Still, even though it is theoretically possible to form a collection having either a Sharp Details or a Full Details specimen for each variety, to my knowledge no such collection has ever been assembled. Nevertheless, for the benefit of those collectors who might like to accept the challenge, this second list estimates the combined availability of the two classifications.

The opening notation in each group expresses the percentage of specimens seen with *either* Sharp Details *or* Full Details for each variety in that group. For example, of all 1929 Buffalo nickels seen, 10% are either Sharp Details or Full Details. The figures in parentheses give the percentage of coins reported with Sharp Details, followed by the percentage of those reported with Full Details for that variety. The groups are ranked in order of increasing availability.

Please keep in mind that the use of combined classifications is a new approach to availability ranking. Therefore, these lists are only preliminary and are subject to modification as additional information becomes available. Also remember that these numbers refer to percentages of populations that have been seen, not to the *absolute* number that may exist. A 1929 Buffalo nickel in MS-65 or finer grade, for instance, has a total certified population of more than 600 coins. Since 10% of them are either Sharp Details or Full Details, we know that there are at least 60 such coins to be found among those 600 coins. In contrast, while 15% of 1920-S coins in the same range are Sharp Details or Full Details, the 1920-S has a certified population of only 25; therefore, that 15% represents only about four coins.

10%—1929 (10% + 0%) A cherrypicker's delight, this coin seems to be the most elusive of all Buffalo nickels when compared to examples with light details; however, it is a common, inexpensive date, so enough sharp coins are out there that one can be found with a bit of searching.

11%—1931-S (11% + 0%) Another cherrypicker's delight, this is also an elusive Buffalo nickel, but it is common and inexpensive and can be found with some searching.

12%—1928-D (12% + 0%) Isn't it interesting that 1928 San Francisco nickels are usually found sharp (53% in this list, see below), while those minted in Denver are most often poorly defined? The nature of the 1928-D is not widely known, so you can look for one *quietly*—a comment relevant to most of the other nickels at this end of the list. • **1930** (12% + 0%) This is another relatively rare issue, but it is inexpensive as 1930-S is a common variety.

13%—1934-D (13% + 0%) The laziness of the Denver Mint press technicians caused the weakness of these pieces, as well as for the 1927-D below.

14%—1927-D (14% + 0%) This one, though hard to find, will be inexpensive when located. (Don't tell anyone, but the highly sought-after *1927-S* may be easier to find than this "lowly" variety!) • **1935-S** (14% + less than 1%) Even though these are relatively rare, quite a few of them are around because they are part of a common date and mint. (If you are interested in collecting Buffalo nickels as an investment, inexpensive varieties, such as this one, that are rare if sharply struck make excellent candidates.)

15%—1920-S (15% + 0%) The 1920-S is *very rare*, both in absolute numbers and in availability of coins with Sharp Details or Full Details. Most of the dates and mints that are rare with strong details are plentiful with weak details. Not so with the 1920-S; it is scarce in Mint State, regardless of sharpness. This might well be the "poster coin" in the Buffalo nickel series—a real plum! This is an ideal example of an occasion when it could be worthwhile to pay well over catalog price to acquire a Sharp Details coin. Given the opportunity, I would buy one at twice the current listing if necessary. (This approach is also useful with other coins at this end of the rarity scale.)

16%—1929-D (16% 1 0%) Few collectors pay attention to this date, making it ripe for cherrypicking. • **1935-D** (16% 1 less than 1%) This is yet another instance of poor workmanship—a common occurrence throughout numismatics. For example, among Morgan dollars, sharp definition of details is the rule for San Francisco coins, while most New Orleans coins have weak details.

19%—1914/3 (18% 1 1%) Data are incomplete on this issue because it is a relatively recent discovery. • **1919-S** (19% 1 less than 1%) • **1926-D** (19% 1 0%) This 19% figure is based on observations made over the past 20 years, during which time some Sharp Details coins have appeared on the market. However, I have been watching and making notes on 1926-D nickels since the 1950s. At that time, rolls came to hand now and then, but none included a sharply struck coin! It is possible that a few sharp pieces were filtered onto the market quietly in the late 20th century, or there may be some other explanation for their sudden emergence.

21%—1916-S (18% + 3%) • **1934** (20% + 1%) Even though there are relatively few sharp pieces, there are a lot of coins around from which to choose.

22%—1913-S Type II (20% 1 2%) In terms of strike sharpness, this key issue is in the cellar among Buffalo nickels of this date. • **1914** (20% 1 2%) • **1918-S** (20% 1 2%) Another nemesis for the connoisseur, the 1918-S is in the same category as the highly elusive 1920-S. It is convenient that most buyers don't care about sharpness of detail, so if you can track one down, the price will be a fraction of what it might be if the guides and grading services made notations for "Sharp Details" and "Full Details"! • 1918/7-D (20% 1 2%) This variety is usually encountered in circulated grades. At those levels, Sharp Details and Full Details do not make much difference. • 1926-S (20% 1 0%) This is a key issue in all grades. A surprising number are sharply struck. If you can afford a coin from MS-63 to MS-65, just stalk this variety quietly, and eventually you will find one. When you do, it would be good practice to pay a nice premium, if you have to, to get it. In an auction, it may well be that other bidders won't notice. • 1927 (20% 1 0%) Although rare in terms of percentage, quite a few of these coins are around, so finding one of the 20% with sharply struck details is doable.

23%—1918-D (20% 1 3%) • **1924-S** (23% 1 0%) In terms of absolute numbers, this is a scarce, expensive coin. finding one with sharply truck details will be an accomplishment. • **1925-D** (20% 1 3%) This is also a scarce, expensive coin in terms of absolute numbers. As is true of several branch mint issues of the decade, finding one with sharply truck details will be difficult.

24%—1930-S (24% + 0%) Quite a few of these are around, so finding one is just a matter of time.

25%—1924-D (25% + 0%) This is another scarce and expensive coin denomination. Locating one with sharply struck details will not be easy.

26%—1925-S (25% 1 1%) This is one of the scarcer issues of the era, but finding a specimen with Full Details is possible. • **1928** (26% 1 less than 1%)

28%—1915-D (25% 1 3%) • **1916-D** (25% 1 3%) • **1917-S** (25% 1 3%) • **1918** (25% 1 3%) • **1935** (28% 1 less than 1%)

31%—1924 (30% + 1%)

33%—1917-D (30% + 3%) • **1920-D** (30% + 3%) • **1926** (33% + less than 1%)

35%—1936-D (33% + 2%)

36%—1919-D (32% + 4%)

38%—1920 (35% + 3%)

40%—1913 Type II (35% + 5%) • **1914-D** (35% + 5%) • **1925** (39% + 1%)

41%—1927-S (40% + 1%) Surprisingly, most specimens of this key date found in the marketplace are relatively sharply struck—poles apart from the situation with, for example, the 1920-S. Take your time and shop around.

42%—1914-S (35% + 7%) • **1937** (40% + 2%)

43%—1923-S (40% + 3%) • **1937-D** (33% + 10%)

44%—1929-S (44% + less than 1%)

45%—1917 (40% + 5%) • **1936** (43% + 2%)

47%—1915-S (35% + 12%)

50%—1913-D Type II (45% + 5%)

53%—1928-S (50% + 3%)

54%—1913-S Type I (45% + 9%) This, the first San Francisco coin of this design, exists in varying degrees of sharpness, but truly well-detailed examples are the scarcest among the three Type I mint varieties.

55%—1936-S (45% + 10%)

58%—1916 (50% + 8%)

63%—1923 (58% + 5%)

65%—1937-S (55% + 10%)

67%—1919 (62% + 5%)

70%—1921-S (55% + 15%) A scarce variety by any reckoning, the 1921-S can be found quite sharp, making it easy to cross off the connoisseur's want list. Would it be an oxymoron to suggest that 1921-S is the commonest rare variety if with Sharp Details or Full Details?

87%—1913-D Type I (65% 1 22%) As was true for this issue at the other mints, the Coining Department took care to create a sharply detailed product. • **1938-D/S** (80% 1 7%) Perhaps a particularly careful press operator was on duty when these and the related 1938-D coins were minted, for both have exceptional detail.

88%—1938-D (80% + 8%) This coin probably has the same availability as the 1938-D/S, since the difference in the figures is not statistically significant. In any event, there are so many of these coins in existence that a sharp coin will attract little notice.

90%—1915 (70% + 20%) Coins of this particular issue are usually very nice overall.

91%—1913 Type I (71% + 20%) This one is an easy winner—and nice in this regard because examples are essential for inclusion in type sets. The press operators at the Philadelphia Mint took care in striking these new nickels, and the coins show it.

95%—1921 (40% + 55%) In *relative* terms of sharp versus not-sharp coins, the 1921 takes the prize for being the most often seen with well-defined details. Perhaps, because business might have been very slow at the Philadelphia Mint during this year of national economic recession, operators of coin presses may have been able to take more care in producing nickels. (By contrast, dimes and quarter dollars of this date are among the most weakly defined in their respective series and the Liberty Walking half dollars are often weak at the centers.)

SUMMARY OF SHARPNESS IMPORTANCE

If you have read the chapter to this point and have absorbed the material in a general way, you probably have more knowledge than nine out of ten of your competitors in the marketplace. Some of the characteristics are difficult to remember. Even though I have been immersed in the Buffalo nickel world for a long time, I often have to go back and look up a variety to see how rare it is if sharply struck.

While I give several steps to success in buying Buffalo nickels, I emphasize that finding *sharply detailed* coins is exceedingly important—or at least it should be. However, because the commercial grading services, registry set listings, the Red Book, various market charts, and the like take little or no notice of this, the point cannot be overemphasized in terms of money-making opportunities for you.

Although no study has been done regarding strike sharpness, the general situation is hardly a secret. In his article in *The Numismatist*, January 1949, Charles I. Altman states:

> It is when one comes to the Buffalo nickels that he gets his real surprise. Although this popular coin was issued for a period of 25 years, many of the dates in large quantities, brilliant Uncirculated, finely-struck copies of many of

the dates are hard to find; this is especially true of those struck at the Denver and San Francisco mints, which, as a rule, were in much smaller quantities than were issued at the Philadelphia Mint.

Starting with the first issue of 1913 the D and S coins of nearly every year to and including 1927 are getting scarcer each year as the great increase of collectors creates a greater demand for the few fine copies of these dates that seem to be available. It seems quite possible the 1925-6 and 7 from the S mint may become real rarities in the years ahead.

Now, set as your goal that every Mint State Buffalo in your collection must have Sharp Details or Full Details! With this little secret, you'll leave the competition in the dust.

OTHER ASPECTS OF EYE APPEAL

"TIRED DIES"

Among various date and mintmark varieties of Buffalo nickels there are many that were struck from "tired dies," where one or both dies showed metal-flow lines, graininess, or indistinct areas, particularly around the rims. Sometimes the higher areas of the coin will have sharply defined details, but the rims will be weak. Such pieces are sometimes described as "mushy."

Mushy coins are apt to have dull or poor luster, sometimes with "shiny spots." Still others have very bright luster, but with a somewhat "greasy" appearance. Certification doesn't help, for again the grading services take no note of such matters.

BRILLIANT VS. TONED

In the Buffalo nickel series there are quite a few pieces certified in high grades, on the long side of MS-65, that are deeply toned, often with iridescent colors, but so heavily patinated that their true nature cannot be determined. Before the last few decades nearly all buyers wanted "brilliant" rather than toned coins, so dealers routinely dipped the coins to make them brilliant and thus saleable. As a rule, these coins proved to have friction or light wear. As recently as the 1980s there were countless "Mint State" Buffalo nickels on the market, particularly of dates from about 1914 to 1926, that had been dipped, dipped again, and then dipped some more—giving them a silvery, but dull and lifeless appearance.

Mind-sets changed, though, after *naturally toned* coins from old-time collections and estates came on the market, and attractively toned coins began to bring record prices. Then, after some hoopla about the desirability of rainbow-toned Morgan dollars (which, by the way, can be quite nice) appeared in print, toned coins—including Buffalo nickels—became popular.

Not to worry, a solution was a hand! Coin doctors heated and treated nickels, creating vast numbers of "Mint State" coins with toning ranging from brown to vivid iridescent. Buyers scrambled to write checks!

For those involved, this was a very profitable business, ethical considerations aside. Coins from AU into lower Mint State levels, dipped to death, were subjected to heat and/or chemicals, and ended up with grades of MS-64 or higher, including MS-66 or MS-67! Coin doctors like to play cat-and-mouse games with certification services. Many doctored coins are rejected, but others make the cut. Once in a "slab," doctored coins tend to remain there!

Whether we are talking about artificial toning, natural toning, or whatever, there are a lot of "doggy" coins out there. As part of his discussion on the 1915-S (although the situation is hardly unique to this variety), David Lange comments:

> There seem to be quite a number of toned examples, with this toning rarely being attractive. Dull, monochromatic toning of brownish gold is typical. There's no point in attempting to remove this toning, as the underlying luster has probably already been impaired.

My recommendation is to buy only coins ranging from medium-toned—with the character of the *original luster* fully evident, including on the all-important higher areas and any gradations—up to fully brilliant. This means that rich luster must be present. Let investors and bargain-seekers buy all of those wondrous toned coins that have very little if any real luster.

Buying Buffalo Nickels: Four Steps to Success

If you want to be a connoisseur and form a truly outstanding collection of Buffalo nickels, there is much more than just the grading numbers to consider. In my opinion, numbers, while important, may not be any more significant than other aspects such as quality and eye appeal. I have mentioned this elsewhere in this book and will mention it again.

If I were forming a set of Buffalo nickels and wanted a nice specimen of the very common 1934 date, I know that while Mint State coins abound in the marketplace, only a few have both Full Details (FD) and good eye appeal. I would much rather have an MS-65 1934 with FD that an MS-67 that is flatly struck. The preceding paragraphs on the significance of striking are, indeed, important!

Step 1:
Consider the Numerical Grade Assigned to the Coin

Suppose you are holding a dealer's coin in your hand. Should you buy it? Your first step is to look at the assigned grade of the coin, or, if you are familiar with grading, to assign your own number. Experienced collectors and dealers will often share their opinions with you, so, short of becoming a nuisance, you can ask around for help. The chances are excellent that if you are aspiring to collect Buffalo nickels, most of the coins offered to you will be already be graded and in certified holders. These holders will have just a number—such as MS-63, MS-65, or whatever—and will tell you little if else. Aha! Herein lies *your* opportunity!

If you are just entering numismatics, you would do well in the Buffalo nickel series to consider only coins that have been certified by one of the four leading grading services. Listed alphabetically, these are ANACS, Independent Coin Grading Service (ICG), Numismatic Guaranty Corporation (NGC), and the Professional Coin Grading Service (PCGS). NGC and PCGS are the two largest by far, and ANACS, NGC, and PCGS each publish population reports delineating the coins that have passed through their hands. There are other grading services that you might want to check out. However, at present these seem to be the most widely used by advanced collectors, with

NGC and PCGS capturing the lion's share of the business. Price information for many commercially graded coins is available in many places, in particular *The Certified Coin Dealer Newsletter.* To learn about grading, not only for Buffalo nickels, but to become acquainted with general guidelines applied elsewhere, review the earlier section in this chapter entitled "Learning the Techniques of Grading."

When you visit a coin shop or a convention, or contemplate a catalog or Internet offering, you will want to have an approximate grade in mind for each coin you are seeking. If you are looking for a rare 1913-S Type II Buffalo nickel and have $300 to spend, there is no point in asking to see MS-65s or other high-grade coins, but neither is there any reason to waste your time looking at well-worn pieces in G-4 or VG-8 grades. Here are the prices from the 2006 *Guide Book of U.S. Coins:*

1913-S Type II Buffalo nickel—G-4: $250 • VG-8: $300 • F-12: 350 • VF-20: $400 • EF-40: $450 • AU-50: $500 • MS-60: $650 • MS-63: $900

At a coin show, or in sending a "want list" to a dealer, ask to see coins in the range of VG-8 to Fine-12, as these are within the price range you want to pay. However, if I were looking at the above price list, I might notice that, for not too much more money, I could buy a Mint State coin—and I probably would.

Having said that, let's take a look at Red Book prices for a 1920-S nickel, which would seem to require a different approach to making a buying decision:

1920-S Buffalo nickel—G-4: $4 • VG-8: $7 • F-12: $20 • VF-20: $90 • EF-40: $175 • AU-50: $300 • MS-60: $500 • MS-63: $2,000

Unlike with the 1913-S Type II nickel, there are huge jumps in price between grades for the 1920-S. You will have to think carefully whether you want a sharp EF-40 at $175, or an MS-63 at 10 times the price.

A good way to approach this problem is to look at popular price guides, consider your budget, and develop goals for the grades you want. If you are on a budget, perhaps you can opt for VF and EF coins for the rarer earlier dates in the Buffalo nickel series, and Mint State for those in the 1930s. If you can afford it, MS-65 or 66 would be a great goal, but only for coins with Full Details. Amazing as it sounds, to my knowledge no one has ever formed even an MS-*63* set of Buffalo nickels with Full Details!

STEP 2:
CONSIDER EYE APPEAL AT FIRST GLANCE

Although beauty is in the eye of the beholder, if I were buying Buffalo nickels in circulated grades, I would seek pieces with light gray or gray-silver surfaces, without serious nicks or marks, and with no areas of roughness or dullness. For Mint State coins I would insist on pieces that are either brilliant (realizing that they may have been dipped to become that way—but not so overdipped as to become dull) or very lightly toned. As to toning, I prefer light shades of blue, yellow, or gold. I do not like deep rainbow toning and believe that many coins, including ones in certified holders, received their vivid colors from "coin doctors." Nevertheless, some buyers delight in owning these.

If you are contemplating buying a Buffalo nickel illustrated in an auction catalog or pictured on the Internet, remember that, although the picture will be helpful, photographs are easy to enhance. It is a simple matter to adjust the brightness, contrast, color, and shading in a photo—so unless you know that a seller is trustworthy, it is always wise to examine coins in person. If experience demonstrates that what you see in a picture of an offering is actually what you will receive, fine; however, if you are not sure, be careful. Always check the terms of sale before bidding or ordering. Many if not most direct sale offerings of Buffalo nickels have a return privilege if you send the coin back quickly.

If the coin you are considering is not beautiful in your eyes, reject it immediately. There is absolutely no need to compromise. I am not aware of a single date or mint-mark among Buffalo nickels that does not include specimens with good eye appeal—quite unlike the situation with, for example, certain federal half cents of the year 1797 or certain Vermont copper coins of the 1785–1788 era. Furthermore, do not be tempted by overgraded and/or ugly coins offered at "below wholesale" prices. The reason these are "bargains" is that dealers, most of whom eagerly buy for inventory, don't want them either!

If the coin is attractive to your eye, then in some distant year when the time comes to sell it, it will be attractive to the eyes of others as well. If you are satisfied with the appearance of the coin, you have a candidate for your *further consideration.*

STEP 3:
EVALUATE SHARPNESS AND RELATED FEATURES

At this point, you have a Buffalo nickel that you believe to be more or less in the correct numerical grade and that has passed your test for excellent eye appeal. Now you want to use the information I gave earlier in this chapter to determine the coin's sharpness, and to check the available population according to the individual date and mint-mark listings in chapter 6.

Aspire to obtain a coin with Full Details, meaning that the area above the braid ribbon, the word LIBERTY, and other features on the obverse are sharp, and that the bison has full fur on its head and upper flank, and that the mintmark (if present) is bold on the reverse, and so on. (See Bill Fivaz's comments on page 58.) Photographs can be useful for determining sharpness if the pictures are clear and of high resolution; however, an in-person examination is usually required to be certain.

Check the coin for surface quality. Is the luster satiny or frosty? Does it have full sheen—or does it show metal flow and granularity because it was struck from overused dies? Again, assigned numerical grades reveal nothing about this. Is the planchet of good quality, or is it rough? Generally, Matte Proofs of 1913 to 1916 and mirrored Proofs of 1936 and 1937 have Full Details.

If the Buffalo nickel you are considering buying has passed the preceding tests, chances are good that you are holding a very nice coin! You are now ready to *move on to step four!*

STEP 4:
ESTABLISH A FAIR MARKET PRICE

If you have followed the first three steps carefully, you are holding a Buffalo nickel that is correctly graded, of superb eye appeal, and is sharply struck. Only now should you consider the price you will pay.

For starters, use one or several handy market guides for a ballpark estimate. Unlike many other series, all Buffalo nickel date and mintmark issues are actively traded, so there is no lack of information.

Now comes the fun part: If the coin is common enough in a given grade, with Full Details, with fine planchet quality, and with good eye appeal, then the market price is very relevant because you can shop around. Find out how rare a given variety is with Full Details checking the individual listings in the next chapter. If, say, 20% or more of the Mint State coins are estimated to have Full Details, and the coin is not a rare date or mintmark, shop around. There is no hurry.

On the other hand, if the variety is relatively rare with Full Details, say below 10% of those in existence, I would recommend paying a premium to get it. Possession, while possibly not nine points of the law, will get you across the finish line for that particular variety while others are still looking. There is something to be said for taking advantage of the opportunity at hand. If coins with Full Details constitute an estimated 5% or less of the population, go ahead and pay a sharp premium *if you have to.* However, right now the opportunity exists to cherrypick Full Details rarities at everyday prices.

You will also want to consider what I call the *Optimal Collecting Grade,* or OCG. In cases where a very small difference in grade makes a very large difference in price, you should opt for the lower grade. For example, if a Buffalo nickel is priced at $600 in MS-64 and $2,500 in MS-66, the MS-64 might offer you the most coin for the money, if you cherrypick the 64 for sharpness and eye appeal. Overall, it may even be a better coin! In any event, I believe that sharpness and eye appeal overwhelm any minor differences between two adjacent numerical grades.

Congratulations. You now own a *wonderful* Buffalo nickel!

BUILDING YOUR COLLECTION

If you follow these four steps, each coin you acquire will be a very nice example of its date and mint. In terms of the prices you pay, your money will be well spent because you will know what is rare and what is not, and what degree of striking sharpness is available. Do not be a slave to grading numbers. Remember, the top coins in today's population reports often fail the test for Full Details.

The difficult side of all this is that connoisseurship takes time. You cannot simply go to a convention, walk by bourse tables, write checks willy-nilly, and come home with a high-level, connoisseur-quality set of Buffalo nickels. I suggest you begin with the less expensive varieties in the Buffalo series. It is unwise to start out with the rarities because mistakes, and you will make some, will be expensive. Start slowly, and before you know it, you will become confident in your abilities.

Remember, too, that basic rarity does not change much over time. Issues such as the 1913-S Type II and the 1926-S were elusive 20 years ago and will remain key issues 20 years hence. On the other hand, that "rare" common-date Buffalo nickel now standing as the only certified MS-68 might have dozens of companions 20 years from now!

The more practical—and enjoyable—way to build your collection is to buy your coins one at a time, using the four steps I have described. If, after several years, you are still lacking a certain variety with Full Details, you will be able to *knowledgeably* compromise and buy one that has Sharp Details instead.

Highways and Byways of Collecting
Early Circulated Coins Rare

It is not generally known, but nevertheless true, that early issues—especially branch mint coins of the Type II design through the early 1920s—are quite rare in grades such as EF or AU. The reason is that it was not until the 1930s, when Wayte Raymond popularized his "National" albums and later, when J.K. Post, Whitman, and others sold "boards" widely, that collecting Buffalo nickels by date and mint became popular. By that time, the vast majority of earlier varieties had been worn by circulation, making even VF coins rare for many issues. (This is also the case with Barber silver coins minted from 1892 to 1916. However, by the 1930s, the Barber coins were *really* worn, so that coins in even Fine grade were, and still are, rare.)

By the mid-1930s, Buffalo nickels in circulation had been largely picked over. However, some scarce dates could still be found now and then, as evidenced by this comment from Edgar Levy printed in *The Numismatist*, August 1946:

> After reading the advertisements offering worn coins, particularly the Buffalo nickels, I decided to see if they were as "scarce" and "rare" as the "dealers" claim. In the first two weeks after I started, I picked out of circulation all except nine of the entire series. Strangely enough the nine I lack, from 1913 to date, are not "rare" dates, but instead quite common.
>
> Living as I do, in the Denver Mint area, the dates I could not find, are mostly from the Philadelphia Mint. So I attribute my failure to find the missing dates to the fact that they do not circulate as freely out here as do the mint marks. Understand, these are not Uncirculated, but neither were those advertised.

Although I never met him, Edgar Levy was no doubt a fine fellow. I remember when his collection, which had some particularly rare quarter dollars in it, was auctioned by Abe Kosoff on May 24, 1955. Levy's 1946 letter, however, reflects a prejudice against dealers that remains common today. One of the worst manifestations of this (said to have been in fun, but then prejudice is often dismissed as fun) was the "Pirate's Den" lounge at the 1942 ANA convention, with its sketches of dealers drawn as pirates. When I was president of the ANA, I registered a complaint at a regional show when a well-meaning bourse chairman announced, "Thieves' Row is now open." And it was damaging to the Professional Numismatists Guild when a member of the ANA Board of Governors characterized dealers as a "necessary evil" at conventions.

Of course, some dealers may deserve condemnation, as may some collectors, but it has been my experience that there are many more truly wonderful people than scoundrels in the professional community.

Returning to the subject of circulated Buffalo nickels, these were common in circulation in the 1950s, although many had the dates worn completely away. Some acid-based liquids were available and advertised widely, to "restore" the dates. The acid worked because the metal in the date numerals had a different compaction, due to its flow in the die, than did the field around. The ghostlike numerals "1913" and others could be revealed this way. Nickels of the 1930s were common and usually graded Fine to VF. Then, in the 1960s, when coin collecting entered a boom period, the remaining pieces were plucked from circulation, and a trade developed in circulated rolls.

COLLECTING CIRCULATED NICKELS TODAY

While sets of Buffalo nickels in Mint State are exciting and capture a lot of ink in the press and auction catalogs, most demand by collectors of modest means is for circulated examples, sometimes mixed with Mint State coins of the later dates. With regard to basic dates and mints—not overdates or other varieties—the series is eminently affordable.

In general, the lower the mintage, the higher the price will be; and the earlier the date, the higher the price will be. Because of this, an early date with a low mintage, such as the key 1913-S Type II, is known as the star coin in the set. Certain other mintmarks are hard to find, even if worn down to Good or Very Good levels. These include the 1921-S and 1926-S in particular, as well as a few others. The low mintage 1931-S is probably harder to find in, say, VG grade than in Mint State because they were popular with investors in the 1930s and many were saved.

In higher circulated grades such as VF, EF, and AU, there are many scarce or even rare nickels. These were not plucked out of circulation until the 1930s, by which time many of the earlier issues had sustained significant wear.

As noted earlier, until the late 20th century, conventional wisdom stated that, in order for a Buffalo nickel to be graded "Fine," the full outline of the bison's horn had to be visible. As might be expected, some wily people used tools to cut away metal, giving lesser grade pieces a full-horn appearance. This trick is no longer necessary today because grading interpretations have become relaxed, and a Buffalo nickel without a full horn can still be called Fine! Actually, the horn situation is a bit overblown (no pun intended), for more than a few Buffalo nickels, particularly among mintmarked issues of the 1920s, were poorly struck and did not have full horns when they tumbled from the coining press.

Putting together a set of circulated Buffalo nickels can be very enjoyable. Frequently, local dealers, regional coin shows, or even antique shops offer buying opportunities—many more than for the collector of Mint State coins.

Remember the guidelines: familiarize yourself with grading, check the information in this book regarding quality of details and striking, and be sure each coin you buy has good eye appeal. Although details are not as important for low-grade coins, a variety such as 1926-D graded Good or Very Good will be nicer if the details were sharp to begin with (i.e. the mintmark was not a blob or mushy, etc.). Do not be in a hurry.

If you opt for higher circulated grades, you will find my advice below, under "How to Be a Smart Buyer," to be relevant. It is far better to have a nicely detailed EF or AU coin than a poorly defined one.

COLLECTING MINT STATE NICKELS

In the mid-1930s, albums and holders started to become more popular, and collectors who could afford to do so bought Uncirculated coins from dealers. Enthusiasts learned quickly that 1913 Type I coins were fairly plentiful, while quite a few Philadelphia Mint coins throughout the series had been saved. Among mintmarks, the 1926-D turned up in quantity, but the 1926-S was very rare, and the 1927-S was elusive. Rolls of 1928 to 1930-S issues could be found now and then; the 1931-S was plentiful and later mintmarks were also common, the 1938-D being especially abundant. The last Buffalo nickels were issued in 1938, so collectors and investors saved them in inordinate quantities.

On September 10 and 11, 1943, through his Numismatic Gallery in New York City, Abe Kosoff sold the Michael F. Higgy Collection, which brought in over $30,000—a grand sum at the time. The Mehl's sale of the Dunham Collection in 1941 had realized about three times that amount, but it had included great rarities such as the 1804 one dollar coin and the 1822 five-dollar piece. The Higgy sale was more of a bread-and-butter event, offering lots of basic coins, among which were Uncirculated Buffalo nickels. These five-cent pieces created a great sensation, selling for far more than their *Standard Catalogue* values. Some sample prices are shown here, with the catalog values in parentheses: 1913-D Type I ($2 catalog) $6 at the auction, 1913-S Type II ($8) $15, 1914 ($1) $2.50, 1915-S ($3) $7, 1918-S ($6) $12, 1926-S ($12.50) $28, and 1927-S ($16) $30.

Kosoff later wrote, "Yes, September 1943 has been marked as the start of the coin boom, and the Higgy Sale touched it off."[3] The sale had taken place in the middle of World War II, when cash was common and consumer goods were scarce, so a lot of money was spent chasing rare coins. In November of the same year *The Numismatist* ran a detailed article, "The Nickel," by A.T. Duffield, which imparted a great deal of interesting information, and the rush was on. Buffalo nickels have been popular ever since.

Years later Abe Kosoff took a survey of his customers and found that Buffalo nickels were the most desired series—even outranking Lincoln cents!

Collecting by Type

Buffalo nickels can be collected in several different ways. If you are forming a type set of designs, you need just two, a 1913 Type I and any date of the 1913 to 1938-D Type II design. If you opt for Mint State and desire sharply detailed coins, a 1913 Type I will be no problem, with the Philadelphia and Denver issues being the easiest to find.

Among Type II nickels, an easy solution is to find a nice 1938-D or 1938-D/S, perhaps the latter, for the variety is so interesting to contemplate. Both are common in gem Mint State and with sharp details.

Quite a few numismatists have opted to add Proofs to their collections. This entails finding a 1913 Type I Matte Proof and either a Type II Matte Proof of any year from 1913 to 1916, or one of the different-finish Proofs of 1936 or 1937.

Collecting Matte Proof Nickels

No one reading old-time comments about Matte Proofs would think of collecting them now. Times change, though, and Matte Proofs are in strong demand today. If there is a fly in the ointment, it is that there seems to have been some fudging on what is a real Matte Proof and what is not. *Real* Matte Proofs, if viewed edge-on, have *completely mirrored edges*. In addition, they have squared-off rims. I examined hundreds of such pieces in the inventory of the late William L. Pukall, taking them from their original Mint wrappers. There were *no* exceptions.

The matter is further complicated by the likelihood that certain Matte Proof dies were used to coin circulation strikes after the Proofs had been made. In *The Complete Guide to Buffalo Nickels*, p. 176, David Lange makes this comment: "It is believed that Proof dies were used to produce regular issues once their elite service had ended. . . ."

These pieces, however, do not have mirror edges. Today, with many coins in "slabs," this all-important feature is difficult to verify. In an undisguised effort to rewrite history, a grader for one of the services recently told me, "Some Matte Proofs have mirrored edges and others do not." This is just plain wrong! If I were spending a lot of money on Matte Proofs, I would crack them out of the holders, perhaps at a convention in the presence of a grading service employee, to assure myself of authenticity.

From 1913, when Edgar H. Adams complained about them in *The Numismatist*, until today, Matte Proofs have bewildered and confused collectors and dealers alike. In 1977, *Walter Breen's Encyclopedia of United States and Colonial Proof Coins* included this:

> I used to make lunch money buying unrecognized [Matte Proof] examples of these dates as Uncirculated, but that was many years ago. In the meantime many sharp-eyed youngsters have gone and done likewise, pretty well exhausting the supply. Now the problem is to find coins offered as Matte Proofs that are not mere Uncirculateds.

The late Walter Breen was often willing to certify this coin or that, given the appropriate fee. To his doorstep can be laid the so-called "Proof" 1917 nickels, which even made their way into the Red Book, but are candidates for removal, like the pseudo-reeded-edge 1937 Buffalo nickels before them. In his *Complete Guide*, page 178, David W. Lange notes that the "Breen Proofs" have a curious wire rim that "is not a feature seen on the Proof nickels of 1913 to 1916." He states further:

> No Proof nickels were reported or offered to the public in 1917, yet Breen allegedly authenticated as many as seven! I have had the opportunity to see only one. . . . I examined it carefully when it was submitted to NGC for certification as a Proof.
>
> While it did exhibit an extremely strong strike from unworn dies, it simply did not possess the characteristics of the 1913 to 1916 Proofs. Its surfaces were of a slightly different texture, and it simply lacked the overall "look" of a Proof. I agreed with the NGC grading team that it did not merit Proof status.

Lange includes an illustration of Breen's September 17, 1977, letter, written on First Coinvestors, Inc., stationery, that came with this coin and states, in part:

> This certifies that I have examined the accompanying coin and that I unhesitatingly declare it a genuine 1917 Matte Proof nickel. . . . [Discussion.] The above absolutely confirm this coin as a 1917 Matte Proof. It is, by a small margin, the finest of the four I have seen to date. . . .

Breen authenticated as "Proof" even larger numbers of what I consider circulation strike MCMVII double eagles, notwithstanding that, as far as I know, there had been no prior mention of such Proof coins in any Mint or numismatic record. The problem gets even more troublesome when coins authenticated by Breen wind up in certification service holders, as some have! Standard practice seems to be to sell coins according to the labels marked on them by the services, tacitly holding the services out as experts.

What to do about the unfortunate investors who bought these coins based on Breen's say-so? Over the years, I have returned their coins to them saying, "Sorry."

All Matte Proofs are superbly detailed, making them showcase examples of their particular dates. This factor alone adds considerable allure. Most also have excellent eye appeal.

My advice is this: buy only Matte Proofs certified by a leading service willing to verify that they have mirrored edges. Also, be sure the coin has a flat rim of consistent width around both sides. This is not always easy to discern because sometimes the plastic of a holder will overlap the edge. Be sure the surface is grainy, satiny, and matte, not deeply frosted. Be sure it has good eye appeal. Most coins certified as Matte Proof-65 (usually the word "Matte" is missing from the label) are actually quite nice.

INTERESTING VARIETIES OF BUFFALO NICKELS

DATE DIFFERENCES

Many interesting differences among Buffalo nickels are revealed by comparing the assorted dates. For instance, placement of the date varies. It can be at a slight distance to the left of the ribbon strand, or it may touch the strand, or cover it. Compare, for example, the 6 in 1926, which covers the ribbon, and the 5 in 1925, which is clear of it. The incuse initial F (for Fraser) below the date is also a point of reference, as are the horizontal lines on the Indian's braid ribbon.

The digit 1 appears as a vertical "stick" on all dates except 1921, which has a slight extension or suggestion of a serif at the upper left. The 2 is seen only as the third digit of dates in the 1920s, and is narrow and without knob or serif. The 3 on 1913 and 1923 nickels has a flat top, while the 3 on dates in the 1930s has a round top. Within the decade of the 1930s, the 3 can be fairly solid and compact, as on the 1934, or tall and skinny, as on the 1938-D. The 4 on 1914 has just a tiny bit of the crossbar to the right of the vertical stand, while coins of 1924 and 1934 have a larger projection. On the 1915 nickel, the top flag of the 5 is thick and close to the curved area below it, while on the 1925 and 1935 it is thin, distant from the curve, and slopes upward to the right. All instances of a 6 resemble an inverted 9 of the same date. The top of the 6 is open and does not have a knob.

The 7 in 1917 is delicate and has a gently curving stem. On the 1927, it is heavier, but is also gently curved. The 7 on 1937 nickels is lower than the other digits and is sharply angled with a straight stem. The 8 of 1918 is delicate, well formed, and has the top slightly smaller than the bottom, while the 8 on the 1928 is small at the top and has a much larger bottom. The 8 in 1938 appears somewhat heavy and compressed vertically, with the top slightly smaller. Every Buffalo nickel has at least one 9, and some have two. These typically have the bottom tip curved upward and distant from the curve above it. The 0 on an 1920 nickel is tall and narrow, while that on 1930 is wider and with a larger opening at the center.

Sometimes the date numerals are crowded together, as on 1938, while for other years, such as 1929, they are slightly separated. Although the style, spacing, and positioning of the numerals vary from year to year, they remain constant within each year—for all dies for each of the mints.

MINTMARK DIFFERENCES

The mintmarks D and S appear on the Buffalo nickels for most of the years. Their positions vary because they were punched into the working dies by hand. Some are centered below the space separating FIVE and CENTS, while others are closer to the E or the C. The vertical spacing (i.e. the distance from the bottom rim) can vary as well. Sometimes a mintmark is tilted slightly to one side or the other.

Slight repunchings of a D or an S mintmark are common and command no particular premium unless the two punchings are dramatically off-register. Among Buffalo nickels, there are several varieties with doubled mintmarks—the same mintmark punched twice into a working die, but with slight overlapping.

The mintmark positions can vary within a given year and mint. A 1914-S can have the S low, or have it punched partly into the lower left of the C in CENTS. A certain 1923-S has the S high with its top protruding into the space between the E and the C. Another 1923-S has the S low and close to the C. One 1925-S die has the S high, nearly touching the E and C, and tilted to the left. Another has the S lower, closer to the C, and with the top of the S light and the base heavy. Still another has the S high, straight, and close to the C. Many 1927-D nickels have the mintmark touching the E and distant from the C. There is almost no end to the possibilities, but interest in the position differences is limited.

Apart from the 1938-D/S, which earns a separate listing among date and mintmark issues, the other mintmark varieties—such as positional and doubling—have stirred relatively little attention, but can be interesting to specialists.

DOUBLED DIES

The working dies for Buffalo nickels were made by impressing working hubs, complete with the date on the obverse, into the blanks for working dies. These were then hardened. On certain reverse dies, a D or S mintmark was punched in separately.

Sometimes during the making of the working die, the hub was impressed again, slightly off-register, causing some doubling of features, usually minor, as on certain issues of 1913 Type II (obverse), 1925-D (obverse), 1927-S (obverse; a bit more distinctive), 1935 (reverse; this is especially popular), and 1937-D. For these and others, the Fivaz-Stanton *Cherrypickers' Guide*, the Breen *Encyclopedia*, and the Lange *Complete Guide* give more information.

The 1916 Doubled Die Obverse is exceedingly popular, with certain features—most dramatically the date—off-register. It seems incredible that this variety evaded publication until Herbert S. Perlin, of Pasadena, CA, sent notice of it to the *Numismatic Scrapbook Magazine*, where it appeared in July 1962. This was on the very cusp of widespread interest in such curiosities, which went into overdrive the following year when Frank G. Spadone published his *Major Variety and Oddity Guide*. After that, magnifying glasses and microscopes came out in force, and all sorts of new and interesting varieties surfaced! Today, the 1916 Doubled Die has been listed in the *Guide Book of United States Coins* for more than 30 years, and is highly sought by specialists. Unfortunately, this variety is rare in all grades and in Mint State—well, you'd better forget about getting one!

Although real doubled dies are interesting, quite a few Buffalo nickels show *machine doubling*, or slight doubling of features caused by wobbling of one of the dies in the coining press during the striking process. These have little premium value.

RELAPPED DIES

An outsider coming into numismatics for the first time might think that a coin struck from a worn, tired die would be worth quite a bit less than one issued from a fresh die pair. For most issues this is so; however, there are a few remarkable exceptions. The most famous of these is the 1922 "Plain" Lincoln cent, which is simply a 1922-D cent from an obverse die so worn and filled that the D was not visible on the finished coin.

Clashmarks occur when two dies came together without an intervening planchet, often damaging both dies. These damaged dies are often *relapped* or resurfaced. Sometimes, though nothing is done, and the resultant coins show evidence of the clashmarks. In March 1944, when hardly anything was known about this phenomenon, and when Buffalo nickels were abundant in circulation (and San Francisco Mint coins were especially plentiful in California), *The Numismatist* printed a letter from California collector R. Romer, who wrote in part:

> About two years ago I noted certain markings on a few copies of Buffalo nickels in my collection. These marks appeared on the obverse of the coin directly under the chin and along the throat of the Indian head.
>
> Having been interested in die breaks and freak variety type coins for some time, these interested me until I studied them more closely and seemed to detect a resemblance of letters among the marks. However, the letters made no sense. Some weeks later I struck upon the idea of placing a mirror against the face of the coin, and to my surprise by this reversal of the marks I plainly found appearing several letters of the word PLURIBUS. On further checking as to how these letters could. be appearing on the obverse, I found them located directly on the opposite side from the regular motto E. PLURIBUS UNUM on the reverse.
>
> Since that time I have been on the watch for this variety and have found it on the following 8 mint coins: 1913-S Type I, 1913-S Type II, 1914- S. 1916- S, 1918- S. 1923-S, 1924-S. 1925-S, and 1928- S. I have found only two copies from the Philadelphia Mint: 1914 and 1921. No copies have been found of the D mint to date. Of the above, only one or two copies of each date have been found with these marks. out of a total of approximately 100,000 examined. As much as half a roll of the scarcer dates in about Fine or better condition were found and retained at the time, and yet a recent check of my entire nickel collection showed a total of only 14 pieces with the freak appearing. I would be interested to hear from any other collectors who have observed this variety or who have any further explanation as to its cause.

One variety attributed to the effects of clashmarks, this time with the die relapped, is the well-known 1937-D 3-Legged Buffalo nickel. At the Denver Mint, the obverse and reverse dies came together and caused clash marks. The reverse die was filed down to remove these marks. In the process, the technician ground away the foreleg of the bison, creating the variety. This story has been widely publicized, and today most collectors assembling sets of dates and mintmarks eagerly seek the coin.

Varieties of 1913 Type I, 1917-D, 1926-D, 1927-D, and 1936-D are all described as "3½ legs" and are sought by specialists, but these are not as well known as the 1937-D 3-Legged.

On sharply detailed examples, the Indian on the obverse has *three* feathers, with the third feather being in the form of a small raised area high in the space between the back of the neck and the large feather behind it. On some coins, relapping of the die has removed all or part of this third feather, creating a "Two Feathers" variety. According to Bill Fivaz, such Two Feathers coins, once ignored, have attracted notice in recent times.[4]

Although there are other sources of information, two important books on this subject are the *Cherrypickers' Guide to Rare Die Varieties*, fourth edition, by Bill Fivaz and J. T. Stanton, and *Treasure Hunting Buffalo Nickels*, by John A. Wexler, Ron Pope, and Kevin Flynn.

"HOBO" NICKELS

At some point, people with time on their hands discovered that the appearance of Buffalo nickels could be altered by carving away some of the features. An early mention of this practice appeared in *The Numismatist*, June 1918, under the title of "The Kaiser's Head on U.S. Nickels!"

> Collectors frequently have brought to their attention coins on which the device has been altered by someone skilled in the use of engraver's tools, giving the piece a humorous or satirical effect.
>
> The present type of nickel seems to offer a splendid field for these artists to display their ability, and some ludicrous specimens have been out. The latest of these alterations . . . is one on which the head of the Indian has been transformed into the head of the Kaiser by the addition of a spiked helmet, an upturned mustache, and a close-fitting uniform, with other slight alterations. . . .

A related item appeared under the signature of Will W. Neil in *The Numismatist*, September 1926. Neil told of curious coins received across the counter in his Baldwin, Kansas pharmacy:

> Among the interesting things I have taken in at face value are: One brilliant, Uncirculated Panama-Pacific half dollar, one 1866 half dollar without motto or mintmark, which may or may not be an altered job, but the weight is good, and one Buffalo nickel which some expert engraver has altered by turning the Indian to a Hebrew, derby and all.

In time, a story arose that such pieces, today referred to as "hobo nickels," were the work of hobos or tramps during the Depression of the 1930s, who perhaps whittled away at nickels in the light of a campfire in a "railroad jungle." Another notion was that the carved nickels often featured men resembling hobos.

In any event, hobo nickels became very popular in numismatic circles. Occasionally a particularly fine example would be reproduced in electrotype form so that other collectors could enjoy it.[5]

The interest was further spurred by the publication in 1982 of *Hobo Nickels, Prisoner Nickels, Shop Tokens, Modern Engravings; An Extensive Study of Hobo Nickels* by Delma K. Romines. Articles also appeared in numismatic journals such as *The Numismatist*, which published Michael Wescott's "Bumming Around With a Hobo Nickel," in its July 1989 issue.

Anything one person can make by hand in one era, another can re-make later. So it was with hobo nickels . . . newly carved varieties, some very elegant, began appearing in the marketplace. The Original Hobo Nickel Society (*original* referring to old-time pieces) with its journal, *Bo Tales*, edited by Don Farnsworth, plays to the purists, although the casual collector cannot resist adding a new version now and then if the price is right. Bill Fivaz, author of the foreword to this book, is a long-time hobo nickel enthusiast and specialist.

CHAPTER SIX

INDIAN HEAD/BUFFALO NICKELS 1913–1938
ANALYSIS BY DATE AND MINTMARK

1913 TYPE I

Circulation-Strike Mintage: 30,992,000
Matte Proof Mintage: 1,520
Optimal Collecting Grade (OCG™): MS-65, PF-65

1913 Type I • Market Values • Circulation Strikes and Matte Proof Strikes

VG-8	F-12	VF-20	EF-40	AU-50	AU-55	MS-60	MS-63	MS-64	MS-65
$12.	$14.	$16.	$22.	$32.	$38.	$45.	$60.	$85.	$150.
MS-66	MS-67		PF-60	PF-63	PF-64	PF-65	PF-66	PF-67	PF-68
$350.	$500.		$800.	$1,400.	$2,400.	$3,500.	$4,500.	$5,800.	—

Availability (Certified Populations) • Circulation Strikes and Matte Proof Strikes

<MS-60	MS-60	MS-61	MS-62	MS-63	MS-64	MS-65	MS-66	MS-67	MS-68	MS-69	MS-70
665	71	125	508	1,682	4,778	9,607	2,404	532	8	0	
< PF-60	PF-60	PF-61	PF-62	PF-63	PF-64	PF-65	PF-66	PF-67	PF-68	PF-69	PF-70
0	0	0	3	15	134	193	170	71	8	0	

Field populations: Circulation strikes (AU-59 and lower), 600,000–900,000; circulation strikes (MS-60+), 90,000–150,000; Matte Proof strikes, 1,000–1,300.

Key to Collecting: The 1913 Type I Buffalo nickel is ideal in many ways. As the first and only year of its type, it is in great demand. However, supplies are generous in the marketplace, and when found in Mint State, examples are apt to be sharply detailed and with good eye appeal. Finding a high-quality specimen will be easy to do—in sharp contrast to many later dates.

Matte Proofs were not popular in their time, due to their similarity in appearance to circulation strikes. Today, however, numismatists appreciate them, examples are avidly sought, and most are very attractive.

CIRCULATION STRIKES

Sharpness of Design Details: *Weak, <1% • Typical, 9% • Sharp, 71% • Full, 20%.* Sharply detailed coins are the rule for this issue. When weakness is seen, it is usually minor and is on the fur on the bison's head and/or at the center of the obverse. On a few the date numerals are not sharp, and on some there is lightness at LIBERTY and the obverse rim.

Quality of Luster: Usually somewhat satiny and very attractive. The satiny finish is common to Type I nickels from all three mints and has an artistic aspect that to me seems nicer than the "deep frosty" luster of many later varieties.

Mintage and Distribution Notes: The new Buffalo nickels reached circulation early in 1913. Although their release was not a nationwide sensation in the sense that the 1909 V.D.B. cent was, the nickels did attract a lot of attention, and many were saved as souvenirs. Examples have always been plentiful on the coin market, but usually as singles or in small groups, not in bank-wrapped rolls or other quantities.

A few dealers, including Henry Chapman, John Zug, and David Proskey, laid in stocks of these and other minor coins; however, most simply wanted examples of the *date*, and paid little attention to mintmarks.

MATTE PROOF STRIKES

Strike, Contrast, and Other Aspects: All examples seen are with Full Details (FD). Nearly all have excellent eye appeal. Much of the demand for this variety comes from type set collectors. However, as circulation strikes are readily available with Sharp Details and are inexpensive, the price of the 1913 Type I Matte Proof is not as high as it might be if this were not the case.

The visual distinction between certain high-quality circulation strikes and Matte Proofs is not great; therefore, I recommend that any Matte Proof considered for purchase be certified as such by one of the leading grading services.

INTERESTING VARIETY

1913 Type I "3-1/2 Legs" (FS-05-1913-901): The relapping of a reverse die caused the lower part of the bison's right foreleg to be reduced in outline to a fuzzy raised area, giving this scarce variety its name.

1913-D TYPE I

Circulation-Strike Mintage: 5,337,000
Optimal Collecting Grade (OCG™): MS-65

1913-D Type I • Market Values • Circulation Strikes

VG-8	F-12	VF-20	EF-40	AU-50	AU-55	MS-60	MS-63	MS-64	MS-65	MS-66	MS-67
$15.	$18.	$24.	$35.	$50.	$55.	$65.	$75.	$150.	$350.	$1,000.	$2,500.

Availability (Certified Populations) • Circulation Strikes

<MS-60	MS-60	MS-61	MS-62	MS-63	MS-64	MS-65	MS-66	MS-67	MS-68	MS-69	MS-70
502	48	64	303	769	1,445	1,014	382	46	1	0	

Field populations: Circulation strikes (AU-59 and lower), 75,000–120,000; circulation strikes (MS-60+), 18,000–27,000.

Key to Collecting: Although the 1913-D Type I is scarcer than its Philadelphia Mint cousin, enough are in numismatic channels that finding one will be easy. Most Mint State coins are fairly well struck and with nice luster—an easy win and a delightful coin to own. If you are buying on the Internet, zoom in to view the details of striking—a handy procedure for other Buffalo nickels as well. In my view, the 1913-D is somewhat undervalued. It has everlasting appeal as a type coin.

Sharpness of Design Details: *Weak, 3% • Typical, 10% • Sharp, 65% • Full, 22%.* On some coins the D mintmark is filled or mushy; avoid these. The head of the bison is often flat. The letters in PLURIBUS and UNUM are sometimes run together. David W. Lange writes, "The D mintmark is small and of the type first used on the cents of 1911. It remained in use as late as 1917."

Quality of Luster: Satiny and very attractive, somewhat matching that on other Type I nickels. On flat strikes, the luster is sometimes "greasy" in appearance, though very rich—a characteristic also seen on light strikes of other issues.

Mintage and Distribution Notes: As the first year of issue of the design, the 1913-D nickel was saved in quantity by collectors, dealers, and the public. Although I have never handled a bank-wrapped roll of this issue, until the 1960s it was not unusual to find a handful of Mint State coins all at once. Today, they are widely dispersed and are usually seen one at a time. Because sharply struck examples are readily available, the 1913-D has been popular for a long time.

Interesting Variety: Two Feathers (FS-05-1913D-401)—Relapping of the obverse die caused the removal of the vestigial third feather.

1913-S TYPE I

Circulation-Strike Mintage: 2,105,000
Optimal Collecting Grade (OCG™): MS-64

1913-S Type I • Market Values • Circulation Strikes

VG-8	F-12	VF-20	EF-40	AU-50	AU-55	MS-60	MS-63	MS-64	MS-65	MS-66	MS-67
$40.	$45.	$55.	$75.	$95.	$100.	$120.	$160.	$500.	$1,000.	$2,000.	$4,200.

Availability (Certified Populations) • Circulation Strikes

<MS-60	MS-60	MS-61	MS-62	MS-63	MS-64	MS-65	MS-66	MS-67	MS-68	MS-69	MS-70
456	17	55	257	613	1,008	454	127	23	1	0	

Field populations: Circulation strikes (AU-59 and lower), 24,000–36,000; circulation strikes (MS-60+), 7,200–10,800.

Key to Collecting: As the mintage suggests, the 1913-S Type I is the most elusive of the three different Type I nickels. It is also the one least likely to be found sharply struck. Although examples are hardly rare in Mint State, finding a truly nice one, from a fresh die pair, will take some looking. Year in and year out this has been a numismatic favorite.

Sharpness of Design Details: *Weak, 6% • Typical, 40% • Sharp, 45% • Full, 9%.* Some are quite sharp, except for the fur on the bison's head. Others were struck using tired dies, hence clashmarks and minor defects are common. On some, the S mintmark is somewhat thick and filled.

Quality of Luster: The luster is matte-like and satiny, similar to the Philadelphia and Denver varieties of this type. On some, the luster is dullish, and eye appeal can be lacking. Some are struck from tired dies, resulting in less attractive luster. David W. Lange makes this telling comment in his *Complete Guide:* "The poorly struck pieces may have very brilliant and satiny surfaces that often assist them in obtaining high certified grades, while the better struck pieces are usually characterized by more subdued luster."

Mintage and Distribution Notes: As the first year of issue, the 1913-S Type I was saved by the public in larger numbers than might otherwise be the case. However, I am not aware of any caches or hoards, and I have never seen a bank-wrapped roll.

Interesting Variety: Two Feathers (FS-05-1913S-402).

1913 TYPE II

Circulation-Strike Mintage: 29,856,186
Matte Proof Mintage: 1,514
Optimal Collecting Grade (OCG™): MS-64, PF-65

1913 Type II • Market Values • Circulation Strikes and Matte Proof Strikes

VG-8	F-12	VF-20	EF-40	AU-50	AU-55	MS-60	MS-63	MS-64	MS-65
$9.	$10.	$12.	$18.	$25.	$28.	$30.	$65.	$100.	$350.
MS-66	MS-67		PF-60	PF-63	PF-64	PF-65	PF-66	PF-67	PF-68
$1,500.	$5,000.		$600.	$1,000.	$1,800.	$2,500.	$3,500.	$4,000.	—

Availability (Certified Populations) • Circulation Strikes and Matte Proof Strikes

<MS-60	MS-60	MS-61	MS-62	MS-63	MS-64	MS-65	MS-66	MS-67	MS-68	MS-69	MS-70
383	25	57	290	717	1,439	697	194	10	0	0	
< PF-60	PF-60	PF-61	PF-62	PF-63	PF-64	PF-65	PF-66	PF-67	PF-68	PF-69	PF-70
0	6	3	7	25	117	155	149	72	9	0	

Field populations: Circulation strikes (AU-59 and lower), 300,000–360,000; circulation strikes (MS-60+), 24,000–36,000; Matte Proof strikes, 1,000–1,300.

Key to Collecting: Although the mintage of the 1913 Type II far exceeded that of the Type I, by the time they were released, the novelty of the design had passed. Accordingly, relatively few were saved. Today, examples are plentiful in all grades. Sharpness and eye appeal can present a challenge, much more so than for the Type I. While this is hardly a "tough" date, it is not easy pickings either. In addition to demand by specialists, many collectors who form type sets desire one to illustrate the first year.

CIRCULATION STRIKES

Sharpness of Design Details: *Weak, 5% • Typical, 55% • Sharp, 35% • Full, 5%.* As the dies became worn, certain details, not always the deepest ones, lost resolution. In the Buffalo nickel series, coins with graininess from "tired dies," are not as attractive as those from fresh dies, but not many buyers are aware of the difference. Some of this issue have unusually bold rims on both sides.

Quality of Luster: The luster ranges from somewhat satiny, as on the Type I nickels, to frosty. The eye appeal is usually good, but specimens can vary widely.

MATTE PROOF STRIKES

Matte Proof Mintage: 1,514 • Beginning with the 1913 Type II and continuing through 1916, the Matte Proofs are usually very well detailed. However, the surface is quite similar to that of the circulation strikes—so much so that, until ANACS developed die characteristics, many circulation strikes were sold as Matte Proofs. As these were easily obtained at the time of issue, many numismatists who collected nickels by date opted for a Matte Proof, resulting in many of these coins turning up in old-time collections.

Strike, Contrast, and Other Aspects: Full Details (FD) and usually attractive, but sometimes more "lustrous" and less "matte" than the 1913 Type II. Popular for type set purposes, these provide an easy but expensive way to obtain a definitive specimen of the design.

INTERESTING VARIETY

Slightly Doubled Date: On some a slight die doubling is seen at the date (FS-05-1903-1801). The doubling is not dramatic, but is of interest to collectors of Buffalo nickel die varieties. However, FS notes it as a very popular variety.

1913-D TYPE II

Circulation-Strike Mintage: 4,156,000
Optimal Collecting Grade (OCG™): MS-64

1913-D Type II • Market Values • Circulation Strikes

VG-8	F-12	VF-20	EF-40	AU-50	AU-55	MS-60	MS-63	MS-64	MS-65	MS-66	MS-67
$115.	$140.	$170.	$190.	$210.	$225.	$250.	$350.	$600.	$1,800.	$4,000.	$15,000.

Availability (Certified Populations) • Circulation Strikes

<MS-60	MS-60	MS-61	MS-62	MS-63	MS-64	MS-65	MS-66	MS-67	MS-68	MS-69	MS-70
641	47	106	203	365	486	187	54	8	0	0	

Field populations: Circulation strikes (AU-59 and lower), 45,000–60,000; circulation strikes (MS-60+), 3,600–4,800.

Key to Collecting: The 1913-D Type II nickels were not saved to any great degree, and today choice pieces are elusive. When found, however, the details are apt to be sharper than on those from the two other mints.

Sharpness of Design Details: *Weak, 5%* • *Typical, 45%* • *Sharp, 45%* • *Full, 5%.* Full Details coins are elusive, but enough exist that finding one is a realistic possibility.

Quality of Luster: Usually somewhat subdued, but frosty (not satiny). As is true of other issues, though, one rule does not fit all. The coins were struck from many die pairs, creating different qualities of luster as they became worn.

1913-S TYPE II

Circulation-Strike Mintage: 1,209,000
Optimal Collecting Grade (OCG™): MS-64

1913-S Type II • Market Values • Circulation Strikes

VG-8	F-12	VF-20	EF-40	AU-50	AU-55	MS-60	MS-63	MS-64	MS-65	MS-66	MS-67
$325.	$375.	$425.	$475.	$550.	$620.	$700.	$1,000.	$2,000.	$5,000.	$10,000.	$22,000.

Availability (Certified Populations) • Circulation Strikes

<MS-60	MS-60	MS-61	MS-62	MS-63	MS-64	MS-65	MS-66	MS-67	MS-68	MS-69	MS-70
1,149	26	76	268	455	505	150	41	3	0	0	

Field populations: Circulation strikes (AU-59 and lower), 7,200–9,000; circulation strikes (MS-60+), 1,080–1,320.

Key to Collecting: When collecting Buffalo nickels by date and mint became popular during the 1930s, the 1913-S Type II was considered *the* key issue. Now however, we know that in certain higher number categories in Mint State, others are rarer. Nevertheless, the 1913-S remains hard to find. My feeling is that *foundational rarity*—rarity across all grades—is a more comfortable situation than *conditional rarity*—rarity in some grades, but not in others.

To many collectors, including myself, this is a favorite among the Buffalo nickel series. Striking can be a problem, though—more so than with any other 1913 Buffalo nickel. Accordingly, some cherrypicking is advisable when buying.

Sharpness of Design Details: *Weak, 18%* • *Typical, 60%* • *Sharp, 20%* • *Full, 2%.* Most are rather average in their details, but quite a few are weak and blurry. Sharp pieces exist, but it will require some searching to find them. Clashmarks are common. **Quality of Luster:** Luster is usually satisfactory, sometimes a bit more glossy than frosty on coins struck from worn dies. The combination of good luster, Sharp Details, and excellent eye appeal is elusive.

1914/3

Circulation-Strike Mintage: 220,000 to 330,000 (estimated)
Optimal Collecting Grade (OCG™): MS-60

1914/3 • Market Values • Circulation Strikes

VG-8	F-12	VF-20	EF-40	AU-50	AU-55	MS-60	MS-63	MS-64	MS-65	MS-66	MS-67
$300.	$350.	$550.	$850.	$1,800.	$2,250.	$3,500.	$10,000.	$20,000.	$35,000.	—	—

Availability (Certified Populations) • Circulation Strikes

<MS-60	MS-60	MS-61	MS-62	MS-63	MS-64	MS-65	MS-66	MS-67	MS-68	MS-69	MS-70
234	1	13	29	29	24	6	2	0	0	0	

Field populations: Circulation strikes (AU-59 and lower), no data available; circulation strikes (MS-60+), no data available.

Key to Collecting: This variety is readily discernible upon close study, but the over-date feature—a lightly defined horizontal ridge across the top of the 4—is not bold, so the demand is limited. It has been my experience that those who collect by date and mint want the famous and bold 1918/7-D overdate as a matter of course, but often ignore the 1914/3 and its cousin, the 1914/3-S.

Sharpness of Design Details: *Weak, 9%* • *Typical, 72%* • *Sharp, 18%* • *Full, 1%.*

Quality of Luster: Probably typical, but most show wear, and no wide survey of Mint State coins has been done.

Mintage and Distribution Notes: This variety was probably made by punching a 1914 hub or master die, complete with date, into a working die already dated 1913. David W. Lange describes two or three known variations in obverse dies in *Complete Guide to Buffalo Nickels.* R.A. Medina discovered the first one in 1996 and sent it to Bill Fivaz for confirmation. Later, the 1913-D turned up. To date, there has been no 1914/3-S, but the variety might be worth looking for, since logic suggests that it would have been created. Listed as FS-05-1914-101 and FS-05-1914S-101.

The total mintage for 1914 nickels was 20,665,738; therefore, if a Type II obverse die lasted for about 109,000 impressions,[1] there would have been 190 dies. There are possibly three known variations of this overdate, indicating that the mintage might have been 220,000 to 330,000, and that the overdates (assuming three obverses) are perhaps 60 to 100 times rarer than non-overdates. This is guesswork, but the premise is probably correct.

1914

Circulation-Strike Mintage: 20,665,463
Matte Proof Mintage: 1,275
Optimal Collecting Grade (OCG™): MS-64, PF-65

1914 • Market Values • Circulation Strikes and Matte Proof Strikes

VG-8	F-12	VF-20	EF-40	AU-50	AU-55	MS-60	MS-63	MS-64	MS-65
$17.	$20.	$22.	$30.	$40.	$45.	$50.	$80.	$200.	$400.
MS-66	MS-67		PF-60	PF-63	PF-64	PF-65	PF-66	PF-67	PF-68
$1,000.	$5,500.		$600.	$900.	$1,500.	$2,500.	$3,500.	$4,000.	—

Availability (Certified Populations) • Circulation Strikes and Matte Proof Strikes

<MS-60	MS-60	MS-61	MS-62	MS-63	MS-64	MS-65	MS-66	MS-67	MS-68	MS-69	MS-70
424	19	48	219	577	907	434	163	22	0	0	
< PF-60	PF-60	PF-61	PF-62	PF-63	PF-64	PF-65	PF-66	PF-67	PF-68	PF-69	PF-70
0	0	0	5	23	186	226	211	101	15	0	

Field populations: Circulation strikes (AU-59 and lower), 240,000–360,000; circulation strikes (MS-60+), 12,000–18,000; Matte Proof strikes, 800–1,000.

Key to Collecting: The 1914 is not difficult to locate in just about any grade desired. Mint State coins are usually very attractive; one with Sharp Details can be found with a little effort. However, some were struck from overused dies and are grainy. The date on this particular year is especially bold, due to the master hub that produced the working dies.

CIRCULATION STRIKES

Sharpness of Design Details: *Weak, 13%* • *Typical, 65%* • *Sharp, 20%* • *Full, 2%.* The sharpness is usually above average, but many weak coins exist.

Quality of Luster: The luster varies due to the large number of die pairs used and the wearing of the dies, but is usually satisfactory—lustrous, rather than satiny. Fresh dies generated deep, frosty luster; overused dies produced metal flow and "greasy" luster. (This criticism also holds true for many other date and mintmark varieties.)

MATTE PROOF STRIKES

Strike, Contrast, and Other Aspects: Specimens are sharply detailed with flat rims and satiny surfaces.

1914-D

Circulation-Strike Mintage: 3,192,000
Optimal Collecting Grade (OCG™): MS-64

1914-D • Market Values • Circulation Strikes

VG-8	F-12	VF-20	EF-40	AU-50	AU-55	MS-60	MS-63	MS-64	MS-65	MS-66	MS-67
$90.	$115.	$160.	$250.	$300.	$325.	$375.	$500.	$1,500.	$3,000.	$4,000.	$8,000.

Availability (Certified Populations) • Circulation Strikes

<MS-60	MS-60	MS-61	MS-62	MS-63	MS-64	MS-65	MS-66	MS-67	MS-68	MS-69	MS-70
726	16	47	191	356	472	187	44	5	0	0	

Field populations: Circulation strikes (AU-59 and lower), 12,000–18,000; circulation strikes (MS-60+), 2,400–3,600.

Key to Collecting: The typical 1914-D is attractive in Mint State, often having decent details and satisfactory luster. The Denver Mint, in particular, produced poorly struck coins across several different denominations during the 1920s; however, in 1914 all was in good order.

Higher level circulated specimens of this and other branch mint issues of the era are scarce because by the time such coins were widely sought, in the 1930s, most of the early dates had sustained extensive wear.

Sharpness of Design Details: *Weak, 5%* • *Typical, 55%* • *Sharp, 30%* • *Full, 10%.*

Quality of Luster: Varies, as this was a large mintage issue with many different die pairs. Some are dull; however, specimens with attractive surfaces turn up frequently. Some have an attractive "orange peel" matte obverse field area.

Interesting Variety: Does one exist? Because all dies were made in Philadelphia, it is possible to find a 1914/3-D overdate.

1914/3-S

Circulation-Strike Mintage: 110,000 (estimated)
Optimal Collecting Grade (OCG™): *n.a.*

1914/3-S • Market Values • Circulation Strikes

VG-8	F-12	VF-20	EF-40	AU-50	AU-55	MS-60	MS-63	MS-64	MS-65	MS-66	MS-67
—	$2.	—	—	—	—	—	—	—	—	—	—

Availability (Certified Populations) • Circulation Strikes

<MS-60	MS-60	MS-61	MS-62	MS-63	MS-64	MS-65	MS-66	MS-67	MS-68	MS-69	MS-70
2	0	0	2	0	1	0	0	0			

Field populations: Circulation strikes (AU-59 and lower), no data available; circulation strikes (MS-60+), no data available.

Key to Collecting: The 1914/3-S overdate was unknown to numismatists until *Coin World* published Thomas K. DeLorey's discovery of it on June 2, 1997. DeLorey has been an asset to the hobby for a long time and has made many significant discoveries.

The San Francisco overdate resembles its Philadelphia cousin, with the shadow of the top of the 3 visible to the left and right of the peak of the 4. Because it is difficult to discern, the 1914/3-S is sought primarily by dedicated specialists (see "Quality of details" below). It is not listed in the *Guide Book of United States Coins* and is, by any account, an also-ran in popularity.

Sharpness of Design Details: For this coin, the details of the *overdate* are more important than the details of the coin itself. In his *Complete Guide to Buffalo Nickels* (2000) David W. Lange comments:

> While the Philadelphia Mint [overdates of this year] are difficult to identify, the S-Mint edition is extremely so. The horizontal top of the numeral 3 is just barely evident on even the sharpest early die state specimens. As the attributor for NGC I've examined several dozen coins submitted as this variety and have had to reject the majority, even when some diagnostic features of the overdate were evident. This is because the overdate itself was obscured through either wear on the die or wear on the coin.

Not enough examples have been studied to give information on sharpness of details.

Quality of Luster: Not studied.

Mintage and Distribution Notes: If just one die pair was used, the estimated mintage would be about 110,000[2] of the total mintage of 3,470,000 pieces, making this variety about 30 times rarer than the normal 1914-S.

1914-S

Circulation-Strike Mintage: 3,470,000
Optimal Collecting Grade (OCG™): MS-64

1914-S • Market Values • Circulation Strikes

VG-8	F-12	VF-20	EF-40	AU-50	AU-55	MS-60	MS-63	MS-64	MS-65	MS-66	MS-67
$30.	$40.	$55.	$80.	$140.	$160.	$185.	$425.	$800.	$3,800.	$6,500.	$9,800.

Availability (Certified Populations) • Circulation Strikes

<MS-60	MS-60	MS-61	MS-62	MS-63	MS-64	MS-65	MS-66	MS-67	MS-68	MS-69	MS-70
719	23	69	339	440	688	134	40	2	1	0	

Field populations: Circulation strikes (AU-59 and lower), 24,000–36,000; circulation strikes (MS-60+), 2,400–3,600.

Key to Collecting: Many of this issue were made, thus it is not a key date. However, finding a really choice one can be a challenge. Like the little girl with a curl in the middle of her forehead, examples can be very, very good or they can be horrid. This applies to many other varieties from the 1920s, as well. Since commercially graded coins are simply marked MS-64, MS-65, and so on, knowing this will give the cherrypicker a fine advantage in the marketplace!

Sharpness of Design Details: *Weak, 13%* • *Typical, 45%* • *Sharp, 35%* • *Full, 7%.* Sharp Details coins are not difficult to find, but enough Full Details coins exist that it may be best to wait until you have a chance to locate one.

Quality of Luster: Again, luster varies from dull to deep and frosty, not necessarily in relation to sharpness of details.

1915

Circulation-Strike Mintage: 20,986,220
Matte Proof Mintage: 1,050
Optimal Collecting Grade (OCG™): MS-64, PF-65

1915 • Market Values • Circulation Strikes and Matte Proof Strikes

VG-8	F-12	VF-20	EF-40	AU-50	AU-55	MS-60	MS-63	MS-64	MS-65
$6.	$7.	$10.	$22.	$40.	$45.	$50.	$75.	$120.	$300.
MS-66	MS-67	PF-60	PF-63	PF-64	PF-65	PF-66	PF-67	PF-68	
$900.	$2,100.	$750.	$1,100.	$2,000.	$3,000.	$4,000.	—	—	

Availability (Certified Populations) • Circulation Strikes and Matte Proof Strikes

<MS-60	MS-60	MS-61	MS-62	MS-63	MS-64	MS-65	MS-66	MS-67	MS-68	MS-69	MS-70
289	15	43	189	487	1,008	665	296	37	0	0	
< PF-60	PF-60	PF-61	PF-62	PF-63	PF-64	PF-65	PF-66	PF-67	PF-68	PF-69	PF-70
0	1	1	8	35	142	220	192	78	4	1	

Field populations: Circulation strikes (AU-59 and lower), 240,000–360,000; circulation strikes (MS-60+), 12,000–18,000; Matte Proof strikes, 700–900.

Key to Collecting: The 1915 nickel is a good case in point—of something or other! Here is a high-mintage issue of which the majority of pieces are sharply detailed and very attractive—which proves that it can be done! As noted in the introduction, sharpness of details has nothing to do with minting quantities, but is a function of correct annealing of the planchets, together with the diligence of the press technicians who set the die spacing and tend the dies as the coins are struck.

Circulation Strikes

Sharpness of Design Details: *Weak, <1%* • *Typical, 10%* • *Sharp, 70%* • *Full, 20%.* An easy find, but be sure to check other aspects, such as metal flow from worn dies.

Quality of Luster: Luster can vary widely, but most are frosty and quite attractive—a no-problem situation.

Matte Proof Strikes

Strike, Contrast, and Other Aspects: Matte Proofs are well struck with satiny luster. Some closely resemble gem Mint State circulation strikes, and the two are easily confused. A true Matte Proof has a flat rim all around on both sides, and the edge, when viewed edge-on, is deeply mirrorlike without any vertical press-ejection lines. On some, a tiny die crack is present in the fur between ITE of UNITED and the top of the leg. Since reverse dies could be used for more than one issue, it would be interesting to see if this same die was used on Matte Proofs of other dates. David W. Lange suggests the possibility that this die could have been consigned to regular presses to make circulation strikes.

Interesting Varieties

Slightly Doubled Die (FS-05-1915-101): On some a slight die doubling is seen at the date and at the Indian's profile. While not dramatic, it is of interest to collectors of Buffalo nickel die varieties.

Two Feathers (FS-05-1915-401): Relapping of the obverse die caused the removal of the vestigial third feather.

1915-D

Circulation-Strike Mintage: 7,569,500
Optimal Collecting Grade (OCG™): MS-64

1915-D • Market Values • Circulation Strikes

VG-8	F-12	VF-20	EF-40	AU-50	AU-55	MS-60	MS-63	MS-64	MS-65	MS-66	MS-67
$20.	$30.	$50.	$100.	$140.	$200.	$250.	$325.	$500.	$2,500.	$5,000.	$11,000.

Availability (Certified Populations) • Circulation Strikes

<MS-60	MS-60	MS-61	MS-62	MS-63	MS-64	MS-65	MS-66	MS-67	MS-68	MS-69	MS-70
651	21	77	248	361	359	153	28	2	0	0	

Field populations: Circulation strikes (AU-59 and lower), 42,000–36,000; circulation strikes (MS-60+), 4,200–5,400.

Key to Collecting: The 1915-D nickel was made in quantity, but most were coined rather casually, with the result that sharply detailed coins with excellent eye appeal are

very elusive. Finding a nice one is a cherrypicker's challenge, but when found, it is quite a prize. Otherwise, the 1915-D is available in proportion to its mintage and is not a key issue.
Sharpness of Design Details: *Weak, 12% • Typical, 60% • Sharp, 25% • Full, 3%.* Sharp coins are in the minority. This, in combination with generally unattractive luster, makes the 1915-D a challenge for the connoisseur.
Quality of Luster: Varies, but is often subpar. Attractive, frosty examples are in the distinct minority.
Interesting Variety: Large D Over Small D (FS-05-1915D-501)—One reverse die has a large heavy D punched over a smaller, more delicate D. The variety is quite dramatic under magnification and would be an interesting addition to any collection that emphasizes varieties.

1915-S

Circulation-Strike Mintage: 1,505,000
Optimal Collecting Grade (OCG™): MS-64

1915-S • Market Values • Circulation Strikes

VG-8	F-12	VF-20	EF-40	AU-50	AU-55	MS-60	MS-63	MS-64	MS-65	MS-66	MS-67
$50.	$85.	$165.	$385.	$450.	$500.	$575.	$850.	$1,500.	$3,500.	$7,500.	$14,000.

Availability (Certified Populations) • Circulation Strikes

<MS-60	MS-60	MS-61	MS-62	MS-63	MS-64	MS-65	MS-66	MS-67	MS-68	MS-69	MS-70
436	8	25	89	212	395	141	45	3	0	0	

Field populations: Circulation strikes (AU-59 and lower), 15,000–24,000; circulation strikes (MS-60+), 2,100–2,700.

Key to Collecting: The 1915-S is often seen with Sharp Details or, less often, with Full Details, and with good luster and eye appeal. There are many exceptions, however, so use care when buying.
Sharpness of Design Details: *Weak, 2% • Typical, 51% • Sharp, 35% • Full, 12%.* David W. Lange comments in his *Complete Guide:*

> The existence of numerous 1915-S nickels having extremely sharp strikes has led to speculation that Proof dies were used to produce those coins. There are instances known in other coin series of retired Proof dies being placed into general service, so this is not as far-fetched as it may seem. Of course, there's really little difference between a Proof die and a regular die that's unworn, as both are capable of producing a sharp impression. It's likely that at least one press run of 1915-S nickels enjoyed a fresh pair of dies set closely together. This would result in very well struck examples. It's interesting to note that there are also many 1915-S Lincoln Cents having similarly sharp strikes.

Quality of Luster: The luster varies but is usually quite good. There are many dull, lifeless coins on the market—victims of too much dipping. Often these have been recolored with brown or golden toning. Beware.

Interesting Varieties: Repunched Mintmark (FS-05-1915S-501 and FS-05-1915 S-502)—Bold remnants of two early punchings can be seen on two different reverse dies.

1916

Circulation-Strike Mintage: 63,497,466
Matte Proof Mintage: 600
Optimal Collecting Grade (OCG™): MS-64, PF-65

1916 • Market Values • Circulation Strikes and Matte Proof Strikes

VG-8	F-12	VF-20	EF-40	AU-50	AU-55	MS-60	MS-63	MS-64	MS-65
$5.	$6.	$7.	$10.	$15.	$25.	$42.	$70.	$120.	$700.
MS-66	MS-67	PF-60	PF-63	PF-64	PF-65	PF-66	PF-67	PF-68
$1,500.	$6,500.	$1,000.	$1,650.	$2,500.	$4,000.	$5,500.	$7,000.	—

Availability (Certified Populations) • Circulation Strikes and Matte Proof Strikes

<MS-60	MS-60	MS-61	MS-62	MS-63	MS-64	MS-65	MS-66	MS-67	MS-68	MS-69	MS-70
535	37	63	317	806	1,477	664	178	15	1	0	
< PF-60	PF-60	PF-61	PF-62	PF-63	PF-64	PF-65	PF-66	PF-67	PF-68	PF-69	PF-70
3	0	0	1	3	68	119	123	49	8	0	

Field populations: Circulation strikes (AU-59 and lower), 600,000–780,000; circulation strikes (MS-60+), 27,000–36,000; Matte Proof strikes, 400–500.

Key to Collecting: There was a slight adjustment of the obverse design in this year; however, the change often goes unnoticed. Specifically, the word LIBERTY is more distinct and is set slightly farther in from the rim. This issue is usually found with a decent strike and good luster—a beacon of quality.

CIRCULATION STRIKES

Sharpness of Design Details: *Weak, 2% • Typical, 40% • Sharp, 50% • Full, 8%.*
Quality of Luster: Usually somewhat frosty. Overly dipped coins and coins struck from overused dies can appear slightly "greasy."

MATTE PROOF STRIKES

Most likely, not all of them were sold.
Strike, Contrast, and Other Aspects: Usually sharp and attractive. Authentic Proofs have wide rims of even width all around and have mirrored edges when viewed edge-on. This date harbors more false "Matte Proofs" than just about any other!

INTERESTING VARIETY

1916 Doubled Die Obverse (FS-05-1916-101, Breen-2599; URS-9): The date is boldly doubled, as are certain other features. This issue, unpublished until 1962, is one of the most sought-after of all Buffalo nickel varieties and is listed in the Red Book and other popular references. It turns up with some frequency, but usually in worn grades. The number known is undetermined. Ronald Pope noted 33 offerings in a period of two and a half years. A good guess would probably be 150 to 250.

1916-D

Circulation-Strike Mintage: 13,333,000
Optimal Collecting Grade (OCG™): MS-64

1916-D • Market Values • Circulation Strikes

VG-8	F-12	VF-20	EF-40	AU-50	AU-55	MS-60	MS-63	MS-64	MS-65	MS-66	MS-67
$15.	$20.	$32.	$80.	$110.	$125.	$150.	$250.	$600.	$2,500.	$8,000.	$14,000.

Availability (Certified Populations) • Circulation Strikes

<MS-60	MS-60	MS-61	MS-62	MS-63	MS-64	MS-65	MS-66	MS-67	MS-68	MS-69	MS-70
718	37	77	373	592	608	128	12	0	0	0	

Field populations: Circulation strikes (AU-59 and lower), 300,000–360,000; circulation strikes (MS-60+), 5,400–7,200.

Key to Collecting: The 1916-D is available in most grades through MS-65 and occasionally higher. The typical Mint State coin is attractive and lustrous, but with Typical Details—lightness on both sides. Finding an MS-65 coin will be easy; finding one with Full Details will not be!

Sharpness of Design Details: *Weak, 15% • Typical, 57% • Sharp, 25% • Full, 3%.* Sharpness varies, but nearly all show weakness in some areas, most noticeably on the fur of the bison. The D mintmark is filled or indistinct on some.

Quality of Luster: The luster is usually quite good.

1916-S

Circulation-Strike Mintage: 11,860,000
Optimal Collecting Grade (OCG™): MS-64

1916-S • Market Values • Circulation Strikes

VG-8	F-12	VF-20	EF-40	AU-50	AU-55	MS-60	MS-63	MS-64	MS-65	MS-66	MS-67
$11.	$17.	$30.	$70.	$100.	$125.	$175.	$280.	$600.	$2,000.	$5,000.	$19,000.

Availability (Certified Populations) • Circulation Strikes

<MS-60	MS-60	MS-61	MS-62	MS-63	MS-64	MS-65	MS-66	MS-67	MS-68	MS-69	MS-70
499	24	58	226	389	447	103	32	5	0	0	

Field populations: Circulation strikes (AU-59 and lower), 360,000–480,000; circulation strikes (MS-60+), 4,800–6,600.

Key to Collecting: The 1916-S nickel in Mint State is usually fairly well struck, with good luster, and a nice overall appearance. Examples with Sharp Details or Full Details are elusive. Some AU coins have been toned brown and marketed as Mint State, and some "iridescent wonders" have been created to attract those in the market for such things. Be careful.

Sharpness of Design Details: *Weak, 21% • Typical, 56% • Sharp, 18% • Full, 5%.* Some have an inner ridge on the reverse rim.

Quality of Luster: Lightly frosty is the rule. Some have streaky toning, owing to incomplete mix of the alloy.

1917

Circulation-Strike Mintage: 51,424,029
Optimal Collecting Grade (OCG™): MS-64

1917 • Market Values • Circulation Strikes

VG-8	F-12	VF-20	EF-40	AU-50	AU-55	MS-60	MS-63	MS-64	MS-65	MS-66	MS-67
$5.	$6.	$7.	$13.	$30.	$40.	$50.	$125.	$250.	$750.	$1,500.	$5,000.

Availability (Certified Populations) • Circulation Strikes

<MS-60	MS-60	MS-61	MS-62	MS-63	MS-64	MS-65	MS-66	MS-67	MS-68	MS-69	MS-70
112	3	14	93	309	695	442	138	13	3	0	

Field populations: Circulation strikes (AU-59 and lower), 480,000–600,000; circulation strikes (MS-60+), 21,000–30,000.

Key to Collecting: In higher grades, the 1917 Buffalo nickel usually exhibits a very nice strike and excellent luster. Some dies remained in service too long, resulting in pebbly or grainy surfaces, usually most visible around the border of the obverse and in the area below the bison's belly.

Sharpness of Design Details: *Weak, 5%* • *Typical, 50%* • *Sharp, 40%* • *Full, 5%.* Enough Sharp Details coins exist that finding one is easy. Most are oh so close to Full Details, but not quite.

Quality of Luster: The luster is usually rich and satiny, yielding excellent eye appeal. However, there are enough exceptions that careful inspection is warranted.

Interesting Varieties: *Doubled Die Reverse*—At least two varieties of this are known, the most significant being FS-05-1917-801 (a find made by Tim Hargis of ANACS). In "The Collector's Edge: Buffalo Nickel Die Varieties," *The Numismatist*, November 1991, Don Bonser called this "a dramatic new discovery." *"Proof" Pretenders*—As David Lange points out in his study, the late Walter Breen "certified" a number of ordinary Mint State coins as "Matte Proofs," accompanying his determinations with fancy prose. Elsewhere, some 1917 nickels, identifiable by a die scratch from the lower left of the Y of LIBERTY, have been called—or even certified as—*Specimens*, whatever that means. At least one was marketed at auction with the story that "Specimens" were made at the Mint to the order of Philadelphia dealer Ira S. Reed. The truth is that Reed was not in Philadelphia until the late 1930s and, in fact, was not even in the coin business in 1917!

A popular ploy when offering false Proofs of various denominations dated from about 1916 to the mid-1920s and involved a claim that they came from the "estate of George T. Morgan" or, for later issues such as "Matte Proof" and "Sand Blast Proof" phonies (usually made by acid etching), the "estate of John R. Sinnock." Both Morgan and Sinnock were assistant engravers who later became chief engravers.

1917-D

Circulation-Strike Mintage: 9,190,800
Optimal Collecting Grade (OCG™): MS-64

1917-D • Market Values • Circulation Strikes

VG-8	F-12	VF-20	EF-40	AU-50	AU-55	MS-60	MS-63	MS-64	MS-65	MS-66	MS-67
$20.	$35.	$70.	$125.	$230.	$275.	$300.	$750.	$2,000.	$4,000.	$10,000.	$18,000.

Availability (Certified Populations) • Circulation Strikes

<MS-60	MS-60	MS-61	MS-62	MS-63	MS-64	MS-65	MS-66	MS-67	MS-68	MS-69	MS-70
590	30	90	180	346	324	117	13	0	0	0	

Field populations: Circulation strikes (AU-59 and lower), 60,000–75,000; circulation strikes (MS-60+), 3,000–4,200.

Key to Collecting: The 1917-D is among the earlier Denver Mint Buffalo nickels frequently seen with so-so or "typical" details and below-par eye appeal. Although examples with Sharp Details exist, there are not many.

This date and mint seems to have an overly generous share of recolored coins posing as choice Mint State. Be careful when shopping.

Sharpness of Design Details: *Weak, 17% • Typical, 50% • Sharp, 30% • Full, 3%.* Sharply defined coins are elusive, a true challenge to find.

Quality of Luster: It is often the case with this issue that the poorer the strike, the richer the luster. In general, the luster will vary because of the number of die pairs used.

Interesting Variety: *3-1/2 Legs (FS-05-1917D-901; URS-5)*—The die was relapped, removing much of the bison's foreleg. FS notes this variety as very popular.

1917-S

Circulation-Strike Mintage: 4,193,000
Optimal Collecting Grade (OCG™): MS-64

1917-S • Market Values • Circulation Strikes

VG-8	F-12	VF-20	EF-40	AU-50	AU-55	MS-60	MS-63	MS-64	MS-65	MS-66	MS-67
$35.	$65.	$90.	$175.	$300.	$325.	$375.	$1,250.	$2,500.	$5,000.	$10,000.	$18,000.

Availability (Certified Populations) • Circulation Strikes

<MS-60	MS-60	MS-61	MS-62	MS-63	MS-64	MS-65	MS-66	MS-67	MS-68	MS-69	MS-70
466	7	29	78	140	279	99	30	0	0	0	

Field populations: Circulation strikes (AU-59 and lower), 27,000–36,000; circulation strikes (MS-60+), 1,800–2,400.

Key to Collecting: The typical 1917-S in a Mint State grade earns a "gentleman's C" for sharpness. Most examples show lightness of details on the bison's head, the obverse center, and other key points. The luster is often "greasy," but pleasing in appearance. Recolored coins seem to be less of a problem than with the 1917-D.

Sharpness of Design Details: *Weak, 12% • Typical, 60% • Sharp, 25% • Full, 3%.* Most coins in the marketplace are so-so in sharpness. Some have ridges or metal flow areas from overly used dies.

Quality of Luster: These are usually finely grained or "greasy," but with decent eye appeal.

1918

Circulation-Strike Mintage: 32,086,314
Optimal Collecting Grade (OCG™): MS-64

1918 • Market Values • Circulation Strikes

VG-8	F-12	VF-20	EF-40	AU-50	AU-55	MS-60	MS-63	MS-64	MS-65	MS-66	MS-67
$5.	$6.	$12.	$30.	$45.	$75.	$95.	$300.	$800.	$1,500.	$3,000.	$15,000.

Availability (Certified Populations) • Circulation Strikes

<MS-60	MS-60	MS-61	MS-62	MS-63	MS-64	MS-65	MS-66	MS-67	MS-68	MS-69	MS-70
212	12	20	102	270	504	212	44	8	0	0	

Field populations: Circulation strikes (AU-59 and lower), 240,000–360,000; circulation strikes (MS-60+), 15,000–21,000.

Key to Collecting: The 1918 Buffalo is plentiful in all grades, providing the opportunity to cherrypick for quality. Nickels of this date tend to be lightly struck and unattractive, ideal for bargain hunters and misguided investors. Connoisseurs who take their time can find sharp coins with good eye appeal.

Sharpness of Design Details: *Weak, 7% • Typical, 65% • Sharp, 25% • Full, 3%.* Usually lightly struck in areas.

Quality of Luster: Luster varies. On the sharper coins it tends to be frosty; on the usually seen light strike it is somewhat "greasy."

1918/7-D

Circulation-Strike Mintage: 100,000 (estimate)
Optimal Collecting Grade (OCG™): Buyer's choice

1918/7-D • Market Values • Circulation Strikes

VG-8	F-12	VF-20	EF-40	AU-50	AU-55	MS-60	MS-63	MS-64	MS-65	MS-66	MS-67
$1,500.	$2,700.	$5,500.	$9,500.	$12,000.	$17,000.	$28,000.	$60,000.	$100,000.	$200,000.	$225,000.	$250,000.

Availability (Certified Populations) • Circulation Strikes

<MS-60	MS-60	MS-61	MS-62	MS-63	MS-64	MS-65	MS-66	MS-67	MS-68	MS-69	MS-70
797	1	4	18	13	38	5	0	0	0	0	

Field populations: Circulation strikes (AU-59 and lower), 900–1,800; circulation strikes (MS-60+), 18–30.

Key to Collecting: The 1918/7-D overdate was not known in numismatic circles until Barney Bluestone, of Syracuse, New York published it in an auction catalog in 1931. Even then, it attracted almost no attention, not even that of compilers of references and check lists. By the time it did catch on, the opportunity to find high-grade coins was gone.

Today, the typical 1918/7-D is in a grade from VG to VF. AU. Mint State coins are very scarce and choice Mint State examples are rare. Interestingly, among Mint State coins, the quality varies considerably—some are lightly struck and show annoying metal flow from tired dies, while others are quite sharp. As nearly all coins show some wear, the sharpness of details is not as important as for an issue generally collected in Mint State.

Sharpness of Design Details: *Weak, 28% • Typical, 50% • Sharp, 20% • Full, 2%.* Usually seen struck from worn dies.

Quality of Luster: Most are grainy with metal flow, but this is evident only with higher-grade coins. One cannot be too choosy if offered a choice or gem Mint State coin, but a sharp, lustrous one would, without question, be best.

About the Dies: All authentic 1918/7-D nickels were struck from a single pair of dies. J.P. Martin made these comments in an ANACS report:

> Most known specimens appear to have been struck from fairly well-eroded dies that display a die break at the Indian's braid. Very few represent an earlier die state that shows no break. . . . The position of the mintmark on genuine 1918/7-D nickels is consistent. Mintmark placement on the regular 1918-D is similar, but not the same as the overdate. On coins representing advanced die states, the die break at the braid extends to the Indian's mouth. Even on low-grade specimens, the break is nearly always visible near the braid. However, be advised that the 1918-D Indian Head nickel is known to display a similar die break.[3]

1918-D

Circulation-Strike Mintage: 8,362,000
Optimal Collecting Grade (OCG™): MS-64

1918-D • Market Values • Circulation Strikes

VG-8	F-12	VF-20	EF-40	AU-50	AU-55	MS-60	MS-63	MS-64	MS-65	MS-66	MS-67
$25.	$40.	$100.	$200.	$325.	$350.	$375.	$1,200.	$2,000.	$5,000.	$10,000.	$20,000.

Availability (Certified Populations) • Circulation Strikes

<MS-60	MS-60	MS-61	MS-62	MS-63	MS-64	MS-65	MS-66	MS-67	MS-68	MS-69	MS-70
570	14	21	119	228	314	80	24	1	0	0	

Field populations: Circulation strikes (AU-59 and lower), 27,000–36,000; circulation strikes (MS-60+), 2,400–3,600.

Key to Collecting: Although the 1918-D is common in lower grades, in gem Mint State (MS-65 or higher) and with a decent strike, it is a rarity. Sharpness ranges from relatively decent, with rich luster, to some with large areas of flatness. This date and mint can be a cherrypicker's delight.

Sharpness of Design Details: *Weak, 27% • Typical, 50% • Sharp, 20% • Full, 3%.*

Quality of Luster: Luster ranges from frosty on some of the sharper pieces to somewhat dull on flat strikes.

1918-S

Circulation-Strike Mintage: 4,882,000
Optimal Collecting Grade (OCG™): MS-64

1918-S • Market Values • Circulation Strikes

VG-8	F-12	VF-20	EF-40	AU-50	AU-55	MS-60	MS-63	MS-64	MS-65	MS-66	MS-67
$25.	$42.	$90.	$185.	$300.	$400.	$500.	$3,000.	$8,000.	$20,000.	$40,000.	$45,000.

Availability (Certified Populations) • Circulation Strikes

<MS-60	MS-60	MS-61	MS-62	MS-63	MS-64	MS-65	MS-66	MS-67	MS-68	MS-69	MS-70
453	13	38	106	195	104	36	1	0	0	0	

Field populations: Circulation strikes (AU-59 and lower), 24,000–33,000; circulation strikes (MS-60+), 1,200–1,800.

Key to Collecting: The 1918-S offers contrasts in striking from weak to sharp; however, most are typical, with light details in areas. Luster and eye appeal are usually good. Cherrypicking for quality can produce excellent results, but watch out for coins that have been doctored with golden or brown toning, thus concealing evidence of friction and wear.

Sharpness of Design Details: *Weak, 38% • Typical, 40% • Sharp, 20% • Full, 2%.* Sharp coins are elusive. One example studied was flat at the centers, but had excellent fur detail on the bison's head and was sharp around the borders—simply proving that one rule does not fit all.

Quality of Luster: These are usually frosty and attractive, but there are exceptions.

1919

Circulation-Strike Mintage: 60,868,000
Optimal Collecting Grade (OCG™): MS-64

1919 • Market Values • Circulation Strikes

VG-8	F-12	VF-20	EF-40	AU-50	AU-55	MS-60	MS-63	MS-64	MS-65	MS-66	MS-67
$2.	$3.	$6.	$12.	$30.	$35.	$45.	$100.	$250.	$750.	$1,300.	$5,200.

Availability (Certified Populations) • Circulation Strikes

<MS-60	MS-60	MS-61	MS-62	MS-63	MS-64	MS-65	MS-66	MS-67	MS-68	MS-69	MS-70
129	7	12	103	339	863	454	143	11	1	0	

Field populations: Circulation strikes (AU-59 and lower), 600,000–780,000; circulation strikes (MS-60+), 24,000–36,000.

Key to Collecting: The 1919 nickel was made in large quantities just after the crest of the World War I economic boom, but while business was still strong. So many die pairs were used that coins are all over the map in terms of sharpness and luster. Enough exist on an absolute basis that finding one with Full Details is possible, although only about one in 20 coins will qualify.

Sharpness of Design Details: *Weak, 2% • Typical, 30% • Sharp, 63% • Full, 5%.* The sharpness varies, but is generally good.

Quality of Luster: The luster is above average on most 1919 nickels. Beware AU coins that have been recolored to brown. Lightly toned Mint State coins are more naturally light blue or gold.

1919-D

Circulation-Strike Mintage: 8,006,000
Optimal Collecting Grade (OCG™): MS-64

1919-D • Market Values • Circulation Strikes

VG-8	F-12	VF-20	EF-40	AU-50	AU-55	MS-60	MS-63	MS-64	MS-65	MS-66	MS-67
$25.	$50.	$100.	$300.	$400.	$500.	$600.	$1,500.	$3,000.	$7,500.	$10,000.	$30,000.

Availability (Certified Populations) • Circulation Strikes

<MS-60	MS-60	MS-61	MS-62	MS-63	MS-64	MS-65	MS-66	MS-67	MS-68	MS-69	MS-70
632	11	32	81	140	290	63	15	0	0	0	

Field populations: Circulation strikes (AU-59 and lower), 42,000–60,000; circulation strikes (MS-60+), 1,800–2,400.

Key to Collecting: The 1919-D is available in circulated grades in proportion to its mintage—not a key date, but not plentiful either. The variety is quite scarce in Mint State, especially with decent details.

Sharpness of Design Details: *Weak, 12% • Typical, 52% • Sharp, 32% • Full, 4%.* Most coins are indifferently struck. Full Details coins are very elusive in combination with nice luster.

Quality of Luster: Luster is usually good. Some of the shallowest strikes have the richest luster—a perplexing situation, but generally true throughout the series. Dull coins are apt to have resulted from repeated dipping.

1919-S

Circulation-Strike Mintage: 7,521,000
Optimal Collecting Grade (OCG™): MS-64

1919-S • Market Values • Circulation Strikes

VG-8	F-12	VF-20	EF-40	AU-50	AU-55	MS-60	MS-63	MS-64	MS-65	MS-66	MS-67
$20.	$40.	$100.	$250.	$350.	$400.	$500.	$1,800.	$2,500.	$7,500.	$17,500.	$35,000.

Availability (Certified Populations) • Circulation Strikes

<MS-60	MS-60	MS-61	MS-62	MS-63	MS-64	MS-65	MS-66	MS-67	MS-68	MS-69	MS-70
730	20	27	130	279	259	40	1	0	0	0	

Field populations: Circulation strikes (AU-59 and lower), 36,000–60,000; circulation strikes (MS-60+), 1,500–2,100.

Key to Collecting: The 1919-S is readily available in most grades, from well worn through MS-65 or higher. If you go to a large convention and are lucky enough to view a dozen Mint State coins, nearly all will lack detail at the center, and the bison will be rather glossy and smooth, with little fur detail. A Full Strike coin is a great rarity. A contributor to this study reported finding just *one* among 395 pieces surveyed!

Sharpness of Design Details: *Weak, 26% • Typical, 55% • Sharp, 19% • Full, <1%.* Likely, even if you become a connoisseur, you will have to settle for a Sharp Details, Full Details being one of the great challenges in the series. (It is remarkable that scarcely anyone knows this—except for those who have read and remember David W. Lange's *Complete Guide to Buffalo Nickels*. It is also remarkable that investors and collectors, who think nothing of spending a few thousand dollars on Buffalo nickels, will balk at spending a fraction of that to buy either the Lange book or this one.)

Quality of Luster: The luster varies, but is often glossy or "greasy," rather than deeply frosty.

1920

Circulation-Strike Mintage: 62,093,000
Optimal Collecting Grade (OCG™): MS-64

1920 • Market Values • Circulation Strikes

VG-8	F-12	VF-20	EF-40	AU-50	AU-55	MS-60	MS-63	MS-64	MS-65	MS-66	MS-67
$2.	2.50	$5.	$12.	$25.	$35.	$50.	$125.	$300.	$1,000.	$2,000.	$6,000.

Availability (Certified Populations) • Circulation Strikes

<MS-60	MS-60	MS-61	MS-62	MS-63	MS-64	MS-65	MS-66	MS-67	MS-68	MS-69	MS-70
177	14	21	131	347	717	287	119	11	0	0	

Field populations: Circulation strikes (AU-59 and lower), 935,000–1,190,000; circulation strikes (MS-60+), 34,000–51,000.

Key to Collecting: The bad news is that Buffalo nickels made at the Philadelphia Mint in 1920 are usually weak in areas and have unsatisfactory luster. The good news is that this is a very common date. Many Mint State coins exist, and although Full Details coins with good eye appeal are in the minority, there are enough of them around for you to find an example.

Sharpness of Design Details: *Weak, 12% • Typical, 50% • Sharp, 35% • Full, 3%.* Most are Typical Details, often with metal flow and stress lines in the fields, from overused dies.

Quality of Luster: These vary widely, but are usually attractive.

1920-D

Circulation-Strike Mintage: 9,418,000
Optimal Collecting Grade (OCG™): MS-64

1920-D • Market Values • Circulation Strikes

VG-8	F-12	VF-20	EF-40	AU-50	AU-55	MS-60	MS-63	MS-64	MS-65	MS-66	MS-67
$15.	$25.	$100.	$275.	$325.	$395.	$500.	$1,800.	$2,500.	$7,500.	$15,000.	$27,500.

Availability (Certified Populations) • Circulation Strikes

<MS-60	MS-60	MS-61	MS-62	MS-63	MS-64	MS-65	MS-66	MS-67	MS-68	MS-69	MS-70
538	7	30	76	140	345	60	2	0	0	0	

Field populations: Circulation strikes (AU-59 and lower), 76,500–102,000; circulation strikes (MS-60+), 2,975–4,250.

Key to Collecting: Although the 1920-D comes with a large mintage figure, Mint State coins are scarce in general and rare if both Full Details and excellent luster. This issue will be a challenge for the connoisseur.

The press attendants at the Denver Mint became increasingly inattentive during this period, with the result that the quality of details varies considerably. Nevertheless, quite a few have Sharp Details and cost no more than poorly struck examples. The bison's head is a good place to check first. Take your time and find a nice one.

Sharpness of Design Details: *Weak, 22% • Typical, 45% • Sharp, 30% • Full, 3%.* Usually lightly struck in areas. The 1920-D is often seen with Weak Details, generally flat at the centers and on the bison's head. Let investors buy these; they don't know the difference! (Connoisseurs can be thankful for investors—they take up the dregs in the Buffalo nickel series, a practice abetted by the unstinting belief that a grading number on a slab tells all!)

Quality of Luster: Luster ranges from dull and lifeless to deeply frosty.

1920-S

Circulation-Strike Mintage: 9,689,000
Optimal Collecting Grade (OCG™): MS-64

1920-S • Market Values • Circulation Strikes

VG-8	F-12	VF-20	EF-40	AU-50	AU-55	MS-60	MS-63	MS-64	MS-65	MS-66	MS-67
$7.	$20.	$90.	$175.	$300.	$400.	$500.	$2,000.	$5,000.	$20,000.	$40,000.	$50,000.

Availability (Certified Populations) • Circulation Strikes

<MS-60	MS-60	MS-61	MS-62	MS-63	MS-64	MS-65	MS-66	MS-67	MS-68	MS-69	MS-70
659	23	65	110	301	260	19	1	0	0	0	

Field populations: Circulation strikes (AU-59 and lower), 85,000–110,500; circulation strikes (MS-60+), 2,763–3,825.

Key to Collecting: The 1920-S is scarce in any Mint State grade, and when found is apt to have lightly defined details. Coins with Sharp Details are *very rare*, and seem to constitute only about 15% of the population. Luster and eye appeal are usually subpar. Here, indeed, is a fantastic opportunity for the informed connoisseur!

For the buyer who simply looks at labels on a certified holder, the 1920-S will be an easy acquisition. For the connoisseur, this may well be one of the last coins acquired. And as to finding one with Full Details—forget it, unless you get *very* lucky.
Sharpness of Design Details: *Weak, 25% • Typical, 60% • Sharp, 15% • Full, 0%.* This is the earliest variety for which no Full Details coins have been seen. • David W. Lange's comment in *Complete Guide to Buffalo Nickels* is eminently quotable and relevant:

> Well-struck coins are scarce and highly prized. Fully struck examples are virtually unknown. Most seen range in strike from fair all the way to awful, the reverse being particularly subject to extreme die erosion and incompleteness. The worst ones look like wax coins left to melt in the sun.

Quality of Luster: The luster is usually subdued and below par, not deeply frosty or flashy. This is due in part to the poor quality of striking.

1921

Circulation-Strike Mintage: 10,663,000
Optimal Collecting Grade (OCG™): MS-64

1921 • Market Values • Circulation Strikes

VG-8	F-12	VF-20	EF-40	AU-50	AU-55	MS-60	MS-63	MS-64	MS-65	MS-66	MS-67
$4.	$6.	$20.	$50.	$75.	$85.	$100.	$300.	$500.	$1,000.	$2,000.	$5,000.

Availability (Certified Populations) • Circulation Strikes

<MS-60	MS-60	MS-61	MS-62	MS-63	MS-64	MS-65	MS-66	MS-67	MS-68	MS-69	MS-70
197	8	13	71	208	459	338	176	23	0	0	

Field populations: Circulation strikes (AU-59 and lower), 127,500–191,250; circulation strikes (MS-60+), 10,200–12,750.

Key to Collecting: The 1921 is a plentiful issue. Mint State coins tend to be very well struck and have excellent eye appeal. Finding a gem will be easy—a pleasant situation, for ahead lie many entries with dates and mintmarks that will pose problems. Because this was a slow time both in the American economy and at the Philadelphia Mint, employees had the time to do their jobs with care and pride. (Things started hopping later that year, though, when millions of silver dollars were struck, for the first time since 1904).
Sharpness of Design Details: *Weak, 0% • Typical, 5% • Sharp, 40% • Full, 55%.* The 1921 is the only Buffalo nickel in which the numeral 1 in the date is other than a vertical "stick." On the 1921, the 1 has a slight projection, the hint of a serif, at the upper left. • Ron Pope contributed this additional comment:

> On the 1921 and 1921-S nickels several details are completely unlike previous or subsequent dates. It appears that the central details of the braid were reworked—not merely more deeply impressed into the master die—the hairline configuration is different-perhaps someone in the engraving department

(with some idle time on their hands?) decided to strengthen a major area of weakness seen on earlier dates. I can easily tell a dateless 1921 or 1921-S just from this one characteristic.

This characteristic is noticeable most often at the separation of the hair-strand groups immediately over the Indian's braid ribbon.

Quality of Luster: Luster varies, but is usually excellent.

1921-S

Circulation-Strike Mintage: 1,557,000
Optimal Collecting Grade (OCG™): MS-64

1921-S • Market Values • Circulation Strikes

VG-8	F-12	VF-20	EF-40	AU-50	AU-55	MS-60	MS-63	MS-64	MS-65	MS-66	MS-67
$110.	$175.	$525.	$850.	$1,200.	$1,350.	$1,500.	$2,200.	$3,500.	$7,500.	$15,000.	$30,000.

Availability (Certified Populations) • Circulation Strikes

<MS-60	MS-60	MS-61	MS-62	MS-63	MS-64	MS-65	MS-66	MS-67	MS-68	MS-69	MS-70
1,148	5	8	26	105	277	75	10	0	0	0	

Field populations: Circulation strikes (AU-59 and lower), 11,900–17,000; circulation strikes (MS-60+), 765–1,020.

Key to Collecting: The 1921-S is somewhat scarce in all grades; however, market offerings at the Mint State level are frequent. Most have decent details, although some are flat. The first place to check is the head of the bison. You can use your time and find a nice one, since quality is seldom more expensive in a marketplace where buyers are generally ignorant about sharpness of strike. Although high-grade 1921-S nickels are valuable and are considered scarce, Full Details examples are surprisingly available, although it takes some searching to find them.

Sharpness of Design Details: *Weak, 15%* • *Typical, 15%* • *Sharp, 55%* • *Full, 15%*. In general, the 1921-S is well struck with Sharp Details. Full Details coins are relatively more available than other mintmarked nickels of this era. (See note for 1921 above concerning a one-year modification to the obverse.)

Quality of Luster: Luster varies, but is usually quite good, with excellent eye appeal.

1923

Circulation-Strike Mintage: 35,715,000
Optimal Collecting Grade (OCG™): MS-64

1923 • Market Values • Circulation Strikes

VG-8	F-12	VF-20	EF-40	AU-50	AU-55	MS-60	MS-63	MS-64	MS-65	MS-66	MS-67
$2.50	$3.	$6.	$13.	$30.	$40.	$50.	$150.	$250.	$750.	$1,200.	$6,500.

Availability (Certified Populations) • Circulation Strikes

<MS-60	MS-60	MS-61	MS-62	MS-63	MS-64	MS-65	MS-66	MS-67	MS-68	MS-69	MS-70
162	14	27	105	331	705	404	122	15	0	0	

Field populations: Circulation strikes (AU-59 and lower), 510,000–680,000; circulation strikes (MS-60+), 21,250–29,750.

Key to Collecting: The 1923 nickel is a beacon of beauty in its era, as is the 1921 Philadelphia issue. Most are decently struck and have excellent luster. Coins with Sharp Details are plentiful, but nearly all have some lightness, usually at the center of the obverse, keeping them from crossing the finish line to Full Details.

Sharpness of Design Details: *Weak, 1%* • *Typical, 36%* • *Sharp, 58%* • *Full, 5%.* Although Full Details coins are elusive, Sharp Details specimens are easy to find.

Quality of Luster: Luster is usually very frosty and attractive, although there are exceptions.

1923-S

Circulation-Strike Mintage: 6,142,000
Optimal Collecting Grade (OCG™): MS-64

1923-S • Market Values • Circulation Strikes

VG-8	F-12	VF-20	EF-40	AU-50	AU-55	MS-60	MS-63	MS-64	MS-65	MS-66	MS-67
$8.	$18.	$125.	$275.	$350.	$400.	$450.	$900.	$1,800.	$15,000.	$30,000.	$45,000.

Availability (Certified Populations) • Circulation Strikes

<MS-60	MS-60	MS-61	MS-62	MS-63	MS-64	MS-65	MS-66	MS-67	MS-68	MS-69	MS-70
901	11	41	212	397	606	49	5	0	0	0	

Field populations: Circulation strikes (AU-59 and lower), 38,250–51,000; circulation strikes (MS-60+), 2,550–3,400.

Key to Collecting: The 1923-S is readily available in lower grades but becomes scarce in Mint State. The details of striking vary, but most are reasonably sharp. Examples in most of the higher grades have good eye appeal. On the other hand, some have weak details and mushy mintmarks and are absolutely horrid.

Sharpness of Design Details: *Weak, 19%* • *Typical, 38%* • *Sharp, 40%* • *Full, 3%.* More than a few Sharp Details coins are only a hair's breadth from Full Details, but have lightness above the braid ribbon (the usual spot) or weak fur details on the bison's head.

Quality of Luster: These are usually of nice quality, finely grained rather than deeply frosty.

1924

Circulation-Strike Mintage: 21,620,000
Optimal Collecting Grade (OCG™): MS-64

1924 • Market Values • Circulation Strikes

VG-8	F-12	VF-20	EF-40	AU-50	AU-55	MS-60	MS-63	MS-64	MS-65	MS-66	MS-67
$2.	$5.	$10.	$20.	$45.	$55.	$65.	$150.	$800.	$1,500.	$3,000.	$4,500.

Availability (Certified Populations) • Circulation Strikes

<MS-60	MS-60	MS-61	MS-62	MS-63	MS-64	MS-65	MS-66	MS-67	MS-68	MS-69	MS-70
136	9	11	89	255	528	258	80	4	0	0	

Field populations: Circulation strikes (AU-59 and lower), 255,000–340,000; circulation strikes (MS-60+), 11,900–15,300.

Key to Collecting: With such a large mintage, you might expect that quite a few 1924 nickels would rank high in striking sharpness. However, nearly all have weakness on the fur of the bison. David W. Lange suggests that the prevalence of such pieces might indicate incomplete hubbing during the making of master dies. Luster is often subpar. A high-quality 1924 is hard to find.

Sharpness of Design Details: *Weak, 5%* • *Typical, 64%* • *Sharp, 30%* • *Full, 1%.* Most are light at the centers, particularly on the fur details of the bison. Some appear to be "shallow" on the reverse.

Quality of Luster: Often dull or "greasy," rarely deeply frosty with good eye appeal.

1924-D

Circulation-Strike Mintage: 5,258,000
Optimal Collecting Grade (OCG™): MS-64

1924-D • Market Values • Circulation Strikes

VG-8	F-12	VF-20	EF-40	AU-50	AU-55	MS-60	MS-63	MS-64	MS-65	MS-66	MS-67
$8.	$25.	$75.	$225.	$300.	$325.	$350.	$1,000.	$1,500.	$5,000.	$15,000.	$19,000.

Availability (Certified Populations) • Circulation Strikes

<MS-60	MS-60	MS-61	MS-62	MS-63	MS-64	MS-65	MS-66	MS-67	MS-68	MS-69	MS-70
525	16	19	79	166	505	99	2	0	0	0	

Field populations: Circulation strikes (AU-59 and lower), 42,500–59,500; circulation strikes (MS-60+), 1,190–1,530.

Key to Collecting: The 1924-D is somewhat scarce in all grades. Mint State coins were considered quite rare until the 1990s, when the Connecticut State Library released a number of them, and dozens were auctioned by Heritage. Today, most high-quality Mint State coins are from that hoard. These wonderful pieces could be bought at face value in 1924.

The combination of Sharp Details and frosty luster can yield a specimen with a great deal of eye appeal. However, avoid the many pieces that have been overdipped, and those that have been toned to various shades of brown or purple.

Sharpness of Design Details: *Weak, 15%* • *Typical, 60%* • *Sharp, 25%* • *Full, 0%.* Light striking is the rule for the 1924-D, although finding a Full Details coin is possible.

Quality of Luster: Luster is usually quite good.

1924-S

Circulation-Strike Mintage: 1,437,000
Optimal Collecting Grade (OCG™): MS-64

1924-S • Market Values • Circulation Strikes

VG-8	F-12	VF-20	EF-40	AU-50	AU-55	MS-60	MS-63	MS-64	MS-65	MS-66	MS-67
$30.	$100.	$475.	$1,250.	$1,800.	$2,200.	$2,400.	$4,000.	$5,000.	$10,000.	$20,000.	$40,000.

Availability (Certified Populations) • Circulation Strikes

<MS-60	MS-60	MS-61	MS-62	MS-63	MS-64	MS-65	MS-66	MS-67	MS-68	MS-69	MS-70
1,056	4	9	44	89	215	52	2	0	0	0	

Field populations: Circulation strikes (AU-59 and lower), 17,000–25,500; circulation strikes (MS-60+), 425–680.

Key to Collecting: Because of its low mintage, the 1924-S is scarce in all grades. Those in the VF and EF ranges were plucked out of circulation in the 1930s when collecting by date and mintmark varieties became popular. Striking is usually light in some areas, so Full Details coins are few. (Although some may exist, I have never seen one.) The publication of this book may intensify interest in finding such pieces—many coins thought to be rare come out of the woodwork after they are publicized. I don't expect this to happen with 1924-S, but it is possible.

Avoid the many recolored AU and low-range Mint State coins. One way to spot them is by their dull, lifeless luster—which brown or iridescent toning cannot change. **Sharpness of Design Details:** *Weak, 32% • Typical, 45% • Sharp, 23% • Full, 0%.* Repeating a familiar scenario, while Sharp Details coins can be found, no Full Details coin has been seen.

Quality of Luster: Varies, but Mint State coins are often frosty.

1925

Circulation-Strike Mintage: 35,565,000
Optimal Collecting Grade (OCG™): MS-64

1925 • Market Values • Circulation Strikes

VG-8	F-12	VF-20	EF-40	AU-50	AU-55	MS-60	MS-63	MS-64	MS-65	MS-66	MS-67
$3.50	$4.	$8.	$15.	$30.	$35.	$40.	$100.	$250.	$750.	$1,500.	$2,300.

Availability (Certified Populations) • Circulation Strikes

<MS-60	MS-60	MS-61	MS-62	MS-63	MS-64	MS-65	MS-66	MS-67	MS-68	MS-69	MS-70
193	918	25	88	270	790	442	169	4	0	0	

Field populations: Circulation strikes (AU-59 and lower), 510,000–765,000; circulation strikes (MS-60+), 17,000–25,500.

Key to Collecting: The 1925 nickel is one of those coins that is very common in "nice" preservation, and has good eye appeal, but for which Full Details examples are almost non-existent. A Sharp Details coin presents a reasonable compromise. Luster ranges from soft to deeply frosty.

Sharpness of Design Details: *Weak, 5% • Typical, 55% • Sharp, 39% • Full, 1%.* Usually with Typical Details or Sharp Details, but scarcely ever with Full Details.

Quality of Luster: Luster varies. Softly struck pieces often have "greasy" or creamy luster, attractive to view. Better strikes usually have a deep frosty luster.

1925-D

Circulation-Strike Mintage: 4,450,000
Optimal Collecting Grade (OCG™): MS-64

1925-D • Market Values • Circulation Strikes

VG-8	F-12	VF-20	EF-40	AU-50	AU-55	MS-60	MS-63	MS-64	MS-65	MS-66	MS-67
$15.	$35.	$90.	$175.	$250.	$300.	$400.	$750.	$1,500.	$5,000.	$15,000.	$22,000.

Availability (Certified Populations) • Circulation Strikes

<MS-60	MS-60	MS-61	MS-62	MS-63	MS-64	MS-65	MS-66	MS-67	MS-68	MS-69	MS-70
507	10	28	148	306	592	134	8	0	0	0	

Field populations: Circulation strikes (AU-59 and lower), 51,000–76,500; circulation strikes (MS-60+), 3,400–5,100.

Key to Collecting: The 1925-D is somewhat scarce in worn grades and elusive in Mint State, especially with Sharp Details. Connoisseurs have long viewed it a challenge to find a decently struck 1925-D that has good eye appeal. Like the 1924-D, this issue was squirreled away by the Connecticut State Library. When dozens were sold by Heritage in the 1990s the availability of choice pieces changed dramatically.

Sharpness of Design Details: *Weak, 33%* • *Typical, 44%* • *Sharp, 20%* • *Full, 3%.* Most 1925-D nickels are lightly struck, sometimes with flat or mushy details, especially at the bottom of the reverse. However, Sharp Details examples do exist.

Quality of Luster: Most of the Connecticut State Library coins are lustrous and attractive; otherwise, luster varies. A number of over-dipped and dull coins have been dressed up with artificial toning and trotted out as choice Mint State, including some in certified holders. Avoid any coin that does not show *frosty* luster.

1925-S

Circulation-Strike Mintage: 6,256,000
Optimal Collecting Grade (OCG™): MS-64

1925-S • Market Values • Circulation Strikes

VG-8	F-12	VF-20	EF-40	AU-50	AU-55	MS-60	MS-63	MS-64	MS-65	MS-66	MS-67
$10.	$18.	$85.	$180.	$250.	$300.	$450.	$2,200.	$5,000.	$30,000.	$54,000.	$60,000.

Availability (Certified Populations) • Circulation Strikes

<MS-60	MS-60	MS-61	MS-62	MS-63	MS-64	MS-65	MS-66	MS-67	MS-68	MS-69	MS-70
836	11	39	131	305	377	31	1	0	0	0	

Field populations: Circulation strikes (AU-59 and lower), 63,750–85,000; circulation strikes (MS-60+), 765–1,105.

Key to Collecting: The 1925-S nickel is complex, especially in Mint State, because certified examples are identified only as MS-64, MS-65, and so on. In reality, quite a few are simply miserable strikes, with flatness of certain date numerals and the lettering at the bottom of the reverse. Others are weak in the usual places—the center of both sides and on the bison's fur. Still others masquerading as "Mint State" are dull, cleaned coins that have been doctored by adding toning.

It is possible to buy a gorgeous Mint State 1925-S nickel with rich luster and superb eye appeal, but you will be on your own; descriptions in commercial listings are not apt to reveal some of the problems mentioned above.

Sharpness of Design Details: *Weak, 27%* • *Typical, 47%* • *Sharp, 25%* • *Full, 1%.* Sharpness varies, but is usually weak in one or more areas, sometimes flat on numerals and lettering. The mintmark on some is just a blob. Sharp coins are elusive.

Quality of Luster: Luster varies and is often subpar.

1926

Circulation-Strike Mintage: 44,693,000
Optimal Collecting Grade (OCG™): MS-65

1926 • Market Values • Circulation Strikes

VG-8	F-12	VF-20	EF-40	AU-50	AU-55	MS-60	MS-63	MS-64	MS-65	MS-66	MS-67
$1.50	$2.50	$4.	$10.	$20.	$25.	$35.	$75.	$100.	$200.	$600.	$2,500.

Availability (Certified Populations) • Circulation Strikes

<MS-60	MS-60	MS-61	MS-62	MS-63	MS-64	MS-65	MS-66	MS-67	MS-68	MS-69	MS-70
80	13	13	61	228	1,273	1,303	431	33	1	0	

Field populations: Circulation strikes (AU-59 and lower), 595,000–765,000; circulation strikes (MS-60+), 25,500–34,000.

Key to Collecting: The 1926 nickel is common in all grades, including Mint State. Most have weakness in one area or another. Full Details coins are exceedingly rare (a fact surprising to many), but Sharp Details coins can be found, usually with only slight weakness at the center of the obverse and on the fur on the reverse—subtle enough that most people wouldn't notice. Eye appeal is generally excellent, although some struck from tired dies are grainy or show metal flow.

Sharpness of Design Details: *Weak, 10% • Typical, 57% • Sharp, 33% • Full, <1%.* Sharpness varies. The 1926 is readily available in all degrees except Full Details.

Quality of Luster: The luster is usually frosty and attractive, although there are exceptions.

1926-D

Circulation-Strike Mintage: 5,638,000
Optimal Collecting Grade (OCG™): MS-64

1926-D • Market Values • Circulation Strikes

VG-8	F-12	VF-20	EF-40	AU-50	AU-55	MS-60	MS-63	MS-64	MS-65	MS-66	MS-67
$12.	$24.	$90.	$175.	$275.	$285.	$300.	$550.	$1,500.	$5,000.	$10,000.	$20,000.

Availability (Certified Populations) • Circulation Strikes

<MS-60	MS-60	MS-61	MS-62	MS-63	MS-64	MS-65	MS-66	MS-67	MS-68	MS-69	MS-70
415	28	45	322	507	279	109	25	1	0	0	

Field populations: Circulation strikes (AU-59 and lower), 46,750–63,750; circulation strikes (MS-60+), 3,400–5,100.

Key to Collecting: The 1926-D mintage was large enough that examples in most grades are plentiful today. As I noted earlier, in the marketplace of the 1950s, nickels of this date were abundant, occasionally seen in roll quantities, when other mintmarked issues of the era were not. However, nearly all were flatly struck, although in recent decades, for reasons unknown to me, quite a few sharp pieces have appeared. Perhaps someone found a cache. Today, Sharp Details coins are *not* among the great rarities of the series, but Full Details pieces are another matter entirely. Those seem to be nonexistent, although some examples come quite close, having only slight lightness above the braid ribbon on the obverse and on the fur details on the bison's head.

Interestingly, the relatively low-mintage 1926-D quarter dollar also appeared with regularly in the 1950s, but other mintmarked quarters did not. These, too, were weakly struck, especially on the head of Miss Liberty.

Sharpness of Design Details: *Weak, 55% • Typical, 26% • Sharp, 19% • Full, 0%.* As mentioned above, Sharp Details coins, once seemingly rare, turn up with some frequency today, but are still in the minority. Some 1926-D nickels are almost completely flat on the reverse.

Quality of Luster: Luster is usually "greasy" or satiny, not deeply frosty.

Mintage and Distribution Notes: In his *Complete Guide to Buffalo Nickels*, David W. Lange states that quantities of 1926-D nickels were not released until 1934.

1926-S

Circulation-Strike Mintage: 970,000
Optimal Collecting Grade (OCG™): MS-64

1926-S • Market Values • Circulation Strikes

VG-8	F-12	VF-20	EF-40	AU-50	AU-55	MS-60	MS-63	MS-64	MS-65	MS-66	MS-67
$30.	$75.	$450.	$900.	$2,800.	$3,250.	$4,500.	$8,000.	$15,000.	$100,000.	$180,000.	$200,000.

Availability (Certified Populations) • Circulation Strikes

<MS-60	MS-60	MS-61	MS-62	MS-63	MS-64	MS-65	MS-66	MS-67	MS-68	MS-69	MS-70
2,019	1	12	39	128	199	16	1	0	0	0	

Field populations: Circulation strikes (AU-59 and lower), 12,750–21,250; circulation strikes (MS-60+), 340–510.

Key to Collecting: The 1926-S has received a fair amount of press in recent years, especially with regard to its scarcity and the rise in price for circulated grades. Mint State coins, always highly prized, went along for the ride—at least partly because of a mention by David W. Lange in the first edition of his *Complete Guide to Buffalo Nickels* (1992) that it was undervalued. That anomaly was corrected with the publication of the second edition in 2000.

Among Mint State 1926-S nickels, many are dull, stained, artificially toned, or otherwise unsatisfactory—including more than a few in certified holders. The striking is unremarkable, the result of inaccurate die spacing and, perhaps, keeping dies in the press too long. The net result is that neither I, nor any contributor to this work, have seen a Full Details coin. Even a Sharp Details coin with rich luster would be a numismatic prize.

Sharpness of Design Details: *Weak, 13% • Typical, 67% • Sharp, 20% • Full, 0%.* The strike is usually light on this variety. No Full Details coin has been reported.

Quality of Luster: Luster is often dull, sometimes "greasy," but a few have attractive luster.

1927

Circulation-Strike Mintage: 37,981,000
Optimal Collecting Grade (OCG™): MS-65

1927 • Market Values • Circulation Strikes

VG-8	F-12	VF-20	EF-40	AU-50	AU-55	MS-60	MS-63	MS-64	MS-65	MS-66	MS-67
$1.25	$2.50	$4.	$10.	$20.	$25.	$35.	$75.	$100.	$300.	$800.	$5,000.

Availability (Certified Populations) • Circulation Strikes

<MS-60	MS-60	MS-61	MS-62	MS-63	MS-64	MS-65	MS-66	MS-67	MS-68	MS-69	MS-70
97	97	12	75	243	872	856	304	10	0	0	

Field populations: Circulation strikes (AU-59 and lower), 637,500–850,000; circulation strikes (MS-60+), 21,250–29,750.

Key to Collecting: In many ways, the 1927 Philadelphia Mint nickel is similar to its 1926 cousin. Examples can be found in all grades, including MS-65 and finer, however most have weakness in one area or another. While Full Details coins are exceedingly rare, Sharp Details coins can be found, usually with only subtle weakness at the center of the obverse and on the fur on the reverse. Eye appeal is usually excellent, although some struck from tired dies are grainy or show metal flow.

As a general rule, artificially toned and doctored coins of this era are plentiful in branch Mint issues, but are not often seen among Philadelphia Mint dates. This is because the Philadelphia coins are less valuable.

Sharpness of Design Details: *Weak, 7% • Typical, 73% • Sharp, 20% • Full, 0%.* Most pieces have weakness in areas. Sharp Details coins are in the minority, and though one may exist, no piece with Full Details has been seen.

Quality of Luster: Luster varies, but is usually quite good, except on coins from overused dies.

Interesting Varieties: *"Specimens"*—Some 1927 nickels have been certified as "Specimens," but to my eye, they are simply nice examples of regular circulation strikes with evidence of careful striking.[4]

1927-D

Circulation-Strike Mintage: 5,730,000
Optimal Collecting Grade (OCG™): MS-64

1927-D • Market Values • Circulation Strikes

VG-8	F-12	VF-20	EF-40	AU-50	AU-55	MS-60	MS-63	MS-64	MS-65	MS-66	MS-67
$5.	$7.	$30.	$75.	$125.	$135.	$150.	$300.	$1,000.	$7,500.	$25,000.	$30,000.

Availability (Certified Populations) • Circulation Strikes

<MS-60	MS-60	MS-61	MS-62	MS-63	MS-64	MS-65	MS-66	MS-67	MS-68	MS-69	MS-70
244	7	27	148	498	531	66	3	0	0	0	

Field populations: Circulation strikes (AU-59 and lower), 63,750–85,000; circulation strikes (MS-60+), 4,845–5,270.

Key to Collecting: The Denver Mint did a sloppy job coining this issue, with the result that most coins range from poorly detailed to minimally average. Congratulations are due if you find one with Sharp Details because this coin is a major *sleeper.* The good news is that the 1927-D is not a key date, so, if you are successful, you will likely pay only a small additional premium to acquire it.

Sharpness of Design Details: *Weak, 31% • Typical, 55% • Sharp, 14% • Full, 0%.* Sharpness varies. Sharp Details coins exist and can be found by cherrypicking. No Full Details coin has been seen.

Quality of Luster: Luster is usually satiny, but can vary to deeply frosty.

Interesting Varieties: *3-1/2 Legs (FS-05-1927D-901)*—The die was relapped, removing much of the bison's foreleg. FS notes that this variety is very popular. Years ago, only the 1937-D 3-Legged variety was well known, but several other issues have been identified since that time, most with a *partially* missing leg. *Repunched mintmark (FS-05-1927D-501; URS-3)*—Traces of two earlier mintmarks, one high and the other low, are visible under the final bold mintmark.

1927-S

Circulation-Strike Mintage: 3,430,000
Optimal Collecting Grade (OCG™): MS-64

1927-S • Market Values • Circulation Strikes

VG-8	F-12	VF-20	EF-40	AU-50	AU-55	MS-60	MS-63	MS-64	MS-65	MS-66	MS-67
$3.	$5.	$32.	$90.	$175.	$250.	$500.	$2,500.	$7,500.	$15,000.	$50,000.	$55,000.

Availability (Certified Populations) • Circulation Strikes

<MS-60	MS-60	MS-61	MS-62	MS-63	MS-64	MS-65	MS-66	MS-67	MS-68	MS-69	MS-70
540	33	100	218	350	37	5	0	0	0	0	

Field populations: Circulation strikes (AU-59 and lower), 38,250–51,000; circulation strikes (MS-60+), 1,275–2,125.

Key to Collecting: Although the 1927-S is generally regarded as a key date, the large mintage resulted in many coins being plucked out of circulation when collecting by date and mintmark varieties became popular in the 1930s. These pieces were usually in grades of VF or EF. Mint State coins have always been elusive. This is the only coin issued from 1927 to 1938 that I have never handled as an original bank-wrapped roll.

Most Mint State coins show light striking overall. Coins classified as Sharp Details usually have the fur of the bison complete, but not needle sharp. Toned coins are often somewhat streaky, owing to incomplete mixing of the nickel alloy. Artificially toned "Mint State" coins are common and should be avoided. If you want a toned coin, be sure it has rich luster under the toning.

Sharpness of Design Details: *Weak, 1% • Typical, 58% • Sharp, 40% • Full, 1%.* This coin usually has some lightness overall. A Sharp Details coin is a realistic expectation and when found will cost no more than one with Typical Details.

Quality of Luster: Luster is usually somewhat satiny, not deeply frosty, but with good eye appeal.

1928

Circulation-Strike Mintage: 23,411,000
Optimal Collecting Grade (OCG™): MS-64

1928 • Market Values • Circulation Strikes

VG-8	F-12	VF-20	EF-40	AU-50	AU-55	MS-60	MS-63	MS-64	MS-65	MS-66	MS-67
$1.25	$2.50	$5.	$10.	$25.	$28.	$30.	$75.	$150.	$500.	$1,500.	$5,500.

Availability (Certified Populations) • Circulation Strikes

<MS-60	MS-60	MS-61	MS-62	MS-63	MS-64	MS-65	MS-66	MS-67	MS-68	MS-69	MS-70
125	9	10	76	275	862	609	187	17	0	0	

Field populations: Circulation strikes (AU-59 and lower), 552,500–680,000; circulation strikes (MS-60+), 17,000–21,250.

Key to Collecting: The 1928 nickel is common in all circulated grades and is one of the more plentiful Mint State issues of its era. However, Sharp Details coins are few, and Full Details coins are rare. As noted in the preceding chapter, the decline in sharpness across the board in this era may have to do with wear on the hubs and masters.

Sharpness of Design Details: *Weak, 9% • Typical, 65% • Sharp, 26% • Full, <1%.* Sharpness varies, but Sharp Details coins can be found by searching for them.
Quality of Luster: Luster ranges from satiny to deeply frosty.

1928-D

Circulation-Strike Mintage: 6,436,000
Optimal Collecting Grade (OCG™): MS-64

1928-D • Market Values • Circulation Strikes

VG-8	F-12	VF-20	EF-40	AU-50	AU-55	MS-60	MS-63	MS-64	MS-65	MS-66	MS-67
$2.50	$5.	$15.	$40.	$45.	$48.	$50.	$100.	$200.	$800.	$3,000.	$6,000.

Availability (Certified Populations) • Circulation Strikes

<MS-60	MS-60	MS-61	MS-62	MS-63	MS-64	MS-65	MS-66	MS-67	MS-68	MS-69	MS-70
75	8	15	118	750	1,874	394	32	0	0	0	

Field populations: Circulation strikes (AU-59 and lower), 59,500–76,500; circulation strikes (MS-60+), 6,800–10,200.

Key to Collecting: The 1928-D shares the condition of the 1927-D: most are sloppily struck. However, it is not considered a rare date, and with a lot of looking you will be able to land one with Sharp Details, paying little if any extra for it. This is a major *sleeper.* Examples are plentiful in all grades, and as recently as the 1950s, it was common to see groups of original bank-wrapped rolls.
Sharpness of Design Details: *Weak, 30% • Typical, 58% • Sharp, 12% • Full, 0%.* As with many other nickels of this era, the 1928-D is available with Sharp Details if you search, but it is not realistic to hope for one with Full Details.
Quality of Luster: Usually lustrous and frosty, the 1928-D typically has nice eye appeal.
Numismatic Notes: In his *Complete Guide to Buffalo Nickels,* David W. Lange states that quantities of 1928-D nickels were not released until 1934.

In the October 1943 issue of *Hobbies* magazine, Frank C. Ross reported that a recent burglary of his office netted the thief 800 1928-D Buffalo nickels, two or three sets of Peace dollars, and a set of Standing Liberty quarters. The total loss was as much as $3,000 to $4,000.

1928-S

Circulation-Strike Mintage: 6,966,000
Optimal Collecting Grade (OCG™): MS-64

1928-S • Market Values • Circulation Strikes

VG-8	F-12	VF-20	EF-40	AU-50	AU-55	MS-60	MS-63	MS-64	MS-65	MS-66	MS-67
$2.25	$3.	$12.	$27.	$100.	$150.	$250.	$650.	$1,500.	$4,000.	$16,000.	$22,000.

Availability (Certified Populations) • Circulation Strikes

<MS-60	MS-60	MS-61	MS-62	MS-63	MS-64	MS-65	MS-66	MS-67	MS-68	MS-69	MS-70
296	13	30	154	334	500	93	9	0	0	0	

Field populations: Circulation strikes (AU-59 and lower), 59,500–76,500; circulation strikes (MS-60+), 2,125–3,400.

Key to Collecting: The 1928-S is usually found with good eye appeal and, often with Sharp Details. All known examples have a small S mintmark, but both Walter Breen (*Encyclopedia*, 1988) and David W. Lange (*Complete Encyclopedia of Buffalo Nickels*, 2000) speculate that a large S, similar to that used on Lincoln cents, might also exist. A few 1928-S nickels have a curious reverse rim treatment with the base of the S of CENTS located well within the rim.

Sharpness of Design Details: *Weak, 2%* • *Typical, 45%* • *Sharp, 50%* • *Full, 3%.* Often seen with Sharp Details.

Quality of Luster: Most Mint State coins have frosty luster and good eye appeal.

1929

Circulation-Strike Mintage: 6,446,000
Optimal Collecting Grade (OCG™): MS-64

1929 • Market Values • Circulation Strikes

VG-8	F-12	VF-20	EF-40	AU-50	AU-55	MS-60	MS-63	MS-64	MS-65	MS-66	MS-67
$1.50	$2.50	$4.	$10.	$20.	$30.	$35.	$70.	$150.	$300.	$1,000.	$3,000.

Availability (Certified Populations) • Circulation Strikes

<MS-60	MS-60	MS-61	MS-62	MS-63	MS-64	MS-65	MS-66	MS-67	MS-68	MS-69	MS-70
93	6	16	84	338	1,204	634	130	1	0	0	

Field populations: Circulation strikes (AU-59 and lower), 765,000–1,020,000; circulation strikes (MS-60+), 29,750–42,500.

Key to Collecting: Psst! The secret here is that the 1929 Buffalo nickel, a common date that is inexpensive even in Mint State, is *rare* if with Sharp Details! Most show light striking in areas and are classified as Typical Details. Forget about finding any with Full Details. However, a Sharp Details coin is a *sleeper*—a landmark in the series—and few people are aware of its significance.

Sharpness of Design Details: *Weak, 28%* • *Typical, 62%* • *Sharp, 10%* • *Full, 0%.* In *Complete Guide to Buffalo Nickels*, David W. Lange comments:

> 1929 nickels are usually well struck but not fully struck. This is typical of nickels from the 1920s. Partly to blame was wear on the master hubs, but incompletely hubbed dies and greater than optimal die-set distance seems to have contributed to this problem as well.

Quality of Luster: Luster is usually attractive, but somewhat subdued—not deeply frosty.

1929-D

Circulation-Strike Mintage: 8,370,000
Optimal Collecting Grade (OCG™): MS-64

1929-D • Market Values • Circulation Strikes

VG-8	F-12	VF-20	EF-40	AU-50	AU-55	MS-60	MS-63	MS-64	MS-65	MS-66	MS-67
$2.00	$2.50	$8.	$35.	$45.	$50.	$60.	$125.	$300.	$1,800.	$4,500.	$12,000.

Availability (Certified Populations) • Circulation Strikes

<MS-60	MS-60	MS-61	MS-62	MS-63	MS-64	MS-65	MS-66	MS-67	MS-68	MS-69	MS-70
87	12	23	120	423	785	181	61	1	0	0	

Field populations: Circulation strikes (AU-59 and lower), 68,000–93,500; circulation strikes (MS-60+), 5,100–8,500.

Key to Collecting: Although the mintage for 1929-D is generous, this variety is surprisingly elusive in MS-65 or better grades. There is no problem for lower levels, though. Sharpness is a real challenge with the 1929-D. In addition, the luster is subpar on most examples; finding one that is just right will require special attention.

Sharpness of Design Details: *Weak, 34% • Typical, 50% • Sharp, 16% • Full, 0%.* Most are lightly struck.

Quality of Luster: Luster is usually below par. Frosty coins with good eye appeal are rare.

Mintage and Distribution Notes: In his *Complete Guide to Buffalo Nickels*, David W. Lange states that quantities of 1929-D nickels were not released until 1934.

1929-S

Circulation-Strike Mintage: 7,754,000
Optimal Collecting Grade (OCG™): MS-64

1929-S • Market Values • Circulation Strikes

VG-8	F-12	VF-20	EF-40	AU-50	AU-55	MS-60	MS-63	MS-64	MS-65	MS-66	MS-67
$1.50	$2.00	$2.50	$14.	$25.	$35.	$50.	$75.	$150.	$600.	$2,000.	$4,500.

Availability (Certified Populations) • Circulation Strikes

<MS-60	MS-60	MS-61	MS-62	MS-63	MS-64	MS-65	MS-66	MS-67	MS-68	MS-69	MS-70
144	5	17	80	311	904	519	189	5	0	0	

Field populations: Circulation strikes (AU-59 and lower), 72,250–93,500; circulation strikes (MS-60+), 8,500–12,750.

Key to Collecting: The 1929-S is easy to find in grades up to MS-65 or finer. Mint State coins usually have nice luster and good eye appeal. Quite a few have Sharp Details, but there are many weakly struck coins around as well.

Sharpness of Design Details: *Weak, 4% • Typical, 52% • Sharp, 44% • Full, <1%.* Sharpness varies, but many Sharp Details coins exist.

Quality of Luster: The luster is usually frosty and attractive. Avoid coins showing graininess and metal flow caused by worn dies.

1930

Circulation-Strike Mintage: 22,849,000
Optimal Collecting Grade (OCG™): MS-64

1930 • Market Values • Circulation Strikes

VG-8	F-12	VF-20	EF-40	AU-50	AU-55	MS-60	MS-63	MS-64	MS-65	MS-66	MS-67
$1.50	$2.50	$4.	$10.	$20.	$25.	$30.	$70.	$100.	$300.	$600.	$4,600.

Availability (Certified Populations) • Circulation Strikes

<MS-60	MS-60	MS-61	MS-62	MS-63	MS-64	MS-65	MS-66	MS-67	MS-68	MS-69	MS-70
135	8	8	73	238	1,138	1,289	290	21	0	0	

Field populations: Circulation strikes (AU-59 and lower), 900,000–1,200,000; circulation strikes (MS-60+), 30,000–40,000.

Key to Collecting: The 1930 nickel is easy to find in all grades, although sharp strikes are elusive. Luster varies, and more than a few are grainy or show metal flow. It takes a connoisseur to land a Sharp Details coin with all other aspects in good order, but it can be done. The *sleepers* in this era of Buffalo nickels are numerous; now is the time to look for them—before the grading services take notice!

Sharpness of Design Details: *Weak, 12% • Typical, 76% • Sharp, 12% • Full, 0%.* Sharpness varies, most show significant lightness.

Quality of Luster: Luster varies. Some are dull or grainy, but many frosty coins exist.

1930-S

Circulation-Strike Mintage: 5,345,000
Optimal Collecting Grade (OCG™): MS-64

1930-S • Market Values • Circulation Strikes

VG-8	F-12	VF-20	EF-40	AU-50	AU-55	MS-60	MS-63	MS-64	MS-65	MS-66	MS-67
$1.50	$2.50	$3.	$12.	$30.	$40.	$50.	$110.	$250.	$750.	$2,500.	$7,200.

Availability (Certified Populations) • Circulation Strikes

<MS-60	MS-60	MS-61	MS-62	MS-63	MS-64	MS-65	MS-66	MS-67	MS-68	MS-69	MS-70
171	13	12	69	191	686	507	120	4	0	0	

Field populations: Circulation strikes (AU-59 and lower), 85,000–105,000; circulation strikes (MS-60+), 10,000–15,000.

Key to Collecting: Although the mintage of the 1930-S was generous, this variety did not capture the fancy of collectors at the time, and relatively few were saved—in sharp contrast to what would happen the following year with the 1931-S. Nevertheless, the 1930-S is inexpensive. It is also a cherrypicker's delight because, while pieces with Sharp Details are scarce, there are enough coins of this date and mint around that you can probably find one before other collectors become aware of the situation.

Sharpness of Design Details: *Weak, 10% • Typical, 66% • Sharp, 24% • Full, 0%.* Repeating a familiar scenario, most have lightness, but Sharp Details coins can be found.

Quality of Luster: Most Mint State coins are richly lustrous and have excellent eye appeal.

Background of the 1930-S Nickel: Although there was little popular interest in 1930-S nickels because of the generous mintage, supplies of Mint State coins remained on hand in banks and elsewhere for the next several years. After coin collecting became popular in the mid-1930s, dealers, including William Pukall and Norman Shultz, rescued some rolls.

1931-S

Circulation-Strike Mintage: 1,200,000
Optimal Collecting Grade (OCG™): MS-64

1931-S • Market Values • Circulation Strikes

VG-8	F-12	VF-20	EF-40	AU-50	AU-55	MS-60	MS-63	MS-64	MS-65	MS-66	MS-67
$16.	$18.	$20.	$22.	$40.	$50.	$60.	$80.	$150.	$300.	$1,000.	$12,000.

Availability (Certified Populations) • Circulation Strikes

<MS-60	MS-60	MS-61	MS-62	MS-63	MS-64	MS-65	MS-66	MS-67	MS-68	MS-69	MS-70
211	9	13	53	323	1,860	1,737	355	3	0	0	

Field populations: Circulation strikes (AU-59 and lower), 35,000–50,000; circulation strikes (MS-60+), 80,000–120,000.

Key to Collecting: Although the mintage of 1931-S nickels was small, it was large enough to meet the demands of commerce at the time. Quantities were saved and thousands of Mint State coins exist today. Most are highly lustrous and have good eye appeal. About one in 10 is sharply struck, but finding one will not be much of a challenge, because there are so many pieces in the marketplace. At present, well-struck coins are high on the *sleeper* list. Circulated examples are relatively scarce.

This variety has always been a favorite of collectors, simply because of its enticingly low mintage figure. This is the only variety in the Buffalo nickel series that can be completely identified by looking only at the obverse.

Sharpness of Design Details: *Weak, 24%* • *Typical, 65%* • *Sharp, 11%* • *Full, 0%*. 1931-S nickels with Sharp Details are *relatively* scarce, perhaps one in 10 coins. This news may come as a surprise to readers who haven't considered the matter of details. However, there are tens of thousands of Uncirculated 1931-S nickels in numismatic hands, so finding a sharp one is not difficult.

Quality of Luster: Luster is usually very frosty, with good eye appeal.

Background of the 1931-S Nickel: In January of 1931, 194,000 nickels were struck, with no plans for any more because there was no call for them. On November 19 of that year, Acting Director of the Mint Mary M. O'Reilly (assistant director of the Mint since 1923, and occasionally acting director) requested that San Francisco strike additional pieces in order to prevent the coins from becoming rare and selling for an immediate premium. Using about $14,700 in old nickels available for recoinage and the regular nickel stock on hand, coinage recommenced. By the end of December, the total 1,200,000 had been struck.[5]

In the early 1930s, the Treasury Department filled orders from numismatists who desired current coins and certain older dates that were still obtainable from supplies kept at the Treasury Building in Washington, DC. There were 1931-S nickels available for several years afterward for face value plus postage. At least for a time there was an ordering limit of two coins per customer; nevertheless, quantities went to collectors and dealers—either from the Treasury Department or from normal distribution through banks. Bank-wrapped rolls of 40 coins were a common stock in trade as late as the 1950s. In contrast, rolls of other dates and mints prior to 1934 were encountered only occasionally. Although I recall handling dozens of 1931-S nickel rolls, I never had a roll of 1930-S coins of higher mintage. The same situation was true for 1931-S Lincoln cents; the mintage was low, but so many coins were saved that rolls were commonly traded. After the late 1950s, when the coin market expanded dramatically, rolls of 1931-S cents and nickels were broken apart. Today they usually appear one at a time.

1934

Circulation-Strike Mintage: 20,213,003
Optimal Collecting Grade (OCG™): MS-64

1934 • Market Values • Circulation Strikes

VG-8	F-12	VF-20	EF-40	AU-50	AU-55	MS-60	MS-63	MS-64	MS-65	MS-66	MS-67
$1.50	$2.50	$4.	$10.	$18.	$30.	$50.	$60.	$120.	$300.	$600.	$3,500.

Availability (Certified Populations) • Circulation Strikes

<MS-60	MS-60	MS-61	MS-62	MS-63	MS-64	MS-65	MS-66	MS-67	MS-68	MS-69	MS-70
165	13	17	87	262	840	707	222	19	0	0	

Field populations: Circulation strikes (AU-59 and lower), 1,200,000–1,600,000; circulation strikes (MS-60+), 100,000–150,000.

Key to Collecting: Psst! Can you keep a secret? You can? Good! The availability of 1934 nickels with Full Details is one of the best-kept secrets of the Buffalo series. Although it is a very common coin in high grades such as MS-65 and MS-66, with Full Details it is one of the great sleepers—a true *rarity*. Now, forearmed with this knowledge, enjoy the hunt!

Sharpness of Design Details: *Weak, 12% • Typical, 67% • Sharp, 20% • Full, 1%.* Examples with Sharp Details can be found with some looking. Full Details coins are sufficiently rare that, unless you are lucky, you will have a hard time finding one. The typical 1934 is slightly weak at the center of the obverse, but both the 193 of the date and LIBERTY are bold. The 4 in the date is often light. On the reverse, the fur details of the bison are usually indistinct in areas.

Quality of Luster: As the large mintage might lead you to expect, quality of luster varies all greatly—from dull to frosty. There are many coins around, and you will have no difficulty finding an example with good eye appeal. As noted above, locating a coin with Full Details is another matter!

1934-D

Circulation-Strike Mintage: 7,480,000
Optimal Collecting Grade (OCG™): MS-64

1934-D • Market Values • Circulation Strikes

VG-8	F-12	VF-20	EF-40	AU-50	AU-55	MS-60	MS-63	MS-64	MS-65	MS-66	MS-67
$1.50	$2.50	$5.	$15.	$40.	$50.	$70.	$100.	$300.	$900.	$4,500.	$20,000.

Availability (Certified Populations) • Circulation Strikes

<MS-60	MS-60	MS-61	MS-62	MS-63	MS-64	MS-65	MS-66	MS-67	MS-68	MS-69	MS-70
118	11	16	161	710	1,322	377	41	0	0	0	

Field populations: Circulation strikes (AU-59 and lower), 300,000–400,000; circulation strikes (MS-60+), 20,000–30,000.

Key to Collecting: You already know that a Full Details 1934 Philadelphia Mint nickel is a rarity. Well, the 1934-D seems to be even rarer. Neither Ron Pope, who surveyed many coins over a period of several years, nor I have ever seen one! However, some may exist—and if so, finding one would be a cherrypicker's dream come true. In the meantime, finding a Sharp Details coin is only slightly less difficult, and would also delight a cherrypicker.

Most Mint State nickels of this date are attractive and lustrous. A good goal is to find one with Sharp Details and rich luster.

Sharpness of Design Details: *Weak, 32%* • *Typical, 55%* • *Sharp, 13%* • *Full, 0%.* The sharpness of 1934-D nickels can vary considerably. Generally, the obverse is well struck except at the center; the date is bold, as is LIBERTY. The reverse is a mixed bag. Sometimes the bison has decent sharpness, but the mintmark is mushy. Sometimes the mintmark is sharp, but the bison is weak.

Quality of Luster: The luster is usually subpar, but there are exceptions.

Distribution Notes: In his *Complete Guide to Buffalo Nickels*, David W. Lange includes this interesting information:

> When production of nickels resumed in the latter part of 1934, these pieces appear to have been released almost concurrently with much of the 1926-D, 1928-D and 1929-D mintage. Speculators hoarded the earlier dates, while permitting the 1934-D nickels to become relatively scarce in Uncirculated condition.

1935

Circulation-Strike Mintage: 58,264,000
Optimal Collecting Grade (OCG™): MS-64

1935 • Market Values • Circulation Strikes

VG-8	F-12	VF-20	EF-40	AU-50	AU-55	MS-60	MS-63	MS-64	MS-65	MS-66	MS-67
$1.50	$1.75	$2.	$3.	$9.	$15.	$20.	$40.	$60.	$120.	$300.	$1,500.

Availability (Certified Populations) • Circulation Strikes

<MS-60	MS-60	MS-61	MS-62	MS-63	MS-64	MS-65	MS-66	MS-67	MS-68	MS-69	MS-70
239	17	56	108	240	669	1,284	658	82	0	0	

Field populations: Circulation strikes (AU-59 and lower), 5,500,000–6,000,000; circulation strikes (MS-60+), 70,000–100,000.

Key to Collecting: The 1935 Buffalo nickel is another unheralded rarity as far as finding one that is a needle-sharp strike. Inspection of about 2,000 examples of this date, from various sources, yielded only 10 with Full Details! Otherwise, the issue is plentiful, with Mint State coins sometimes popping up in roll quantities. Luster ranges from miserable to frosty, but the total population is such that a coin with good eye appeal should be easy to find.

Sharpness of Design Details: *Weak, 4%* • *Typical, 67%* • *Sharp, 28%* • *Full, <1%.* Most have lightness in one or more areas. On the obverse, the 19 in 1935 can be light. On the reverse, the bison's fur is apt to be indistinct in areas.

Quality of Luster: This issue was struck in large quantities over many different production runs, therefore, luster varies widely. Finding a frosty coin with good eye appeal should be easy to do, but you might need to look at several pieces before locating one.

Interesting Variety: *Doubled Die Reverse (FS-05-1935-801, Breen-2644)*—Strong traces of doubling are most prominent in the letters on this very popular variety. The sharpness of strike is usually just so-so. Most examples are well worn.

1935-D

Circulation-Strike Mintage: 12,092,000
Optimal Collecting Grade (OCG™): MS-64

1935-D • Market Values • Circulation Strikes

VG-8	F-12	VF-20	EF-40	AU-50	AU-55	MS-60	MS-63	MS-64	MS-65	MS-66	MS-67
$1.50	$2.50	$6.	$15.	$40.	$50.	$60.	$75.	$150.	$500.	$2,400.	$5,800.

Availability (Certified Populations) • Circulation Strikes

<MS-60	MS-60	MS-61	MS-62	MS-63	MS-64	MS-65	MS-66	MS-67	MS-68	MS-69	MS-70
78	4	11	70	486	1,507	616	146	7	0	0	

Field populations: Circulation strikes (AU-59 and lower), 700,000–900,000; circulation strikes (MS-60+), 50,000–70,000.

Key to Collecting: Finding a 1935-D with Sharp Details should be easy. This is a common date and almost any group of 10 coins is apt to yield one or two—making the day for the cherrypicker who finds them. On the other hand, Full Details coins, with sharp definition of the fur on the bison and with superb details elsewhere, are extremely rare. Ron Pope surveyed 732 coins and found only *one!*

Sharpness of Design Details: *Weak, 24%* • *Typical, 60%* • *Sharp, 16%* • *Full, <1%.* Although Full Details coins are very rare, Sharp Details examples that are quite close turn up frequently. Once this is widely known, some coins with Sharp Details may be advertised—especially on the Internet—as having Full Details. Buy wisely.

Quality of Luster: Luster varies from dull or poor on coins struck from worn-out dies, to richly frosty.

Interesting Variety: *Repunched Mintmark (FS-05-1935D-502; URS-4)*—Traces of *several* earlier mintmarks are visible under the final, bold D. The engraver really had an unsteady hand when creating this die!

1935-S

Circulation-Strike Mintage: 10,300,000
Optimal Collecting Grade (OCG™): MS-64

1935-S • Market Values • Circulation Strikes

VG-8	F-12	VF-20	EF-40	AU-50	AU-55	MS-60	MS-63	MS-64	MS-65	MS-66	MS-67
$1.50	$2.00	$2.50	$4.	$15.	$25.	$50.	$70.	$150.	$300.	$750.	$3,800.

Availability (Certified Populations) • Circulation Strikes

<MS-60	MS-60	MS-61	MS-62	MS-63	MS-64	MS-65	MS-66	MS-67	MS-68	MS-69	MS-70
83	5	8	37	273	1,212	1,226	409	33	0	0	

Field populations: Circulation strikes (AU-59 and lower), 800,000–1,100,000; circulation strikes (MS-60+), 65,000–80,000.

Key to Collecting: The 1935-S seems to be a repeat of the 1934-D with regard to striking (a generally well-struck obverse with the reverse more hit and miss), and is another *sleeper* to add to our secret list of potential cherrypicks! Full Details coins are very rare, but some that are close are easy enough to find. Luster can vary widely. Some coins show metal flow and other evidence of misused dies.

Sharpness of Design Details: *Weak, 31%* • *Typical, 55%* • *Sharp, 14%* • *Full, <1%*. Full Details coins are very rare. Sharp Details coins are scarce and usually show weakness at the centers.

Quality of Luster: Luster varies, but is usually below average. However, this is a relatively common issue, and you will find a nice one eventually.

1936

Circulation-Strike Mintage: 118,997,000
Proof Mintage: 4,420
Optimal Collecting Grade (OCG™): MS-65, PF-65

1936 • Market Values • Circulation Strikes

VG-8	F-12	VF-20	EF-40	AU-50	AU-55	MS-60	MS-63	MS-64	MS-65	MS-66	MS-67
$1.50	$1.75	$2.	$3.	$9.	$15.	$20.	$40.	$50.	$100.	$150.	$700.

Availability (Certified Populations) • Circulation Strikes

<MS-60	MS-60	MS-61	MS-62	MS-63	MS-64	MS-65	MS-66	MS-67	MS-68	MS-69	MS-70
386	12	32	120	267	1,066	2,361	1,632	116	2	0	

Field populations: Circulation strikes (AU-59 and lower), 9,000,000–10,000,000; circulation strikes (MS-60+), 400,000–500,000.

1936 • Market Values • Satin Proof Strikes and Brilliant Proof Strikes[a]

PF-60	PF-63	PF-64	PF-65	PF-66	PF-67	PF-68
$800.	$1,200.	$2,000.	$3,000.	—	—	—
PF-60	PF-63	PF-64	PF-65	PF-66	PF-67	PF-68
$900.	$1,400.	$2,400.	$3,400.	—	—	—

[a] Satin Proof strikes, red ▮▮ Brilliant Proof strikes, green ▮

Availability (Certified Populations) • Satin Proof Strikes and Brilliant Proof Strikes[a]

< PF-60	PF-60	PF-61	PF-62	PF-63	PF-64	PF-65	PF-66	PF-67	PF-68	PF-69	PF-70
6	0	8	8	40	177	274	444	344	44	1	
< PF-60	PF-60	PF-61	PF-62	PF-63	PF-64	PF-65	PF-66	PF-67	PF-68	PF-69	PF-70
2	1	1	9	37	235	347	430	180	16	1	

Field populations: Proof strikes (all), 3,500.
[a] Satin Proof strikes, red ▮▮ Brilliant Proof strikes, green ▮

Key to Collecting: The 1936 Buffalo nickel was the first minting of any nickel five-cent piece in a quantity greater than one hundred million. The figure remained a mintage record for the rest of the Indian Head / Buffalo series.

The quality improved considerably for this mintage, and most 1936 nickels have good eye appeal and decent strikes, though Full Strike coins are elusive.

In 1936, the Mint struck Proof nickels for the first time since 1916. Those produced early in the production run have satiny surfaces and are attractive in their own way. However, collectors wanted the full-mirror style, and later coins have mirrored fields—the field area being relatively small on this design. Proofs show Full Details.

CIRCULATION STRIKES

Sharpness of Design Details: *Weak, 1%* • *Typical, 54%* • *Sharp, 43%* • *Full, 2%.* Coins with Sharp Details are common, but finding one with Full Details will take some effort. **Quality of Luster:** Luster varies from dull and grainy to richly lustrous. Many attractive coins are around, and finding one should not be a problem.

PROOF STRIKES

Strike, Contrast, and Other Aspects: Early issues have a Satin Proof finish; later ones have brilliant, mirrored fields. The strike is usually superb. Both Satin Proofs and Brilliant Proofs are in demand, although years ago the Satin Proofs were considered inferior. Today, the two styles are collected as *separate* varieties. Walter Breen states in his *Encyclopedia* (1988) that half of the surviving Satin Proofs are impaired, but my experience has been that most are of nice quality. Some fake "Proofs" have been created by buffing coins or chrome plating them. The leading certification services will not encapsulate these chrome-plated pieces. Beware of any "Proof" offered on the Internet that is not certified.

1936-D

Circulation-Strike Mintage: 24,814,000
Optimal Collecting Grade (OCG™): MS-65

1936-D • Market Values • Circulation Strikes

VG-8	F-12	VF-20	EF-40	AU-50	AU-55	MS-60	MS-63	MS-64	MS-65	MS-66	MS-67
$1.50	$1.75	$2.	$4.	$12.	$20.	$35.	$40.	$45.	$100.	$260.	$1,000.

Availability (Certified Populations) • Circulation Strikes

<MS-60	MS-60	MS-61	MS-62	MS-63	MS-64	MS-65	MS-66	MS-67	MS-68	MS-69	MS-70
68	7	0	22	161	921	2,147	1,068	62	2	0	

Field populations: Circulation strikes (AU-59 and lower), 1,400,000–1,700,000; circulation strikes (MS-60+), 100,000–125,000.

Key to Collecting: The situation with the 1936-D is similar to that of some other issues of its era: Examples with Sharp Details are plentiful, but those with Full Details are elusive. With persistence, though, you will be able to find one.
Sharpness of Design Details: *Weak, 5%* • *Typical, 60%* • *Sharp, 33%* • *Full, 2%.* The striking is usually quite good.

Quality of Luster: Luster varies from subpar to deeply frosty. However, coins with good eye appeal are relatively easy to find.

Interesting Variety: *3-1/2 Legs (FS-05-1936D-901, Breen-2647; URS-7)*—Part of the right front leg of the bison it was removed when the die was relapped. This is a very popular variety and one of the most sought after. Beware examples that have been faked by cutting away part of the leg. Certification by a leading service is your best protection.

1936-S

Circulation-Strike Mintage: 14,930,000
Optimal Collecting Grade (OCG™): MS-65

1936-S • Market Values • Circulation Strikes

VG-8	F-12	VF-20	EF-40	AU-50	AU-55	MS-60	MS-63	MS-64	MS-65	MS-66	MS-67
$1.50	$1.75	$2.00	$3.50	$12.	$20.	$35.	$40.	$45.	$100.	$260.	$1,400.

Availability (Certified Populations) • Circulation Strikes

<MS-60	MS-60	MS-61	MS-62	MS-63	MS-64	MS-65	MS-66	MS-67	MS-68	MS-69	MS-70
143	15	9	35	126	319	1,898	810	76	0	0	

Field populations: Circulation strikes (AU-59 and lower), 800,000–1,100,000; circulation strikes (MS-60+), 90,000–110,000.

Key to Collecting: This is the earliest issue of the 1930s that can be found with both rich luster and Full Details. Coins having this combination, however, comprise less than 10% of the population. Nevertheless, the 1936-S usually has good eye appeal.

Sharpness of Design Details: *Weak, 5% • Typical, 40% • Sharp, 45% • Full, 10%.* This is the first variety for several years for which Full Details coins are not rare.

Quality of Luster: Luster varies, but is usually above average, frosty with a lot of "life."

1937

Circulation-Strike Mintage: 79,480,000
Proof Mintage: 5,769
Optimal Collecting Grade (OCG™): MS-65, PF-65

1937 • Market Values • Circulation Strikes and Proof Strikes

VG-8	F-12	VF-20	EF-40	AU-50	AU-55	MS-60	MS-63	MS-64	MS-65
$1.50	$1.75	$2.	$3.	$9.	$15.	$20.	$40.	$45.	$75.
MS-66	**MS-67**		**PF-60**	**PF-63**	**PF-64**	**PF-65**	**PF-66**	**PF-67**	**PF-68**
$100.	$420.		$650.	$1,000.	$1,500.	$2,000.	—	—	—

Availability (Certified Populations) • Circulation Strikes and Proof Strikes

<MS-60	MS-60	MS-61	MS-62	MS-63	MS-64	MS-65	MS-66	MS-67	MS-68	MS-69	MS-70
405	24	29	109	266	1,541	5,759	6,102	534	7	0	
< PF-60	PF-60	PF-61	PF-62	PF-63	PF-64	PF-65	PF-66	PF-67	PF-68	PF-69	PF-70
4	7	1	18	115	569	935	1,129	633	0	0	

Field populations: Circulation strikes (AU-59 and lower), 7,500,000–8,000,000; circulation strikes (MS-60+), 300,000–400,000; Proof strikes, 5,000.

Key to Collecting: The 1937 Buffalo nickel is extremely common. Mint State coins abound, and most have decent strike quality and good eye appeal. Coins with Full Details, though, are few and far between.

Proofs struck in this year are all of the mirror-field style. Examples with good eye appeal and higher grade designations—Proof-64 and above—frequently appear on the market.

CIRCULATION STRIKES

Sharpness of Design Details: *Weak, 1%* • *Typical, 57%* • *Sharp, 40%* • *Full, 2%.* The 1937 coin is usually fairly well struck, but Full Detail coins are relatively rare. • At the 1941 ANA Convention in Philadelphia, local dealer Ira S. Reed sold pairs of reeded-edge Lincoln cents and Buffalo nickels of the 1937 date, apparently without saying much about their origin. Supposedly, 104 sets were made. They stirred up excitement in some places, and eventually landed a mention in the Red Book. However, we now know they were reeded in a local machine shop, not at the Mint, and they receive little attention. **Quality of Luster:** Luster varies but is usually frosty and attractive. Avoid those that show graininess or metal flow from overused dies.

PROOF STRIKES

Strike, Contrast, and Other Aspects: The field area of these Brilliant Proofs is deeply mirrored. Proofs have Full Details and usually receive higher grade ratings, generally Proof-64 or above. These were sold both singly and in sets.

1937-D

Circulation-Strike Mintage: 17,826,000
Optimal Collecting Grade (OCG™): MS-65

1937-D • Market Values • Circulation Strikes

VG-8	F-12	VF-20	EF-40	AU-50	AU-55	MS-60	MS-63	MS-64	MS-65	MS-66	MS-67
$1.50	$1.75	$3.	$4.	$10.	$15.	$30.	$40.	$45.	$60.	$120.	$1,000.

Availability (Certified Populations) • Circulation Strikes

<MS-60	MS-60	MS-61	MS-62	MS-63	MS-64	MS-65	MS-66	MS-67	MS-68	MS-69	MS-70
2,757	29	54	81	144	1,061	3,929	2,792	131	2	0	

Field populations: Circulation strikes (AU-59 and lower), 800,000–1,100,000; circulation strikes (MS-60+), 150,000 to 200,000.

Key to Collecting: The 1937-D confirms the fact that a coin can be beautiful and desirable—but not rare! This one is an easy pick; a Full Details coin with great luster and eye appeal will be a wonderful addition to your collection.

The 1937-D 3-Legs variety is one of the most sought-after curiosities among 20th century coins. Many exist, including a surprising number in Mint State, but they are expensive because of the demand. **Sharpness of Design Details:** *Weak, 2%* • *Typical, 55%* • *Sharp, 33%* • *Full, 10%.* Coins with Sharp Details, or even Full Details, are easily obtainable in the marketplace. **Quality of Luster:** Luster varies from grainy and dull to frosty and attractive, but is usually quite good.

Interesting Variety: *1937-D 3-Legged*—This variety was created when a worker at the Denver Mint (a Mr. Young, according to Walter Breen in his 1988 *Encyclopedia*) used a tool—some say an emery board—to remove a defect or a clash mark on a reverse die. Whatever the exact scenario, the right foreleg of the bison was removed, creating a three-legged animal. Certain other areas of the die are weak as well. In the 1950s, nearly all coins in the marketplace were in grades such as Very Fine and Extremely Fine. Coins graded About Uncirculated were rare, even though in the late 1930s Aubrey and Adeline Bebee reported having nearly two dozen Mint State coins. Many hundreds of Mint State coins exist today. I have no idea where all of these came from, but it certainly was a surprise when they first appeared in quantity. Perhaps a bunch of rolls turned up that included examples from this particular die. The typical Mint State coin is attractive, with a satiny or slightly grainy luster. Beware of fakes made by grinding away the leg after minting.

1937-S

Circulation-Strike Mintage: 5,635,000
Optimal Collecting Grade (OCG™): MS-65

1937-S • Market Values • Circulation Strikes

VG-8	F-12	VF-20	EF-40	AU-50	AU-55	MS-60	MS-63	MS-64	MS-65	MS-66	MS-67
$1.50	$1.75	$3.	$3.50	$10.	$15.	$30.	$40.	$45.	$60.	$100.	$1,000.

Availability (Certified Populations) • Circulation Strikes

<MS-60	MS-60	MS-61	MS-62	MS-63	MS-64	MS-65	MS-66	MS-67	MS-68	MS-69	MS-70
110	13	6	41	154	1,223	3,927	1,723	90	0	0	

Field populations: Circulation strikes (AU-59 and lower), 225,000–300,000; circulation strikes (MS-60+), 225,000–300,000.

Key to Collecting: Most Mint State 1937-S nickels are fairly well struck and have rich luster. Full Details coins are scarce, but the abundance of 1937-S coins in the marketplace makes it easy enough to find one.

Sharpness of Design Details: *Weak, 1% • Typical, 34% • Sharp, 55% • Full, 10%.* Sharp Details is the norm for this coin. When there is slight weakness, it is usually on the head of the bison. Full Details coins are in the minority.

Quality of Luster: Although there are exceptions, 1937-S is usually deeply lustrous with good eye appeal. In a word, the 1937-S was a *quality* production.

1938-D

Circulation-Strike Mintage: 6,620,000 (estimated)
Optimal Collecting Grade (OCG™): MS-65

1938-D • Market Values • Circulation Strikes

VG-8	F-12	VF-20	EF-40	AU-50	AU-55	MS-60	MS-63	MS-64	MS-65	MS-66	MS-67
$2.50	$3.00	$3.25	$3.75	$10.	$15.	$20.	$40.	$45.	$60.	$100.	$300.

Availability (Certified Populations) • Circulation Strikes

<MS-60	MS-60	MS-61	MS-62	MS-63	MS-64	MS-65	MS-66	MS-67	MS-68	MS-69	MS-70
4,015	43	18	86	356	3,988	250,000	36,084	2,544	16	0	

Field populations: Circulation strikes (AU-59 and lower), 400,000–500,000; circulation strikes (MS-60+), 800,000–1,200,000.

Key to Collecting: The last of Buffalo nickels were struck in 1938, and only at the Denver Mint. The story spread that these would become rare and valuable; as a result, huge numbers of them were hoarded. In his *Encyclopedia* (1988), Walter Breen puts the quantity at "thousands of rolls." Until the 1960s, when coin collecting became widespread, groups of rolls were stock-in-trade items for many dealers.

The 1938-D is usually well struck and has good luster—an ideal closing representative of this popular design. The 1938-D/S, given a separate listing below, has been popular as well.

I estimate the mintage of "perfect" D mintmark coins to be about 6,620,000 coins—or approximately 7,020,000 minus about 400,000 of the 1938-D/S. This is guesswork, though; the exact figure will never be known.

Sharpness of Design Details: *Weak, <1% • Typical, 12% • Sharp, 80% • Full, 8%.* Striking is usually very good, although Full Details coins are scarce. Most Sharp Details coins have some lightness on the fur of the bison.

Quality of Luster: Luster is usually frosty and attractive.

1938-D/S

Circulation-Strike Mintage: 400,000 (estimated)
Optimal Collecting Grade (OCG™): MS-65

1938-D/S • Market Values • Circulation Strikes

VG-8	F-12	VF-20	EF-40	AU-50	AU-55	MS-60	MS-63	MS-64	MS-65	MS-66	MS-67
$7.50	$10.	$15.	$18.	$30.	$40.	$50.	$75.	$100.	$150.	$200.	$750.

Availability (Certified Populations) • Circulation Strikes

<MS-60	MS-60	MS-61	MS-62	MS-63	MS-64	MS-65	MS-66	MS-67	MS-68	MS-69	MS-70
98	18	13	13	86	581	1,750	1,624	718	27	2	

Field populations: Circulation strikes (AU-59 and lower), 15,000–25,000; circulation strikes (MS-60+), 10,000–20,000.

Key to Collecting: The 1938-D/S nickel is fascinating, plentiful in high grades, and affordable! How fortunate we are that this is the case. There are at least six minor variations of the D over S die. I recommend that you look for a coin that shows the top of the S clearly peeking out from the upper sides of the D—easy enough to do.

The mintage is unknown, but I estimate it to be 400,000, or about 1/17 of the total mintage of 1938-DThis would give less than 70,000 impressions from each of the six known dies. The certification figures seem to fall into this general range, with the likely possibility that 1938-D/S coins, being more valuable, are submitted more often. However, die use varied, and the exact figure will never be known. It appears, though, that the dies for this issue were retired before they showed metal flow.

Sharpness of Design Details: *Weak, <1% • Typical, 13% • Sharp, 80% • Full, 7%.* The 1938-D/S usually comes well struck.

Quality of Luster: The 1938-D/S is usually deeply lustrous and frosty.

Story of the 1938-D/S Overmintmark: The 1938-D/S overmintmark is the most curious and interesting of the Buffalo nickel varieties. In my 1979 book *Adventures With Rare Coins*, I devoted a few paragraphs to my involvement with this unusual coin. What follows is an update of that information.

For me, one of the most significant events in the discovery of new die varieties was the 1962 verification of the 1938-D/S *overmintmark* Buffalo nickel. Two Jamestown, New York dealers, C.G. Langworthy and Robert Kerr, came upon a coin with the letter D sharply punched over a previous letter S, and contacted *Coin World*, the weekly numismatic newspaper, to report the find. *Coin World* then asked me to authenticate this startling issue—a coin which appeared to have two distinct and different mintmarks, both a D and an S!

Coin World, then scarcely two years old and without the expert staff it would later acquire, often called on me for advice and consultation. In 1959, its founder, J. Oliver Amos, and I had discussed the formation of such a newspaper before the hobby newspaper became a reality in April 1960. In time, I would launch my column, "Numismatic Depth Study." The title later became "The Joys of Collecting" and the feature has now been running for well over 40 years—the longest record in numismatic history for a column by a single author.

Getting back to the nickel. . . . Although many overmintmarks have been discovered since then, the event was shocking news in 1962. No one had ever heard, seen, or even suspected that such a variety might exist. There were plenty of overdates, where one numeral of the date had been punched over another, but no one knew of any coins with verified overmintmarks. The sensational news made exciting reading on the front page of *Coin World*. It was one of the most spectacular discoveries of modern times.

One theory of how the overmintmark occurred is that in late 1937 or early 1938, as dies were being prepared for the 1938 calendar year, someone realized that, while Denver would be making 1938 Buffalo nickels, San Francisco would not. Moreover, it was common knowledge at the time that the Buffalo design would soon be discontinued. It seems that there were at least half a dozen reverse dies with S mintmarks sitting in San Francisco. Rather than waste them, the S was overpunched with a D and the dies were sent to Denver to be used.

When I saw my first 1938-D/S nickel, I considered it not only a rarity, but perhaps a fantastic rarity. Would just a few specimens be found, or would dozens or hundreds turn up? Perhaps it was as rare as the 1913 Liberty Head nickel. Following the publication of the initial announcement in the September 14, 1962 issue of *Coin World*, I received letters and telephone calls from all over the country. In the ensuing weeks and months more 1938-D/S nickels surfaced—a few at first, then several dozen, and within a year or two, several hundred. Investors and hoarders with rolls of 1938-D Buffalo nickels combed through them in the hopes of finding the coveted D/S variety. Two Kansas City collectors struck a bonanza, finding several rolls. My firm started an active business in the variety, and thousands of dollars went to those two fortunate collectors. I suspect that there are many thousands of 1938-D/S nickels known today. The variety is still much scarcer than the 1938-D nickel without the overmintmark, but it is hardly a great rarity. The point is that new things can be discovered in modern times.

The laurels for reporting the first overmintmark in American numismatics go to Baldwin, Kansas, pharmacist Will W. Neil. A few years after completing *Adventures With Rare Coins*, I was reading the November 1928 issue of *The Numismatist* and was startled to find this comment, submitted by Neil, concerning the Morgan silver dollar:

"Mint Marks, or What Have You?"

Regarding the specimen in question, it is at first glance an ordinary Morgan-type silver dollar of 1900 from the New Orleans Mint, but upon closer examination of the mint mark it has the appearance of the O having been punched in over the letters CC. If this is so, then, undoubtedly, in this instance a reverse die was taken from the Carson City Mint to the mint at New Orleans [*sic*; actually the punching was done in Philadelphia], where the usual O was punched in the die over the CC and used in conjunction with an obverse die of 1900.

The sensation created by 1938-D/S nickel prompted dealers and collectors to begin studying other coins carefully, so that quite a few overmintmarks are known today. Though there are no others among Buffalo nickels, there are the 1949-D/S and the 1954-S/D in the Jefferson series, as well as the 1944-D/S Lincoln cent, the 1950-S/D dime, and the 1950-D/S and 1950-S/D quarters.

CHAPTER SEVEN

JEFFERSON NICKELS 1938 TO DATE
HISTORY AND BACKGROUND

TIME FOR A CHANGE?
EXIT THE BISON

Today, numismatists love Buffalo nickels, what with memories of dealer Abe Kosoff saying that this was the all-time favorite of his customers, and with the trusty bison making reappearances in our own time—on a commemorative *dollar* of all things, and redux on the nickel itself in 2005. Reminiscent of stage great Sarah Bernhardt, who had three grand "final tours," the "buffalo" keeps coming back!

Accordingly, in retrospect it seems rather strange that in 1938, when the Indian Head / Buffalo nickel had used up its 25-year minimum legal life span, there was a big rush to get rid of the design. Actually, for a long time it had been unloved by the several mints, due to the near impossibility of getting them to strike up properly and the pesky problem of die breakage.

ARTISTIC COMPETITION

Although several official and unofficial nationwide contests inviting many artists to improve designs had been held before, none had resulted in any changes to the circulating coinage. The commissions given to Augustus Saint-Gaudens (1907 gold coins), Bela Lyon Pratt (1908 $2.50 and $5 gold), Victor D. Brenner (1909 Lincoln cent), James Earle Fraser (1913 Indian Head / Buffalo nickel), Adolph A. Weinman (1916 dime and half dollar), Hermon A. MacNeil (1916 quarter), and Anthony de Francisci (1921 Peace dollar) had been with limited competition or simply a negotiated contract. Now in 1938 the idea of an open competition was tried again, this time with success.

An announcement was made in late January 1938:

> ### National Competition for New Design for Five Cent Coin
> ### Open to All American Sculptors
>
> The Treasury Department, Procurement Division, Section of Painting and Sculpture invites competition for designs for a new five cent coin to be known as the "Jefferson Nickel." This competition is open to all American sculptors.
>
> The competition requirements are that a sculptor entering the competition must submit two plaster models, one representing the obverse and one the reverse of the coin.
>
> The sum of $1,000 is to be paid to the winner. The sculptor whose designs win the competition will be required to execute a formal contract with the Treasury Department, agreeing to make any revisions required by the Secretary of the Treasury.
>
> All designs will be judged by the following Advisory Committee who have kindly consented to act with the Section of Painting and Sculpture in judging the competition:
>
> Mrs. Nellie Tayloe Ross, Director of the Mint
> Mrs. Sidney Waugh, Sculptor

Mr. Albert Stewart, Sculptor

Mr. Heinz [Henry] Warneke, Sculptor

The models should not be signed. They should be accompanied by a plain, sealed envelope, enclosing the sculptor's name and address. These envelopes will be carefully numbered when received with the same number as the designs they accompany and will remain unopened unless they conform strictly with the foregoing conditions.

Any sculptor may submit as many designs as he desires. Should he submit more than one set of designs he should remember to send a sealed envelope with his address with each entry.

The subject matter must contain on the obverse of the coin an authentic portrait of Thomas Jefferson. On the reverse side the subject matter will be a representation of Monticello, Jefferson's historic home near Charlottesville. In addition to the words required by law to appear on the coin, the coin may contain the inscription "MONTICELLO," in order to identify the architecture. The coinage laws require that there shall appear upon the obverse side of the coin the word "LIBERTY" and the date "1938," and, on the reverse, "UNITED STATES OF AMERICA," and the denomination "FIVE CENTS." The coin should also contain the motto "IN GOD WE TRUST." None of the legends are to be abbreviated and should be all in capital letters.

Neither the United States of America nor any officer, agency, agents, or employee thereof shall be liable to the sculptor for the use by any person of any idea, plan, or design, expressed or executed by the sculptor in connection with the work.

Competitors are invited to participate in this competition subject to the condition, in view of the provisions of the laws of the United States, that any and all sketches, designs, molds, models, and the like, made by them in connection with such competition, whether or not submitted, be delivered to the committee by not later than April 15, 1938 so that they may be ultimately delivered to a representative of the Treasury Department for destruction or such other disposition as the Department may see fit to make of them.

The Treasury Department shall be under no obligation to show, exhibit, or preserve the work of any sculptor.

The models in order to be acceptable to the Treasury Department must be of plaster and should not exceed $8\frac{1}{2}$ inches in diameter and should be executed in such a manner as to be suitable for coinage purposes. The background or field should have a slight radius, that is, the background must curve slightly from the center to meet the edge of the coin or border. A model with an absolutely flat background would be practically impossible to coin. The extreme depth of relief from the border to the deepest part should not exceed 5/32 of an inch and the highest part of the design should be kept slightly under the level of the border. The competition will terminate April 15th, on which date the models should have been delivered, carrying charges prepaid, to the Section of Painting and Sculpture, Procurement Division, Treasury Department, Washington, D.C.

If no designs are submitted which are of sufficient merit to justify an acceptance, no contract will be awarded as a result of this competition.

Photographs of a front and side view of Monticello are available and may be obtained by writing to the Section of Painting & Sculpture.[1]

THE CONTEST RESULTS

Artists were slow in their response, and by mid-March only a few entries had been submitted. However, this belied the activity, as many were working on the project, intending to finish later, but before the deadline.

On April 21, 1938, the *Washington Post* carried this account:

> A new nickel was born yesterday. Art judges peered at 390 plaster models, showing Thomas Jefferson on one side and his Monticello home on the other, and picked a winner to supplant the Indian-buffalo design. It may be a day or two until the winning artist is disclosed, however.
>
> Jefferson, third president and author of the Declaration of Independence, never looked like so many different people as he did yesterday. The models depicted him as everything from a coarse barbarian to a royal dandy. The facial features varied from skinny to the triple-chin type. On a few casts, Jefferson scowled. He smiled on none, usually wearing a calm expression.
>
> On some models, Jefferson wore his hair in a typical colonial pigtail. On others he had bobbed and even marcelled hair. The classic Monticello fared little better, the competitors, in some instances, perching eagles on its roof. In violation of rules for the contest, some artists substituted the Liberty Bell and even an ear of corn for the house.
>
> The new Jefferson nickel will enter circulation some time this fall, the present buffalo nickel having served its minimum statutory life of 25 years.

FELIX SCHLAG

On April 24 it was revealed that Felix Schlag (1891–1974) was the winner of the contest. However, there were extensive modifications still to be made, per this newspaper account of May 11:

> The Treasury today said that news isn't worth a nickel, but the design for the Thomas Jefferson five-cent piece has gone back to artist Felix Schlag for a few changes.
>
> What was the trouble? Was Jefferson's face going to be lifted? Was his jaw too lantern-like?
>
> The Treasury said, "no." There are a few minor revisions, like angles and curves. Further investigation disclosed the nickel won't be ready for the public for a couple of months. It still has to be approved by a lot of people. The Fine Arts Commission must say it is O.K. The Director of the Mint, Mrs. Nellie Tayloe Ross, must nod and tell Secretary Morgenthau it's all right.
>
> When and if the Secretary says all's well, the design goes to the Philadelphia Mint, which will then begin to stamp out the new coins.

The Commission of Fine Arts was not altogether pleased with the designs, particularly the modernistic reverse. Schlag thus revised his models, refining the "lantern jaw" and substituting a more traditional version of Monticello.

On July 17, Commission chairman Charles Moore noted: "The Treasury being anxious for a report as soon as possible, the photographs were submitted to Mr. Lawrie, who reported as follows:

'The models are of good workmanship. I feel that the main lettering on the United States side should be as bold or bolder than the lettering on the Jefferson side; also I feel that UNITED STATES OF AMERICA should be at the top of the coin, thus reversing the position of that and E PLURIBUS UNUM. In looking through a reducing glass at the photograph, which brings the image down to the size of a nickel, the letters FIVE CENTS seem to me too small.'"[2]

JEFFERSON-NICKEL DESIGNER

AUTOGRAPH BY FELIX SCHLAG

PHOTOGRAPH OF THE PRIZE WINNING MODEL

The original Jefferson nickel design by Felix O. Schlag, as shown on a souvenir card the artist created. For the final design the Mint modified the lettering and the details of the Jefferson portrait and for the reverse had Schlag create a different depiction of Monticello.

MODIFICATIONS REQUESTED

Schlag's bold portrait of Jefferson was retained, with modifications to the lettering style, but his depiction of Monticello, a corner view with the building accompanied by foliage, was rejected. This was changed to a direct or plan view of the building, with no foliage. Harry X Boosel, a youthful numismatist and civil servant in Washington, DC, submitted this comment as part of a piece published in the May issue of *Numismatic Scrapbook Magazine*, "The models have been returned to the artist for alterations on the reverse side."

In the meantime, among the original submissions by other artists was a plan view of Monticello, leading Michael Wescott in his 1991 book to comment, "artist

Marcello Rotundo submitted a design of which the building [but not the lettering] looks *stunningly* like the final design."[3] Seeking to resolve the matter I contacted the National Archives, and obtained a file of original correspondence, which revealed that Rotundo had no part in any aspect of the finished design.[4] The depiction of the building by contest entrant Franz Karl Hejda was similar.

In any event, it was Schlag who captured the $1,000 prize and garnered all of the publicity. Presumably, Schlag's revision, in conjunction with Sinnock, was adapted from an illustration of Monticello that may have been seen by other contestants, including Rotundo. In its final form the *lettering* on the reverse follows Schlag's original art, not Rotundo's.

Numismatic scholar R.W. Julian commented on the reverse in a May 18, 2004, article in *Numismatic News*, "Interest in Jefferson Nickels Revitalized," this being a small excerpt from a detailed commentary tracing the origins of the design:

> For the reverse the artist used a view of Monticello—but not the standard one seen today on the nickel. Instead, Schlag prepared an artistic *tour de force* in which Jefferson's home is seen from a three-quarter view. Unfortunately, official busybodies in the Treasury and perhaps the White House took exception to the modernistic view of Monticello, as well as the lettering, and asked that changes be made. One minor point made by officials was that the tree standing by Monticello had to be eliminated. It seems that everyone saw it as a palm tree and no one thought that Jefferson had been growing this sort of thing!
>
> The request for changes was made in late May 1938, but Schlag by then had made other commitments for his artistic time, so it was not until mid-June that he was able to make the alterations. These were done by July 15 and submitted to the Commission of Fine Arts. The commission quickly approved the basic models, although it is not clear if the lettering had yet been changed to the traditional style. Perhaps it was merely understood that this would be the case. The Treasury secretary then gave formal approval.

For his 1966 *U.S. Mint and Coinage* book, Don Taxay unearthed this comment in the *Anderson* (Indiana) *Herald*, published on August 21, 1938:

> The prize winning design for the new Jeffersonian nickel has been altered by order of the Federal Fine Arts Commission. They didn't like the view of Thomas Jefferson's home, Monticello, so they required the artist to do another picture of the front of the home. They did not like the lettering on the coin. It wasn't in keeping, but they forgot to say what it wasn't in keeping with.
>
> The Commission compelled the artist to use the classical Roman letters that have been used on coins for decades. They are more familiar and perhaps easier to read, but who reads the lettering on a five cent piece, anyway?
>
> Originally the letters were akin to the slim, graceful type without serifs (those curley-cues at the top or bottom of a letter) that are seen in up-to-date newspapers today. The letters on coins, as on public buildings, are purely decorative and should express the contemporary American spirit. There is no more reason for imitating the Romans in this respect than there would be for modeling our automobiles after the chariot of Ben Hur's day.

Felix Schlag with the revised model for the obverse of the Jefferson nickel. (United States Mint)

Schlag's "working plaster" model for the revised view of Monticello used on the reverse of the Jefferson nickel. (United States Mint)

COINAGE TO COMMENCE

Taxay's account also includes this from the St. Louis *Globe-Democrat*, September 12:

> The new Jefferson nickel which will be in initial production at the Philadelphia Mint this week, will present a kindlier likeness than the original design on which it was based. Original lines by Felix Schlag, who won a $1,000 prize contest over 400 competitors, have been softened and the pictured face of the author of the Declaration of Independence lifted. That is, on order of the Federal Fine Arts Commission.
>
> Mr. Felix Schlag removed the hollow from the great Democrat's cheek, smoothed hard lines around the mouth into a pleasant smile and even cut down the size of Jefferson's collar. And the original side view of Monticello, which is for the obverse [*sic*] side of the coin, has been changed somewhat. Under orders of the Commission, Monticello was twisted around to a front view and a modernistic tree, which was shown in the foreground, was chopped down.
>
> So it will be a handsome and somewhat pleasing coin that, starting production this week, will begin trickling into circulation from Federal Reserve banks the first week in November, when supplies will be of circulating stature.

HOW MUCH DID SCHLAG CONTRIBUTE?

The Numismatist, January 1939, had this comment:

> Why did the Treasury Department select a winning design and award the prize for the new nickel and then not use the design?
>
> This appears like an extreme view, but it seems to be confirmed by the new coin recently placed in circulation. At the time of the award it was announced that the prize-winning design was selected with the understanding that certain changes were to be made in it before final acceptance.
>
> As issued, not a single feature of the original reverse design has been retained. Everything is new. A front view of Jefferson's home replaces the corner view, the name "Monticello" has been placed beneath it, the style of lettering has been changed, and the impossible tree has been removed.
>
> On the obverse the head of Jefferson has been retained with slight modifications, but the style of lettering has also been changed. Since the head of Jefferson is the only thing remaining from the original design, it may be assumed that this head was the best of all the heads presented (we understand there were 300 designs submitted), and that the award committee based its decision on this feature. As it appears on the new coin, the head is the best feature. It is large, but not nearly as large as the Indian head it replaces.
>
> A building on the reverse of a regular issue of United States coins an innovation, and a welcome one. Whatever criticism may be directed against it is probably because it is an innovation. It is time to realize that something besides wreaths and eagles may fittingly be placed on our coins. . . . An editorial opinion of the new nickel is worth no more than that of any other collector. But we like it, particularly the obverse.

WHAT THEY ARE SAYING

The Numismatist, January 1939, also included "Short comments on the Jefferson nickel," not attributed as to the authors:

Oh! The new nickel. It's nice.

It's smaller than the old one.

Hey, Joe, here's one of the new nickels I read about in the paper. Is it thicker?

I think it's an awful looking job.

We don't take that kind of money here. Gimme a nickel.

Whose picture is that on the front?

From the pictures I thought it would look terrible, but I like the coin. I call it a token. I have lots of transportation tokens that look better. It went into the turn-stile all right.

I think it will wear much better. The jaw and portico will go first. Oh! World's Fair?

That building looks like the Aquarium.

Will have to get up some new Scotch gags now.

It reminds me of an Austrian coin.

The obverse is fine, but I don't like the reverse at all.

I liked the old buffalo.

Give me one, please. I want to put it away.

OTHERS CRITIQUE THE DESIGN

In the annals of American coin designs special homage should be paid to French sculptor Jean Antoine Houdon, for the busts he created of George Washington, Benjamin Franklin, and Thomas Jefferson were used on the quarter dollar, half dollar, and nickel respectively. His depiction of Washington was also used on commemorative coins, medals, and tokens, becoming the essential numismatic definition of the Father of Our Country.

Regarding Jefferson, a circa 1789 bust by Houdon, done while the subject was in the ambassadorial service in Paris, was used by Schlag. Multiple copies were produced by Houdon, a particularly fine one being in the Boston Museum of Fine Arts since 1934, described by art historian H.H. Amason as follows:

> The marble *Jefferson* in Boston is a superb interpretation of the third President of the United States. Jefferson is shown in modern dress, his face tilted upward and angled slightly to the right. The hair is dressed in a manner similar to that of Washington, worn rather long at the sides. The eyes are large and cut unusually deep, shadowed under heavy brows in a manner which gives them an exceptional sense of vitality. The lean symmetrical face, with its sharply

aquiline nose, compressed lips and jutting chin is the perfect reflection of the intellectual man of affairs that we know Jefferson to have been. It is at the same time a face of great sensitivity and the face of an aristocrat.[5]

Cornelius Vermeule in *Numismatic Art in America, Aesthetics of the United States Coinage,* 1971, reviewed the design, admired the obverse (and furnished the citation given above). However, the other side of the coin left much to be desired:

> The reverse is a disappointment, but evidently this is not Schlag's fault. The original model showed Jefferson's home somewhat enlarged and cleverly fore-shortened at a three-quarters angle with a tree masking the left (facing) or (properly) right front wing. The house is even tilted upward and back slightly, as if the viewer were approaching it while ascending an incline. Official taste eliminated this interesting, even exciting, view and substituted the mausoleum of Roman profile and blurred forms that masquerades as the building on the finished coin. On the trial reverse the name "Monticello" seemed scarcely necessary and was therefore, logically, omitted. On the coin as issued it seems essential lest one think the building portrayed is the vault at Fort Knox, a state archives building, or a public library somewhere. Again, lettering is well balanced and well defined, with slender clarity. The high rim has preserved the broad bust and the blurry, inarticulate columns and windows of the house from much abuse.

The depiction of front-on or plan views of buildings has been an artistic failure in most instances, garnering poor reviews from artists and numismatists alike. A particularly ubiquitous modern example is the Lincoln Memorial on the reverse of the Lincoln cent.

IN THE WORDS OF FELIX O. SCHLAG

At the 1964 ANA convention Felix O. Schlag delighted listeners with his reminiscences, giving what must be considered to be the authoritative version of what actually happened:

> Twenty six years ago an American numismatic event moved me in the spotlight for a short time. It is the general opinion that it made me rich and famous. Recently, Jefferson nickel collectors have taken me out of the mothballs, and I must admit that I enjoy it and am glad to be at this convention.
>
> The story of the Jefferson nickel has interwoven in it many personal and human elements. In order to impress upon you that winning the competition was more than just an accidental achievement, as some may think, I shall have to relate to you something of my background and education. I won more than fifteen monetary awards and numerous honorable mentions—all in open competitions here and abroad. The reason that I inject personal references in my conversation is that the exacting details, specifications, and terms of contracts with statistics may be very dry to an outsider. . . .
>
> Just to set the record straight and to correct errors concerning the disputed Jefferson Nickel competition, I wrote my life story for the reason that it might be of interest someday to a Jefferson nickel collector or numismatist.
>
> My life story describes my studies at the former Royal Academy of Art in Munich, Germany, which I attended for seven years and which was at that time

an exclusive school of classical tradition. Here I received an education in the practical arts as well as art history, architecture—and lectures and demonstrations in anatomy. Emphasis was placed on the spatial relationship of sculpture.

A chapter refers to my life as a front line soldier—my long hospitalization due to shrapnel wounds—my convalescence—my struggle to find my way back to normal life. During the last period of my convalescence I won first prize for my models for a monumental fountain and first prize for a Red Cross medal.

The revolution of 1918–1919 affected my life directly and seriously. Another phase of my story touches on my experience as a mountain climber in the European Alps. Mountain climbing is exhilarating and challenging. It is beset with danger and adventure—like a call or defense to a personal contest.

Climbing the peak of a mountain solo—you are very much alone, confronting an awesome spectacle such an enormity of dimensions, a closeness to the universe. There is an unearthly silence. You feel the tremendous power of all creation. After such revelation and drama you hesitate to return to daily city life—the contrast is so great, so startling. It influenced my mind and spirit, my attitude toward life, and prepared me well to endure all the hardships and struggles in later years, when at times everything around me seemed crashed.

Now my story comes to the 1930s. The life of most sculptors in the Depression years was rather hard, not at all lived in splendor. Sometimes I worked in ivory, other times I made window displays, other times I worked in silver, and for a half year I earned my living with a pick and a shovel, at the same time spending nights as a bus boy. Always on the move—New York, Chicago, Detroit, New York, and back to Chicago, where I finally could rent a studio, find artist friends, where I lived on big hopes, working long hours. Artists love good conversation, and our talks were interesting and lively.

The reward was that it lifted you spiritually, hardships were forgotten, and imagination raised beyond this world into one of eternal art—a dream. Sculptures were seen in a fabulous light—an inspiration to work, to fight with the material, that continued quest to find the concrete form, that elusive goal. The aim was always high and the works of the great artists of bygone days are where the shining star is. It is the mission of the artist to translate his time to which he is fixed, arrested, into a definite shape.

In the thirties the section of Fine Arts, Washington, DC, sent leaflets to artists announcing competitions and news pertaining to government activities in relation to art. Late in 1937 or very early 1938, the department invited all American sculptors to compete for a new five-cent coin to be known as the Jefferson nickel. I believe it was the first and only open competition of this kind ever held in this country. Prospective competitors were admonished that there were specific legal and other conditions which must be accurately complied with in creating a model, and that before proceeding, the competitors should get the specifications.

After receiving the detailed form announcement (regarding subject matter, size of models, coinage rules, etc.) I made a series of pencil sketches, without having an actual portrait in mind, just a composition—but the fundamental object for me was to find a likeness that portrayed the character and the strong facial features of the great American as I imagined him. None of the portraits of Jefferson in my collection satisfied me.

In my search I read everything I could find about Jefferson. I felt that unless I could somehow discover what I was looking for, my participation in the competition was uncertain. One night around 10 p.m., after a hard day's work, I entered an old bookstore in my neighborhood to browse. To my great surprise and excitement, in the first magazine I opened I found a portrait of Jefferson that inspired me and which I intuitively knew depicted the noble qualities of a true American statesman. The search was over—my decision to compete was certain!

In an open competition one has to strive harder than when the commission is given outright to a favored son. In open competition, the winning design is bound to be criticized more severely. Contemplate the disappointment of the other artists in the competition who also worked hard, spent many uncounted hours, and received no compensation whatsoever. In submitting the design all the names of the participants were in individual sealed envelopes so that the jury would not be influenced by the name of someone known to them.

As I was occupied with other sculptural projects, the work on my interpretation, within the rules set up by the Treasury Department, forced me to work on the Jefferson nickel in the time spot from 10 p.m. to 4 a.m., at which time I retired for some rest.

To me as a sculptor, the Greek coins were always of the greatest interest. This is not to imply that other nations and cultures in different centuries did not create beautiful coins of the highest artistic value. I marveled at the freshness, technique, and beauty of Greek coins. There was an intensive drive and constant challenge to create the most beautiful designs, backed by a general understanding of art. They represented a living force. Complete independence of Greek cities and communities was one reason for the variety of Greek coins. Even small cities had their own mints and jealously protected their rights and privileges.

The Greek coins are still exciting to me. Created in the negative, they give an effect one cannot imitate by modeling in clay or wax. And I applied the very same procedure, cutting the portrait as well as the reverse in plaster, always making tests.

The competition requirements were to submit the obverse and reverse sides of the coin. The subject matter on the obverse of the coin called for an authentic portrait of Jefferson. On the reverse side a representation of Monticello.

The sculptor whose design won was required to execute a formal contract with the Treasury Department, agreeing among other things to make any revisions required by the Secretary of the Treasury without receiving any additional compensation.

Here are some quotes from the specifications [omitted here as they are given in the text above]. But even winning the competition—if the corrections asked were not made or accepted you received no compensation at all.

It is interesting to note by comparison that the sculptor of the Peace silver dollar, who was given an outright commission by the government, received $2,500, and when the Treasury Department requested a minor change, the government paid all his expenses to come to Washington with his wife where they occupied the bridal suite at a first-class hotel with the government as host! This was back in 1921.

The models in order to be acceptable had to be of plaster not exceeding eight and one-half inches in diameter. The extreme depth of the relief was to be 5/32 of an inch. I finished all the models one day before the deadline, photographed them myself, and had to race to the proper train to get them off, for all the time spent would have been lost without even having a chance.

There were 390 pairs of models submitted by various artists. The reason for the large number of entries was the Depression, the prize money, and also the genuine desire to create a new coin, breaking the tradition of designs. The best sculptors in the country competed.

On April 20, 1938, I received a telegram from the superintendent of the Section of Painting and Sculpture asking for my biography. And the next day a telephone call gave me the good news that I had won the competition. But changes were requested. Nine suggestions were offered and I was advised to submit black and white drawings indicating the revisions. It meant starting all over again!

After submitting a new set of drawings, the director of the Mint advised me that they were very pleasing and that the fine qualities indicated in these drawings should be retained in the finished work and I should proceed with the modeling in clay and that photographs must be submitted before casting any plaster.

As I mentioned before, since my technique was to carve directly negative in plaster, I had no photos of any clay models to send for approval, but I submitted photos of the finished plaster models (which was a risk I took). Luckily enough they were accepted and I sent in the final models.

On July 21, 1938, Mrs. Nellie Tayloe Ross advised me that the acting secretary of the Treasury had approved the models and that Philadelphia was being instructed to surrender the prize money, $1,000. Considering the actual time involved to create the models, the reward in itself was nominal.

When the check arrived every cent was spent to pay debts accumulated due to sickness, death, and funeral expenses for someone close to me.

In that year, 1938, I finished a sculptural relief for the Whitehall, Illinois, Post Office. In 1939 I made twice life-size stone carvings for Chicago Heights, and also I created a smaller athletic group for Champaign, Illinois. In 1940 I worked on a relief of three runners.

The future seemed bright and promising. There were inspiring offers for the Governor Horner Monument, one for Admiral Moffet, and an appointment with President Roosevelt was planned for the creation of a Marines Monument.

Then the war came. Planned commissions and promises of commissions were halted. Materials were difficult to obtain. All national, state, and personal interest in art was at a low. It seemed that everything that meant life to me was crashing. I spent time and money to get other commissions. My economic situation became desperate. I was over 50 years of age. I had no mechanical training—never worked in a factory. As a sculptor I had always maintained an optimistic and hopeful view. Even though I went through many adversities I kept my faith.

At the beginning of the war I tried to enlist in the United States Army. As I was still in good physical condition, I expected to be accepted. I had all my belongings packed and stored. Then came the letter from the War Department commending me for my patriotism, but refusing me because they said a man of my age could not stand the rigors of army life.

Since early youth photography was my hobby. I used it to photograph my own work. Now it appeared to be the only avenue of livelihood left to me. I opened my own portrait studio in Owosso [Michigan], and luck was with me. One of the first photographs I took was of a young lady who was so pleased with it that she entered the portrait in a contest in California. It won her a first prize and a modeling career. This kind of news spread fast in a small city, and soon my appointment book was full.

After I had established a going business in photography, I had calls to do sculptural work, but by now I was accustomed to eating regularly and not having to wonder where my next meal was coming from or where I would obtain the next commission. It was the first time in my adult life that I felt a sense of security. I refused all offers of sculpture as none was a definite commission.

A few years ago I retired. The Jefferson nickel popped up again, and I was rediscovered due to the upsurge of interest in coin collecting. There were requests for my signature from collectors. One dealer came with a load of coin books to be signed. I found out that my signature was being sold, my letters of correspondence were used for personal advantage, books that I signed were being advertised for sale. At one coin show I saw memento that I had given away priced at $500! I thought: I have the name so I might as well have the game. When I began asking $1.50 for a signature and $5 for an autographed card with a montage of the prize-winning designs of the nickel. The flood stopped. By this time you will have realized that the story of the Jefferson nickel is not an isolated event, but the story of a sculptor's trials and tribulations. It did not make me rich and famous.

Do not draw the conclusion that I have grown bitter toward life. Far from it—I still keep looking in the sky and at the stars and admire the often monumental beauty of creation.[6]

In the early 21st century the Gallery Mint created a "pattern" coin, a beautifully struck modern issue with the obverse similar to that of a regular issue 1938 Jefferson nickel and so dated, and with the reverse depicting Schlag's unadopted reverse design, with a corner view of Monticello. These were offered for sale in "Matte Uncirculated" for $38 and Proof for $42, with 1,938 struck of each. As might be expected, it was not long before an example turned up in an Internet auction site, incompletely described, and was sold to a naïve buyer for over $500.

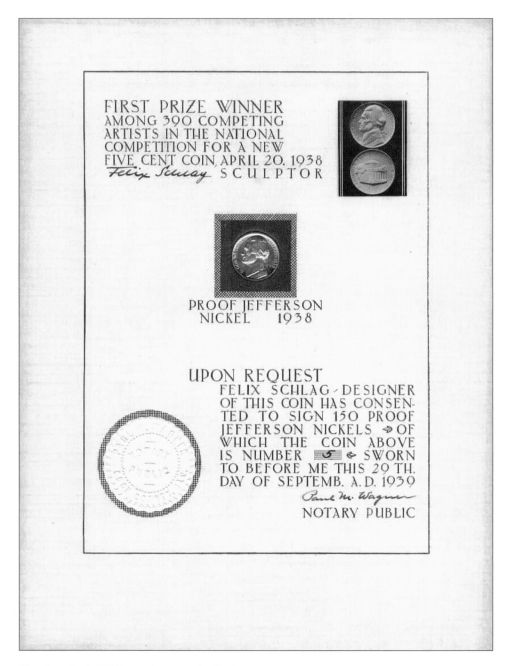

Number 5 of 150 framed souvenir displays Felix Schlag had made in 1939. Each was signed by him and notarized. At the center is a Proof 1938 nickel with obverse facing; at upper right is a photograph of his original 1938 Monticello design.

EVOLUTION AND USE OF THE JEFFERSON NICKEL

Getting Ready

The Numismatist, May 1938, included this news:

> It was announced from Washington on April 20 that the winning designs for the new five-cent nickel coin had been selected. The winner of the competition is Felix Schlag, of Chicago. The obverse has a large bust of Jefferson facing left, with "In God We Trust. Liberty 1938" surrounding. The reverse has a view of Monticello, Jefferson's home. Above, "E Pluribus Unum." Below, "Five Cents. United States of America." 390 plaster models were submitted. Coins with the new designs will not be placed in circulation until fall, it was said. Mrs. Nellie Tayloe Ross, director of the Mint, was chairman of the judging. The artist-judges were Sidney Waugh and Albert Stewart, of New York, and Heinz Warneke, of East Haddam, Connecticut. So far this year nickels have been struck only at the Denver Mint.

The June issue of the same magazine illustrated the nickel, but with Schlag's unadopted reverse with an angle view of Monticello. Apparently, the editor did not know that another version had been substituted. In nearby pages, James F. Kelly, of Dayton, Ohio, announced that he was entering the coin business full time—this being the same dealer who made headlines years later in 1967 with the sale of the J.V. McDermott 1913 Liberty Head nickel.

Collectors of coins have always had a cross to bear with the term *numismatic*, unfamiliar to the public. On another page of the same issue was a commentary from ANA librarian William S. Dewey, who submitted this list of misspellings gleaned from correspondence sent to him:

> numatic, numisatic, nunisatic, munismatic, numesmatic, pneumatic, numismaitic, numisitic, numasmatic, numismutic, nunisnatic, numimatic, nomismatic, newmismatic, amunistac, numusmatic, nuismatic, numastic, numerismatic, numistic, numistatical, numismastic, numismatical, and nunismetic.

Philatelists (stamp collectors) probably don't have any easier time with their word! There was no urgency to rush the new Jefferson nickels into circulation. Treasury and bank stocks of this denomination were adequate, and the country was still in the Depression, although prosperity, thought to be "just around the corner" years earlier, was finally showing a few evidences here and there. The Treasury instructed all three mints to begin coinage on October 3, seemingly for no particular reason. Nickels had last been coined in Philadelphia and San Francisco in 1937, and at Denver the production of 1938-D nickels had ended in April.

R.W. Julian described the scenario:

> Officials then picked the curious figure of 12,700,000 as the necessary number of nickels to be stockpiled before the new coins could be released. One suspects that this number was chosen as some sort of office contest at the Mint Bureau, for the simple reason that the figure means nothing; at any rate the magic number was eventually reached on November 15 and the coins issued to an interested public, which had been reading about them for several months.

While the dies were yet being prepared, numismatists were asking for Proof specimens of the new nickel, even though it was late in the year. Surprisingly, the government agreed to this request and collectors were allowed to purchase specimens for 20 cents each. More than 19,000 were made in the last two months of 1938, easily the year's most popular denomination; the second-place cent saw less than 15,000 being purchased.[7]

In the meantime, production of the new nickel continued apace. By year's end nearly thirty million coins had been struck at the Philadelphia, Denver, and San Francisco mints, with Philadelphia making the lion's share. The official release date was November 15.

Into Circulation

Frank G. Duffield, long-time editor of *The Numismatist*, brought readers up to date with the nickel in December 1938, adding his own opinions:

> Instead of the "proposed" Jefferson nickel, of which so much has been heard during the last six months, it has now become one of our current coins—that is, in a very small way. It was formally placed in circulation on November 15, through the banks of the country, and the supply was far short of the demand. Less than 8 million pieces had been coined to November 1, and many who wanted a chance to see what the coin looked like and own one were disappointed. To have postponed the distribution a month would have caused no hardship to anyone and a larger quantity would have been available to the public.
>
> The designs for the coin by Felix Schlag, the winner in the contest, were accepted by the Treasury Department with the understanding that some changes were to be made, to be dictated by the Mint Bureau, before final acceptance. Mr. Schlag's models were illustrated in our June issue. The revised designs show some changes in the face of Jefferson, and a front view of Monticello has been placed on the reverse, instead of the corner view. The tree so prominent in the original design has been eliminated. The style of lettering on both sides of the coin has been changed to conform to the usual lettering required for United States coins. Altogether, the changes are an improvement.
>
> The Jefferson nickel seems to establish two things: First, that it is perfectly OK with the public to place portraits of deceased presidents on our coins, taken in connection with the Lincoln cent and Washington quarter. Second, that it is also proper to use on the reverse a design that does not include a wreath or an eagle. Of course, the buffalo on the nickel design just discarded was a departure from the time-honored custom, and it has been repeated in the new nickel. The average person cares little about the designs on a coin. He is concerned only with its purchasing power. The collector is more fastidious. He likes occasional new designs and would be glad to have them oftener than once in 25 years. And if new designs bring new departures he will be the last to complain.
>
> One thing, however, has not been decided by the new nickel: In planning for new designs, is it wise to have a free-for-all competition instead of inviting designs or models from a limited number of artists of recognized standing?

At the time coin collecting was a very popular hobby in America, as it had been since the mid-1930s when Raymond "National" albums, followed by J.K. Post and other "penny boards," achieved wide sales. Filling in album holes was like working on a crossword puzzle—another popular diversion during the Depression. However, the investment end of the coin market was reeling from the crash of commemorative coin prices that had commenced in late 1936 and was still going on. Because of this there was little interest in squirreling away quantities of modern Uncirculated coins.

The reception of the new nickels by the collecting community was warm, but not overly enthusiastic. Many numismatists bought one each from the three mints and ordered Proofs as well. At the time, Proof nickels could be bought separately, not necessarily as part of sets. There was a small but unprecedented interest in acquiring the new Proof nickels. Ever since modern Proofs had been issued, beginning in 1936, Lincoln cents had been ordered in the greatest numbers, followed by nickels, then by the silver issues (with quarters being the least popular). In 1938 there was a bubble in the distribution, as reflected by the Proof mintages for the era. In 1939, normal demand resumed:

Proof Coin Mintages, 1936–1940

1936—cent, 5,569; nickel, 4,420; dime, 4,130; quarter, 3,827; half dollar, 3,901

1937—cent, 9,320; nickel, 5,569; dime, 5,746; quarter, 5,542; half dollar, 5,728

1938—cent, 13,734; **nickel, 19,365**; dime, 8,728; quarter, 8,045; half dollar, 8,152

1939—cent, 13,520; nickel, 12,535; dime, 9,321; quarter, 8,795; half dollar, 8,808

1940—cent, 15,872; nickel, 14,158; dime, 11,827; quarter, 11,246; half dollar, 11,279

The next year, in *The Numismatist*, January 1939, Roy Hill, an ANA member in California, wrote to tell of his search for the newly-released Jefferson nickels:

> I have had a lot of fun trying to gather in some of those 1938 Jefferson nickels here, and perhaps the same condition exists elsewhere. The best I did from one bank was to get five all at once. The rest have been in lots of one, two, or three, and many times none at all. So it will probably not reach active circulation until the 1939 coinage is turned loose. I got a Proof from the Philadelphia Mint, the first Proof I have ever sent for, and they are interesting. We are getting a deluge of bright coins here these days, and one is tempted to hang on to them all, but they are getting more numerous—1938 cents and dimes and 1937 quarters.

On September 29, 1939, Schlag had a group of display panels numbered from 1 to 150 and notarized. Each one was personally signed, and fitted with a Proof 1938 nickel, obverse facing up, and a small photograph which showed both sides of a Jefferson nickel, the reverse being his unadopted angle-view of Monticello. These are highly prized display items today.

A Step Change in 1939, and a Nomenclature Note
In early 1939, the Mint made a minor modification to the reverse hub, strengthening the steps on the likeness of Monticello. Such steps had presented difficulty with the

striking of Full Details, and it was hoped that this change would help solve the problem. Actually, the steps would continue to be a nuisance for a long time, not only to the Mint but to collectors as well. Collector-specialists began to focus on the six tiny steps on the building as the place to determine whether a nickel was sharply struck; in time, *Full Steps*, or *FS*, became part of the numismatic lexicon. Colloquial usage varies today, with some numismatists using *Full Step* (singular) as an adjective, as with the Full Step Nickel Club, and others using the plural *Full Steps*. (Quoted passages in the present work have been edited to conform to modern style and in this way may differ from the originals.) Some modern collectors distinguish between 5 Full Steps (5FS; all but one step full) and 6 Full Steps (6FS). Although 5FS and 6FS coins are sometimes discussed herein, *FS* can indicate *any* nickel with at least 5 Full Steps. According to popular wisdom and tradition, starting with published comments in 1939, a wider change in the hub was made. However, long-time Jefferson nickel specialist Bernard Nagengast has set the record straight. Only the aforementioned steps were involved.[8]

As to a description of the old-style steps on the Reverse of 1938, the Fivaz-Stanton *Cherrypickers' Guide* (p. 306) calls them "wavy" and "ill defined." This hub was necessarily used on all 1938 Proof nickels and on *most* of 1939, as by the time the hub had been modified early in the year, either old reverses continued to be used for Proofs, or new Proof reverse dies from the old hub were made. In any event, relatively few Proofs of 1939 have the "Reverse of 1940" or new hub with sharp steps. Most have the "Reverse of 1938." The term "Reverse of 1940" is the suggestion of Bernard Nagengast, for both hubs styles were used in 1939.

To the observer the steps on nickels with the Reverse of 1938 are usually blended or touching in at least some areas. Even Proofs are not sharply defined. The Reverse of 1940 has the top "step" heavy—actually not a step, but the edge of the deck from the front door. The five real steps are small ruled parallel lines. These can be sharp on some coins, especially Proofs, but can be indistinct or incomplete on circulation strikes. As to the distribution of the Reverse of 1938 vis-à-vis the Reverse of 1940 cents across the three mints, Bernard Nagengast and others have found the 1939 Philadelphia Mint circulation strikes to be mostly the Reverse of 1940 and Proofs to be mostly the Reverse of 1938. Among 1939-D nickels the reverses seem to be about evenly divided, while 1939-S coins are seen more often with the new reverse. A few *1940* Proof nickels were made with the Reverse of 1938. Such rare reverses on certain 1939 and 1940 Proofs can be finds for cherrypickers, for their existence is not widely known, and they are not listed in the *Guide Book of United States Coins*. The Reverse of 1940 hub was used through the year 1970.

The 1939 Doubled Die

The idea of a larger-scope modification, beyond just the steps, was presented by Malcolm O.E. Chell-Frost in a letter published in *The Numismatist*, November 1942:

> This is probably news to a great many collectors of nickels, but the truth is that the 1939, Jefferson nickel was re-engraved in the early part of the year. Sometime before Feb. 21, 1939, the word MONTICELLO and the words FIVE CENTS were quite weak and the Mint decided to develop a new hub to strengthen these two or three words.

Before this new hub was completed the old hub was cut over through MONTICELLO and FIVE CENTS. How many were made is strictly a guess; however, to give collectors an idea of how few are to be found they may be interested in a few figures.

During the past two months I have had many collectors searching for this nickel, and up to the present 12 have been found. Here is a chance to do something during the day. I would greatly appreciate fellow collectors letting me know if any more are found and the amount.

I quote a letter from the U.S. Mint written to me Sept. 18, 1939, as follows:

"Please be advised that a new hub was completed on the reverse Jefferson nickel with a slight increase in weight of MONTICELLO and FIVE CENTS, Feb. 21, 1939. Since that date all the dies have been drawn from the new hub. No change has been made in the hub since Feb. 21, 1939."

(Signed) Paul J. Dowd, acting superintendent.

Bernard Nagengast suggests that Acting Superintendent Dowd's letter of September 18, 1939, referring to changes of the preceding February, was an erroneous recollection, possibly based not on first-hand experience with the change, but the knowledge that, in broad terms, Monticello had been modified on the five-cent piece, not a reference to the specific words MONTICELLO and FIVE CENTS. The modification of Monticello was simply the steps. Nagengast and others can find no difference in the "weight" (strength or boldness) between the Reverse of 1938 and the Reverse of 1940 issues.

The variety showcased by Chell-Frost is today referred to as the 1939 Doubled Die reverse, Breen-2665, FS-05-1939-801, and in the Red Book, "Doubled MONTICELLO and FIVE CENTS." This die was made by double-impressing the master hub into a working die, the second impression being off-register. This variety is a doubling of the Reverse of 1939, with strong steps, thus precluding the possibility that it is a 1939 hub punched over an 1939 hub. Some other dies exist with slight doubling (notably the collectible FS-05-1939-802), but none as dramatic as this.

In August 1984, Bernard Nagengast wrote to me about the 1939 Doubled Die:

This variety was discovered in the early 1940s in New York City by subway token collectors, and a copy of a letter from one of them [L. Friedman] is enclosed. Incidentally, I had an opportunity to purchase a number of circulated Doubled Die reverse (Variety 1) pieces from a retired New York subway man recently. He said, "Everybody was looking for them at the time—this must have been like the 1955 Doubled Die cent craze!"

Because the variety was discovered a few years after issue, Uncirculated specimens are quite rare. I have seen personally, or know of about 12 pieces in various Uncirculated gradations, four of which were found by a collector in an Uncirculated roll of 1939 nickels which he examined in 1980. I would estimate that fewer than 50 Uncirculated coins exist.

The letter from Louis Friedman, dated July 23, 1979, which had been published in *Coin World*, noted that from 1937 to 1946 he had worked as a subway token taker and had searched for rare and interesting coins, most notably 1942/1 dimes, but also 1939 Doubled Die nickels. About 35 other subway men were also in the coin-finding game and were said to have comprised about 25% of the advertisers in *The Numismatist* and the *Numismatic Scrapbook Magazine*. Max L. Kaplan and Herbert Tobias went on to become prominent in the profession, Morris Moscow less so, and the others all profited to an extent. As to the curious 1939 nickels, Friedman reported that over a long period of years he found about 500 total, in grades from Very Good to AU.

As to my own experience, I have always found the 1939 Doubled Die nickel to be fascinating and, in fact, illustrated it in the first book I ever wrote, *Coins and Collectors*, 1964. In the 1950s I had called on Malcolm O.E. Chell-Frost to discuss this variety and, in general, to interview him as an old timer—an interest then and an interest now. After discovering the variety in the summer of 1939 he set about looking for them, and by 1941 had found about 20 coins. His pursuit continued. Mint State coins were viewed as being exceedingly rare, even in early times. In my own search for them I found this to be true. However, in the 4th edition of the *Cherrypickers' Guide*, Bill Fivaz and J.T. Stanton comment, "several Mint State rolls have come on the market in recent years."

THE NICKEL GOES TO WAR

In 1942, the first full year of World War II, nickel was in demand for strategic and military use. It was decided to eliminate it from the five-cent piece, so as to free up more supplies. Public Law 507, of March 27, 1942, made the necessary provision to do this, suggesting that future coins were to be 50 percent silver and 50 percent copper, but that the director of the Mint could "vary the proportions of silver and copper and add other metals of such as would be in the public interest."

The Numismatist, April 1942, revealed that not all was going according to plan:

> According to reports in the daily press, the proposition to save 435 tons of nickel and copper, through the substitution of silver in our 5-cent piece, has been stymied because of technical considerations. The factor which is operating against the use of nickel substitutes in vending machines, slot machines, and the host of other mechanically operated coin machines is based upon the magnetic failure of silver, and the fact that many of these mechanisms are operated on a scales system, which tests the weight of each coin, and all of these would have to be readjusted if not manufactured specially.
>
> At the present time, numismatists will be interested to know that silver is less valuable than nickel. Nickel can do work which silver cannot. For example, the nickel which goes into our coinage can be redirected into channels which will supply adequate metal to harden the steel for 1,000 heavy tanks. This task cannot be relegated to any other metal. Some weeks ago reports were rife that the Mint might indicate the changed alloy in our coinage (since changed designs for the nickel are contrary to law until about 1963) by the addition of a star. We hope, however, that the well-established Mint precedent of the use of arrows at the sides of the date will not be abandoned, as the arrows were indicators of a changed coinage, which did not vary in design otherwise. In many ways it would be desirable to continue an old mint practice which commenced in 1853.

As noted above, certain coin-operated machines had detectors that measured the approximate electrical resistance of the standard alloy (75 percent copper and 25 percent nickel). The Mint conducted experiments to devise a nickel-less alloy that could be used in such devices, without the coins being rejected as counterfeit. Some thought was given to reviving the silver half dime, and Chief Engraver John R. Sinnock prepared some sketches, including those which closely resemble the obverse of his later 1948 Franklin half dollar.

More on the subject appeared in *The Numismatist*, July 1942. What had been envisioned as a simple change was becoming more complicated:

> According to a press dispatch from Washington in the *Philadelphia Record*, the new nickel will not contain silver at all and electrolytic manganese will be substituted. The dispatch says:
>
> "The Treasury recently was on the verge of coining a new nickel without any nickel in it when Congressman Charles Dewey, of Chicago, stepped in and pointed out that the new nickel could not be used in the New York subway turnstiles, nor in thousands of slot machines which sell refreshments in factories and elsewhere. Behind all this is the fact that nickel is one of the scarcest of defense metals; so the government had decided the new 5-cent piece should not be made of nickel at all, but of 50 per cent copper and 50 per cent silver.
>
> "But suddenly Congressman Dewey discovered that it is not entirely the weight or size of the 5-cent piece which moves turnstiles or slot machines, but a magnetism coming from the quantity of nickel in the coin. Copper and silver, it was found, would not set off the mechanism. So the Mint suddenly held up making the new coins. Since then it has been discovered that electrolytic manganese, not a critical war material, can be used to supply the magnetism, and it will be used instead of nickel. So the new 5-cent piece will function in slot machines and subway turnstiles after all."

After many tests it was found that an alloy of 56% copper, 35% silver, and 9% manganese filled the bill, and the "nickel" five-cent piece could continue to be made, although now its nickname would be inappropriate (which did not matter).

To distinguish coins of the new alloy, the mintmark position was moved from the right side of the Monticello building, greatly enlarged, and placed over the dome. For the first time a P mintmark was used to designate Philadelphia. This was done with foresight, anticipating the time when the Treasury would be redeeming worn nickels and melting them. By viewing incoming coins reverse-up, those of the special alloy could be easily sorted out from regular ones.

Production of regular-alloy nickels took place at the Philadelphia and Denver mints through the end of the summer. On October 8, 1942, the silver-content began to be used, after which, through the end of the year, the Philadelphia and San Francisco mint produced the new coins. The wartime silver alloy was continued in use past the end of World War II, until December 1945. From 1943 through 1945, coinage was effected at all three mints.

The coins of this alloy were especially beautiful when first struck, exhibiting a dazzling silver brilliance. Also, the striking of the details was sharper. However, after the coins had been in circulation for a time they tended to become dull gray and stained, quite unattractive (the same thing happened to the zinc-coated Lincoln cents of 1943). In 1946 the regular alloy was resumed, and it has been continued ever since.

In an insightful article in *The Numismatist* in 2000, Mark A. Benvenuto, a chemistry professor, provided data suggesting that about 827,163 pounds of nickel metal might have been saved by the alloy switch, but "statistically, this figure is pretty insignificant" in view of about 300 *million* pounds of nickel produced annually during World War II, about 60% of which was available for use of the Allies. Further:

> If the savings afforded by changing the composition of the 5-cent piece was so minimal, why did the Mint even bother? My theory is that the action was intended simply to be a morale booster. Every time John Q. Public saw the enlarged mintmark atop Monticello, he knew that even the United States Mint was doing its part for the war effort. . . .
>
> Although no official records corroborate (or discredit) this theory, contemporary figures for worldwide nickel production tend to support it. It appears the United States was in little danger of running out of nickel for coins or the manufacture of steel. It also would seem that the Mint was willing and able to do its duty by doing without.[9]

In the meantime, after 1942 no Proof coins were minted. It was not until 1950 that collectors could again order such coins from the Mint.

The 1950-D Nickel Scramble

The most famous of all Jefferson nickel "rarities" is the 1950-D. Indeed, this is the most famous Jefferson nickel, rare or otherwise. More excitement, more hoopla has surrounded this particular coin than any other in the series. Today, the curtain has fallen on the 1950-D, the press agents have turned elsewhere, and it is generally ignored, sort of like Mount Baker in the 21st century. Now and then its low mintage figure of 2,630,030 attracts the attention of readers of the Red Book and other popular references.

In early 1951, when Mint reports seemed to indicate that a very rare nickel had been produced at the Denver Mint the year before, a wild scramble ensued. A few banks still had undistributed supplies, especially in the Midwest. Some energetic numismatists, most notably A.J. Mitula of Texas, succeeded in finding large quantities. Two collectors struck it rich, sort of, and drove around the Midwest unloading $2 rolls at $5 to $7, the last being the going price in May and June 1951.

It was difficult *not* to get excited about the 1950-Ds. I remember buying rolls for $15, the lowest price for me, and wondering where the rise would end. During the mid and late 1950s there was a strong and growing interest in investment in bank-wrapped rolls of coins. These were simply traded as "BU" (Brilliant Uncirculated), with no thought at all as to whether the coins were nicked all over or were gems. Most rolls remained unopened as they passed from seller to buyer to seller again.

In 1960 the coin market went into overdrive. The reasons for this have been well documented, but can be mainly laid at the doorstep of *Coin World*, founded in April of that year, and soon a sensation as the only *weekly* coin publication (*Numismatic News* was then a monthly, and the *Coin Dealer Newsletter* did not hatch until 1963). At the same time, at the Philadelphia Mint the Die Department turned out a small batch of Lincoln cent dies with the date 1960 in small numerals, in addition to scads of "regular" dies with large numerals. Notice of these was published in *Coin World* and elsewhere, everybody and his brother just had to own some, and before you knew it, a $50 bag of bank-wrapped rolls was selling for over $10,000, then over $12,000! *Time* magazine picked up the story, newspapers did likewise, and television hosts were excited, too. Several dealers specialized in the 1960 Small Date cents, most prominently Jonah Shapiro in Syracuse, NY, and

Harry Forman in Philadelphia. Soon the passion for 1960 Small Dates calmed, but those who dipped their toes in numismatic waters stayed to look around at other investment opportunities. Front row center was the 1950-D nickel, what with so few minted. It was bound to be *the* rarity of the future. The price went up and up, to over $1,200 per roll by 1964. Then the market ran out of steam, investors in the hottest items in the market fled, and, over a period of time, this pet nickel dropped to about $300 per roll. In the meantime, most dealers, aware of market fads, had lowered or eliminated their inventories. With his profits A.J. Mitula maintained a summer place in Cascade, Colorado, on the slopes of Pikes Peak. He was fond of calling it "the house that 1950-D nickels built." In the 1970s and 1980s, when I taught classes at the ANA Summer Seminar, a day was devoted to a field trip to Cripple Creek. On the way our tour bus would slow as we passed Mitula's log-cabin style place, and the story would be told. Walter Breen in his 1988 *Encyclopedia* noted, "One Milwaukee dealer had 8,000 rolls = 160,000 pieces, all Uncirculated," a cache now dispersed if the dealer was sharp.

The 1950-D nickel indeed proved to be rare—in *circulation*. Today worn pieces are seen far less often than are Uncirculated coins.

Continuing Events

In 1950 the coinage of Proofs was resumed by the Philadelphia Mint. Coins were sold only in sets of five, from the cent to the half dollar, for $2.10 per set. In San Francisco a few years later the 1954-S/D overmintmark Jefferson nickel was created, but no numismatists were aware of it at the time. The San Francisco Mint, which had been in operation since 1854 and which had struck nickel five-cent pieces for most years since 1912, stopped producing coins in 1955. It was announced that the facility would thereafter be used for storage and other purposes. There was a great investment rush to acquire quantities of the final S-mint coins, the cents and dimes being the only values made in 1955. In the meantime, 10 or more Jefferson nickel reverse dies with useless S mintmarks were overpunched with D mintmarks, creating the 1955-D/S, made at the Denver Mint.

In 1964, Eva Adams, director of the Mint, was distressed by a nationwide passion for hoarding modern coins as soon as they reached circulation, a fad stimulated by the new Kennedy half dollar, but extending to other denominations as well. She blamed coin collectors and decided to punish them collectively by no longer putting mintmarks on Denver coins and by stopping the mintage of Proofs. Numismatists reacted angrily, as they were involved only peripherally in the accumulation of modern coins. Later, Ms. Adams "got religion" and even started attending ANA conventions! Still later, she ran for office as an ANA governor and also became a member of the Numismatic Literary Guild. By this time she was no longer director of the Mint. Collectors are of a forgiving nature, and Ms. Adams was warmly welcomed.

If you are looking at certain nickels from this era and ask, "When were they struck," the date on the coins may not be of much help. Late in 1965, Assistant Secretary of the Treasury Robert A. Wallace announced that nickels made throughout the year had been dated 1964, but beginning on December 29, 1965, the 1965 date would be used (with only three days remaining in the year) and would be continued in use in 1966![10]

In the meantime, Special Mint Sets (SMS) of coins were struck at the *San Francisco Mint*, from 1965 through 1967, from polished dies and with care. No S mintmark was on the dies, part of the aforementioned punishment to rascally numismatists. SMS coins of 1965 are somewhat satiny, while those of 1966 and 1967 generally resemble Proofs.

In 1966 a change was made by adding the letters FS, the first and last initials of Felix O. Schlag, on the obverse of the coin. Agitation by *Coin World* and by columnist Mort Reed was largely responsible for this long-overdue recognition of Schlag's 1938 accomplishment. The artist, however, stated that he would have preferred use of his full initials, FOS. This can be considered to be a new type for collecting purposes, just as the 1909 V.D.B. cent is considered a separate type.

In 1968 the mintmark position was moved to the obverse below the date. In the same year the Mint resumed making Proofs for collectors, but at the San Francisco Mint rather than Philadelphia, as earlier. The San Francisco Mint, once considered to be closed for coinage forever, was reactivated for limited regular coin striking and special issues such as Proofs and commemoratives.

After the use of silver in circulating dimes, quarters, and half dollars was discontinued, the price of silver metal rose on international markets. In the 1970s there was a great "silver rush," as vast quantities of worn silver coins were melted into bullion. Silver-content nickels of the 1942 through 1945 years, most of which were worn and unattractive when found in circulation, were melted in large quantities as well. This was not much of a loss to the numismatic community, as Mint State coins continued to be preserved and were and still are plentiful. However, anyone looking through pocket change in the 1980s to find Jefferson nickels was apt to find very few of the silver-content coins.

Later Hub Modifications

The Reverse of 1940 hub continued to be used through 1967 and was modified very slightly in the period 1968 to 1970. The hubs and masters experienced wear and deteriorated, resulting in lessening of definition, especially evident on the steps of Monticello. Numismatic considerations regarding steps are discussed separately below.

The Reverse of 1971, a modification was used through 1976, now with sharp, thin steps. When seen, the steps are often well defined. However, on some strikings they are absent. This reverse was used into 1982, with later years having less definition than earlier ones.

On all the dies for circulation strikes and Proofs of 1957 and 1958 the star between LIBERTY and the date is larger and stronger. After 1958, the star is smaller, similar to that used in 1956 and earlier. No reason for this short-lived modification has been found.

For circulation strike Jefferson nickels of the next decade, Bernard Nagengast says this:

> Many of the P and D mint issues of 1960 through 1967 show five steps at the right side of Monticello, but the steps will not connect to the left side of the *stairs*. This is unlike previous issues which almost always have connected steps at each side, the missing area being below the second pillar from the right. By now, the master hub is showing extreme wear, and the steps are usually shallow. Six step coins probably do not exist for most dates, except on Proofs.

The Reverse of 1982 was the next modification, with sharper steps. In 1987 the hair of Jefferson and the details of Monticello were strengthened, after which 6 Full Steps coins became more available, indeed common on many issues. In 1991 and again in 1993 the details of Jefferson's hair were strengthened.

Modern mint technology increased the average life of a nickel five-cent die to over 300,000 impressions by the 1980s, but many numismatists would be quick to say that this was at the expense of quality and eye appeal. Current striking pressure is about 55 tons, and a pair of dies can stamp out about 120 nickels per minute.

THE WESTWARD JOURNEY DESIGNS

By 2003 the Jefferson nickel with portrait obverse and Monticello reverse had been minted continuously for well over 60 years. The basic design had remained the same, with a few modifications along the way, and the addition of the FS initials in 1966.

Now, in the early 21st century, under the administration of Mint Director Henrietta Holsman Fore, the Mint envisioned other possibilities for the five-cent piece. By this time the Mint had earned high marks from collectors and the public for its panorama of state-reverse quarter dollars, five designs per year produced since 1999, and for its other programs, including commemoratives, special Proof coins (such as silver strikings of dimes, quarters, and half dollars), and other products.

The time was ripe for a change. The 1803 Louisiana Purchase, orchestrated by President Thomas Jefferson, added vast territory to the American West. The Lewis and Clark expedition was organized to depart from St. Louis in 1804, travel up the Missouri River, and report on what they saw in the newly acquired district. The American 5-Cent Coin Continuity Act of 2003 provided for five special reverses to be used on Jefferson nickels in 2004, 2005, and 2006, to observe the bicentennial of the Lewis and Clark travels. In some publicity, these were referred to as the "Westward Journey Nickel Series." This name sparked interest, and later it was widely used in Mint literature and offerings.

In 1904 the same travels by Meriwether Lewis and William Clark were memorialized by the Louisiana Purchase Exposition, popularly known as the St. Louis World's Fair, and through commemorative gold dollars dated 1903. In 2000 the Sacagawea "golden dollar" was related to the same exploration.

The Peace Medal Reverse of 2004

The first of the new nickel motifs to be released featured the standard Jefferson obverse by Felix Schlag paired with a reverse copied by Mint engraver Norman E. Nemeth from the design of an Indian peace medal of 1801, featuring a tomahawk, peace pipe, and clasped hands.

The new Peace Medal nickels were first publicly distributed on March 14, 2004, at the Three Flags Ceremony on the shore of the Mississippi River at the St. Louis Arch (Jefferson National Expansion Memorial). An estimated 10,000 people attended. Each child age 12 and younger received a free nickel, while others could buy them for face value, limit $500 face value per person. However, it seemed that the $50,000 stock on had was in danger of running out too soon, so the limit was lowered to $200 face value, then to $20. By three in the afternoon, all were gone, save for a small reserve held back for the kids.[11]

Before production was halted in June, the Philadelphia Mint struck about 361,440,000 and the Denver Mint made 372,000,000 of the coins. Where they all went is a minor mystery, for they have not been plentiful in circulation since. No doubt there novelty value intervened, and most are preserved as souvenirs.

Regarding the original peace medal, sometimes this is attributed to Robert Scot, engraver at the Mint at the time. However, John Reich is also a possibility, likely a better candidate.[12] The medals were ready by the end of 1801. Reich, born Johann Matthias Reich in Fürth, Germany in 1768, came from Hamburg to America on board the *Anna*, arriving in Philadelphia in August 1800, after which time he was indentured for a year to a Philadelphia coppersmith. He was released from that covenant through he efforts of Henry Voigt, chief coiner at the Mint, suggesting that Reich may have been put to work on projects there. In March 1807 Reich was hired full-time as an assistant engraver. Members of the expedition took Jefferson-portrait medals as well as three varieties of Washington "Seasons" medals, the last struck in Birmingham, England, from dies by the exceptionally talented Conrad Küchler, whose artistry on American-related items bids fair to challenge the work of the later Charles Cushing Wright. If the U.S. Mint *really* wants to cause a stir with collectors, they could resurrect some of these Seasons designs, namely *The Home*, *The Farmer*, and *The Shepherd*, the elegance of which is nowhere matched elsewhere in the Indian peace medal series.

The Keelboat Reverse of 2004
The second reverse motif in the Westward Journey Nickel Series features a design depicting the largest of three boats used on inland rivers by the Lewis and Clark expedition of 1804 to 1806. The keelboat is shown with a fully billowed sail. The two explorers are shown in the bow with a crew standing behind, many manning poles to push the boat. The original design was by Alfred F. Maletsky, who retired from the Mint's Engraving Department on December 31, 2003. Maletsky also created dies for several varieties of state-reverse quarter dollars. The new nickels were officially released on August 2, 2004. Ceremonies were held in Nebraska and Iowa on August 3 and 20 to publicize the new nickels.[13]

The Artistic Infusion Program
In 2003, Mint Director Henrietta Holsman Fore and her staff created the Artistic Infusion Program. The intent was to improve the artistry of motifs on coins and medals produced by the Mint. In recent times there had been stinging criticisms of the quality of art on certain of the state quarters issued since 1999.[14]

On November 20, 2003, the Mint announced a "Call for Artists," inviting professional as well as student artists to apply, with the deadline set as January 9, 2004. As many as 20 "master" designers and 20 students or "associate" designers were to be chosen. On the Internet, thousands of responses were received, resulting in 306 formal applications. Staffers of the Mint and officials of the National Endowment for the Arts (NEA) made the final selections. The judges selected 18 master designers and six associates:

> **Master designers:** Leonard E. Buckley, Damascus, MD, former bank note designer with the Bureau of Engraving and Printing, now doing watercolor painting and calligraphy. • Stephen M. Clark, Post Falls, ID, wildlife painter, freelance designer and medallic sculptor. • Thomas S. Cleveland, Houston, TX, commercial graphic designer. • Charles Danek, Los Angeles, CA, photographic producer. • Joe Fitzgerald, Silver Spring, MD, computer graphics, woodcuts, pastels and oil paintings. • Jamie N. Franki, Concord, NC, illustrator, associate professor, University of North Carolina, Charlotte. • Sharon Fullingim, Socorro, NM, sculptor in bronze, limestone and marble. • Susan Gamble, Tinker Air Force Base, OK., graphic designer and illustrator. • Howard Koslow, Toms River, NJ, painter and illustrator. • Bill Krawczewicz, Sevema Park, MD, bank note designer, currently with Bureau of Engraving and Printing, designer of U.S. commemorative coins and the

Maryland state quarter dollar. • Justin Kunz, Sandy, UT, contemporary realist painter and graphic designer. • Michael Leidel, Marietta, GA graphic designer, acrylic and oil painter. • Richard Masters, Appleton, Wis., illustrator, associate professor, University of Wisconsin, Oshkosh. • Erik Must, Lakewood, NJ, illustrator. • John Nordyke, West Hartford, CT, graphic designer, assistant professor, University of Hartford. • Garland "Neal" Taylor, Durant, OK, western and historical illustrator in oils and sculpture. • Joanne C. Wasserman, Silver Spring, MD, commercial designer and calligrapher. • Mary Beth Zeitz, Marlton, NJ, graphic designer and illustrator.

Associate designers: Rebecca Armstrong, illustration major, Virginia Commonwealth University. • Analee Kasudia, graphic design major, Columbia College, Chicago, IL • Joseph LiCalzi, bas-relief study, Fleischer Art Memorial, the Frank Gasparro Studio, Philadelphia, PA. • Amy Mortensen, photographic illustration major, University of Connecticut, Storrs, CT. • Patrick J. Quill, marketing and art studio double major, University of Notre Dame. • Georgina Smigen-Rothkopf, painting, drawing and illustration, the School of Art Institute of Chicago.

Finalists were invited to create at least one new design each year for a coin or medal. Master designers were to receive an honorarium of $1,000 for each submission, while the payment to associate designers was set at $500. Any designs chosen for use on a coin or medal would be modeled by the engraving staff at the Mint.

The initials of the designer will appear on the left side of a coin or medal, and the initials of the Mint sculptor-engraver will appear on the right. In instances in which a Mint engraver is also the designer, only one set of initials will appear, and at the right.[15]

The Great Design Competition for the 2005 Nickels

Visitors to the 2004 ANA Convention held in Pittsburgh were treated to a virtual art gallery set up by the U.S. Mint, featuring sketches and proposals for obverse and reverse designs for new nickel five-cent pieces. A spread of these sketches, with titles, accompanies the present text, courtesy of the U.S. Mint.

The search for public input, which began in a large way with the Statehood Reverse series of Washington quarters, has created a coinage truly by the people, for the people, a dynamic program which at once has delighted numismatists and has brought extensive profit to the Mint—a win-win situation. The proposed designs for 2005 nickels were from artists participating in the Artistic Infusion Program as well as Mint staff sculptor-engravers.

In an August 17, 2005, interview with Paul Gilkes of *Coin World,* former Mint Director Henrietta Holsman Fore reflected on her administration, which extended from August 2001 through July 2005.[16] Included were her remarks about nickels:

> The redesign of the nickels has an historical significance. It's made a lot of Americans look over their coins and think about their nation and the history of the United States in the 1800s. When Americans think about history, it is an addition to their lives. It certainly reconnects them with their country. I've found the nickel series to be educational, interesting and historical.
>
> We also launched the Artistic Infusion Program with those new nickels and the results are we have some designs that will stand the test of time.

GALLERY OF 2005 NICKEL DESIGN PROPOSALS

Mint and Artistic Infusion Program staff contributed many designs for consideration for use on the obverse and reverse of the 2005 Jefferson nickel. Certain of the motifs are shown here with the creator of each and its title. (All illustrations courtesy of the United States Mint)

Leonard E. Buckley "Jefferson Classic"

Richard Masters "Jefferson—Close Up"

Joe Fitzgerald "Jefferson—Houdon"

Joe Fitzgerald "Jefferson—Close Up With Handwritten 'Liberty'"

Joe Fitzgerald "Jefferson—Peale Portrait"

Joanne C. Wasserman "Jefferson—Design E"

Justin Kunz "Jefferson Portrait 3/4 View With Chin Up"

Charles Danek "Jefferson 2"

Richard Masters "Jefferson—Classic Profile"

Don Everhart "Gilbert Stuart Jefferson Facing West"

Donna Weaver "Jefferson After Rembrandt Peale"

Donna Weaver "Jefferson After Houdon 3/4 with 17 Stars"

John Mercanti "3/4 Jefferson Portrait Facing West"

Don Everhart "Houdon Jefferson Facing Right"

Don Everhart "Houdon Jefferson Looking Up"

Mary Beth Zeitz "Salmon With Mountains"

Mary Beth Zeitz
"Flying Eagle"

Mary Beth Zeitz
"Peace Pipes"

Mary Beth Zeitz
"Teepee With Corn"

Mary Beth Zeitz
"Helpful Indian With
Herb Border"

**Joseph N.
LiCalzi** "Beaverhead
Rock"

Jamie N. Franki
"Chinook Salmon"

Mary Beth Zeitz
"Eagle Head"

**Joseph N.
LiCalzi** "Friendship /
Peace Pipe"

**Joseph N.
LiCalzi** "Jumping
Salmon"

**William J.
Krawczewicz**
"Eagle With Peace Pipe
and Laurel Branch"

**William J.
Krawczewicz**
"Bear Claw Necklace"

Jamie N. Franki
"Corn"

**William J.
Krawczewicz**
"Eagle With Peace
Pipe"

**William J.
Krawczewicz**
"Petroglyph"

Jamie N. Franki
"Grazing Buffalo"

Howard Koslow
"Plains Indians,
Peace, and Security"

Garland Neal Taylor "The Native Americans' Gifts"

Garland Neal Taylor "The Sacred Eagle"

Howard Koslow "Mandan Village, Peace, and Friendship"

Rebecca Armstrong "Peace Pipe"

Georgina Smi-gen-Rothkopf "Peace Pipe, Corn, and Mountains"

John Nordyke "Feather/Guidance"

Stephen Clark "Pacific Salmon"

Stephen Clark "Buffalo Skull"

Amy Mortensen "Bear Claw Necklace and Bear Track"

Eric Must "Peaceful Hands to the Gateway of the West"

Michael Leidel "Indian Corn"

Michael Leidel "Calumet"

John Nordyke "Grace/Horse"

Michael Leidel "Staples"

John Mercanti "Feathers and Bear Claw Necklace"

John Mercanti "Prairie Dog, Feathers, and Bear Claw Necklace"

Donna Weaver
"Feathers"

Thomas Scott Cleveland "From Sea to Shining Sea / Sextant and Mountains"

Thomas Scott Cleveland "Charging Buffalo"

Sharon Fullingim
"Blacktail Prairie Dogs"

Susan Gamble
"Circle of Life With Buffalo Skull With 'American Indian' Inscription"

Georgina Smigen-Rothkopf "Corps of Discovery 1804–1806"

Patrick Quill
"The Grizzly Bear"

Sharon Fullingim
"Curious Grizzly"

Stephen Clark
"Standing Grizzly"

Stephen Clark
"Pronghorn Antelope"

John Nordyke
"Magpie/Return"

Susan Gamble
"Horizon: Sunset With Canoe"

Susan Gamble
"Explorers: Lewis and Clark and Sacagawea on Coast"

Howard Koslow
"Western Grandeur and Nature"

Joe Fitzgerald
"Culmination—Joy"

Joe Fitzgerald
"Culmination—Liberty"

Joseph N. LiCalzi "Growling Bear"

Joseph N. LiCalzi "Lewis and Clark Compass With Salmonberry Tree"

Jamie N. Franki "Grizzly Bear"

Richard Masters "Grizzly Bear"

Jamie Franki "Route of Lewis and Clark"

Joanne C. Wasserman "Scene of Black Cottonwood Trees"

Garland Neal Taylor "The Pacific Goal"

Justin Kunz "Pronghorn Antelope Head"

Donna Weaver "Eagle 2"

Don Everhart "Antelope"

Don Everhart "Eagle With Compass"

Don Everhart "Culmination of Journey"

Donna Weaver "Culmination of Journey"

Donna Weaver "Eagle 1"

Changes of 2005

A revised portrait of Jefferson, with a closely cropped profile to the right, made its debut on the obverse of the 2005 nickel and was used that year in combination with two new reverses. The image, based on the Houdon bust, but revised to show Jefferson as he might have appeared to Meriwether Lewis and William Clark in the era of their expedition, was created by Joe Fitzgerald. The Silver Spring, Maryland artist and graphics designer is a member of the Artistic Infusion Program. Jefferson is to the left, with the date and inscriptions to the right, including *Liberty* reproduced in the president's cursive handwriting. Originally, *Liberty* was in lower case, but at the suggestion of the Mint, the artist gave it an upper case L. Mint sculptor engraver Don Everhart did the model.

The first reverse used on 2005 nickels, titled "American Bison," featured this famous animal of the plains, facing right, as drawn by North Carolina art professor Jamie N. Franki, also a member of the artistic infusion program, and modified by Mint sculptor engraver Norman E. Nemeth. On the final version by Nemeth, the bison was made smaller and was centered on the coin. FIVE / CENTS, originally in two lines under the bison, was moved to the bottom border in an arc. UNITED STATES OF AMERICA was placed at the tom border, and E / PLURIBUS / UNUM was given three lines below the bison.

To create the bison Franki drew inspiration from James Earle Fraser's 1913 nickel design as well as other investigations. Franki signed his JNF, to prevent confusion with the JF initials used by Joe Fitzgerald on the obverse. The first coins were released at noon, February 28, 2005. A special ceremony inaugurating the nickel was held in the Upper Senate Park in Washington, DC on the next day. Mint Director Henrietta Fore was on hand, accompanied by Cody (a 2,000-pound American bison), U.S. Treasurer Anna Escobedo Cabral and other human dignitaries, and an estimated five thousand or more attendees. The Adams National Bank, armed with a supply of $100,000 face value of the new coins, passed out $56,000 worth at a kiosk in nearby Union Station by late afternoon. There was no limited placed. One collector bought 52 boxes, each with $100 face value, totaling 104,000 coins.[17]

Perhaps attracting the greatest admiration from numismatists was the Ocean in View, the second reverse of 2005, by Joe Fitzgerald, who created the obverse motif this year.

The journal of Captain William Clark recorded this on November 7, 1805, as the expedition crossed the Columbia River about 20 miles from sea:

> Great joy in camp we are in *View* of the *Ocian*, this great Pacific Ocian which we been So long anxious to See. and the roreing or noise made by the waves breaking on the rockey Shores (as I Suppose) may be heard distictly. *Ocian in View!* O! the joy.[18]

Clark's emotions were translated by Fitzgerald into a sketch, "Culmination—Joy!" which became the essence of the reverse of an 2005 quarter, with *Ocian* appearing on the coin as *Ocean*, a revision made by the Mint. The artist suggested that the original *Ocian* would have been more historical and educational. However, Mint spokeswoman Becky Bailey stated, "We didn't want to confuse anyone into thinking we couldn't spell."[19] This was the fourth and last of the four distinctive Westward Journey series reverses of 2004 and 2005, representing the arrival of the Corps of Discovery at the Pacific Coast.

Rolls, bags, and other quantities of the new Ocean in View nickels went on sale on August 1, 2005. A special launch ceremony began at 10:00 a.m. on Friday, August 5, 2005, at Cape Disappointment State Park in the state of Washington, with a vista of the Pacific. Adults could buy nickels for face value, and children under 18 were each given a free sample. U.S. Mint Deputy Director David Lebryk was the ranking Treasury Department official on hand. Lebryk had been in the post only since August 2, taking the place of recently resigned Mint Director Henrietta Holsman Fore.

Somewhat after the fact, on September 8, 2005, the U.S. Mint included this in a news release:

> The United States Mint is crediting a photograph by Andrew E. Cier of Astoria, Oregon, as a basis for artist Joe Fitzgerald's image on the reverse of the 2005 Ocean in View nickel. Cier, a professional photographer, took this photograph of a rocky, western coast line. He said the image captured what Captain William Clark might have seen upon reaching western waters. The United States Mint will include attribution to Mr. Cier's photograph in its future materials about the new nickel and will note Mr. Cier's contribution to the design in its historical archives. . . .

The Ocean in View nickel was widely admired, and many collectors considered it to be the high point in the recent new designs.

Changes of 2006

On July 28, 2005, at the American Numismatic Association annual convention, held this year in San Francisco, long-time Mint spokesman Michael White issued this release:

> The United States Mint announced today that the 1938 classic rendition of President Thomas Jefferson's Virginia home of Monticello by Felix Schlag will return to the reverse of the Nation's 2006 nickel. However, the design will be crisper and more detailed than Americans have seen it in recent years, having been carefully restored by United States Mint Sculptor-Engraver John Mercanti, using Schlag's original artwork. Over more than 65 years of production, the United States Mint had slightly modified the design for technical reasons, such as die life extension. But now the Nation's five-cent coin will display more of Schlag's artistry.
>
> "Numismatists who examine the new 2006 nickel carefully will see an image that is now closer to the detail that Schlag intended," said United States Mint associate director for sales and marketing, Gloria Eskridge. . . .
>
> "I strengthened the architecture of the image and re-established elements that reflect the original Schlag model," explained Sculptor-Engraver Mercanti. "For instance, the facets of the dome of Monticello had just disappeared on the nickel over the years. They are back now."
>
> Among the changes discussed by Ms. Eskridge and Mr. Mercanti were: Facets of the dome of Monticello have been restored. The balconies of the building have been reworked. *The* detail around the door and windows has been incised and restored.

The 2006 nickel, "Return to Monticello," is the last in the United States Mint's Westward Journey Nickel Series™ and signifies both the return of the Lewis & Clark Expedition from its 8,000 mile journey and the return of the nation's nickel to the reverse design of Monticello. . . .

John Mercanti, sculptor-engraver of the U.S. Mint, at a press conference held by associate marketing director Gloria Eskridge and staff at the American Numismatic Association convention in San Francisco, July 28, 2005. Details of the modified reverse of the "Return to Monticello" nickel were revealed and discussed. (Donn Pearlman photograph)

The obverse of the 2006 nickel features a new image of Thomas Jefferson, by Jamie N. Franki, who designed the 2005 obverse. The new version features Jefferson facing nearly forward, called "Jefferson, 1800" by the Mint, and is based on an 1800 painting by Rembrandt Peale. Mint sculptor engraver Donna Weaver created the model from Franki's concept.

The 2006 nickels were released into circulation on Thursday, January 12, 2006.

CHAPTER EIGHT

JEFFERSON NICKELS 1938 TO DATE
GUIDE TO COLLECTING

GRADING STANDARDS AND INTERPRETATIONS

As a prelude to the collecting of Jefferson nickels, the standard below are given. While they and any other standards are subject to interpretation, those propounded by the American Numismatic Association are the most widely used in the marketplace, including by all of the leading grading services.

OFFICIAL ANA GRADING STANDARDS:
JEFFERSON NICKELS 1938–2003

These grade descriptions are based on average strikes, but coins often have weaknesses other than those specifically mentioned. Coins with "Full Details" are exceptional and deserve special commentary. Examples include Standing Liberty quarters with Full Head details, Franklin half dollars with Full Bell Lines, Winged Liberty ("Mercury") dimes with Full Bands, and Jefferson nickels with Full Steps. Exceptional Liberty Walking half dollars and early gold coins also exist with Full Details. Jefferson nickels are frequently seen weakly struck and with the horizontal step lines joined, even on Uncirculated coins. Many 1950 and 1955 nickels are unevenly struck, with weak spots in the details. 1953-S and 1954-S coins were often struck from worn dies.[1]

Mint State (MS)
Coin is Uncirculated and shows absolutely no trace of wear.

MS-70 • A flawless coin exactly as it was minted, with no trace of wear or injury. Must have full mint luster or attractive light toning.

MS-67 • Virtually flawless, but with very minor imperfections.

MS-65 • No trace of wear; nearly as perfect as MS-67, except for some small weakness or blemish. Has full mint luster but may be unevenly toned, or lightly fingermarked. A few noticeable nicks or marks may be present.

MS-63 • A Mint State coin with attractive mint luster, but noticeable detracting contact marks or minor blemishes.

MS-60 • A strictly Uncirculated coin with no trace of wear, but with blemishes more obvious than for MS-63. May lack full mint luster, and surface may be dull or spotted.

About Uncirculated (AU)

Coin shows small traces of wear is visible on highest points.

AU-58 *(Very Choice)* • Has some signs of abrasion: cheekbone and high points of hair; collar; triangular roof above pillars. Shallow or weak spots in the relief, particularly in the steps below the pillars, are usually caused by improper striking (and not wear).

AU-55 *(Choice)* • OBVERSE: Only a trace of wear shows on cheekbone. REVERSE: A trace of wear shows on the beam above pillars. SURFACE: Most of the mint luster is still present.

AU-50 *(Typical)* • OBVERSE: Traces of wear show on cheekbone and high points of hair. REVERSE: Traces of wear show on the beam and triangular roof above pillars. SURFACE: About half of the mint luster is still present.

Extremely Fine (EF)

Coin shows very light wear on only the highest points.

EF-45 *(Choice)* • OBVERSE: Slight wear shows on cheekbone and central portion of hair. There is a trace of wear at bottom of the bust. REVERSE: High points of the triangular roof and beam are lightly worn. SURFACE: Traces of mint luster still show.

EF-40 *(Typical)* • OBVERSE: Hair is lightly worn but well defined and bold. Slight wear shows on cheekbone and bottom of bust. High points of hair are worn but show all details. REVERSE: Triangular roof and beam are worn but all details are visible.

Very Fine (VF)

Coin shows light to moderate even wear. All major features are sharp.

VF-30 *(Choice)* • OBVERSE: Hair is worn but shows nearly Full Details. Cheek line and bottom of bust are worn but sharp. REVERSE: Triangular roof and beam are worn nearly flat. Most of the pillar lines show plainly.

VF-20 *(Typical)* • OBVERSE: Cheek line shows considerable flatness. More than half the hair lines are clear. Parts of the details still show in the collar. REVERSE: Pillars are worn but clearly defined. Triangular roof is partially visible.

Fine

Coin shows moderate to heavy even wear, but it's entire design is clear and bold.

F-12 • OBVERSE: Some details show in hair around face. Cheek line and collar are plain but very weak. REVERSE: Some details are visible behind pillars. Triangular roof is very smooth and indistinct.

Very Good (VG)

Coin is well worn. Design is clear but flat and lacking details.

VG-8 • OBVERSE: Cheek line is visible but parts are worn smooth. Collar is weak but visible. Only a few hair lines show separations. REVERSE: Slight detail shows throughout the building. The arch is worn away. Pillars are weak but visible.

Good

Coin is heavily worn. Design and legend are visible, but faint in spots.

G-4 • OBVERSE: Entire design is well worn with very little detail remaining. Motto is weak and merged with rim. REVERSE: Building is nearly flat but is well outlined. Pillars are worn flat. Rim is worn to tops of letters.

About Good (AG)

Coin's design is only outlined. Parts of date and legend are worn smooth.

AG-3 • OBVERSE: Design is outlined, with nearly all details worn away. Date and legend are readable but very weak and merging into rim. REVERSE: Entire design is partially worn away. Rim is merged with the letters.

Nearly all of the lower range of this system is useless in the marketplace, as I doubt if anyone, not even a beginner with pocket change as a budget, would seek a Jefferson nickel in the lower grades. For 90% of the people who read this book, the descriptions below Mint State can be discarded.

INTRODUCTION TO JEFFERSON NICKELS

A Lot Is Going On!

Jefferson nickels, first minted in 1938, present a vast panorama of *opportunity* for anyone interested in pursuing the series. While at quick glance at popular reference guides, it seems to be rather simple—a string of dates and mintmarks—upon investigation it is fascinatingly complex.

Although I have bought, sold, and enjoyed Jefferson nickels for many years, during the preparation of this section of the book my knowledge advanced by leaps and bounds, surprising me as to how much I did *not* know! After spending many hours with Bernard Nagengast's *Jefferson Nickel Analyst*, the *Cherrypicker's Guide to Rare Die Varieties*, by Bill Fivaz and J.T. Stanton, issues of *The Portico* by the Full Step Nickel Club, and other references, I became very impressed.

It was quickly revealed that the nuances of varieties, striking, and the like, were almost beyond count, and that certain items that seem to be plentiful if not indeed common could be great rarities, or even unknown, with sharply struck features. Of course, I had known *some* of this before and, in fact, had written about it—but not in recent years. I was amazed as to the depth and breadth of the modern market and all of the material in print and on the Internet.

Some time ago, in December 1989, in *The Numismatist*, under "Major Jefferson Nickel Varieties, ANA Certification Service," Don Bonser made this meaningful comment:

> What comes to mind when you think of Jefferson nickels—a lifeless, 20th-century series? Something nobody collects or wants? This series of coins has long languished from the inattention of collectors and dealers.
>
> Some people have turned this lack of attention to their advantage: they collect and cherry-pick scarce and valuable Jefferson varieties! A small but active collector base exists for these coins, and looking for them can be as exciting as trying to find that 1909-S V.D.B. cent or 1916-D dime in circulation 30 years ago.

Step by Step

For nickels, most people equate *sharply struck* with the number of horizontal steps on the porch or portico of Monticello, that can be counted under magnification. The best coins of all are those with six steps, clearly defined, and without being connected. Second best are five steps.

Somewhat overlooked is the curious aspect that a coin can have six steps and be very pleasing, but can be lightly struck on the *obverse*, particularly on the shoulder of Jefferson, and that isn't noticed. Of course, such inconsistencies have counterparts in other numismatic series—such as "full head" Standing Liberty quarters from 1916 to 1930 that might have shield rivets weak or missing, and so on. I think it is desirable to look at *both* sides of a coin, and in all areas—not just the steps.

The Jefferson nickel was born through a popular competition, the details of which can be found in chapter 7, in which the winning artist was awarded a grand prize, but half of his design wasn't used! From then the Jefferson nickel went through many evolutions, including changes in the hubs and master dies, (but not in the main design), a switch to the silver-content alloy of World War II (which produced coins with gorgeous mint luster), the incredible 1950-D nickel, and more.

Along the way, most collectors simply acquired one of each date and mint, placing them in an album or holder and not paying much attention otherwise. Then arose a generation of dedicated specialists, equipped with magnifying glasses, who began studying the pieces carefully. Today we have a dynamic band of enthusiasts and a club to accommodate them, probably the only niche numismatic organization that has a name reflecting the sharpness of detail on a particular coin.

In 2004 the numismatic community was excited with new designs commemorating the Lewis and Clark Expedition, seemingly launching what beckons to be a panorama of interesting motifs in the future. Success builds upon success, and by 2004 the Mint enjoyed the profits, publicity and enthusiasm engendered by the state quarter program. Now, we all wait and see how the nickels evolve.

Becoming an Expert

I believe if you read the following pages carefully, especially when you contemplate buying or acquiring a particular variety, you will know as much from a historical aspect about these coins as just about anyone today, save details for some mintmark repunching and die doubling variations, to which I refer you to several excellent modern texts (in the entirety comprising hundreds of pages of information, and thus out of the realm of possibility for inclusion here).

Jefferson nickels are very egalitarian. A nice set in, say, MS-63 or MS-64 grade can be purchased very reasonably, for just a few hundred dollars as this book goes to press in 2005. On the other hand, if you aspire to acquire a complete collection from 1938 to date, in MS-65 or better grade, with five full steps as a minimum, six full steps when you can find them, get set to spend thousands of dollars and to dedicate a few years of your life!

Take the popular path and put together a basic set, or take the road less traveled and go for sharp strikes and die varieties—either way you will have a lot of fun.

Bernard Nagengast, whose research and writing efforts have created and defined much of what specialists refer to as an authoritative source today and whose comments are quoted *in extenso* in the following pages, contributed this comment for the present text:

Despite the disguise of a common coin, the Jefferson nickel can present a collecting challenge for a discriminating numismatist. Large quantities were struck, but often they were poorly made. Thus the challenge—looking through many examples to find that one eye appealing, fully struck coin! Wading through rolls of coins with ugly luster and mushy appearance can be frustrating, but with patience nice coins can be found for every date and mint. One of the greatest joys of collecting is that "Eureka" moment when a nice coin is discovered in a roll or a dealer's inventory!

INTERESTING VARIETIES

There are many interesting varieties in the Jefferson nickel series. These generally fit into the following categories:

- *Hub changes*—Sometimes, as with 1939 Proof nickels, an old-style hub was used for part of the production run, and a new-style hub was used for the later part. Such variations can be collected for several years in the series. Hub changes have not been widely studied outside of the realm of specialists, most certification services have ignored them in the past, and today there are many scarce combinations awaiting discovery, possibly by you. On the other hand, the demand for these is limited.

- *Overdate*—The 1943/2 was caused by using two master dies, each of a different date, on the same working die. Presumably, existing 1942 working dies were softened then repunched with 1943 working dies to make them useful in 1943.

- *Die doubling*—During the making of a working die, a master hub was slowly impressed into the working die blank by a powerful hydraulic press. The working die was then inspected, often heated to soften it, slowly cooled, then impressed again with the master hub to bring up more details, after which it was heated, then quenched to harden. During the second impression, and in a few instances a third impression, the master hub was slightly off-register, creating a doubling of features in *some* areas. The most dramatic is the 1939 Doubled Die (doubled MONTICELLO and FIVE CENTS) and the 1943 "Doubled Eye," the popularity of both being considerable due to their listing in the Red Book and their recognition on certified holders.

- *Mintmark differences*—Mintmarks were punched into working dies by hand. To do this, an engraver at the Philadelphia Mint selected an S, D, or P punch from many arranged in a small wooden box, with the tapered end of each punch facing upward. Generally, mintmarks used on nickels were identified as such, as were sometimes different-sized mintmarks for other denominations. Sometimes, the wrong punch was used, as with 1941-S, which occurs with small (normal for the nickel) and large mintmark (an anomalous mintmark not used elsewhere in the series) sizes. From one year to another, and over a long span, there are differences in the shape of some mintmarks—such as height in relation to width, the prominence of the serifs, and the size. They can be vertical, as usual and normal, or they can be tilted slightly to one side or another. Variations of tilting command little interest or premium. Also, for a given die if a mintmark is punched deeply into the die it will appear to be heavier and larger on the finished coin, than if it is punched lightly. The relapping or resurfacing of dies, seemingly not a widespread practice in this series, can result in making the features seem smaller and lighter.

- *Mintmark errors*—Mintmark errors, intentional (as in the case of overmintmarks) or otherwise, are highly important and command significant premiums. Overmintmarks are fascinating and include 1949-D/S, 1954-S/D, and 1955-D/S. A variety of 1942-D has the D punched over an earlier "lazy D" that was entered into the die horizontally, and the 1946-D over inverted D is worthy of mention. All 1971 Proofs were made in San Francisco and have S mintmarks, as 1971-S, except for an estimated 1,655 from a die made in error, without the S.

Mint errors, or errors made during the coining process, are a separate subject treated in chapter 2.

Factors Affecting Popularity and Value
Popularity refers to the number of people desiring a particular variety, and value is built upon that, in combination with the availability of specimens in the marketplace.

The more places a variety is listed, the more demand there will be for it. If it is listed in the *Guide Book of United States Coins*, the best-selling coin book of all time, it will play to a very wide audience. Listing in *Walter Breen's Complete Encyclopedia of U.S. and Colonial Coins* is helpful as well. Bill Fivaz's and J.T. Stanton's *Cherrypickers' Guide to Rare Die Varieties* has much clout, is used by many, and the statements of the authors are viewed as being very authoritative (rather than market driven). Moreover, the FS guide, as it is called, provides superb illustrations, assigns rarity ratings on the URS scale, and gives market values. However, it does not appear annually, and prices in an older edition may have been surpassed in the marketplace.

Bernard Nagengast's *Jefferson Nickel Analyst* (second edition), is a primer to the entire series and includes much basic narrative, an essential guide to getting started and developing an understanding.

The Best of the Jefferson Nickel Doubled Die Varieties, by John A. Wexler and Brian A. Ribar, is a fine addition to the specialist's library, as is *The Jefferson Nickel RPM Book: An Attribution and Pricing Guide*, by James Wiles. Consult the bibliography for additional titles.

If the leading commercial grading ("certification") services recognize the variety on their holders, this will increase demand and price. If there is "talk" or "buzz" about the variety on the internet, or a spread in one of the coin publications, or a splash in a retail or auction catalog, these contribute to popularity and price.

Last, if you want immersion, camaraderie, and more, do all of the above, and also sign up for membership in the Full Step Nickel Club, publisher of the *Portico*, which refers to that portion of Monticello with those challenging steps. Perhaps it would have been easier for all of us had architect and owner Thomas Jefferson used a ramp there instead!

The Bottom Line

There are so many varieties, some minor, others spectacular, some common, others rare, and with more constantly being discovered, that no one can collect them all. Appeal is apt to vary from viewer to viewer. In 2004, in the *Portico*, Darrell Crane described several that he considered to be sleepers, these including the 1939 Doubled MONTICELLO and FIVE CENTS, the 1942-D with doubled mintmark, the 1942-D over horizontal D, the 1943/2 Doubled Die obverse, the 1943 Doubled Eye, the 1945-P Doubled Die reverse, the overmintmarks of 1949-D/S, 1954-D/S, and 1955-D/S, and the S-less 1971 Proof.

Not that you asked, but I consider the 1949-D/S, 1954-D/S, and 1955-D/S, and the S-less 1971 Proof to be *essential*, the overmintmarks deserving of separate listings, as they are neither man nor beast, not D and not S, but both, perhaps *centaur* coins!

The bottom line is for you to collect what you enjoy and find the most interesting, perhaps after reviewing the illustrations and descriptions in the books mentioned above. Most varieties are very inexpensive in "nice" grades such as MS-63 and MS-64, and there are thousands of such coins unidentified in dealers' stocks, investors' groups of rolls, and elsewhere. Happy hunting!

FOCUS ON FULL-STEP AND SIX-STEP NICKELS

Interest in Full-Step Nickels

Bernard Nagengast, in *The Jefferson Nickel Analyst* (second edition), traces the collecting history of the full-step emphasis. The following, with permission, is liberally adapted from that source.

It is not known when the first specialist determined that full steps to Monticello would give a high grade coin the passport to be added to his or her collection. In later years some old-timers said they were doing this in the early 1940s, but documentation is lacking. I recall that at Empire Coin Company in Johnson City, NY, local collector Warren Snow was seeking such pieces in the 1950s, much to the amusement of other members of the Triple Cities Coin Club, who found the effort to be a waste of time.

In any event, in 1977 three collectors of such sharply detailed coins banded together to form the PAK Full Step Nickel Club in Montclair, NJ. The PAK initials came from the first names of Philip Petrillo, Adolf Weiss, and Karl Nenninger, the organizers. Nenninger dropped out within a year, and Petrillo and Weiss, both part-time coin dealers, continued. By about 1980 Weiss operated it on his own. The organization continued to grow, and in time Jay Ess and, later, Rich and Sue Sisti, came on board. By 1986 the membership stood at about 1,000. PAK published a monthly newsletter, sponsored an essay contest for young numismatists (the prize being a paid trip to the ANA Summer Seminar), and did other fine things.

Adolf Weiss was operated on for eye cataracts in 1986, afterward leaving Montclair, taking with him most of the club records, and leaving no forwarding address, the reason for this being unexplained to the present day. He was occasionally seen at later coin shows, but remained silent on the subject. He died in Oregon in 1989.

The gauntlet was picked up, or perhaps *reconstructed* would be a better word, by Richard and Sue Sisti, earlier associated with PAK, who reorganized the group as the Full Step Nickel Club under the aegis of CONECA, the national club featuring error coins. The new club held occasional auctions, produced a 35-minute video program on full-step nickels, and continued in operation into the 1990s.

In the meantime, about 1987, Michael Wescott, a teenage student, formed the American Nickel Collectors Association, which he conducted from his home in South Carolina. In 1991 Westcott wrote a fine book, with Walter Breen as an advisor, which was published under the title, *The United States Nickel Five-Cent Piece*. His club seems to have simply faded away.

In September 2000 in Burbank, CA, collector Darryl Crane organized the Full Step Nickel Club, which caught on quickly, published a newsletter, and issued reports on the rarity of various full-step nickels. This club is still very active.

The Challenge of Sharply Defined Steps
Again, Bernard Nagengast has contributed his expertise on the subject; and from his second edition of *The Jefferson Nickel Analyst*, the following is largely adapted.

At the lower center front of the Monticello building are six steps—actually the front edge of the porch plus the edges of five steps. In theory it would be nice to have a complete set of Jefferson nickels from 1938 onward, each with nicely defined steps, six—count them—six, in all. However, this is an impossibility, as for some issues the *working die* used to produce the coins only had five steps. So, that is how it is! This is particularly true for many issues dated prior to 1971.

Because of this, a 5 Full Steps nickel can be the ultimate for some issues in which 6 Full Steps coins do not exist. As to guidelines for employing these terms, the subject of nicks enters into the equation (unlike the situation for Full Details nickels of other types). In the words of Bernard Nagengast:

> Use a 7 to 10x, and not higher than a 20x magnifying glass to inspect the steps on the reverse. A full step coin (here, 5 Full Steps or 6 Full Steps) must have complete steps and those steps must be free of deep nicks or abrasions. Nickel collectors seek steps that are clean and sharp, and anything less is not worth as much or as desirable. Any bagmarks in the step area, usually showing as nicks and abrasions, must not be deep enough to cut all the way into the depressions between the steps.
>
> Jefferson nickels before 1970 are prone to show what at first appears to be complete steps, but upon careful inspection, bridges can be seen between the raised lines of some of the steps. The bridges are usually no longer than 1/8 inch. The presence of even one of these bridges means that the coin is not full step.
>
> Usually, the weakest area of the steps on nickels dated before 1971 is under the third pillar counted from the left. This area is opposite the high point on the obverse, thus the planchet metal often did not readily flow into that area. It is not uncommon to find a nickel with the first three steps complete, and the fourth and fifth steps missing in a pinhead area just below the third pillar. Design changes after 1970 seem to have eliminated this problem.

The Nagengast Guidelines

As might be expected, nickels with the Reverse of 1938 present special problems, and other hub changes also have effects. Here are the Nagengast outlines, hub by hub:

5 Full Steps Reverse of 1938

> The steps appear mushy and not clearly defined, even on Proofs. The steps are uneven and wavy and the indentations between the steps vary in depth. There are many bridges present between the raised portions of the steps.
>
> The best way to grade the Reverse of 1938 is by *overall definition* of the step area. The steps should be overall reasonably struck with most of the definition present, especially at the left. A five-step coin will have a defined, although thin, raised line all the way across at the fifth step. The line must be defined below the third pillar. If you begin looking from the left, you will probably see the fifth step clearly. As you move from left to right, the step will get thinner, and will tend to merge with the fourth step. For five full steps the fifth step must not merge with the field below the third pillar, but instead must have some definition.
>
> A six-step coin will have a very thin sixth step going all the way across. Even on proofs, six-step coins are seldom found. Properly defining a five-step Reverse of 1938 nickel is difficult due to the nature of the design. A good way to familiarize yourself with this reverse is to inspect a 1938 Proof coin. All of them have at least five steps, and you will be able to see what fully struck five-step coins look like. Circulation strikes will have the same characteristics, but not as sharp a detail.

Reverse of 1940

The reverse of 1940, used on Jefferson Nickels through 1967, and with modification 1968–1970, has straight, sharply defined steps. This definition, however progressively deteriorated as the master hub wore. Thus the steps found on earlier dates will be sharper and deeper than on later dates.

A five-step coin must have four defined indentations between the raised portions of the steps and the raised lines and the indentations must be complete from left to right. If the raised portions bridge together at any point, then the coin does *not* have five full steps. In some cases, all five or six steps will be present, but there will be a small bridge somewhere within the steps. Such a coin is *not* a full step coin.

Bagmarks and struck in marks, depressions, etc. are commonly seen on this reverse, especially on later issues. These detractions must be minor and not cut deeply into the steps. Even when these detractions are minimal, they do decrease the desirability of the coin as far as a Jefferson specialist is concerned. Thus the most desirable nickel is one with sharp, clean steps. Such coins are easier to find in earlier years, and this fact should be taken into account when considering nickels after the mid-1940s. Many later dates are difficult to find with perfect steps.

Six-step coins should have a sharply defined last step going all the way across. On later issues the sixth step is thinner than the preceding steps.

Reverse of 1971

The reverse of 1971, used through 1976, possesses sharp though thin steps. This reverse does not seem prone to bridges between the steps, and the only problem, besides the steps not being there at all, is presence of bagmarks. Because of the thin steps, cuts and nicks easily spoil an otherwise full step coin. The sixth step when present is always very thin.

The reverse of 1977 was used into 1982. The steps are somewhat thicker than the reverse of 1971. As with the reverse of 1971, the major problem is presence of five steps or more, and marks in the steps. The steps are not as sharp after 1979, due to master hub wear. Also, die wear became a major problem after 1979, thus many coins will show worn lettering and orange-peel effect. The sixth step when present usually has the same thickness as the preceding steps.

5 Full Steps Reverse of 1982

The reverse of 1982 was used until 1987, after which it was re-engraved, with subsequent touchups and re-engravings since. The steps are sharper than the reverse of 1977, and the modifications of 1989 and later made them even bolder. The 1982 through 1986 issues show progressive master hub wear resulting in more poorly defined steps. After 1986, the Mint maintained the hub often enough that five- and six-step coins are easy to find. This is particularly true for the issues of the last decade.

Certification

In February 2004, NGC announced that Jefferson nickels submitted for grading, formerly designated as FS, for Full Steps, would henceforth be evaluated as either 5FS, for 5 Full Steps or Full Steps, and 6FS for 6 Full Steps. A spokesperson for NGC said that coins formerly labeled as FS could be resubmitted for finessed attribution at a reduced charge. Further, henceforth the NGC census reports would reflect the new attributions.[2]

These attributions do not necessarily reflect sharp striking on *all* areas of a nickel (such might be called Full Details), and it may be the case that 5FS or 6FS coins could show incomplete striking on the obverse, such as graininess or original planchet marks on the portrait.

ANACS, PCGS, and SEGS (Sovereign Entities Grading Service) have added step information to nickel holders for some time. Nomenclature is not consistent, but in time may be standardized—hopefully. To me the NGC designations are just fine. As adding step information has not been done until recent years, the population reports issued by ANACS, NGC, and PCGS do not reflect what they viewed in earlier times. Accordingly, coins with sharp steps are not as rare as the reports indicate.

Partial Step Coins

While coins with 5 Full Steps or 6 Full Steps are eminently desirable, there are some issues for which such pieces are so rare as to be virtually unobtainable. A compromise is to acquire a coin with partial steps, but as many as possible. Describing each step in detail is the best method, but one that is difficult to standardize and, for some, a cumbersome process. Often, a shortcut is used, such as "almost 6 Full Steps," indicating that most, but not all six steps are complete.

Bernard Nagengast reports on this system, here adapted:

> Darrell Crane of the Full Step Nickel Club revised the PAK method to number the steps in each quarter 1 through 6. Envision the group of steps being divided by hypothetical vertical lines, so the leftmost group of five or six steps is in the first quarter, the two center groups are in the second and third quarter, and the rightmost group is in the fourth quarter. To describe the number of steps in each quarter a number from 0 (no steps at all) to 5 or 6. A coin with 6 Full Steps, complete across that section of the coin, would be called 6666. One with 5 Full Steps would be called 5555.
>
> A coin that had six steps in the first quarter, six in the second, five in the third, and four in the fourth, would be designated as 6654. The system takes some getting used to, but seems to work better than using adjectives.

SHARPNESS, PLANCHETS, AND OTHER MATTERS

Many Aspects

By now you know that nickel five-cent pieces can require knowledge and sophistication to evaluate carefully. The Liberty Head nickel, with its often weak corn ear on the reverse and usually sharp stars on the obverse can be tricky, and sometimes the horn is sharp and some stars are weak. To understand Indian Head / Buffalo nickels from 1913 to 1938 requires quite a bit of experience—where to look for Full Details, how to check the fur on the head of the bison, and more.

By now you realize that in the field of Jefferson nickels, checking the steps to Monticello is a great challenge in its own right, and a club exists just to focus on and appreciate this! As a smart buyer of Jefferson nickels you need to pay attention to the steps—the more, the better. However, as you might expect, they are only part of the story.

If you were to close your eyes and order a full set of, say, MS-63 to MS-65 Jefferson nickels from a dealer, or fill out a set at a convention, you can achieve completion quickly. No problem. All regular date and mintmark issues are available, many in quantity. However, if you insist upon *high quality*, and I am not only referring to having a decent number of steps (the highest number that is a combination of availability, price, and common sense), but to other aspects of striking, the quality of the surface, and more, a great challenge awaits!

Years ago in the hobby it was the usual thought that rolls of Uncirculated Jefferson nickels from 1938 to date were generally attractive for 1938, less so for 1939, and after that apt to be dull and lifeless, lacking eye appeal, but that the silver-content "wartime" nickels were sparkling beauties. Few people stopped to actually look at them, not even the famous 1950-D (which, if inspected, would be found to be indistinctly struck in areas and with just moderate luster).

Today, the situation is much the same. But for specialists who look at the coins there are many aspects to consider, and the formation of a truly beautiful set can be an absorbing project taking several years.

Sharpness of Details

An inviolable rule in American coinage is that if there are two deep areas in the dies, on the obverse and on the reverse, and if these areas are opposite each other when the dies are in a coining press, there will be problems. Unless the dies are precisely adjusted the correct distance apart, the metal will not flow in each direction to completely fill the recesses. As related under Indian Head / Buffalo nickels, the authorized weight of nickel planchets was 77.16 grains, "with no greater deviation than two grains to each piece."

If for a Jefferson nickel, a press was adjusted so that a planchet on the heavy side, weighing 79.16 grains, was used, then all details would be complete. However, a planchet could also be 75.16 and be legal. Such a planchet would not have enough metal to completely fill out the design.

No matter what the distance set might be, there would still be problems with the varying weights. It is seen that to strike a perfectly detailed coin on a high-speed press was difficult to do. Often, the dies were spaced about midway, meaning that most coins were slightly light in their details, others were very light, but just a few, if any, were sharp.

For the Jefferson nickel, the deepest parts are the hair above the ear on the obverse and the famous steps on the reverse. On many nickels there is not only lightness on the hair, but the cheek of Jefferson, also deep in the die, is apt to show what many consider to be handling or circulation marks, but which are really marks in the original planchet that have not been flattened out by striking pressure. This can be a puzzlement when a coin is observed that has frosty, flawless luster in the fields, but appears to have a lot of circulation marks on the portrait! Often in the past, these marks have been attributed to mixing with other coins in a bag, or even "worn dies."

In addition to this obvious cause of weak details, it was often the case that in the process of using die hubs and masters, details of some of them became worn, and thus lack of details was passed on to the working dies.

The equivalent of Full Details (FD) is non-existent for many Jefferson nickels, but to see what a FD coin looks like, *Proofs* usually measure up.

So far as I know, no one has ever assembled a complete FD set of dates and mint-marks of Buffalo nickels, Standing Liberty quarters, or Liberty Walking half dollars. To this list can be added Jefferson nickels.

The challenge, then, is to come as close as you can. Seeking coins with as many full steps (5, or, better yet, 6) is the starting point. Beyond that, when such coins are found, check the hair and cheek on the obverse, then check all other points.

Tired Dies

As with other series, often a coin will show grainy, pebbly surfaces and metal-flow lines. Sometimes the edges of letters and features will be blurred or even slightly doubled. Such coins are struck from tired dies—that have been used to strike tens of thousands of impressions and have lost their sharpness. Sometimes just one die shows these features, sometimes both do.

Improper annealing and hardening of working dies often caused problems. Bernard Nagengast commented: "Many coins of the 1980s have a severe 'orange-peel' effect from severe die erosion that resulted when the coinage dies were improperly heat treated."

By now it is understandable why Jefferson nickel specialists enjoy the company of others in clubs with those who think alike! Perhaps some members of the Full Step Nickel Club are envious of those who belong to the Early American Coppers Club (EAC), an area in which the striking of a coin is not often mentioned when the subjects of grade, quality, and price come up!

Planchet Problems

Again with permission, I quote from Bernard Nagengast's *The Jefferson Nickel Analyst* (second edition):

> Most Jefferson Nickels are brilliant, however some coins minted by the Philadelphia Mint in the 1950s are very dark in color, ranging from gray to charcoal black.
>
> The Philadelphia Mint in the 1950s was known to be having annealing oven problems, particularly with the atmosphere in the ovens. The annealing process normally causes planchets to darken, and for this reason they may be washed and tumbled dry to brighten them. It is possible that at times, planchets were much darker than usual, and/or the post-annealing washing/tumbling was done haphazardly or even not done at all. The fact is that many of the coins produced at Philadelphia in the 1950s are dark and quite ugly in appearance.
>
> Dark Philadelphia coins seem to have sporadically appeared after 1945, as I have seen examples from 1946, 1948, and 1949. However dark coins from 1946 through 1950 are uncommon. The situation began to change in 1951, when many more dark nickels appear to have been released. After 1951, the situation got generally worse. Much of the 1952, 1953, and 1954 issues are dark. In 1955 things sunk to a new low, and virtually all of the 1955 Philadelphia coins have a darkish cast. For some reason, 1956 saw a sudden improvement, since most 1956 nickels are brilliant. Not satisfied with success, the Philadelphia Mint returned to whatever it had been doing before, resulting in steady deterioration of coin

quality in 1957 and 1958. In 1959, bright white coins became more prevalent. After that, the mint apparently solved its dark coin problem, for I have never seen any dark nickels after 1959.

Curiously, the Philadelphia Mint did such a uniformly good job in producing black nickels in 1958, that some enterprising coin dealers promoted the coins, selling them as "Black Beauties." These coins actually have a certain eye-appeal, being uniformly glossy or satiny black. There are some 1959 black beauties as well, but they are much less common. . . .

Many San Francisco nickels exhibit a grayish color combined with a unique appearance of being slightly circulated. The effect is seen on S mint issues from 1938 through 1941 and from 1946 through 1952. It is so prevalent on 1940 and 1941 issues, that some dealers were convinced that some unscrupulous person had assembled "slider rolls" of AU coins. The effect is also very common on 1947-S nickels as well. I am convinced that the so-called sliders are in fact Uncirculated. Close inspection shows no wear at all, and I have seen varying numbers of these coins in original BU rolls.

The cause is a mystery. The possibilities are poor metal quality, and unusual die wear.

In addition for seeking Jefferson nickels on bright, clean planchets without discoloration, there can be problems of porosity, planchet lamination (rifts or flakes in the surface), etc. Often, dirt, debris, or grease was on the surface of one or both dies, causing discoloration, weakness, or lint marks on the coin.

Being a Smart Buyer of Jefferson Nickels

Action Plans for Smart Buying
Bernard Nagengast concludes his discussion of striking, dies, etc., with this: "In searching out fully struck Jefferson Nickels, experience will be your guide as to what is the best you can reasonably expect." To some, such a solution will be a disappointment. They want a magic bullet, a quick formula, a notation on a certified holder that will tell them, "this is a sharply struck Full Steps coin, with Full Details everywhere else, on a good planchet, with excellent luster."

Perhaps someday someone will devise such a service, as Rick Snow has done with his "Photo Seal" review of certified Indian Head cents. Certain cents that he has inspected and passed with flying colors are recorded photographically and by "slab" serial number, and can be bought and sold with confidence.

Returning to Jefferson nickels, you are likely to be either a casual collector, as most buyers are, or a specialist.

The Casual Buyer
If you are a casual buyer, here is what to do: Buy a copy of the Nagengast book, *The Jefferson Nickel Analyst*, to determine what is available in the way of quality for a given issue. Consult the present book (the one you are now holding) also. If a given date and mintmark is very rare or expensive with 5 Full Steps or 6 Full Steps, compromise and settle for a nice one, not stepless, but with just a few steps. Do not compromise on anything else, and within the grade category you seek, say MS-64 or higher, buy only coins with good luster, on good planchets, and with good eye appeal. Probably the best way to

do this is either to form an alliance with a mail order dealer and give him/her your requirements, or spend some time at coin shows. It will probably be a waste of time to simply order coins you see listed, without knowing their quality. Visual images on the Internet can be a help, but the appearance of a coin can be enhanced by turning it at certain angles, varying the lighting, etc.—many sellers know all the tricks. Other coins you need may be so inexpensive that dealers will not bother to list them, and yet you will want to find choice ones.

As to certified coins, this choice is up to you. Quite a few collectors think nothing of spending $10 to buy a $1 coin that has been certified. My own feeling is that if you collect casually, buy a convenient album or set of plastic holders, so you can watch your collection grow coin by coin and can enjoy seeing them easily.

The Specialist

If you want to specialize, buy the Nagengast book, join the Full Step Nickel Club, and jump in by buying whatever you can among coins that are available (without spending a fortune) in 5 Full Steps or 6 Full Steps quality. In every instance, be sure the rest of the coin is well struck and that it has good eye appeal. While not everyone might agree, I would rather have a 5 Full Steps coin with sharp obverse details as well, than a 6 Full Steps coin with a flat or grainy area on the obverse.

If you desire to collect Proofs alongside your circulation strikes, these make good beginning acquisitions, and choice, well-struck pieces are easy to find. Proofs themselves can be complex if you get into "frosted cameo" surfaces, which for some early issues are rare. There is a lot of literature to consult and many offerings in the marketplace, so you will learn quickly.

In time you will be guided by experience, as Bernard Nagengast has suggested. So long as you follow rules for sharpness, quality, and eye appeal you will not have to retrace your steps (pun) and upgrade any pieces you bought when you first started.

Everything has a price, and part of your experience will be to find out what is available and for what cost. You do have the great advantage that you can cherrypick 5 Full Steps and 6 Full Steps nickels at coin shows, by looking through dealer stocks—assuming that a specialist has not preceded you. Chances are 10 to 1 that the cost of the Nagengast book and this book too will be repaid quickly once you start looking! Many treasures await your eyes!

Sometimes at coin shows dealers become annoyed with variety collectors, call them "weenies" or similar, and even shoo them away. The best way to avoid this treatment is to tell the dealer what you want to do, and that you will probably buy at least *something*. Then, if you spend a half hour browsing the stock and do not find a prize, buy something else as a gesture—a duplicate common variety, or a book.

On the other hand if you are building a registry set or are trying to outdo the Joneses, then certified coins permit comparing numbers and step designations. However, it might be well to consider the matter carefully. Can the pursuit of the elusive 6 Full Steps coins dampen your basic enjoyment of old-fashioned collecting?

BEING A SMART BUYER OF JEFFERSON NICKELS

For general advice on collecting, see chapter 3, "How to Be a Smart Buyer," including the four steps to success. To these you can add the following information relating to the Jefferson nickel specialty.

BUYING JEFFERSON NICKELS: FOUR STEPS TO SUCCESS

Stop, Consider, Go!

Buying Jefferson nickels involves a different mind set from assembling a set of Buffalo nickels. The rarity and value of Full Details coins, which have 6 Full Steps, is becoming realized in the marketplace. Some varieties that in lustrous, attractive MS-65 grade, but with, say, just four steps on Monticello visible, might sell for just a few dollars, while an example of the same issue with 6 Full Steps may not exist, or it may be priced into the thousands of dollars!

The Full Steps situation is evolving, and rapidly, and rarity ratings, evaluations, and prices are subject to change. However, it is likely true that a variety now considered to be rare with 5 Full Steps or, better yet, 6 Full Steps, will remain hard to find.

Contemplate the possibilities before following the advice I give below. As I see it, if you are a connoisseur you have three choices:

Option 1: To build a "nice" set of Jefferson nickels in, say, MS-65 or MS-66 grades, with each coin having superb eye appeal. This is very doable, and for surprisingly modest cost. The result will be an attractive set that you can mount in an album and add to as new issues become available.

Option 2: To build a significantly above average set in terms of Full Steps, adding 5 Full Steps or, better, 6 Full Steps, when they are affordable.

Option 3: Shoot the moon: Aspire to acquire each date and mark in a combination of good eye appeal, as above, plus with as many steps to Monticello that are known to exist. This will automatically project you into competition for assembling a registry set in competition with others. For good measure, you will want to become acquainted with other specialists with the same ambition, you will want to join the Full Step Nickel Club, and when the *Portico* (the publication of the FSNC) arrives in the mail, you will want to drop everything and read it immediately. While doing all of this, you will need to regularly add deposits to your checking account.

Each of the three options yields its own pleasure, but number 3 involves a deep commitment of time and money. Go for whatever option is most appealing and sensible for you.

Step 1:
Numerical Grade Assigned to the Coin

Your first step is to look at the grade of a Jefferson nickel offered to you. Some may be in certified holders, but most will likely be "raw," but be graded by the seller. Learn basic grading for the Jefferson series, or call upon an experienced numismatist to help you. Grading is not difficult, and with an hour or so spent examining nickels at a coin convention or dealer's shop, you will become fairly knowledgeable.

Determine that a coin offered to you in a given grade is in that grade. As to what grades to seek, in the Jefferson series all are affordable in grades of MS-64 and MS-65, and many are inexpensive beyond that. I would avoid seeking "ultra grades," such as MS-69 or MS-70, as certified populations of such pieces tend to expand as more coins are certified, and price structures may weaken or even crash. Be careful and select a grading goal that is just right for you.

While some Jefferson nickels can be bought at auction, especially on the Internet, most numismatists buy the majority of their coins directly for fixed prices, from dealers at conventions, in their shops, or by mail. Although buying coins at a shop or show may not come with a return privilege if tomorrow you decide you do not like the grade, most mail-order sellers offer the opportunity to send something back if you do not like it. Check the appropriate terms of sale.

Step 2:
Eye Appeal at First Glance

Now, look at the Jefferson nickel in question. Is it brilliant or lightly toned, and attractive to your eyes? I would avoid coins that are dull, deeply toned, vividly iridescent (mostly through the application of heat or chemicals), and the like.

There are so many Jefferson nickels in the marketplace that if you are troubled by even the slightest aspect of visual appeal, reject the coin immediately.

If the Jefferson nickel is attractive to your eye, then in some distant future year when time comes to sell it, the piece will be attractive to the eyes of other buyers, an important consideration. While at present, most Jefferson nickels are of low values, I can envision that a generation from now some of the scarcer issues will be valuable and will be traded individually, perhaps accompanied by enthusiastic descriptions. Even though a coin might be inexpensive on the current market, take the time to complete this and the other four steps. Now, with an attractive coin in hand, you have a candidate for your *further consideration.*

Step 3:
Evaluating Sharpness and Related Features

At this point you have a Jefferson nickel which you believe to be properly graded and with superb eye appeal. The next step (no pun intended) is to check it for sharpness of strike. You will need a magnifying glass to do this. First, count the steps on the portico of Monticello. If you see 6 Full Steps, complete and distinct, you have a coin that for some will rank at the top of the list. However, for you it might not! Check all other areas of the coin, including the shoulder of Jefferson on the other side, which can sometimes be nicked or grainy if the original planchet surface did not strike up completely. Also inspect the lettering and other features. A coin with Full Details will have not only 6 Full Steps, but will have everything else well defined. Do *not* rely upon notations on certified holders, as these deal with the step count, not the rest of the coin!

An element of practicality enters into this if a coin with 6 Full Steps is not known to exist or is very expensive. Review the options above. It is okay to compromise and have a coin with three, four, or five full steps if these are affordable, but sharper coins are not.

Generally, Proofs in the Jefferson nickel series are fairly sharp and have good eye appeal. However, some are cleaned and/or spotty, so these require careful inspection as well.

If the coin you are considering buying has passed the preceding tests, it is ready for *further consideration.* Chances are good that you are holding a very nice Jefferson nickel in your hand!

Step 4:
Establishing a Fair Market Price

At this point you are ready to buy. Check published values in numismatic periodicals to learn the average market price for the coin you are considering. As most Jefferson nickels are inexpensive, even in MS-65 or MS-66 grades, my advice is to simply write a check, as long as the price is in the ballpark. If the market price for a MS-65 is, say, $10, I would buy a coin offered in this range, even at $12 or $13, if it had exceptional eye appeal. You have already invested some time in this coin, and now you can take it home. On the other hand, if the asking price is $20, I would wait for another opportunity.

Also consider what I also call the "Optimal Collecting Grade," abbreviated OCG. In instances in which a very small difference in grade makes a very large difference in price, opt for the lower grade. This is not as important in the Jefferson series as it is in some other numismatic specialties, but it is still worth considering.

Enjoying the Pursuit

If you follow each of these steps, each Jefferson nickel in your collection will be a very special coin, even if it is not expensive. You should complete your collection within a month if you really delve into it, or perhaps a year if you pursue the pieces in a more leisurely fashion.

If you elect Option 3, given above, and want the sharpest of the sharp, the finest of the fine, be prepared to spend several years in the quest, and even then you will not be able to complete a set with Full Details, including 6 Full Steps. However, this is okay and, actually, is an important part of the challenge.

The three options given above will each yield a great set of Jefferson nickels. Take your pick, then jump in!

CHAPTER NINE

JEFFERSON NICKELS 1938 TO DATE
ANALYSIS BY DATE AND MINTMARK

1938

Circulation-Strike Mintage: 19,496,000
Proof Mintage: 19,365

1938 • Market Values • Circulation Strikes and Proof Strikes

AU-55	MS-60	MS-63	MS-64	MS-64FS	MS-65	MS-65FS	MS-66	MS-66FS
$1.50	$2.50	$3.50	$6.	$45.	$11.	$150.	$50.	$425.
MS-67	MS-67FS	PF-60	PF-63	PF-64	PF-65	PF-66	PF-67	PF-68
—	—	$30.	$60.	$110.	$125.	$200.	$450.	—

Availability (Certified Populations) • Circulation Strikes and Proof Strikes

< MS-60	MS-60	MS-61	MS-62	MS-63	MS-64	MS-65	MS-66	MS-67	MS-68	MS-69	MS-70
33	1	4	9	50	222	489	408	200	0	0	
< PF-60	PF-60	PF-61	PF-62	PF-63	PF-64	PF-65	PF-66	PF-67	PF-68	PF-69	PF-70
2	4	3	23	117	576	1,038	1,098	353	17	0	

Key to Collecting: Mint State coins are usually attractive with satiny luster. The steps are usually ill-defined and blend together in some areas. Finding a 5 Full Steps coin is very doable, although such bring a good premium. Proofs are mirrorlike and attractive. A few have slight cameo contrast, not deeply frosty, and are very desirable. Five Full Steps coins are available, but "most Proofs do not have a full sixth step all the way across. When all of step 6 is present it will be thin at the third pillar," noted Bernard Nagengast. Many of the 150 cards containing a Proof nickel, signed by Schlag and notarized, made in 1939, fell into the hands of Detroit dealer Earl Schill in the early 1960s, who marketed them for $225 or so each. Such cards, once often seen at coin shows, are widely dispersed now. One sold for $1,500 in 2004.

Step-Detail Availability (MS-65 and Higher): *5 Full Steps*—1 in 20 coins • *6 Full Steps*—Extremely rare or unknown; opinions vary.

Step-Detail Availability (Proof): *5 Full Steps*—1 in 20 • *6 Full Steps*—Extremely rare.

Minor Die Doubling: Breen-2660, "Large over small date," is dismissed as simply minor die doubling by Fivaz and Stanton who list it as FS-05-1938-1101, noting that at one time it attracted much attention, but no longer.

Optimal Collecting Grades—The OCG™ for Jefferson nickels is your choice between MS-65 and Proof-65, or slightly higher—in nearly all instances, very affordable. To these grades can be added a "nice" strike that does not necessarily have Full Steps, among issues for which Full Steps are rare or expensive.

Market Values, 5 vs. 6 Full Steps—Circulation-strike coins with 6 Full Steps can be so rare as to make it impossible to compile a meaningful set of sale-price data (Proofs, of course, are commonly found with 6 Full Steps). Thus, the market values for circulation-strike FS coins have generally been derived from sale prices for coins graded at 5FS; values for coins with 6 Full Steps will be notably higher.

The values of extreme FS rarities can sometimes be *drastically* higher than those for non-FS coins of the same year and grade (e.g., $0.50 for an MS-64, vs. $5,000 for an MS-64FS). When you encounter such discrepancies in these value charts, rest assured that your eyes are not fooling you—but always check the most recent auction records (which may be much lower or higher), and consult with specialists in the field, before bidding!

1938-D

Circulation-Strike Mintage: 5,376,000

1938-D • Market Values • Circulation Strikes

AU-55	MS-60	MS-63	MS-64	MS-64FS	MS-65	MS-65FS	MS-66	MS-66FS	MS-67	MS-67FS
$2.	$4.	$7.	$10.	$30.	$14.	$90.	$40.	$250.	—	$1,500.

Availability (Certified Populations) • Circulation Strikes

<MS-60	MS-60	MS-61	MS-62	MS-63	MS-64	MS-65	MS-66	MS-67	MS-68	MS-69	MS-70
10	0	0	2	10	90	481	1,577	848	8	0	

Key to Collecting: Mint State coins are usually sharply detailed with 5 Full Steps a possibility, although not sharply delineated due to the nature of the hub. Most have excellent eye appeal.

Step-Detail Availability (MS-65 and Higher): *5 Full Steps*—1 in 20 • *6 Full Steps*—Extremely rare or unknown, opinions vary.

1938-S

Circulation-Strike Mintage: 4,105,000

1938-S • Market Values • Circulation Strikes

AU-55	MS-60	MS-63	MS-64	MS-64FS	MS-65	MS-65FS	MS-66	MS-66FS	MS-67	MS-67FS
$2.00	$4.50	$7.50	$12.	$200.	$15.	$350.	$20.	$800.	—	—

Availability (Certified Populations) • Circulation Strikes

<MS-60	MS-60	MS-61	MS-62	MS-63	MS-64	MS-65	MS-66	MS-67	MS-68	MS-69	MS-70
25	2	4	10	23	120	507	877	284	1	0	

Key to Collecting: Mint State coins are easy to find, despite the status of 1938-S having the lowest production of the three mints. Many are struck from tired or overused dies. Weakness is the rule. Some have very lustrous surfaces with an attractive "greasy" luster—as often seen on coins struck from worn dies in other series (e.g., Buffalo nickels and Peace silver dollars).

Step-Detail Availability (MS-65 and Higher): *5 Full Steps*—1 in 50 • *6 Full Steps*—Unverified.

1939

Circulation-Strike Mintage: 120,615,000
Proof Mintage: 12,535

The 1939 variety with doubled MONTICELLO and FIVE CENTS.

1939 • Market Values • Circulation Strikes and Proof Strikes[a]

AU-55	MS-60	MS-63	MS-64	MS-64FS	MS-65	MS-65FS	MS-66	MS-66FS
$2.00	$2.25	$2.50	$3.	$55.	$4.	$60.	$15.	$90.
MS-67	MS-67FS	PF-60	PF-63	PF-64	PF-65	PF-66	PF-67	PF-68
—	$900.	$30.	$45.	$100.	$125.	$375.	$2,000.	—

Availability (Certified Populations) • Circulation Strikes and Proof Strikes

<MS-60	MS-60	MS-61	MS-62	MS-63	MS-64	MS-65	MS-66	MS-67	MS-68	MS-69	MS-70
84	4	11	28	33	50	94	210	436	3	0	
< PF-60	PF-60	PF-61	PF-62	PF-63	PF-64	PF-65	PF-66	PF-67	PF-68	PF-69	PF-70
0	0	1	4	18	65	136	193	51	3	0	

[a] Full Steps values are for coins with Reverse of 1940. For those with Reverse of 1938, values for MS-64FS, MS-65FS, MS-66FS, and MS-67FS are $175, $300, $1,200, and $2,500, respectively.

Key to Collecting: Among circulation strikes, relatively few, perhaps 10%, are of the Reverse of 1938, with indistinct lettering with perhaps 1 in 1,000 having 5 Full Steps (see Nagengast). The rest are with the Reverse of 1940 with sharper details in the hub and master die. The vast majority of Proofs are with the Reverse of 1938 with somewhat indistinct areas to the steps. Relatively few Reverse of 1940 coins exist (including a remarkable cache of 30 in the 1985 Bowers and Merena sale of the Abe Kosoff estate), but most have 6 Full Steps.

REVERSE OF 1938
Step-Detail Availability (MS-65 and Higher): *5 Full Steps*—1 in 400 • *6 Full Steps*—Unknown.
Step-Detail Availability (Proof): *5 Full Steps*—Scarce • *6 Full Steps*—Very rare.

REVERSE OF 1940
Step-Detail Availability (MS-65 and Higher): *5 Full Steps*—1 in 5 • *6 Full Steps*—Scarce.
Step-Detail Availability (Proof): *5 Full Steps*—Not seen • *6 Full Steps*—Standard.

DOUBLED DIE REVERSE

Breen-2665, FS-05-1939-801. This is the much-discussed die with MONTICELLO and FIVE CENTS dramatically doubled (see narrative in the preceding chapter). Perhaps 1,000 or more, virtually all with signs of circulation, were in numismatic hands by 1960. At that point I had never seen a choice Mint State coin! In his 1988 *Complete Encyclopedia*, Breen noted, "Very rare Uncirculated." However, the FS text modifies that with later information: "Scarce in Mint State. Several Mint State rolls have come on the market in recent years." Listed in the Red Book and widely sought for a long time, whatever the supply of Mint State coins may be, say fewer than 200, it is a drop in the bucket in comparison to the desire for them.

1939-D

Circulation-Strike Mintage: 3,514,000

1939-D • Market Values • Circulation Strikes[a]

AU-55	MS-60	MS-63	MS-64	MS-64FS	MS-65	MS-65FS	MS-66	MS-66FS	MS-67	MS-67FS
$30.	$55.	$75.	$85.	—	$100.	$400.	$125.	$1,500.	—	—

Availability (Certified Populations) • Circulation Strikes

<MS-60	MS-60	MS-61	MS-62	MS-63	MS-64	MS-65	MS-66	MS-67	MS-68	MS-69	MS-70
6	0	1	5	5	13	52	208	288	0	0	

a Full Steps values are for coins with Reverse of 1940. For those with Reverse of 1938, values for MS-64FS, MS-65FS, and MS-66FS are $300, $650, and $850, respectively, with insufficient data to estimate an MS-67FS value.

Key to Collecting: The 1939-D is the key issue in the Jefferson nickel series, regarding basic availability in Mint State (not considering numerical gradations of Mint State and not considering the step count). It has been a favorite for a long time. Likely, about 25% of the mintage is from the Reverse of 1938, and the remainder or larger portion is from the Reverse of 1940. Few numismatists have sought one of each, so there is no market differential, except for sharp steps. Mint luster and eye appeal are usually very good.

REVERSE OF 1938

Step-Detail Availability (MS-65 and Higher): *5 Full Steps*—1 in 150; *6 Full Steps*—Unverified.

REVERSE OF 1940

Step-Detail Availability (MS-65 and Higher): *5 Full Steps*—1 in 10; *6 Full Steps*—Very rare.

Notes on Rarity: The 1939-D was once at the peak of collector interest as the lowest-mintage issue among the earlier dates (until 1950-D came along) and for its general scarcity in Mint State. By 1939 the novelty of the design had passed, and the public did not save them. Numismatists with an investment turn of mind were still taking hits from the crash in the commemorative market, which started its slide in autumn 1936 and did not hit bottom until about this year. Survival of bank-wrapped rolls was a matter of chance—such as some being found years later tucked away with cash in a vault.

1939-S

Circulation-Strike Mintage: 6,630,000

1939-S • Market Values • Circulation Strikes[a]

AU-55	MS-60	MS-63	MS-64	MS-64FS	MS-65	MS-65FS	MS-66	MS-66FS	MS-67	MS-67FS
$10.	$16.	$22.	$28.	$115.	$38.	$450.	$150.	$1,100.	—	—

Availability (Certified Populations) • Circulation Strikes

<MS-60	MS-60	MS-61	MS-62	MS-63	MS-64	MS-65	MS-66	MS-67	MS-68	MS-69	MS-70
26	5	3	9	21	50	92	204	110	0	0	

[a] Full Steps values are for coins with Reverse of 1940. For those with Reverse of 1938, values for MS-64FS, MS-65FS, and MS-66FS are $350, $500, and $5,000, respectively, with insufficient data to estimate an MS-67FS value.

Key to Collecting: Two varieties exist, the Reverse of 1938, comprising slightly over half of the production. The luster is very good, and 5 and 6 Full Steps coins can be found, but, of course, the steps, while complete, are not sharp. The rest are with the Reverse of 1940, which *should* be sharp, but in this case are often unsatisfactory. The luster is frequently sub-par and details are lacking on the steps. Bernard Nagengast reports that a gem 6 Full Steps coin swept everyone away at $2,640 way back in 1982. Today in the early 21st century, what with so much interest in Jefferson nickels, the market is more stable.

REVERSE OF 1938

Step-Detail Availability (MS-65 and Higher): *5 Full Steps*—1 in 100; *6 Full Steps*—Ultra rare.

REVERSE OF 1940

Step-Detail Availability (MS-65 and Higher): *5 Full Steps*—1 in 10; *6 Full Steps*—Rare.

1940

Circulation-Strike Mintage: 176,485,000
Proof Mintage: 14,158

1940 • Market Values • Circulation Strikes and Proof Strikes

AU-55	MS-60	MS-63	MS-64	MS-64FS	MS-65	MS-65FS	MS-66	MS-66FS
$0.50	$1.00	$1.50	$2.50	$8.	$4.	$20.	$15.	$50.
MS-67	MS-67FS	PF-60	PF-63	PF-64	PF-65	PF-66	PF-67	PF-68
—	—	$30.	$45.	$90.	$125.	$175.	$550.	—

Availability (Certified Populations) • Circulation Strikes and Proof Strikes

<MS-60	MS-60	MS-61	MS-62	MS-63	MS-64	MS-65	MS-66	MS-67	MS-68	MS-69	MS-70
23	1	2	11	30	107	551	565	211	1	1	
< PF-60	PF-60	PF-61	PF-62	PF-63	PF-64	PF-65	PF-66	PF-67	PF-68	PF-69	PF-70
2	0	2	5	30	213	501	170	8	0	0	

Key to Collecting: Many were made, and years ago roll quantities were common. Today, singles are easily enough found. All have the Reverse of 1940. Proofs are mostly of the Reverse of 1940 style. Concerning the Proof Reverse of 1938: This anachronistic reverse was taken from a vault and used to strike a small number of Proofs. Instantly recognizable by the lack of definition and "wavy" character of the all-important steps, this variety was first identified by Bill Fivaz. The variety remains rare (URS-8) today. Breen-2670, FS-05-1940-901.
Step-Detail Availability (MS-65 and Higher): *5 Full Steps*—1 in 5; *6 Full Steps*—Very scarce.

Reverse of 1938
Step-Detail Availability (Proof): *5 Full Steps*—Standard; *6 Full Steps*—Unknown.

Reverse of 1940
Step-Detail Availability (Proof): *5 Full Steps*—Common; *6 Full Steps*—Common.

1940-D

Circulation-Strike Mintage: 43,540,000

1940-D • Market Values • Circulation Strikes

AU-55	MS-60	MS-63	MS-64	MS-64FS	MS-65	MS-65FS	MS-66	MS-66FS	MS-67	MS-67FS
$1.00	$2.00	$2.50	$4.	$9.	$6.	$12.	$25.	$45.	—	$225.

Availability (Certified Populations) • Circulation Strikes

<MS-60	MS-60	MS-61	MS-62	MS-63	MS-64	MS-65	MS-66	MS-67	MS-68	MS-69	MS-70
21	4	8	16	25	176	683	1,197	547	1	0	

Key to Collecting: Most Mint State coins are attractive and well struck (5 Full Steps or, less often, 6 Full Steps), although spotting and eye appeal can be a problem.
Step-Detail Availability (MS-65 and Higher): *5 Full Steps*—1 in 3 • *6 Full Steps*—Scarce.

1940-S

Circulation-Strike Mintage: 39,690,000

1940-S • Market Values • Circulation Strikes

AU-55	MS-60	MS-63	MS-64	MS-64FS	MS-65	MS-65FS	MS-66	MS-66FS	MS-67	MS-67FS
$1.00	$2.25	$3.	$4.	$25.	$6.	$45.	$25.	$175.	—	—

Availability (Certified Populations) • Circulation Strikes

<MS-60	MS-60	MS-61	MS-62	MS-63	MS-64	MS-65	MS-66	MS-67	MS-68	MS-69	MS-70
15	0	0	6	22	154	577	367	76	0	0	

Key to Collecting: Mint State coins *per se* are plentiful, but most have problems of one sort or another—erratic luster, weak details, and sub-par eye appeal. Five Full Steps and 6 Full Steps coins exist and can be found with good eye appeal, but are few and far between. The 1940-S is a good example of the necessity to look beyond the step count and insist on eye appeal as well.

Step-Detail Availability (MS-65 and Higher): *5 Full Steps*—1 in 10; *6 Full Steps*—Scarce.

1941

Circulation-Strike Mintage: 203,265,000
Proof Mintage: 18,720

1941 • Market Values • Circulation Strikes and Proof Strikes

AU-55	MS-60	MS-63	MS-64	MS-64FS	MS-65	MS-65FS	MS-66	MS-66FS
$0.25	$0.75	$1.50	$2.	$20.	$6.	$20.	$20.	$110.
MS-67	**MS-67FS**	**PF-60**	**PF-63**	**PF-64**	**PF-65**	**PF-66**	**PF-67**	**PF-68**
—	—	$30.	$40.	$75.	$125.	$175.	$500.	—

Availability (Certified Populations) • Circulation Strikes and Proof Strikes

<MS-60	MS-60	MS-61	MS-62	MS-63	MS-64	MS-65	MS-66	MS-67	MS-68	MS-69	MS-70
18	0	2	4	15	67	335	410	202	2	0	
< PF-60	**PF-60**	**PF-61**	**PF-62**	**PF-63**	**PF-64**	**PF-65**	**PF-66**	**PF-67**	**PF-68**	**PF-69**	**PF-70**
1	0	2	10	47	386	853	821	140	3	0	

Key to Collecting: As so many were produced, Mint State coins are common today. Some have water spots that look easily removable, but are not. Some are struck from tired dies and should be avoided. Eye appeal can be a problem across all grades. Proofs can have planchet roughness on the portrait from incomplete striking, but the rest of the coin is usually sharply struck with 6 Full Steps. Cherrypick for a choice obverse!

At the 1941 ANA Convention, Philadelphia dealer Ira S. Reed displayed and sold as novelties some 1937 cents and nickels for which he had the edges reeded by a local machine shop. However, these were later taken seriously by some collectors and, in fact, were even listed for a time in *A Guide Book of United States Coins*. These have no particular value, and you can make your own!

Step-Detail Availability (MS-65 and Higher): *5 Full Steps*—1 in 5; *6 Full Steps*— Very scarce.

Step-Detail Availability (Proof): *5 Full Steps*—Common; *6 Full Steps*—Common.

Nickels With Reeded Edges: This appeared in *The Numismatist*, November 1941: "One of the novelties of the Philadelphia Convention Bourse tables was sale of the U.S. 5-cent nickel with reeded edges. It has been stated on excellent authority that the coins were prepared in the U.S. Mint." Ira S. Reed, Philadelphia coin dealer, had a machine shop add reeded edges to a few hundred current Lincoln cents and Jefferson nickels, in a process that had nothing to do with the Mint. It seems that many collectors and dealers were fooled, and later this variety was even listed in the Red Book, until the editor was informed of their true nature.

1941-D

Circulation-Strike Mintage: 53,432,000

1941-D • Market Values • Circulation Strikes

AU-55	MS-60	MS-63	MS-64	MS-64FS	MS-65	MS-65FS	MS-66	MS-66FS	MS-67	MS-67FS
$1.00	$2.50	$3.50	$4.	$15.	$6.	$20.	$35.	$30.	—	$150.

Availability (Certified Populations) • Circulation Strikes

<MS-60	MS-60	MS-61	MS-62	MS-63	MS-64	MS-65	MS-66	MS-67	MS-68	MS-69	MS-70
28	2	2	6	18	103	750	1,569	709	1	0	

Key to Collecting: The 1941-D in Mint State is often found sharply detailed, 5 Full Steps or, occasionally, 6 Full Steps. Now and then a rare prooflike example is seen.

Step-Detail Availability (MS-65 and Higher): *5 Full Steps*—1 in 3; *6 Full Steps*—Scarce.

D Over Horizontal D: Breen-2678. D first punched horizontally, curved side facing down, then corrected. Originally reported by Bob Salawasser,[1] the coin is not in Fivaz Stanton or Wiles and is ignored by Nagengast, possibly indicating that confirmation by current experts is desired? Rare. Also see the same error for 1942-D; same die?

1941-S

Circulation-Strike Mintage: 43,455,000

1941-S • Market Values • Circulation Strikes

AU-55	MS-60	MS-63	MS-64	MS-64FS	MS-65	MS-65FS	MS-66	MS-66FS	MS-67	MS-67FS
$2.	$3.	$4.	$5.	$30.	$7.	$90.	$25.	$625.	—	—

Availability (Certified Populations) • Circulation Strikes

<MS-60	MS-60	MS-61	MS-62	MS-63	MS-64	MS-65	MS-66	MS-67	MS-68	MS-69	MS-70
14	0	1	3	9	115	285	221	90	1	0	

Key to Collecting: Mint State examples issue is usually seen weakly struck and with unsatisfactory luster, dull and lifeless. Five and 6 Full Steps coins are hard to find with good eye appeal, necessitating some cherrypicking. Use "step information" on a holder as a *starting point.* Bernard Nagengast suggests that fewer than 10 die pairs were used (one with large S), which would mean extraordinarily extended press runs for the pairs—perhaps an explanation for the poor quality produced.

Step-Detail Availability (MS-65 and Higher): *5 Full Steps*—1 in 10; *6 Full Steps*—Scarce.

Small S Mintmark: The usual size seen on 1941-S, this is the size used 1938–1940. Breen-2675.

Small *Inverted* S Mintmark: FS-05-1941S-503 rated as URS-2, rare, but more may be found as the variety is not well known.

Large S Mintmark: Breen-2676, FS-05-1941S-501. Rare in relation to the small mint-mark. Apparently from a single die pair, and likely a short run (seemingly unusual in the context of output of this issue; see above). This style of "S" is unique to 1941, and has a triangular shaped lower serif. It was used on some 1941-S cents, fewer 1941-S nickels, and extremely few 1941-S quarters.

1942 TYPE I

Circulation-Strike Mintage: 49,789,000
Proof Mintage: 29,600

1942 Type I • Market Values • Circulation Strikes and Proof Strikes

AU-55	MS-60	MS-63	MS-64	MS-64FS	MS-65	MS-65FS	MS-66	MS-66FS
$2.	$4.	$6.	$7.	$30.	$10.	$90.	$40.	$1,700.
MS-67	MS-67FS	PF-60	PF-63	PF-64	PF-65	PF-66	PF-67	PF-68
—	—	$30.	$45.	$50.	$125.	$150.	$250.	—

Availability (Certified Populations) • Circulation Strikes and Proof Strikes

<MS-60	MS-60	MS-61	MS-62	MS-63	MS-64	MS-65	MS-66	MS-67	MS-68	MS-69	MS-70
4	2	1	8	73	193	273	150	7	0	0	
< PF-60	PF-60	PF-61	PF-62	PF-63	PF-64	PF-65	PF-66	PF-67	PF-68	PF-69	PF-70
0	0	0	9	60	430	1,318	1,725	642	18	0	

Key to Collecting: Quality varies on circulation strikes, with Mint State coins apt to be lustrous but with irregular surfaces, the last from tired or overused dies. Many 5 Full Steps and 6 Full Steps coins exist, but good surfaces and eye appeal can make finding one that is just right a difficult task. Proofs are plentiful, per the mintage, and are occasionally lightly hazy from storage. By now, most have been dipped to brighten them. Many Proofs are lightly struck on the shoulder, showing marks and roughness from the original planchet; avoid these!
Step-Detail Availability (MS-65 and Higher): *5 Full Steps*—1 in 50; *6 Full Steps*—Rare.
Step-Detail Availability (Proof): *5 Full Steps*—Common; *6 Full Steps*—Common.
Die Doubling: All 1942 Type I nickels show microscopic die doubling. Two are significant enough to be collected as Doubled Dies (Nagengast), FS-05-1942-101 and 102, there illustrated.

1942-D TYPE I

Circulation-Strike Mintage: 13,938,000

1942-D Type I • Market Values • Circulation Strikes

AU-55	MS-60	MS-63	MS-64	MS-64FS	MS-65	MS-65FS	MS-66	MS-66FS	MS-67	MS-67FS
$20.	$27.	$36.	$40.	$45.	$45.	$50.	$60.	$80.	—	$850.

Availability (Certified Populations) • Circulation Strikes

<MS-60	MS-60	MS-61	MS-62	MS-63	MS-64	MS-65	MS-66	MS-67	MS-68	MS-69	MS-70
135	7	2	14	20	135	525	679	332	0	0	

Key to Collecting: Mint State coins are usually choice, with 5 Full Steps being readily available and 6 Full Steps being seen on occasion. Years ago I determined that the 1942-D was underrated in Mint State, simply because in the handling and seeing countless thousands of rolls of early Jefferson nickels, this was the rarest roll next to 1939-D. Bernard Nagengast considers it to be equally as rare as the 1939-D. In the modern market with much attention being paid to ultra-high grades of certified coins of later, high-mintage dates (not necessarily paying attention to strike), the 1942-D has become lost in the shuffle. However, there is something basically appealing about *foundational rarity*, or basic rarity in all grades. The 1942-D has a lot to recommend it. Walter Breen reported, "no bag lots saved," but at least one bag, original or put together I do not know, was sold by an Indiana dealer as part of a "bag set" of dates and mintmarks in the 1950s. I have never heard of another bag of 1942-D or of 1939-D.

Step-Detail Availability (MS-65 and Higher): *5 Full Steps*—1 in 3; *6 Full Steps*—Scarce.

D Over Horizontal D: Breen-2681. D first punched horizontally, curved side facing down, then corrected. FS-05-1942-501 as URS-11, very rare, even a worn example would be a prize.

1942-P TYPE II

Circulation-Strike Mintage: 57,873,000
Proof Mintage: 27,600

1942-P Type II • Market Values • Circulation Strikes and Proof Strikes

AU-55	MS-60	MS-63	MS-64	MS-64FS	MS-65	MS-65FS	MS-66	MS-66FS
$5.	$7.	$10.	$12.	$20.	$16.	$75.	$20.	$100.
MS-67	MS-67FS	PF-60	PF-63	PF-64	PF-65	PF-66	PF-67	PF-68
—	$500.	$80.	$125.	$175.	$250.	$300.	$400.	—

Availability (Certified Populations) • Circulation Strikes and Proof Strikes

<MS-60	MS-60	MS-61	MS-62	MS-63	MS-64	MS-65	MS-66	MS-67	MS-68	MS-69	MS-70
32	1	3	10	125	655	2,709	1,915	2	0		
< PF-60	PF-60	PF-61	PF-62	PF-63	PF-64	PF-65	PF-66	PF-67	PF-68	PF-69	PF-70
3	9	7	45	225	1,235	2,348	2,144	325	13	1	

Key to Collecting: The 1942-P was the first nickel minted in the wartime silver-content alloy. Mint State coins are usually brilliant, lustrous, sharply detailed, and with good eye appeal. Proofs are plentiful and until the 1960s were often found in groups of dozens or even hundreds of pieces in dealers' stocks. Those left in the cellophane envelopes of issue tended to develop gray and yellow haze, easily removable with acetone or an inert solvent. Many Proofs are lightly struck on the shoulder, showing marks and roughness from the original planchet; avoid these! Proofs are in great demand as the only "wartime silver" Proof issue.

Step-Detail Availability (MS-65 and Higher): *5 Full Steps*—1 in 10; *6 Full Steps*—Very rare.

Step-Detail Availability (Proof): *5 Full Steps*—Common; *6 Full Steps*—Common.

1942-S TYPE II

Circulation-Strike Mintage: 32,900,000

1942-S Type II • Market Values • Circulation Strikes

AU-55	MS-60	MS-63	MS-64	MS-64FS	MS-65	MS-65FS	MS-66	MS-66FS	MS-67	MS-67FS
$5.	$7.	$10.	$12.	$20.	$16.	$120.	$50.	$250.	—	$2,100.

Availability (Certified Populations) • Circulation Strikes

<MS-60	MS-60	MS-61	MS-62	MS-63	MS-64	MS-65	MS-66	MS-67	MS-68	MS-69	MS-70
21	3	2	4	27	174	664	2,536	1,251	3	0	

Key to Collecting: Usually seen brilliant, lustrous, sharply detailed if in Mint State, and with good eye appeal. Bernard Nagengast mentions a variety with a die crack through the mintmark, giving it the appearance of a dollar.

Step-Detail Availability (MS-65 and Higher): *5 Full Steps*—1 in 30; *6 Full Steps*—Very rare.

Reverse of 1941-S With Large Mintmark to *Right* of Building: Breen-2684. A circulated example in "wartime silver" alloy was found circa 1961 and passed through several hands. Called "the rarest of all Jefferson nickels" by Breen, with the notation: "Unique?" Not in Fivaz-Stanton.

1943/2-P

Circulation-Strike Mintage: 200,000 (estimated)

1943/2-P • Market Values • Circulation Strikes

AU-55	MS-60	MS-63	MS-64	MS-64FS	MS-65	MS-65FS	MS-66	MS-66FS	MS-67	MS-67FS
$130.	$180.	$260.	$350.	$550.	$620.	$1,100.	$850.	$2,250.	—	—

Availability (Certified Populations) • Circulation Strikes

<MS-60	MS-60	MS-61	MS-62	MS-63	MS-64	MS-65	MS-66	MS-67	MS-68	MS-69	MS-70
266	6	5	35	71	203	191	77	21	1	0	

Key to Collecting: This overdate was made when a 1942-P working die was repunched with a 1943-P master die, causing slight doubling and also leaving parts of the earlier 2 still visible. Vestiges include a thin trace diagonally from the upper part of the lower space in the 3, down to the left, through the base of the 3. A horizontal line, the base of the 2, fills in the top side of the curve of the 3 at the base. This variety was discovered by Delma K. Romines, confirmed by Tom DeLorey, and first published in December 1978. Since then many 1943 nickels have been inspected, bringing thousands more to light, mostly in worn grades. A few hundred Mint State coins exist. Many coins are from later die states with graininess and metal flow. Finding one with good eye appeal can be a challenge. The reverse die shows light triple punching. Breen-2687, FS-05-1943P-101.

Step-Detail Availability (MS-65 and Higher): *5 Full Steps*—Plentiful; *6 Full Steps*—1 reported.

Old Alloy: A few strikings are known on old-style (resumed in 1946) alloy of 75% copper and 25% nickel, presumably made in error from leftover planchets.

1943-P

Circulation-Strike Mintage: 271,165,000

The 1943 Doubled Eye variety.

1943-P • Market Values • Circulation Strikes

AU-55	MS-60	MS-63	MS-64	MS-64FS	MS-65	MS-65FS	MS-66	MS-66FS	MS-67	MS-67FS
$2.	$5.	$7.	$10.	$11.	$13.	$20.	$25.	$50.	—	$950.

Availability (Certified Populations) • Circulation Strikes

<MS-60	MS-60	MS-61	MS-62	MS-63	MS-64	MS-65	MS-66	MS-67	MS-68	MS-69	MS-70
130	7	6	12	45	218	847	3,333	1,735	16	0	

Key to Collecting: The mintage for the 1943-P is the highest for any of the 11 varieties in the wartime silver series. From the mintage figure the amount for 1943/2-P should be deducted.

Step-Detail Availability (MS-65 and Higher): *5 Full Steps*—1 in 5: *6 Full Steps*—Scarce.

Old-Style Planchet: A few strikings are known on old-style planchet with alloy of 75% copper and 25% nickel, made in error from leftover planchets.

Doubled Eye Variety: Breen-2688, FS-05-1943P-106 as URS-9. Further from Fivaz-Stanton: "The doubling is visible on the date, LIBERTY, the motto, and most noticeably the eye. There is a secondary eye below the primary eye, hence the nickname 'double eye' variety." One in 20 coins are 5 Full Steps, and no 6 Full Steps are known (see Nagengast).

1943-D

Circulation-Strike Mintage: 15,294,000

1943-D • Market Values • Circulation Strikes

AU-55	MS-60	MS-63	MS-64	MS-64FS	MS-65	MS-65FS	MS-66	MS-66FS	MS-67	MS-67FS
$3.	$6.	$10.	$12.	$16.	$15.	$20.	$25.	$30.	—	$115.

Availability (Certified Populations) • Circulation Strikes

<MS-60	MS-60	MS-61	MS-62	MS-63	MS-64	MS-65	MS-66	MS-67	MS-68	MS-69	MS-70
9	5	1	6	41	342	1,708	5,577	3,360	10	0	

Key to Collecting: The 1943-D is the lowest-mintage issue in the wartime silver series. In the days in the 1950s (especially) and 1960s when roll sets of the 11 different silver-content nickels traded regularly, this was viewed as the most desired issue. As most have good details, this is a great coin for a type set. Some are prooflike.

Step-Detail Availability (MS-65 and Higher): *5 Full Steps*—1 in 2; *6 Full Steps*—Common.

1943-S

Circulation-Strike Mintage: 104,060,000

1943-S • Market Values • Circulation Strikes

AU-55	MS-60	MS-63	MS-64	MS-64FS	MS-65	MS-65FS	MS-66	MS-66FS	MS-67	MS-67FS
$2.	$5.	$7.	$8.	$10.	$13.	$30.	$25.	$75.	—	$600.

Availability (Certified Populations) • Circulation Strikes

<MS-60	MS-60	MS-61	MS-62	MS-63	MS-64	MS-65	MS-66	MS-67	MS-68	MS-69	MS-70
26	1	3	921	15	118	676	3,103	1,776	3	0	

Key to Collecting: Usually with superb eye appeal, brilliant and lustrous. Some are from highly polished dies, but with microscopic striae; these are very attractive. This is the only San Francisco Mint silver-content nickel that is fairly easy to find with 5 Full Steps.
Step-Detail Availability (MS-65 and Higher): *5 Full Steps*—1 in 10; *6 Full Steps*—Scarce.

1944-P

Circulation-Strike Mintage: 119,150,000

1944-P • Market Values • Circulation Strikes

AU-55	MS-60	MS-63	MS-64	MS-64FS	MS-65	MS-65FS	MS-66	MS-66FS	MS-67	MS-67FS
$3.	$7.	$10.	$15.	$20.	$20.	$55.	$50.	$175.	—	$3,750.

Availability (Certified Populations) • Circulation Strikes

<MS-60	MS-60	MS-61	MS-62	MS-63	MS-64	MS-65	MS-66	MS-67	MS-68	MS-69	MS-70
23	4	3	5	33	174	854	2,120	745	0	0	

Key to Collecting: This issue is very plentiful and is nearly always seen with excellent eye appeal. Quite a few are prooflike. Avoid pieces with rough surfaces, such as incomplete striking revealing original planchet details on the shoulder.
Step-Detail Availability (MS-65 and Higher): *5 Full Steps*—1 in 15; *6 Full Steps*—Rare.
Old-Style Planchet: A few strikings are known on old-style planchets of 75% copper and 25% nickel, presumably made in error from stray leftovers.
Famous Counterfeit: Many counterfeit 1944-dated nickels *without* P mintmark and *none* in silver-content alloy were made by a numismatically naive New Jersey miscreant, Francis Leroy Henning, who was tracked down when these "rarities" attracted the attention of collectors. The scenario was played out in the numismatic magazines.[2]

1944-D

Circulation-Strike Mintage: 32,309,000

1944-D • Market Values • Circulation Strikes

AU-55	MS-60	MS-63	MS-64	MS-64FS	MS-65	MS-65FS	MS-66	MS-66FS	MS-67	MS-67FS
$3.	$6.	$10.	$12.	$14.	$18.	$20.	$30.	$35.	—	$175.

Availability (Certified Populations) • Circulation Strikes

<MS-60	MS-60	MS-61	MS-62	MS-63	MS-64	MS-65	MS-66	MS-67	MS-68	MS-69	MS-70
12	9	0	3	25	147	907	3,929	2,316	6	0	

Key to Collecting: Another silver-content winner, the 1944-D usually has good details and excellent eye appeal. Surfaces are satiny.

Step-Detail Availability (MS-65 and Higher): *5 Full Steps*—1 in 2; *6 Full Steps*—1 in 2.

1944-S

Circulation-Strike Mintage: 21,640,000

1944-S • Market Values • Circulation Strikes

AU-55	MS-60	MS-63	MS-64	MS-64FS	MS-65	MS-65FS	MS-66	MS-66FS	MS-67	MS-67FS
$2.	$5.	$8.	$10.	$27.	$16.	$150.	$40.	$275.	—	$1,100.

Availability (Certified Populations) • Circulation Strikes

<MS-60	MS-60	MS-61	MS-62	MS-63	MS-64	MS-65	MS-66	MS-67	MS-68	MS-69	MS-70
9	3	0	4	16	76	654	3,028	1,516	3	0	

Key to Collecting: Somewhat scarce in Mint State in the context of silver-content nickels. Usually seen with a typical strike, sometimes with original planchet roughness on the shoulder, and often from tired dies. Among silver-content nickels with 6 Full Steps this is the rarest collectible issue (the 1945-S being unknown). This one requires connoisseurship! Some have a die crack through the S, a fanciful dollar sign.

Step-Detail Availability (MS-65 and Higher): *5 Full Steps*—1 in 100; *6 Full Steps*—Very rare.

1945-P

Circulation-Strike Mintage: 119,408,000

1945-P • Market Values • Circulation Strikes

AU-55	MS-60	MS-63	MS-64	MS-64FS	MS-65	MS-65FS	MS-66	MS-66FS	MS-67	MS-67FS
$2.	$5.	$7.	$10.	$50.	$18.	$110.	$35.	$425.	—	$5,500.

Availability (Certified Populations) • Circulation Strikes

<MS-60	MS-60	MS-61	MS-62	MS-63	MS-64	MS-65	MS-66	MS-67	MS-68	MS-69	MS-70
33	1	5	7	29	200	727	2,674	317	2	0	

Key to Collecting: This is a very common coin in Mint State, but well-struck gems, without roughness, and with good eye appeal constitute only a fraction of the populations. Seeking sharp steps adds another challenge. The good news is that there are scads of coins out there for the cherrypicker to sort through.

Step-Detail Availability (MS-65 and Higher): *5 Full Steps*—1 in 80; *6 Full Steps*—Very rare.

Doubled-Die Reverses: Three doubled die reverses are popular, listed as FS-05-1945P-801, 803, and 804, with the first and last being the two rarest.

1945-D

Circulation-Strike Mintage: 37,158,000

1945-D • Market Values • Circulation Strikes

AU-55	MS-60	MS-63	MS-64	MS-64FS	MS-65	MS-65FS	MS-66	MS-66FS	MS-67	MS-67FS
$2.	$5.	$7.	$10.	$20.	$16.	$35.	$30.	$50.	—	$400.

Availability (Certified Populations) • Circulation Strikes

<MS-60	MS-60	MS-61	MS-62	MS-63	MS-64	MS-65	MS-66	MS-67	MS-68	MS-69	MS-70
7	4	0	3	16	134	1,003	3,469	2,243	5	0	

Key to Collecting: The Denver Mint's good performance in turning out wartime nickels with far above average eye appeal ended here, and most of 1945-D are lustrous enough, but lack the flash and sharpness of earlier ones. There can be some roughness on the shoulder. Connoisseurship is advised.

Step-Detail Availability (MS-65 and Higher): *5 Full Steps*—1 in 5; *6 Full Steps*—Scarce.

1945-S

Circulation-Strike Mintage: 58,939,000

1945-S • Market Values • Circulation Strikes

AU-55	MS-60	MS-63	MS-64	MS-64FS	MS-65	MS-65FS	MS-66	MS-66FS	MS-67	MS-67FS
$2.	$5.	$7.	$10.	$165.	$16.	$300.	$25.	$750.	—	$4,500.

Availability (Certified Populations) • Circulation Strikes

<MS-60	MS-60	MS-61	MS-62	MS-63	MS-64	MS-65	MS-66	MS-67	MS-68	MS-69	MS-70
30	5	3	3	19	157	715	3,377	1,505	3	0	

Key to Collecting: Bernard Nagengast has the platform: "The 45-S is similar in appearance to the 44-S, but generally worse! The coins are usually frosty, but are often seen with moderate to severe surface roughness. Much of the issue was struck from worn dies. This date is the 'stopper' in assembling a set of Five Full Steps war nickels, as it is much rarer than the second toughest date, the 44-S. Finding indisputable five-step coins is a terrific challenge, since the steps are usually shallow and weakly struck. Many of what to appear to be 5 Full Steps coins have small bridges between the steps. Sharp, deep 5 Full Steps coins are rare. Six Full Steps are extremely rare. Again cherrypicking (to use a word popularized by Bill Fivaz) can pay rich dividends. However, the time is *now*. As certification services pick up on step details and if they ever add the aspect of Full Details (sharp shoulder, etc., in addition to steps), the game will be over, and sharp gems will sell for much more than they do now!

Step-Detail Availability (MS-65 and Higher): *5 Full Steps*—1 in 300; • *6 Full Steps*—Extremely rare or unknown, opinions vary.

1946

Circulation-Strike Mintage: 161,116,000

1946 • Market Values • Circulation Strikes

AU-55	MS-60	MS-63	MS-64	MS-64FS	MS-65	MS-65FS	MS-66	MS-66FS	MS-67	MS-67FS
$0.25	$0.75	$2.	$4.	$50.	$6.	$300.	$20.	$2,000.	—	—

Availability (Certified Populations) • Circulation Strikes

<MS-60	MS-60	MS-61	MS-62	MS-63	MS-64	MS-65	MS-66	MS-67	MS-68	MS-69	MS-70
13	0	0	3	16	118	226	96	13	0	0	

Key to Collecting: In 1946, the alloy of 75% copper and 25% nickel resumed. Mint State examples are as plentiful as can be, but most, while lustrous, have rough areas or other problems. Those with decently defined steps often have many marks, likely mostly from the original planchet, not that this makes a difference. Some are struck from tired, overworked dies as evidenced by granular fields. Cherrypicking is the order of the day, if you can find a dealer who will accommodate your interests.

Step-Detail Availability (MS-65 and Higher): *5 Full Steps*—1 in 10; *6 Full Steps*— Very scarce.

Wartime Alloy: Several impressions in silver-content wartime alloy have been reported, presumably made in error from a leftover planchet.

Die Doubling: Several variations occur on reverses and are illustrated and described in the literature, Breen-2697, FS-05-1945P-801 being the most notable, with ELLO and NTS with significant doubling, rated as URS-11.

1946-D

Circulation-Strike Mintage: 45,292,000

1946-D • Market Values • Circulation Strikes

AU-55	MS-60	MS-63	MS-64	MS-64FS	MS-65	MS-65FS	MS-66	MS-66FS	MS-67	MS-67FS
$0.50	$1.	$2.	$4.	$10.	$6.	$20.	$30.	$50.	—	—

Availability (Certified Populations) • Circulation Strikes

<MS-60	MS-60	MS-61	MS-62	MS-63	MS-64	MS-65	MS-66	MS-67	MS-68	MS-69	MS-70
6	2	1	1	9	96	660	657	106	0	0	

Key to Collecting: Usually found with nice luster and overall satisfactory appearance. As is the case with all regular Jefferson nickel issues, multiple die pairs were used, and one rule does not fit all coins.

Step-Detail Availability (MS-65 and Higher): *5 Full Steps*—1 to 5; *6 Full Steps*— Scarce.

D Over Inverted D: The mintmark was first punched upside down, the corrected, but the under-mintmark is still visible. Breen-2708, FS-05-1946D-501, rated as URS-8 by the last, with this comment: "This is considered to be the second rarest of the original Jefferson 'Top 10' in Mint State, second only to the 1942-D over horizontal D."

1946-S

Circulation-Strike Mintage: 13,560,000 (all kinds)

1946-S • Market Values • Circulation Strikes

AU-55	MS-60	MS-63	MS-64	MS-64FS	MS-65	MS-65FS	MS-66	MS-66FS	MS-67	MS-67FS
$0.50	$1.00	$1.50	$2.50	$150.	$4.	$90.	$20.	$900.	—	—

Availability (Certified Populations) • Circulation Strikes

<MS-60	MS-60	MS-61	MS-62	MS-63	MS-64	MS-65	MS-66	MS-67	MS-68	MS-69	MS-70
11	0	0	2	22	158	521	349	127	0	0	

Key to Collecting: Despite its relatively low mintage for the era, the 1946-S is readily available in Mint State, usually with good eye appeal. Sharp steps are a challenge for the cherrypicker, but the number of 5 Full Steps coins is greater than the number of collectors desiring them, so when you find one there will be little in the way of a premium. However, if you expect a dealer specialist to locate one and sell it to you, a premium is indeed in order for the effort involved.

Step-Detail Availability (MS-65 and Higher): *5 Full Steps*—1 in 30; *6 Full Steps*—Extremely rare or unknown, opinions vary.

1947

Circulation-Strike Mintage: 95,000,000

1947 • Market Values • Circulation Strikes

AU-55	MS-60	MS-63	MS-64	MS-64FS	MS-65	MS-65FS	MS-66	MS-66FS	MS-67	MS-67FS
$0.50	$0.75	$1.50	$2.50	$17.	$4.	$60.	$15.	$500.	—	—

Availability (Certified Populations) • Circulation Strikes

<MS-60	MS-60	MS-61	MS-62	MS-63	MS-64	MS-65	MS-66	MS-67	MS-68	MS-69	MS-70
5	2	0	6	8	148	318	178	15	0	0	

Key to Collecting: Common enough, including with good luster and eye appeal, but elusive, percentage-wise, if you want one with sharp steps.

Step-Detail Availability (MS-65 and Higher): *5 Full Steps*—1 in 10; *6 Full Steps*—Very rare.

1947-D

Circulation-Strike Mintage: 37,822,000

1947-D • Market Values • Circulation Strikes

AU-55	MS-60	MS-63	MS-64	MS-64FS	MS-65	MS-65FS	MS-66	MS-66FS	MS-67	MS-67FS
$0.50	$1.	$2.	$3.	$15.	$4.	$25.	$20.	$75.	—	$700.

Availability (Certified Populations) • Circulation Strikes

<MS-60	MS-60	MS-61	MS-62	MS-63	MS-64	MS-65	MS-66	MS-67	MS-68	MS-69	MS-70
3	0	0	2	8	90	507	453	117	0	0	

Key to Collecting: Another issue usually seen with nice luster, from flashy to satiny, and with decent eye appeal. Cherrypicking will land you a sharp one. In this era it was very popular for numismatists to tuck away a few rolls of current coins for investment and later trading, accounting for most of the supply available today.

Step-Detail Availability (MS-65 and Higher): *5 Full Steps*—1 in 5; *6 Full Steps*—Scarce.

1947-S

Circulation-Strike Mintage: 24,720,000 (all kinds)

1947-S • Market Values • Circulation Strikes

AU-55	MS-60	MS-63	MS-64	MS-64FS	MS-65	MS-65FS	MS-66	MS-66FS	MS-67	MS-67FS
$0.50	$1.	$2.	$3.	$7.	$4.	$50.	$20.	$550.	—	—

Availability (Certified Populations) • Circulation Strikes

<MS-60	MS-60	MS-61	MS-62	MS-63	MS-64	MS-65	MS-66	MS-67	MS-68	MS-69	MS-70
7	1	1	4	11	132	466	169	10	0	0	

Key to Collecting: Eye appeal ranges from dull and sub-par to pleasingly brilliant and frosty, as created by different die pairs used over a span of time. For the casual collector, picking out a nice one will be easy enough. Sharp steps are another situation, as reflected by the Nagengast-supplied information given below.
Step-Detail Availability (MS-65 and Higher): *5 Full Steps*—1 in 30; *6 Full Steps*—Very rare.

1948

Circulation-Strike Mintage: 89,348,000

1948 • Market Values • Circulation Strikes

AU-55	MS-60	MS-63	MS-64	MS-64FS	MS-65	MS-65FS	MS-66	MS-66FS	MS-67	MS-67FS
$0.50	$1.	$2.	$3.	$80.	$4.	$200.	$15.	$3,000.	—	—

Availability (Certified Populations) • Circulation Strikes

<MS-60	MS-60	MS-61	MS-62	MS-63	MS-64	MS-65	MS-66	MS-67	MS-68	MS-69	MS-70
3	0	0	4	16	117	193	75	12	0	0	

Key to Collecting: Many are lustrous and frosty and when good can be very, very good. Others were struck from tired dies and have granular surfaces. Avoid these.
Step-Detail Availability (MS-65 and Higher): *5 Full Steps*—1 in 10: *6 Full Steps*—Very scarce.

1948-D

Circulation-Strike Mintage: 44,734,000

1948-D • Market Values • Circulation Strikes

AU-55	MS-60	MS-63	MS-64	MS-64FS	MS-65	MS-65FS	MS-66	MS-66FS	MS-67	MS-67FS
$1.	$2.	$3.	$4.	$11.	$5.	$25.	$15.	$55.	—	—

Availability (Certified Populations) • Circulation Strikes

<MS-60	MS-60	MS-61	MS-62	MS-63	MS-64	MS-65	MS-66	MS-67	MS-68	MS-69	MS-70
3	1	0	0	4	69	758	554	95	0	0	

Key to Collecting: Eye appeal varies, but enough lustrous, frosty pieces are around that finding one will be no problem. Sharply defined steps are a challenge, but easy enough.
Step-Detail Availability (MS-65 and Higher): *5 Full Steps*—1 in 10; *6 Full Steps*—Scarce.

1948-S

Circulation-Strike Mintage: 11,300,000

1948-S • Market Values • Circulation Strikes

AU-55	MS-60	MS-63	MS-64	MS-64FS	MS-65	MS-65FS	MS-66	MS-66FS	MS-67	MS-67FS
$1.	$2.	$3.	$4.	$10.	$5.	$30.	$20.	$200.	—	—

Availability (Certified Populations) • Circulation Strikes

<MS-60	MS-60	MS-61	MS-62	MS-63	MS-64	MS-65	MS-66	MS-67	MS-68	MS-69	MS-70
2	2	0	2	11	140	749	486	152	0	0	

Key to Collecting: Generally the 1948-S is the nicest appearing San Francisco nickel from the span beginning in 1946 and continuing through 1954 is the opinion of Bernard Nagengast. This covers the time from the resumption of the standard alloy to the point that the San Francisco Mint stopped making nickels, seemingly forever per notices of the time.
Step-Detail Availability (MS-65 and Higher): *5 Full Steps*—1 in 20; *6 Full Steps*—Rare.

1949

Circulation-Strike Mintage: 60,652,000

1949 • Market Values • Circulation Strikes

AU-55	MS-60	MS-63	MS-64	MS-64FS	MS-65	MS-65FS	MS-66	MS-66FS	MS-67	MS-67FS
$1.50	$3.	$4.	$6.	$400.	$8.	$900.	$20.	—	—	—

Availability (Certified Populations) • Circulation Strikes

<MS-60	MS-60	MS-61	MS-62	MS-63	MS-64	MS-65	MS-66	MS-67	MS-68	MS-69	MS-70
2	1	0	2	10	56	180	109	6	0	0	

Key to Collecting: Although many 1949 nickels were struck, the coin market was in a state of malaise at the time (and would not wake up until after 1951), and fewer rolls were saved by collectors. Of those that do exist today, many are rough, dull, and otherwise with poor eye appeal. Ones with sharp steps are indeed rare, yielding what Bernard Nagengast calls, complete with an exclamation point, "one of the rarest coins in the Jefferson series in gem, full strike, full step!"
Step-Detail Availability (MS-65 and Higher): *5 Full Steps*—1 in 500; *6 Full Steps*—Unverified.

1949-D

Circulation-Strike Mintage: 36,498,000

1949-D • Market Values • Circulation Strikes

AU-55	MS-60	MS-63	MS-64	MS-64FS	MS-65	MS-65FS	MS-66	MS-66FS	MS-67	MS-67FS
$1.	$2.	$3.	$5.	$25.	$6.	$45.	$23.	$200.	—	—

Availability (Certified Populations) • Circulation Strikes

<MS-60	MS-60	MS-61	MS-62	MS-63	MS-64	MS-65	MS-66	MS-67	MS-68	MS-69	MS-70
14	1	0	2	13	128	484	439	103	0	0	

Key to Collecting: Although many Mint State coins exist, the majority have problems of one sort or another, ranging from dull surfaces, spots, to areas of weakness. It will

take some searching to find a sparkling gem. From the mintage figure a small deduction can be taken for the overmintmark variety described in the next listing.
Step-Detail Availability (MS-65 and Higher): *5 Full Steps*—1 in 20; *6 Full Steps*—Rare.

1949-D/S

Circulation-Strike Mintage: 200,000 (estimated)

1949-D/S • Market Values • Circulation Strikes

AU-55	MS-60	MS-63	MS-64	MS-64FS	MS-65	MS-65FS	MS-66	MS-66FS	MS-67	MS-67FS
$20.	$150.	$200.	$300.	—	$350.	—	—	—	—	—

Availability (Certified Populations) • Circulation Strikes

<MS-60	MS-60	MS-61	MS-62	MS-63	MS-64	MS-65	MS-66	MS-67	MS-68	MS-69	MS-70
20	1	1	0	11	85	203	48	0	0	0	

Key to Collecting: To create this variety a die already with an S mintmark was overpunched with a D. Ample traces of the S are still visible. This variety seems to have been discovered in the early 1970s. Rolls were searched, and dozens were found. Probably somewhere around a couple hundred exist today in various grades, all from a single die pair. The dies became worn over a period of time, causing a deterioration in eye appeal. Cherrypicking is advised, but the population is small, and finding a 5 Full Steps gem will take some doing! The mintage is unknown, and the estimate simply reflects the possible life of a die pair. Breen-2720, FS-05-1949D-501. Many of these have been found in the mint sets sold to collectors at the time.
Step-Detail Availability (MS-65 and Higher): *5 Full Steps*—1 in 20; *6 Full Steps*—Unverified.

1949-S

Circulation-Strike Mintage: 9,716,000

1949-S • Market Values • Circulation Strikes

AU-55	MS-60	MS-63	MS-64	MS-64FS	MS-65	MS-65FS	MS-66	MS-66FS	MS-67	MS-67FS
$1.	$2.	$3.	$5.	$175.	$6.	$350.	$20.	$900.	—	—

Availability (Certified Populations) • Circulation Strikes

<MS-60	MS-60	MS-61	MS-62	MS-63	MS-64	MS-65	MS-66	MS-67	MS-68	MS-69	MS-70
7	0	1	6	27	86	308	173	25	0	0	

Key to Collecting: Although this issue is inexpensive, gems with nice eye appeal are hard to find, and those with 5 Full Steps are very rare. This is a cherrypicker's delight—a great quarry to seek at a regional coin show. Throughout this period, roll quantities were saved in few numbers, percentage-wise, than earlier or later.
Step-Detail Availability (MS-65 and Higher): *5 Full Steps*—1 in 150; *6 Full Steps*—Extremely rare or unknown, opinions vary.

1950

Circulation-Strike Mintage: 9,796,000
Proof Mintage: 51,386

1950 • Market Values • Circulation Strikes and Proof Strikes

AU-55	MS-60	MS-63	MS-64	MS-64FS	MS-65	MS-65FS	MS-66	MS-66FS
$1.	$2.	$4.	$5.	$125.	$6.	$300.	$55.	$1,500.
MS-67	MS-67FS	PF-60	PF-63	PF-64	PF-65	PF-66	PF-67	PF-68
—	$7,000.	$30.	$50.	$60.	$65.	—	—	—

Availability (Certified Populations) • Circulation Strikes and Proof Strikes

<MS-60	MS-60	MS-61	MS-62	MS-63	MS-64	MS-65	MS-66	MS-67	MS-68	MS-69	MS-70
2	0	0	1	11	113	283	278	48	0	0	
< PF-60	PF-60	PF-61	PF-62	PF-63	PF-64	PF-65	PF-66	PF-67	PF-68	PF-69	PF-70
0	1	0	5	104	436	802	567	93	1	0	

Key to Collecting: Quality of circulation strikes varies from dull to lustrous and appealing. Enough exist that finding a choice one will be easy to do. A 5 Full Steps coin is another breed of cat, and 6 Full Steps coins are rarer yet. Proofs were made this year for the first time since 1942. Early Proof strikes are satiny rather than fully mirrorlike. 6 Full Steps details are easily enough found. Later ones are mirrorlike, similar to those made in following years. Among the mirrorlike Proofs a minority have frosty cameo contrast and are especially highly prized, especially following the 1991 publication of *Cameo and Brilliant Proof Coinage of the 1950 to 1970 Era*, by Rick Jerry Tomaska.

Step-Detail Availability (MS-65 and Higher): *5 Full Steps*—1 in 150; *6 Full Steps*—Very rare.

Step-Detail Availability (Proof): *5 Full Steps*—Common; *6 Full Steps*—Common.

1950-D

Circulation-Strike Mintage: 2,630,030

1950-D • Market Values • Circulation Strikes

AU-55	MS-60	MS-63	MS-64	MS-64FS	MS-65	MS-65FS	MS-66	MS-66FS	MS-67	MS-67FS
$6.	$12.	$14.	$16.	$18.	$20.	$55.	$60.	$125.	—	$2,750.

Availability (Certified Populations) • Circulation Strikes

<MS-60	MS-60	MS-61	MS-62	MS-63	MS-64	MS-65	MS-66	MS-67	MS-68	MS-69	MS-70
6	11	1	8	53	579	2,111	1,797	220	0	0	

Key to Collecting: This is the showcase rarity of the Jefferson nickel series—rare only in terms of its mintage figure, but in actuality available enough that everyone interested can own a Mint State example. As to *circulated* coins, these are really hard to find! The preceding chapter tells the story of this coin, to which can be added the Nagengast comment, "Despite having the lowest mintage, the 1950-D is actually one of the most common early Jeffersons in Uncirculated, due to excessive hoarding." Although Mint State coins are very common today, most are rather dull or uninspiring in appearance, often struck from worn dies and lackluster. For a sparkling gem with sharp steps the adjective *scarce* can truly be applied.

Step-Detail Availability (MS-65 and Higher): *5 Full Steps*—1 in 10; *6 Full Steps*—Very scarce.

1951

Circulation-Strike Mintage: 28,552,000
Proof Mintage: 57,500

1951 • Market Values • Circulation Strikes and Proof Strikes

AU-55	MS-60	MS-63	MS-64	MS-64FS	MS-65	MS-65FS	MS-66	MS-66FS
$2.	$3.	$4.	$7.	$75.	$9.	$250.	$15.	$3,500.
MS-67	MS-67FS	PF-60	PF-63	PF-64	PF-65	PF-66	PF-67	PF-68
—	—	$30.	$50.	$60.	$65.	—	—	—

Availability (Certified Populations) • Circulation Strikes and Proof Strikes

<MS-60	MS-60	MS-61	MS-62	MS-63	MS-64	MS-65	MS-66	MS-67	MS-68	MS-69	MS-70
1	0	1	0	11	98	160	138	10	0	0	
< PF-60	PF-60	PF-61	PF-62	PF-63	PF-64	PF-65	PF-66	PF-67	PF-68	PF-69	PF-70
2	0	1	9	33	63	362	790	631	206	16	

Key to Collecting: Surface quality varies, many lack eye appeal, and some looking will be needed to find an attractive gem, and a Sherlock Holmes hat will need to be donned to find one with 5 Full Steps. This was the last year of the coin market slump, and quantities set aside in rolls were less than they would be later in the decade. Proofs are of the mirror finish type, as are all Proofs from this year forward. Striking is good with 6 Full Steps detail easily available. Cameo contrast Proofs are in the minority.

Step-Detail Availability (MS-65 and Higher): *5 Full Steps*—1 in 100; *6 Full Steps*—Very rare.

Step-Detail Availability (Proof): *5 Full Steps*—Common • *6 Full Steps*—In the minority.

1951-D

Circulation-Strike Mintage: 20,460,000

1951-D • Market Values • Circulation Strikes

AU-55	MS-60	MS-63	MS-64	MS-64FS	MS-65	MS-65FS	MS-66	MS-66FS	MS-67	MS-67FS
$2.	$4.	$5.	$8.	$30.	$10.	$80.	$30.	$550.	—	—

Availability (Certified Populations) • Circulation Strikes

<MS-60	MS-60	MS-61	MS-62	MS-63	MS-64	MS-65	MS-66	MS-67	MS-68	MS-69	MS-70
1	0	1	0	3	116	399	352	43	0	0	

Key to Collecting: Indifferent quality marks this issue, with dull coins, pieces struck from worn dies, and other negatives combining to put sparkling gems, well struck and with good eye appeal, in the distinct minority. We are now entering the era of Jefferson nickels in which quality can be a big problem—surprisingly so, as an outsider might expect that early Jeffersons had problems, but by the 1950s, when coin collecting was even more popular, that choice pieces would abound. Part of the problem is that in the 1950s and 1960s there was no emphasis on this, and rolls were rolls and were seldom inspected.

Step-Detail Availability (MS-65 and Higher): *5 Full Steps*—1 in 30: *6 Full Steps*—Rare.

1951-S

Circulation-Strike Mintage: 7,776,000

1951-S • Market Values • Circulation Strikes

AU-55	MS-60	MS-63	MS-64	MS-64FS	MS-65	MS-65FS	MS-66	MS-66FS	MS-67	MS-67FS
$1.	$2.	$3.	$4.	$50.	$5.	$300.	$35.	$2,700.	—	—

Availability (Certified Populations) • Circulation Strikes

<MS-60	MS-60	MS-61	MS-62	MS-63	MS-64	MS-65	MS-66	MS-67	MS-68	MS-69	MS-70
0	0	0	0	8	104	349	228	3	0	0	

Key to Collecting: Quality varies all over the place, from dull and unattractive to lustrous and with fairly Sharp Details, excepting the steps. For the latter finding 5 Full Steps will take some doing, and 6 Full Steps may be nearly impossible.

Step-Detail Availability (MS-65 and Higher): *5 Full Steps*—1 in 150; *6 Full Steps*—Extremely rare or unknown, opinions vary.

1952

Circulation-Strike Mintage: 63,988,000
Proof Mintage: 81,980

1952 • Market Values • Circulation Strikes and Proof Strikes

AU-55	MS-60	MS-63	MS-64	MS-64FS	MS-65	MS-65FS	MS-66	MS-66FS
$0.50	$1.	$2.	$3.	$625.	$4.	$800.	$25.	$1,200.
MS-67	MS-67FS	PF-60	PF-63	PF-64	PF-65	PF-66	PF-67	PF-68
—	—	$10.	$15.	$35.	$40.	—	—	—

Availability (Certified Populations) • Circulation Strikes and Proof Strikes

<MS-60	MS-60	MS-61	MS-62	MS-63	MS-64	MS-65	MS-66	MS-67	MS-68	MS-69	MS-70
9	1	0	4	15	71	122	82	13	0	0	
< PF-60	PF-60	PF-61	PF-62	PF-63	PF-64	PF-65	PF-66	PF-67	PF-68	PF-69	PF-70
1	0	0	3	4	54	264	737	797	271	28	

Key to Collecting: Many Mint State coins are around, but most have poor eye appeal, and even those taken from undisturbed bank-wrapped rolls are apt to be discolored or downright ugly. Finding a sharp one will take some searching. The Mint simply was not interested in turning out quality this year. Marks and nicks are common on Mint State coins, many from the surfaces of the original planchets. Proofs are sharply struck with 6 Full Steps detail easily available. Cameo contrast Proofs are in the minority.

Step-Detail Availability (MS-65 and Higher): *5 Full Steps*—1 in 200 • *6 Full Steps*—Unverified.

Step-Detail Availability (Proof): *5 Full Steps*—In the minority, but who cares? • *6 Full Steps*—In the minority.

1952-D

Circulation-Strike Mintage: 30,638,000

1952-D • Market Values • Circulation Strikes

AU-55	MS-60	MS-63	MS-64	MS-64FS	MS-65	MS-65FS	MS-66	MS-66FS	MS-67	MS-67FS
$2.	$4.	$5.	$7.	$80.	$9.	$250.	$25.	$700.	—	—

Availability (Certified Populations) • Circulation Strikes

<MS-60	MS-60	MS-61	MS-62	MS-63	MS-64	MS-65	MS-66	MS-67	MS-68	MS-69	MS-70
9	1	0	0	3	104	296	186	41	0	0	

Key to Collecting: Most Mint State examples of 1952-D are rather decent in appearance. The details can be weak on both sides at the center, from incorrect but practical die spacing. The key here is to seek a sharply detailed coin.
Step-Detail Availability (MS-65 and Higher): *5 Full Steps*—1 in 20 • *6 Full Steps*— Unverified.

1952-S

Circulation-Strike Mintage: 20,572,000

1952-S • Market Values • Circulation Strikes

AU-55	MS-60	MS-63	MS-64	MS-64FS	MS-65	MS-65FS	MS-66	MS-66FS	MS-67	MS-67FS
$0.50	$1.	$2.	$3.	$75.	$4.	$500.	$40.	$1,700.	—	—

Availability (Certified Populations) • Circulation Strikes

<MS-60	MS-60	MS-61	MS-62	MS-63	MS-64	MS-65	MS-66	MS-67	MS-68	MS-69	MS-70
2	0	0	0	7	125	291	247	3	0	0	

Key to Collecting: Quality varies all over the place, from the use of multiple die pairs at different periods. While some 1952-S nickels are attractive gems (MS-65 or better), others are dogs. Finding one with sharp steps is a great challenge—as noted below. In his narrative, not quoted here, Bernard Nagengast notes that some 5 Full Steps can be found, full but not *sharp*. Ah, the nuances of coin hunting!
Step-Detail Availability (MS-65 and Higher): *5 Full Steps*—1 in 300; *6 Full Steps*— Unverified.

1953

Circulation-Strike Mintage: 46,644,000
Proof Mintage: 128,800

1953 • Market Values • Circulation Strikes and Proof Strikes

AU-55	MS-60	MS-63	MS-64	MS-64FS	MS-65	MS-65FS	MS-66	MS-66FS
$0.25	$0.50	$1.00	$1.50	$2,800.	$2.	$6,500.	$40.	$6,600.
MS-67	MS-67FS	PF-60	PF-63	PF-64	PF-65	PF-66	PF-67	PF-68
—	—	$5.	$10.	$35.	$40.	—	—	—

Availability (Certified Populations) • Circulation Strikes and Proof Strikes

<MS-60	MS-60	MS-61	MS-62	MS-63	MS-64	MS-65	MS-66	MS-67	MS-68	MS-69	MS-70
7	0	0	2	14	84	240	154	78	5	0	
< PF-60	PF-60	PF-61	PF-62	PF-63	PF-64	PF-65	PF-66	PF-67	PF-68	PF-69	PF-70
0	0	0	1	4	34	160	521	785	499	34	

Key to Collecting: It would be difficult to add much to this comment by Bernard Nagengast: "Really a common coin if one cares nothing about quality. Most of this issue is of very poor quality. Dark colored, poorly struck, nicked and marked coins are the norm. The 1953 is rare as a full strike, brilliant white coin, and is one of the rarest P mints in full strike condition with unmarked full steps." Proofs vary in their sharpness, and for the first time among modern (1950 onward) Proofs, many pieces are less that 6 Full Steps, although the latter are available. Attention to striking detail seems to have slipped this year. Cameo contrast Proofs are in the minority.

Step-Detail Availability (MS-65 and Higher): *5 Full Steps*—1 in 500; *6 Full Steps*—Unverified.

Step-Detail Availability (Proof): *5 Full Steps*—Usual; *6 Full Steps*—In the minority.

1953-D

Circulation-Strike Mintage: 59,878,600

1953-D • Market Values • Circulation Strikes

AU-55	MS-60	MS-63	MS-64	MS-64FS	MS-65	MS-65FS	MS-66	MS-66FS	MS-67	MS-67FS
$0.25	$0.50	$1.00	$1.50	$35.	$2.	$250.	$40.	—	—	—

Availability (Certified Populations) • Circulation Strikes

<MS-60	MS-60	MS-61	MS-62	MS-63	MS-64	MS-65	MS-66	MS-67	MS-68	MS-69	MS-70
2	5	0	2	14	148	372	231	9	0	0	

Key to Collecting: Most Mint State coins are attractive and highly lustrous. Light details at the center of both sides is common. Sharp strikes are rare.

Step-Detail Availability (MS-65 and Higher): *5 Full Steps*—1 in 200; *6 Full Steps*—Unverified.

1953-S

Circulation-Strike Mintage: 19,210,900

1953-S • Market Values • Circulation Strikes

AU-55	MS-60	MS-63	MS-64	MS-64FS	MS-65	MS-65FS	MS-66	MS-66FS	MS-67	MS-67FS
$0.50	$1.	$2.	$3.	$4,400.	$4.	$12,000.	$40.	—	—	—

Availability (Certified Populations) • Circulation Strikes

<MS-60	MS-60	MS-61	MS-62	MS-63	MS-64	MS-65	MS-66	MS-67	MS-68	MS-69	MS-70
5	1	1	4	43	272	245	119	11	0	0	

Key to Collecting: Lustrous examples are easy enough to find, but usually with weak details in the centers or with surfaces indicating that the dies were used far too long. In an early survey the PAK Full Step Nickel Club nominated the 1953-S to be the second worst struck Jefferson nickel, with only the 1954-S being more miserable. To the extent that market prices can be reflective of rarity, later the 1953-S became slightly more valuable than the 1954-S in MS-65 with Full Steps (now divided into 5 Full Steps and 6 Full Steps). "Most five step coins have a weak strike, and usually that is what the collector must settle for. Such coins are often touted as rare and offered at high prices," this per the Nagengast text.

Step-Detail Availability (MS-65 and Higher): *5 Full Steps*—1 in 5,000: *6 Full Steps*—Unverified.

1954

Circulation-Strike Mintage: 47,684,050
Proof Mintage: 233,300

1954 • Market Values • Circulation Strikes and Proof Strikes

AU-55	MS-60	MS-63	MS-64	MS-64FS	MS-65	MS-65FS	MS-66	MS-66FS
$0.50	$1.00	$1.50	$2.	$95.	$3.	$450.	$15.	$550.
MS-67	MS-67FS	PF-60	PF-63	PF-64	PF-65	PF-66	PF-67	PF-68
—	—	$4.	$8.	$20.	$25.	—	—	—

Availability (Certified Populations) • Circulation Strikes and Proof Strikes

<MS-60	MS-60	MS-61	MS-62	MS-63	MS-64	MS-65	MS-66	MS-67	MS-68	MS-69	MS-70
5	0	2	4	31	184	211	60	6	0	0	
< PF-60	PF-60	PF-61	PF-62	PF-63	PF-64	PF-65	PF-66	PF-67	PF-68	PF-69	PF-70
0	1	0	5	7	70	239	561	941	716	131	

Key to Collecting: Circulation strikes are usually sub-par in appearance. However, enough are around that you will eventually find a nice one. Price listings hardly ever address quality, but just give grade. Take your time on this and most other "common" Jeffersons of this decade and the next. Proofs are sharply struck with 6 Full Steps detail easily available. However, during this era the microscopic details become progressively weaker due to wear on hubs and master dies. Cameo contrast Proofs are in the minority.

Step-Detail Availability (MS-65 and Higher): *5 Full Steps—1 in 200; 6 Full Steps—* Unverified.

Step-Detail Availability (Proof): *5 Full Steps—Available; 6 Full Steps—1 in 7.*

1954-D

Circulation-Strike Mintage: 117,183,060

1954-D • Market Values • Circulation Strikes

AU-55	MS-60	MS-63	MS-64	MS-64FS	MS-65	MS-65FS	MS-66	MS-66FS	MS-67	MS-67FS
$0.50	$1.00	$1.50	$2.	$95.	$3.	$200.	$35.	—	—	—

Availability (Certified Populations) • Circulation Strikes

<MS-60	MS-60	MS-61	MS-62	MS-63	MS-64	MS-65	MS-66	MS-67	MS-68	MS-69	MS-70
9	1	2	7	64	196	117	17	1	0	0	

Key to Collecting: 99% of buyers will find a "nice" coin easily, as most Mint State coins are brilliant with good luster. However, if you want one without bagmarks or original planchet marks, and if you want at least five steps leading into Monticello, you have your work cut out!

Step-Detail Availability (MS-65 and Higher): *5 Full Steps—1 in 200; 6 Full Steps—* Unverified.

1954-S

Circulation-Strike Mintage: 29,384,000

1954-S • Market Values • Circulation Strikes

AU-55	MS-60	MS-63	MS-64	MS-64FS	MS-65	MS-65FS	MS-66	MS-66FS	MS-67	MS-67FS
$1.00	$2.00	$2.50	$3.	$5,000.	$4.	$14,000.	$35.	—	—	—

Availability (Certified Populations) • Circulation Strikes

<MS-60	MS-60	MS-61	MS-62	MS-63	MS-64	MS-65	MS-66	MS-67	MS-68	MS-69	MS-70
7	4	2	9	62	239	332	128	13	0	0	

Key to Collecting: The 1954-S is another one of those issues that the buyer who simply purchases "MS-65" or "gem" will quickly find. However, nearly all are weak at their centers. In an early survey the PAK Full Step Nickel Club crowned the 1954-S with the dubious distinction of being the worst struck of all coins in the series, with the runner-up being the 1953-S. From the mintage a deduction for the overmintmark (see next listing) can be taken.

Step-Detail Availability (MS-65 and Higher): *5 Full Steps*—1 in 3,000; *6 Full Steps*—Unverified.

1954-S/D

Circulation-Strike Mintage: 200,000 (estimated)

1954-S/D • Market Values • Circulation Strikes

AU-55	MS-60	MS-63	MS-64	MS-64FS	MS-65	MS-65FS	MS-66	MS-66FS	MS-67	MS-67FS
$15.	$25.	$40.	$60.	—	$75.	—	—	—	—	—

Availability (Certified Populations) • Circulation Strikes

<MS-60	MS-60	MS-61	MS-62	MS-63	MS-64	MS-65	MS-66	MS-67	MS-68	MS-69	MS-70
32	3	4	3	48	312	155	37	0	0	0	

Key to Collecting: Struck from one pair of dies, the reverse originally being with an D mintmark that was overpunched with an S. Probably over a thousand exist, including many in Mint State. All show lightness in one area or another. As the die continued to be used, the detail of the underlying D was weakened. In the marketplace one with a clearly definable D commands more money than one with a weak D. Breen-2736,FS-05-1954D-501.

Step-Detail Availability (MS-65 and Higher): *5 Full Steps*—Unknown; *6 Full Steps*—Unknown.

1955

Circulation-Strike Mintage: 7,888,000
Proof Mintage: 378,200

1955 • Market Values • Circulation Strikes and Proof Strikes

AU-55	MS-60	MS-63	MS-64	MS-64FS	MS-65	MS-65FS	MS-66	MS-66FS
$0.50	$1.00	$1.50	$2.	$150.	$3.	$1,000.	$30.	—
MS-67	MS-67FS	PF-60	PF-63	PF-64	PF-65	PF-66	PF-67	PF-68
—	—	$3.	$5.	$12.	$15.	—	—	—

Availability (Certified Populations) • Circulation Strikes and Proof Strikes

<MS-60	MS-60	MS-61	MS-62	MS-63	MS-64	MS-65	MS-66	MS-67	MS-68	MS-69	MS-70
1	1	0	2	28	208	241	65	8	0	0	
< PF-60	PF-60	PF-61	PF-62	PF-63	PF-64	PF-65	PF-66	PF-67	PF-68	PF-69	PF-70
3	0	0	1	19	68	217	658	1,155	1,203	228	

Key to Collecting: Help me, Rhonda! Here is what Bernard Nagengast says, enough to turn you on to collecting something else but Jefferson nickels: "Most of this issue is of 'garbage' quality. Expect dark colored, poorly struck, nicked, and marked coins. Very rare as a full strike, brilliant white coin. Although a common roll coin, in the past often promoted as rare." A few years back this was not a problem, as collectors simply added a *Proof* to their date and mint sets. Now, specialists want sharply struck coins, and there is the challenge. Of course, were it not for such stuff, there would be no need for enthusiasts to organize to share their pleasures and frustrations in the Full Step Nickel Club. Proofs are sharply struck with 6 Full Steps detail easily available. Cameo contrast Proofs are in the minority. Sets this year were distributed in gray boxes (old style) and flat packs (new).
Step-Detail Availability (MS-65 and Higher): *5 Full Steps*—1 in 200; *6 Full Steps*—Unverified.
Step-Detail Availability (Proof): *5 Full Steps*—Available; *6 Full Steps*—1 in 5 or so. The detail of the top step becomes increasingly thin as the years progress.
Tripled Die Reverse: Seen only on Proofs, most of which are from flat-pack sets, this variety shows light tripling of features, most prominent on the O (MONTICELLO) and lower parts of UNITED STATES OF AMERICA. Breen-2737, FS-05-1955-801, evaluated by the last as URS-11 and there illustrated. Several slightly *doubled* dies exist but are neither remarkable nor of much interest.

1955-D

Circulation-Strike Mintage: 74,464,000

1955-D • Market Values • Circulation Strikes

AU-55	MS-60	MS-63	MS-64	MS-64FS	MS-65	MS-65FS	MS-66	MS-66FS	MS-67	MS-67FS
$0.25	$0.50	$1.00	$1.50	$1,000.	$2.	$3,500.	$30.	—	—	—

Availability (Certified Populations) • Circulation Strikes

<MS-60	MS-60	MS-61	MS-62	MS-63	MS-64	MS-65	MS-66	MS-67	MS-68	MS-69	MS-70
16	0	2	14	69	249	231	27	0	0	0	

Key to Collecting: Most Mint State coins in the marketplace are fairly attractive, although some struck from worn-out dies are granular (not that most buyers care). Quite a few are baggy and/or lightly detailed the centers.
Step-Detail Availability (MS-65 and Higher): *5 Full Steps*—1 in 200; *6 Full Steps*—Unverified.

1955-D/S

Circulation-Strike Mintage: 74,464,000

1955-D/S • Market Values • Circulation Strikes

AU-55	MS-60	MS-63	MS-64	MS-64FS	MS-65	MS-65FS	MS-66	MS-66FS	MS-67	MS-67FS
$25.	$35.	$55.	$75.	—	$85.	—	—	—	—	—

Availability (Certified Populations) • Circulation Strikes

<MS-60	MS-60	MS-61	MS-62	MS-63	MS-64	MS-65	MS-66	MS-67	MS-68	MS-69	MS-70
38	13	4	31	221	915	369	11	0	0	0	

Key to Collecting: The Mint had a bunch of S-mintmark dies on hand in 1955, with no nickels scheduled to be struck in San Francisco, and with that Mint set to stop coining operations, seemingly forever, by the end of the year. Rather than waste them, at least 10 dies were overpunched with D mintmarks, generating the overmintmark. Thousands exist today, making the variety easily obtainable. From a numismatic viewpoint, some are better defined than others. Buy one with a bold under-S, such as FS-05-1955D-501.

Step-Detail Availability (MS-65 and Higher): *5 Full Steps*—None verified; *6 Full Steps*—None verified.

1956

Circulation-Strike Mintage: 35,216,000
Proof Mintage: 669,384

1956 • Market Values • Circulation Strikes and Proof Strikes

AU-55	MS-60	MS-63	MS-64	MS-64FS	MS-65	MS-65FS	MS-66	MS-66FS
$0.25	$0.50	$1.00	$1.50	$20.	$2.	$50.	$25.	$600.
MS-67	MS-67FS	PF-60	PF-63	PF-64	PF-65	PF-66	PF-67	PF-68
—	—	$1.00	$2.00	$2.50	$3.	—	—	—

Availability (Certified Populations) • Circulation Strikes and Proof Strikes

<MS-60	MS-60	MS-61	MS-62	MS-63	MS-64	MS-65	MS-66	MS-67	MS-68	MS-69	MS-70
6	1	0	0	12	148	409	170	16	0	0	
< PF-60	PF-60	PF-61	PF-62	PF-63	PF-64	PF-65	PF-66	PF-67	PF-68	PF-69	PF-70
0	0	0	1	4	21	71	288	598	471	120	

Key to Collecting: Most Mint State coins are brilliant, lustrous, and with good eye appeal—a remarkable and much-welcome exception to the generally tawdry line up of circulation strikes of this era. Proofs are sharply struck with 6 Full Steps detail easily available, although slight wear to hub and master dies diminishes the crispness. Cameo contrast Proofs are in the minority.

Step-Detail Availability (MS-65 and Higher): *5 Full Steps*—1 in 10; *6 Full Steps*—Rare.
Step-Detail Availability (Proof): *5 Full Steps*—Available; *6 Full Steps*—Common.

1956-D

Circulation-Strike Mintage: 67,222,940

1956-D • Market Values • Circulation Strikes

AU-55	MS-60	MS-63	MS-64	MS-64FS	MS-65	MS-65FS	MS-66	MS-66FS	MS-67	MS-67FS
$0.25	$0.50	$1.00	$1.50	$200.	$2.	$900.	$30.	$2,300.	—	—

Availability (Certified Populations) • Circulation Strikes

<MS-60	MS-60	MS-61	MS-62	MS-63	MS-64	MS-65	MS-66	MS-67	MS-68	MS-69	MS-70
0	2	0	5	7	77	320	168	18	0	0	

Key to Collecting: Most are quite pleasing to view, nice companions to the Philadelphia coins. Sharpness is a challenge, as noted below.

Step-Detail Availability (MS-65 and Higher): *5 Full Steps*—1 in 150; *6 Full Steps*—Unverified.

1957

Circulation-Strike Mintage: 38,408,000
Proof Mintage: 1,247,952

1957 • Market Values • Circulation Strikes and Proof Strikes

AU-55	MS-60	MS-63	MS-64	MS-64FS	MS-65	MS-65FS	MS-66	MS-66FS
$0.25	$0.50	$1.00	$1.50	$35.	$2.	$90.	$30.	$1,500.
MS-67	MS-67FS	PF-60	PF-63	PF-64	PF-65	PF-66	PF-67	PF-68
—	—	$1.00	$1.50	$2.00	2.50	—	—	—

Availability (Certified Populations) • Circulation Strikes and Proof Strikes

<MS-60	MS-60	MS-61	MS-62	MS-63	MS-64	MS-65	MS-66	MS-67	MS-68	MS-69	MS-70
5	0	0	2	26	104	273	80	0	0	0	
< PF-60	PF-60	PF-61	PF-62	PF-63	PF-64	PF-65	PF-66	PF-67	PF-68	PF-69	PF-70
3	0	0	2	0	31	140	424	670	381	78	

Key to Collecting: Eye appeal varies widely. While some are attractive and lustrous, most are dogs. All nickels of this year and the next have a larger, stronger star between LIBERTY and the date, a short-lived modification. In 1959 the smaller star, as used in 1956 and earlier, was employed. Proofs are sharply struck with 6 Full Steps detail easily available, although slight wear to hub and master dies diminishes the crispness, this continuing the trend since modern-era Proofs were issued in 1950. Cameo contrast Proofs are in the minority. The Proof production for this year crossed the million mark for the first time, the result of speculation in Proof sets and rolls that had characterized the market in 1956. Now, in 1957, buyers did not want to be left out. The excitement died in 1957, and in 1958 fewer Proofs were ordered.

Step-Detail Availability (MS-65 and Higher): *5 Full Steps*—1 in 10; *6 Full Steps*—Rare.

Step-Detail Availability (Proof): *5 Full Steps*—Available; *6 Full Steps*—Common.

1957-D

Circulation-Strike Mintage: 136,828,900

1957-D • Market Values • Circulation Strikes

AU-55	MS-60	MS-63	MS-64	MS-64FS	MS-65	MS-65FS	MS-66	MS-66FS	MS-67	MS-67FS
$0.25	$0.50	$1.00	$1.50	$35.	$2.	$150.	$20.	$1,750.	—	—

Availability (Certified Populations) • Circulation Strikes

<MS-60	MS-60	MS-61	MS-62	MS-63	MS-64	MS-65	MS-66	MS-67	MS-68	MS-69	MS-70
7	0	0	2	26	162	293	161	2	0	0	

Key to Collecting: Finding a lustrous coin with good eye appeal is easy enough, finding one with 5 or 6 Full Steps is not.
Step-Detail Availability (MS-65 and Higher): *5 Full Steps*—1 in 100; *6 Full Steps*—Rare.

1958

Circulation-Strike Mintage: 17,088,000
Proof Mintage: 875,652

1958 • Market Values • Circulation Strikes and Proof Strikes

AU-55	MS-60	MS-63	MS-64	MS-64FS	MS-65	MS-65FS	MS-66	MS-66FS
$0.50	$1.00	$1.50	$2.	$65.	$3.	$1,200.	$50.	$2,500.
MS-67	MS-67FS	PF-60	PF-63	PF-64	PF-65	PF-66	PF-67	PF-68
—	—	$1.	$2.	$7.	$8.	—	—	—

Availability (Certified Populations) • Circulation Strikes and Proof Strikes

<MS-60	MS-60	MS-61	MS-62	MS-63	MS-64	MS-65	MS-66	MS-67	MS-68	MS-69	MS-70
8	3	4	18	79	194	83	18	1	0	0	
< PF-60	PF-60	PF-61	PF-62	PF-63	PF-64	PF-65	PF-66	PF-67	PF-68	PF-69	PF-70
0	0	0	1	1	19	116	286	591	384	53	

Key to Collecting: Many are as ugly as sin, probably a combination of shoddy quality planchet stock and indifferent attitudes in the coining press room. Some sharply detailed gems exist and constitute a tiny fraction of the whole.
Step-Detail Availability (MS-65 and Higher): *5 Full Steps*—1 in 10; *6 Full Steps*—Rare.
Step-Detail Availability (Proof): *5 Full Steps*—Available; *6 Full Steps*—Common.

1958-D

Circulation-Strike Mintage: 168,249,120

1958-D • Market Values • Circulation Strikes

AU-55	MS-60	MS-63	MS-64	MS-64FS	MS-65	MS-65FS	MS-66	MS-66FS	MS-67	MS-67FS
$0.25	$0.50	$0.75	$1.	$20.	$2.	$25.	$25.	$70.	—	$300.

Availability (Certified Populations) • Circulation Strikes

<MS-60	MS-60	MS-61	MS-62	MS-63	MS-64	MS-65	MS-66	MS-67	MS-68	MS-69	MS-70
8	3	0	0	15	146	360	222	27	0	0	

Key to Collecting: Some are dreadful, others are beautiful gems—hot and cold, fire and ice. Look around and you'll find a nice one.
Step-Detail Availability (MS-65 and Higher): *5 Full Steps*—1 in 30; *6 Full Steps*—Rare, but among the more available of the era.

1959

Circulation-Strike Mintage: 27,248,000
Proof Mintage: 1,149,291

1959 • Market Values • Circulation Strikes and Proof Strikes

AU-55	MS-60	MS-63	MS-64	MS-64FS	MS-65	MS-65FS	MS-66	MS-66FS
$0.25	$0.50	$0.75	$1.	$8.	$2.	$50.	$35.	$1,250.
MS-67	MS-67FS	PF-60	PF-63	PF-64	PF-65	PF-66	PF-67	PF-68
—	$0.50	$1.00	$1.50	$2.	—	—	—	—

Availability (Certified Populations) • Circulation Strikes and Proof Strikes

<MS-60	MS-60	MS-61	MS-62	MS-63	MS-64	MS-65	MS-66	MS-67	MS-68	MS-69	MS-70
3	4	1	3	44	304	131	39	6	0	0	
< PF-60	PF-60	PF-61	PF-62	PF-63	PF-64	PF-65	PF-66	PF-67	PF-68	PF-69	PF-70
1	1	0	0	4	25	89	351	614	384	69	

Key to Collecting: Once again, quality varies from awful to beauteous. There are so many Mint State coins around that you can find a nice one without difficulty. Pity anyone who buys "sight unseen," a popular method according to investment reports!
Step-Detail Availability (MS-65 and Higher): *5 Full Steps*—1 in 10; *6 Full Steps*—Rare.
Step-Detail Availability (Proof): *5 Full Steps*—Available; *6 Full Steps*—Common.

1959-D

Circulation-Strike Mintage: 160,738,240

1959-D • Market Values • Circulation Strikes

AU-55	MS-60	MS-63	MS-64	MS-64FS	MS-65	MS-65FS	MS-66	MS-66FS	MS-67	MS-67FS
$0.25	$0.50	$0.75	$1.	$25.	$2.	$250.	$50.	$1,000.	—	—

Availability (Certified Populations) • Circulation Strikes

<MS-60	MS-60	MS-61	MS-62	MS-63	MS-64	MS-65	MS-66	MS-67	MS-68	MS-69	MS-70
11	4	0	5	30	213	304	153	13	0	0	

Key to Collecting: This is the swan song of decent and semi-decent Denver nickels, as for the next decade the quality is generally wretched. The 1959-D can be found lustrous and with good eye appeal, but some searching is needed to locate one with full steps.
Step-Detail Availability (MS-65 and Higher): *5 Full Steps*—1 in 20; *6 Full Steps*—Extremely rare.

1960

Circulation-Strike Mintage: 55,416,000
Proof Mintage: 1,691,602

1960 • Market Values • Circulation Strikes and Proof Strikes

AU-55	MS-60	MS-63	MS-64	MS-64FS	MS-65	MS-65FS	MS-66	MS-66FS
$0.25	$0.50	$0.75	$1.	$450.	$2.	$3,800.	$15.	—
MS-67	MS-67FS	PF-60	PF-63	PF-64	PF-65	PF-66	PF-67	PF-68
—	—	$0.50	$1.00	$1.50	$2.	—	—	—

Availability (Certified Populations) • Circulation Strikes and Proof Strikes

<MS-60	MS-60	MS-61	MS-62	MS-63	MS-64	MS-65	MS-66	MS-67	MS-68	MS-69	MS-70
17	4	4	12	34	161	223	107	2	0	0	
< PF-60	PF-60	PF-61	PF-62	PF-63	PF-64	PF-65	PF-66	PF-67	PF-68	PF-69	PF-70
1	0	0	0	2	32	157	439	767	512	112	

Key to Collecting: Brilliant, lustrous coins are available, but most are poorly struck, or from worn dies, or have other afflictions. This was the first year of *Coin World (CW)* and was the time of the 1960 Small Date cent, the launching time for a sizzle-boom in the coin market, led by the 1950-D nickel, that lasted until 1965. The popular "Collectors' Clearinghouse" column in *CW* led to a new interest in examining coins under magnification to find interesting things, leading to many interesting discoveries.

Step-Detail Availability (MS-65 and Higher): *5 Full Steps*—1 in 100; *6 Full Steps*—Unverified. Most *dies* for circulation issues from 1960 to 1967 lack step continuity below the second pillar from the right (see Nagengast).

Step-Detail Availability (Proof): *5 Full Steps*—Available; *6 Full Steps*—Common.

1960-D

Circulation-Strike Mintage: 192,582,180

1960-D • Market Values • Circulation Strikes

AU-55	MS-60	MS-63	MS-64	MS-64FS	MS-65	MS-65FS	MS-66	MS-66FS	MS-67	MS-67FS
$0.25	$0.50	$0.75	$1.	—	$2.	—	—	—	—	—

Availability (Certified Populations) • Circulation Strikes

<MS-60	MS-60	MS-61	MS-62	MS-63	MS-64	MS-65	MS-66	MS-67	MS-68	MS-69	MS-70
4	1	0	4	20	119	203	87	8	0	0	

Key to Collecting: This super-common issue is super-rare if with 5 Full Steps and also Full Details (sharp on portrait, etc.). Most are weakly detailed on both sides. A coin offered as MS-64 Full Steps in the 2004 ANA sale brought $32,200, while at the same time an MS-63 coin (with no mention of step sharpness) catalogued for 25¢. This caused some excited comment in the pages of *Coin World* (Letters to the Editor, November 8, 2004).

Step-Detail Availability (MS-65 and Higher): *5 Full Steps*—1 in 3,000; *6 Full Steps*—Unknown; see note under 1960.

1961

Circulation-Strike Mintage: 73,640,100
Proof Mintage: 3,028,144

1961 • Market Values • Circulation Strikes and Proof Strikes

AU-55	MS-60	MS-63	MS-64	MS-64FS	MS-65	MS-65FS	MS-66	MS-66FS
$0.25	$0.50	$0.75	$1.	$2,500.	$2.	$5,000.	—	—
MS-67	**MS-67FS**	**PF-60**	**PF-63**	**PF-64**	**PF-65**	**PF-66**	**PF-67**	**PF-68**
—	—	$0.50	$1.00	$1.50	$2.	$10.	$20.	$50.

Availability (Certified Populations) • Circulation Strikes and Proof Strikes

<MS-60	MS-60	MS-61	MS-62	MS-63	MS-64	MS-65	MS-66	MS-67	MS-68	MS-69	MS-70
8	1	0	6	18	91	170	93	6	0	0	
< PF-60	PF-60	PF-61	PF-62	PF-63	PF-64	PF-65	PF-66	PF-67	PF-68	PF-69	PF-70
2	2	0	2	3	37	166	536	796	565	122	

Key to Collecting: Luster and brilliance are standard on Mint State coins, but the strike is usually poor and the surfaces can be granular and rough. Coins with 5 Full Steps are few and far between. Also check for sharpness on the portrait, as the other side of the coin is important too!

Step-Detail Availability (MS-65 and Higher): *5 Full Steps*—1 in 150; *6 Full Steps*—Unknown; see note under 1960.

Step-Detail Availability (Proof): *5 Full Steps*—Available: *6 Full Steps*—Common.

1961-D

Circulation-Strike Mintage: 229,342,760

1961-D • Market Values • Circulation Strikes

AU-55	MS-60	MS-63	MS-64	MS-64FS	MS-65	MS-65FS	MS-66	MS-66FS	MS-67	MS-67FS
$0.25	$0.50	$0.75	$1.	$10,000.	$2.	$15,000.	—	—	—	—

Availability (Certified Populations) • Circulation Strikes

<MS-60	MS-60	MS-61	MS-62	MS-63	MS-64	MS-65	MS-66	MS-67	MS-68	MS-69	MS-70
10	1	0	3	33	115	139	22	1	0	0	

Key to Collecting: This issue is on par with the 1960-D, usually weakly detailed from over-used dies. Five Full Steps coins are rare. Exactly *how rare* will probably be played out over the next few years as certification services take increasing note of such things, and as consumer awareness spreads. In the meantime, be aware of losing your reasoning power while working on a registry set for competition! Of course, if your last name is Rockefeller, it doesn't make much difference.

Step-Detail Availability (MS-65 and Higher): *5 Full Steps*—1 in 3,000; *6 Full Steps*—Unknown; see note under 1960.

1962

Circulation-Strike Mintage: 97,384,000
Proof Mintage: 3,218,019

1962 • Market Values • Circulation Strikes and Proof Strikes

AU-55	MS-60	MS-63	MS-64	MS-64FS	MS-65	MS-65FS	MS-66	MS-66FS
$0.25	$0.50	$0.75	$1.	$13.	$2.	$60.	—	$900.
MS-67	MS-67FS	PF-60	PF-63	PF-64	PF-65	PF-66	PF-67	PF-68
—	—	—	—	—	—	—	—	—

Availability (Certified Populations) • Circulation Strikes and Proof Strikes

<MS-60	MS-60	MS-61	MS-62	MS-63	MS-64	MS-65	MS-66	MS-67	MS-68	MS-69	MS-70
7	3	1	11	57	319	401	97	4	0	0	
< PF-60	PF-60	PF-61	PF-62	PF-63	PF-64	PF-65	PF-66	PF-67	PF-68	PF-69	PF-70
1	4	0	4	5	55	137	590	969	849	343	

Key to Collecting: While brilliant, lustrous coins are common, the vast majority are poorly detailed in the center.

Step-Detail Availability (MS-65 and Higher): *5 Full Steps*—1 in 20; *6 Full Steps*—Unknown; see note under 1960.

Step-Detail Availability (Proof): *5 Full Steps*—Available; *6 Full Steps*—Common.

1962-D

Circulation-Strike Mintage: 280,195,720

1962-D • Market Values • Circulation Strikes

AU-55	MS-60	MS-63	MS-64	MS-64FS	MS-65	MS-65FS	MS-66	MS-66FS	MS-67	MS-67FS
$0.25	$0.50	$0.75	$1.	$350.	$2.	$5,000.	—	—	—	—

Availability (Certified Populations) • Circulation Strikes

<MS-60	MS-60	MS-61	MS-62	MS-63	MS-64	MS-65	MS-66	MS-67	MS-68	MS-69	MS-70
10	4	4	18	75	167	56	19	0	0	0	

Key to Collecting: Poor details and rough surfaces combine to create coins that, for the most part, are really miserable. Exceptions are very rare and very highly prized! As to step counts, it is important to remember that if a 5 Full Steps coin is found on the average of 1 in 2,000 coins, still quite a few exist based on the large mintage for this date. Darrell Crane unveiled a "nice little hoard" of 5 Full Steps coins, 1962-D, 1963-D, and 1964-D, in the November–December 2003 issue of the *Portico*.

Step-Detail Availability (MS-65 and Higher): *5 Full Steps*—1 in 2,000; *6 Full Steps*—Unknown; see note under 1960.

1963

Circulation-Strike Mintage: 175,776,000
Proof Mintage: 3,075,645

1963 • Market Values • Circulation Strikes and Proof Strikes

AU-55	MS-60	MS-63	MS-64	MS-64FS	MS-65	MS-65FS	MS-66	MS-66FS
$0.25	$0.50	$0.75	$1.	$50.	$2.	$175.	—	$400.
MS-67	MS-67FS	PF-60	PF-63	PF-64	PF-65	PF-66	PF-67	PF-68
—	—	—	—	—	—	—	—	—

Availability (Certified Populations) • Circulation Strikes and Proof Strikes

<MS-60	MS-60	MS-61	MS-62	MS-63	MS-64	MS-65	MS-66	MS-67	MS-68	MS-69	MS-70
8	3	1	21	188	345	134	5	0	0		
< PF-60	PF-60	PF-61	PF-62	PF-63	PF-64	PF-65	PF-66	PF-67	PF-68	PF-69	PF-70
0	2	0	0	2	19	165	738	1,028	1,271	532	

Key to Collecting: Lustrous coins with good eye appeal are common, but upon inspection most have poor details on both sides. It is *very curious* that mainstream numismatic literature has overlooked original planchet marks on areas that are not struck up fully, such as on Jefferson's shoulder on the nickel and Lincoln's shoulder on the cent.

Step-Detail Availability (MS-65 and Higher): *5 Full Steps*—1 in 20; *6 Full Steps*—Unknown; see note under 1960.

Step-Detail Availability (Proof): *5 Full Steps*—Available; *6 Full Steps*—Common.

1963-D

Circulation-Strike Mintage: 276,829,460

1963-D • Market Values • Circulation Strikes

AU-55	MS-60	MS-63	MS-64	MS-64FS	MS-65	MS-65FS	MS-66	MS-66FS	MS-67	MS-67FS
$0.25	$0.50	$0.75	$1.	$1,600.	$2.	$10,000.	—	—	—	—

Availability (Certified Populations) • Circulation Strikes

<MS-60	MS-60	MS-61	MS-62	MS-63	MS-64	MS-65	MS-66	MS-67	MS-68	MS-69	MS-70
8	0	0	9	47	116	68	11	0	0	0	

Key to Collecting: Usually with poor details, rough surface, and often from worn-out dies, not the sort of coin a director of the Mint would want to take to one of the periodic conferences of world mint directors! Regarding 5 Full Steps coins see note under 1962-D.

Step-Detail Availability (MS-65 and Higher): *5 Full Steps*—1 in 3,000; *6 Full Steps*—Unknown; see note under 1960.

1964

Circulation-Strike Mintage: 1,024,672,000
Proof Mintage: 3,950,762

1964 • Market Values • Circulation Strikes and Proof Strikes[a]

AU-55	MS-60	MS-63	MS-64	MS-64FS	MS-65	MS-65FS	MS-66	MS-66FS
$0.25	$0.50	$0.75	$1.	$80.	$2.	$350.	—	$2,000.
MS-67	MS-67FS	PF-60	PF-63	PF-64	PF-65	PF-66	PF-67	PF-68
—	—	—	—	—	—	—	—	—

Availability (Certified Populations) • Circulation Strikes and Proof Strikes

<MS-60	MS-60	MS-61	MS-62	MS-63	MS-64	MS-65	MS-66	MS-67	MS-68	MS-69	MS-70
15	4	3	18	41	191	187	72	4	0	0	0
< PF-60	PF-60	PF-61	PF-62	PF-63	PF-64	PF-65	PF-66	PF-67	PF-68	PF-69	PF-70
0	3	0	0	4	23	100	360	1,100	2,255	1,658	7

[a] According to Full Step–valuations contributor Mark Hooten, Full Step prices do not exist for SMS coins of 1964 through 1967. Instead, these coins typically sell by the grade and degree of cameo contrast of the major devices. The 17 recognized 1964 pieces are valued strictly by their rarity, not by the absence or presence of Full Steps. For the 1965 through 1967 issues, Full Step pieces of SMS coins are still quite rare, especially for 1965.

Key to Collecting: This year represents the first time that over a billion nickels were made at a single mint. Even more were made at Denver. The nation was entering a coin shortage, spawned in large part by the introduction of the Kennedy half dollar in combination with the news that silver coins were becoming valuable, due to the rising world market price. The passion for hoarding spread to small denominations as well. The anti-numismatic Act of September 3, 1964, resulted in 1964-dated dies for circulation strikes and Proofs being continued in use into 1965.

Step-Detail Availability (MS-65 and Higher): *5 Full Steps*—1 in 30; *6 Full Steps*—Unknown; see note under 1960.

Step-Detail Availability (Proof): *5 Full Steps*—Available; *6 Full Steps*—Common.

1964-D

Circulation-Strike Mintage: 1,787,297,160

1964-D • Market Values • Circulation Strikes

AU-55	MS-60	MS-63	MS-64	MS-64FS	MS-65	MS-65FS	MS-66	MS-66FS	MS-67	MS-67FS
$0.25	$0.50	$0.75	$1.	$110.	$2.	$650.	—	$2,500.	—	—

Availability (Certified Populations) • Circulation Strikes

<MS-60	MS-60	MS-61	MS-62	MS-63	MS-64	MS-65	MS-66	MS-67	MS-68	MS-69	MS-70
33	5	2	13	51	182	206	83	6	0	0	

Key to Collecting: The mintage figure for this issue set an all-time record for the nickel series. Production from 1964-D dies was continued past December 31. Many coins are choice in luster and eye appeal, but are poorly detailed. Still, with nearly two billion minted, the cherrypicker with lots of time on his/her hands stands a sure-thing chance of winning the 1 in 2,000 lottery. Also see note under 1962-D.

Step-Detail Availability (MS-65 and Higher): *5 Full Steps*—1 in 2,000 • *6 Full Steps*—Unknown; see note under 1960.

1965

Circulation-Strike Mintage: 136,131,380
Special Mint Set Mintage: 2,360,000

1965 • Market Values • Circulation Strikes and SMS Strikes[a]

AU-55	MS-60	MS-63	MS-64	MS-64FS	MS-65	MS-65FS	MS-66	MS-66FS	MS-67	MS-67FS
$0.25	$0.50	$0.75	$1.	—	$2.	$30,000.	—	—	—	—
—	—	—	$12.	[b]	$20.	[b]	$40.	[b]	$55.	[b]

Availability (Certified Populations) • Circulation Strikes and SMS Strikes[a]

<MS-60	MS-60	MS-61	MS-62	MS-63	MS-64	MS-65	MS-66	MS-67	MS-68	MS-69	MS-70
6	1	1	5	16	46	84	95	18	0	0	
1	2		7	58	270	977	532	46	0		

[a] Circulation strikes, red ▌   SMS strikes, green ▌

[b] According to Full Step–valuations contributor Mark Hooten, Full Step prices do not exist for SMS coins of 1964 through 1967. Instead, these coins typically sell by the grade and degree of cameo contrast of the major devices. The 17 recognized 1964 pieces are valued strictly by their rarity, not by the absence or presence of Full Steps. For the 1965 through 1967 issues, Full Step pieces of SMS coins are still quite rare, especially for 1965.

Key to Collecting: Circulation strikes are usually with unsatisfactory detail, and 5 Full Steps coins are scarce in proportion to the quantity made overall. Most numismatists elect to use Special Mint Set (SMS) coins. This is the first year of the SMS coins— pieces made with care and with prooflike finish (more satiny than mirrorlike in 1965), sold at a premium to collectors through 1967. SMS coins for these years were made at the San Francisco Mint, but with no mintmark on them, part of the "punishment" exacted upon numismatists as part of the mistaken notion that they caused the nationwide coin shortage (see narrative in preceding chapter). The 1965-dated SMS were not struck until 1966. By a small leap of faith the SMS coins for these years can be collected separately as "S" mint coins. The 1966 and 1967 coins closely resemble Proofs. Although striking varies, generally the SMS coins are sharper and are the place to look for 5 Full Steps or 6 Full Steps coins. The last can be elusive. By this time the hubs and masters were quite worn (modification would take place in 1967, to which refer).

Step-Detail Availability (MS-65 and Higher): *5 Full Steps*—1 in 100; *6 Full Steps*—Unknown; see note under 1960.

Step-Detail Availability (SMS): *5 Full Steps*—Slightly scarce; *6 Full Steps*—Very rare.

1966

Circulation-Strike Mintage: 156,208,283
Special Mint Set Mintage: 2,261,583

The initials FS, for designer Felix Schlag, appeared on the obverse starting in 1966.

1966 • Market Values • Circulation Strikes and SMS Strikes[a]

AU-55	MS-60	MS-63	MS-64	MS-64FS	MS-65	MS-65FS	MS-66	MS-66FS	MS-67	MS-67FS
$0.10	$0.25	$0.50	$0.75	$2,500.	$1.	$10,000.	—	—	—	—
AU-55	MS-60	MS-63	MS-64	MS-64FS	MS-65	MS-65FS	MS-66	MS-66FS	MS-67	MS-67FS
—	—	—	$10.	b	$15.	b	$30.	b	$70.	b

Availability (Certified Populations) • Circulation Strikes and SMS Strikes[a]

<MS-60	MS-60	MS-61	MS-62	MS-63	MS-64	MS-65	MS-66	MS-67	MS-68	MS-69	MS-70
3	0	0	4	4	61	103	105	34	2	0	
<MS-60	MS-60	MS-61	MS-62	MS-63	MS-64	MS-65	MS-66	MS-67	MS-68	MS-69	MS-70
0	0	0	0	2	18	105	612	567	109	1	

[a] Circulation strikes, red ■ SMS strikes, green ■
[b] According to Full Step–valuations contributor Mark Hooten, Full Step prices do not exist for SMS coins of 1964 through 1967. Instead, these coins typically sell by the grade and degree of cameo contrast of the major devices. The 17 recognized 1964 pieces are valued strictly by their rarity, not by the absence or presence of Full Steps. For the 1965 through 1967 issues, Full Step pieces of SMS coins are still quite rare, especially for 1965.

Key to Collecting: Most of these were struck at the Denver Mint, from dies without a mintmark. The Philadelphia Mint struck nickels only early in the year. Mint State coins are just dandy, unless you want one with 5 Full Steps, in which case you might need to look through several rolls to find one. Actually, as roll-searchers know, the matter is not as mathematically simple as that. One roll might contain several, then 40 other rolls none at all. Such 5 Full Steps coins were not distributed evenly over the production run. First year with FS initials for designer Felix O. Schlag on the obverse. Schlag would have preferred that the O be included as well. Mint State coins are not well detailed, and 5 and 6 Full Steps coins are difficult to find. The Special Mint Set coins are of superb quality and closely resemble Proofs. Many numismatists opt to include these in their sets, rather than pieces taken from bankrolls. The striking is better on these, but ultimate 6 Full Steps coins are in the minority among SMS coins and represent a challenge. SMS coins with cameo contrast and with 6 Full Steps represent the ultimate for this year. It has been said, but disputed, that two (or three) full Proofs were given by the Mint to Felix O. Schlag at a ceremony held at the ANA convention.[3] In *Walter Breen's Complete Encyclopedia of U.S. and Colonial Coins* (1988), Breen states forthrightly: "Two Proofs were made for a ceremony honoring Schlag as the unsung designer." However, Bernard Nagengast, *The Jefferson Nickel Analyst*, second edition, seems to have the last word in the matter: "Research by Theodore Riviere revealed that in fact the coins were apparently not Proofs, but were simply the first two coins struck from regular issue dies. Mr. Riviere was backed up by the late Frank Annunzio, chairman of the congressional committee overseeing coinage issues, who wrote to Riviere: 'Mr. Schlag did not receive any Proof nickels at the American Numismatic Association Convention in

1966. He was presented with the first two nickels struck that bear his initials. These were regular circulation strikes and were not Proof coins.'"
Step-Detail Availability (MS-65 and Higher): *5 Full Steps*—1 in 150; *6 Full Steps*—Unknown; see note under 1960.
Step-Detail Availability (SMS): *5 Full Steps*—Slightly scarce; *6 Full Steps*—Very rare.

1967

Circulation-Strike Mintage: 107,325,800
Special Mint Set Mintage: 1,863,344

1967 • Market Values • Circulation Strikes and SMS Strikes[a]

AU-55	MS-60	MS-63	MS-64	MS-64FS	MS-65	MS-65FS	MS-66	MS-66FS	MS-67	MS-67FS
$0.10	$0.25	$0.50	$0.75	—	$1.	—	—	—	—	—
AU-55	MS-60	MS-63	MS-64	MS-64FS	MS-65	MS-65FS	MS-66	MS-66FS	MS-67	MS-67FS
—	—	—	$10.	[b]	$15.	[b]	$25.	[b]	$55.	[b]

Availability (Certified Populations) • Circulation Strikes and SMS Strikes[a]

<MS-60	MS-60	MS-61	MS-62	MS-63	MS-64	MS-65	MS-66	MS-67	MS-68	MS-69	MS-70
2	0	1	0	9	34	67	74	20	0	0	
<MS-60	MS-60	MS-61	MS-62	MS-63	MS-64	MS-65	MS-66	MS-67	MS-68	MS-69	MS-70
0	0	0	0	1	29	146	871	791	134	0	

[a] Circulation strikes, red ■ SMS strikes, green ■
[b] According to Full Step–valuations contributor Mark Hooten, Full Step prices do not exist for SMS coins of 1964 through 1967. Instead, these coins typically sell by the grade and degree of cameo contrast of the major devices. The 17 recognized 1964 pieces are valued strictly by their rarity, not by the absence or presence of Full Steps. For the 1965 through 1967 issues, Full Step pieces of SMS coins are still quite rare, especially for 1965.

Key to Collecting: All of these were struck at the Denver Mint, but without a mintmark. Technically, these are "1967-D nickels." Once again, nice-appearing coins are common, but those with 5 Full Steps are hard to find. There are two reverse varieties this year. The coins produced for general circulation employed the Reverse of 1940 in its original, but by now blunted form, due to wear on hubs and master dies. Such coins are generally poorly detailed. A coin with as many as 3 Full Steps is unusual, and 6 Full Steps pieces may not exist. Writing in the *Portico*, Mark Powell considered the regular (not SMS) 1967 to be the hardest Jefferson nickel to find with step details.[4] As to the Special Mint Set nickels struck in San Francisco, but without a mintmark, these are collectible by dedicated specialists as a separate variety, Bernard Nagengast stated this: "The reverse of 1940 was slightly modified for the Special Mint Set issues of 1967, and used for all business and Proof strikes from 1968 through 1970. The door and window lines within the porch and the steps were strengthened. The steps appear to curve slightly from top to bottom into the field above the word MONTICELLO. This modification significantly increased the possibility of finding 6 Full Steps coins, at least on the Proofs." SMS coins with cameo contrast and with 6 Full Steps represent the ultimate for this year.
Step-Detail Availability (MS-65 and Higher): *5 Full Steps*—1 in 150, if that; *6 Full Steps*—Unknown; see note under 1960.
Step-Detail Availability (SMS, Modified Reverse Die): *5 Full Steps*—Slightly scarce; *6 Full Steps*—Very rare.

1968-D

Circulation-Strike Mintage: 91,227,880

1968-D • Market Values • Circulation Strikes

AU-55	MS-60	MS-63	MS-64	MS-64FS	MS-65	MS-65FS	MS-66	MS-66FS	MS-67	MS-67FS
$0.10	$0.25	$0.50	$0.75	$30,000.	$1.	—	—	—	—	—

Availability (Certified Populations) • Circulation Strikes

<MS-60	MS-60	MS-61	MS-62	MS-63	MS-64	MS-65	MS-66	MS-67	MS-68	MS-69	MS-70
3	3	0	1	6	67	165	96	9	0	0	

Key to Collecting: Although attractive gems are common, those with 5 Full Steps are rarities. The reverse design modification did not help matters with this issue. There was no Philadelphia Mint Jefferson nickel this year.

Step-Detail Availability (MS-65 and Higher): *5 Full Steps*—1 in 4,000 • *6 Full Steps*—Unverified.

1968-S

Circulation-Strike Mintage: 100,396,004
Proof Mintage: 3,041,506

1968-S • Market Values • Circulation Strikes and Proof Strikes

AU-55	MS-60	MS-63	MS-64	MS-64FS	MS-65	MS-65FS	MS-66	MS-66FS
$0.10	$0.25	$0.50	$0.75	$472.	$1.	$1,750.	—	$4,000.
MS-67	MS-67FS	PF-60	PF-63	PF-64	PF-65	PF-66	PF-67	PF-68
—	—	$0.50	$1.00	$1.50	$2.	$5.	$10.	$30.

Availability (Certified Populations) • Circulation Strikes and Proof Strikes

<MS-60	MS-60	MS-61	MS-62	MS-63	MS-64	MS-65	MS-66	MS-67	MS-68	MS-69	MS-70
4	0	0	1	16	105	154	101	7	0	1	
< PF-60	PF-60	PF-61	PF-62	PF-63	PF-64	PF-65	PF-66	PF-67	PF-68	PF-69	PF-70
0	1	0	1	4	8	36	115	468	618	320	

Key to Collecting: Most Mint State circulation strikes are very attractive. Upon close inspection the steps have problems, as reflected below. This represents the new era of Proof coins, not made since 1964. Production was now at the San Francisco Mint, with an S mintmark added by hand to each die; accordingly, there are minute differences in mintmark placement, this continuing through 1984. This was also the first year for the mintmark to appear on the obverse. Beginning in 1985 the S mintmark was added to the hub and master dies, and all have the same placement.

Step-Detail Availability (MS-65 and Higher): *5 Full Steps*—1 in 500; *6 Full Steps*—Rare.

Step-Detail Availability (Proof): *5 Full Steps*—Common; *6 Full Steps*—Common.

1969-D

Circulation-Strike Mintage: 202,807,500

1969-D • Market Values • Circulation Strikes

AU-55	MS-60	MS-63	MS-64	MS-64FS	MS-65	MS-65FS	MS-66	MS-66FS	MS-67	MS-67FS
$0.10	$0.25	$0.50	$0.75	—	$1.	—	—	—	—	—

Availability (Certified Populations) • Circulation Strikes

<MS-60	MS-60	MS-61	MS-62	MS-63	MS-64	MS-65	MS-66	MS-67	MS-68	MS-69	MS-70
3	0	1	2	14	49	44	30	1	0	0	

Key to Collecting: Many Mint State examples are lustrous and attractive, though in grades below the gem level. Others are dull. No one rule fits all from this large mintage. From the standpoint of 5 Full Steps, this is considered by some to be the *rarest* issue in the series. Some of the few known 5 Full Steps coins have about half of step 6, leading to the speculation that the Golden Fleece might be found.

Step-Detail Availability (MS-65 and Higher): *5 Full Steps*—1 in 10,000; *6 Full Steps*—Unverified.

1969-S

Circulation-Strike Mintage: 120,165,000
Proof Mintage: 2,934,631

1969-S • Market Values • Circulation Strikes and Proof Strikes

AU-55	MS-60	MS-63	MS-64	MS-64FS	MS-65	MS-65FS	MS-66	MS-66FS
$0.10	$0.25	$0.50	$0.75	—	$1.	—	—	—
MS-67	MS-67FS	PF-60	PF-63	PF-64	PF-65	PF-66	PF-67	PF-68
—	—	$0.50	$1.00	$1.50	$2.	$5.	$20.	$50.

Availability (Certified Populations) • Circulation Strikes and Proof Strikes

<MS-60	MS-60	MS-61	MS-62	MS-63	MS-64	MS-65	MS-66	MS-67	MS-68	MS-69	MS-70
4	0	0	0	14	79	29	15	2	0	0	
< PF-60	PF-60	PF-61	PF-62	PF-63	PF-64	PF-65	PF-66	PF-67	PF-68	PF-69	PF-70
0	2	0	0	3	26	29	124	448	510	210	

Key to Collecting: Most circulation strikes are very attractive. Once again, steps are a challenge to the dedicated specialists. Proofs have great eye appeal.

Step-Detail Availability (MS-65 and Higher): *5 Full Steps*—1 in 2,000; *6 Full Steps*—Unverified.

Step-Detail Availability (Proof): *5 Full Steps*—Common; *6 Full Steps*—Common.

1970-D

Circulation-Strike Mintage: 515,485,380

1970-D • Market Values • Circulation Strikes

MS-60	MS-63	MS-64	MS-64FS	MS-65	MS-65FS	MS-66	MS-66FS	MS-67	MS-67FS
$0.25	$0.50	$0.75	$5,000.	$1.	$12,500.	—	—	—	—

Availability (Certified Populations) • Circulation Strikes

<MS-60	MS-60	MS-61	MS-62	MS-63	MS-64	MS-65	MS-66	MS-67	MS-68	MS-69	MS-70
6	1	0	10	13	71	69	30	5	0	0	

Key to Collecting: Repeating a familiar scenario, the 1970-D is an easy find in gem state and with good eye appeal, but finding one with 5 Full Steps is another ballgame. **Step-Detail Availability (MS-65 and Higher):** *5 Full Steps*—1 in 3,000; *6 Full Steps*— Unverified.

1970-S

Circulation-Strike Mintage: 238,832,004
Proof Mintage: 2,632,810

1970-S • Market Values • Circulation Strikes and Proof Strikes

MS-60	MS-63	MS-64	MS-64FS	MS-65	MS-65FS	MS-66	MS-66FS
$0.25	$0.50	$0.75	$300.	$1.	$1,000.	—	—
MS-67	**MS-67FS**	**PF-60**	**PF-63**	**PF-64**	**PF-65**	**PF-66**	**PF-67**	**PF-68**
—	—	$0.50	$1.00	$1.50	$2.	$10.	$20.	$40.

Availability (Certified Populations) • Circulation Strikes and Proof Strikes

<MS-60	MS-60	MS-61	MS-62	MS-63	MS-64	MS-65	MS-66	MS-67	MS-68	MS-69	MS-70
2	0	1	2	38	127	79	24	1	0	0	
< PF-60	**PF-60**	**PF-61**	**PF-62**	**PF-63**	**PF-64**	**PF-65**	**PF-66**	**PF-67**	**PF-68**	**PF-69**	**PF-70**
0	3	0	0	14	40	166	422	538	226	0	

Key to Collecting: Gems are easily available, among many that are bagmarked. At long last, 5 Full Steps is a practical goal for the specialist with a modest budget. **Step-Detail Availability (MS-65 and Higher):** *5 Full Steps*—1 in 100; *6 Full Steps*— Rare.
Step-Detail Availability (Proof): *5 Full Steps*—Common; *6 Full Steps*—Common.

1971

Circulation-Strike Mintage: 106,884,000

1971 • Market Values • Circulation Strikes

MS-60	MS-63	MS-64	MS-64FS	MS-65	MS-65FS	MS-66	MS-66FS	MS-67	MS-67FS
$0.50	$1.00	$1.50	$16.	$2.	$9.	—	$45.	—	—

Availability (Certified Populations) • Circulation Strikes

<MS-60	MS-60	MS-61	MS-62	MS-63	MS-64	MS-65	MS-66	MS-67	MS-68	MS-69	MS-70
10	0	0	13	54	200	218	103	8	0	0	

Key to Collecting: The modified reverse with stronger architectural details went into service this year. This reverse was used through 1976. Walter Breen speculates that some of this and also the Denver issue might be found with the old-style reverse; none such reported. Gems are common, and well-stepped pieces are not hard to find.
Step-Detail Availability (MS-65 and Higher): *5 Full Steps*—1 in 3; *6 Full Steps*— Scarce.

1971-D

Circulation-Strike Mintage: 316,144,800

1971-D • Market Values • Circulation Strikes

MS-60	MS-63	MS-64	MS-64FS	MS-65	MS-65FS	MS-66	MS-66FS	MS-67	MS-67FS
$0.25	$0.50	$0.75	$6.	$1.	$9.	—	$40.	—	—

Availability (Certified Populations) • Circulation Strikes

<MS-60	MS-60	MS-61	MS-62	MS-63	MS-64	MS-65	MS-66	MS-67	MS-68	MS-69	MS-70
5	1	0	2	30	197	544	325	134	1	0	

Key to Collecting: A home-run Jefferson nickel—gems are common, and you can have all the steps you want. Coins such as this, and others in this and later years, form an ideal way to begin a specialized set, without having to upgrade it later. Then you can feel your way through the step situations, rarity considerations, and price levels of earlier years.

Step-Detail Availability (MS-65 and Higher): *5 Full Steps*—1 in 2; *6 Full Steps*—Scarce.

1971-S

Proof Mintage: 3,220,733
No-"S" Proof Mintage: 1,655 (estimated)

1971-S • Market Values • Proof Strikes

PF-60	PF-63	PF-64	PF-65	PF-66	PF-67	PF-68
$0.50	$1.00	$1.50	$2.	$5.	$15.	$50.

Availability (Certified Populations) • Proof Strikes

< PF-60	PF-60	PF-61	PF-62	PF-63	PF-64	PF-65	PF-66	PF-67	PF-68	PF-69	PF-70
0	0	0	0	4	39	67	191	366	466	143	

1971-S, No "S" • Market Values • Proof Strikes

PF-60	PF-63	PF-64	PF-65	PF-66	PF-67	PF-68
$500.	$700.	$900.	$1,000.	—	—	—

Availability (Certified Populations) • Proof Strikes

< PF-60	PF-60	PF-61	PF-62	PF-63	PF-64	PF-65	PF-66	PF-67	PF-68	PF-69	PF-70
0	0	0	0	0	1	6	21	47	59	14	

Key to Collecting: In this year the Treasury Department created the first Proof-only nickel since the 1878 Shield issue. A new policy was set, and in years after 1971 the San Francisco Mint would continue to make Proofs for collectors, with no related circulation strikes.

1971 "S" Proof Without Mintmark: All Proofs this year were made at the San Francisco Mint. By inadvertence at the Philadelphia Mint, where an assistant engraver was charged with punching mintmarks into dies one at a time, someone forgot to add an S. It is not known how many S-less Proofs were made, but the estimate of 1,655 comes from the Mint and should be subtracted from the overall mintage of 3,220,733.

Step-Detail Availability (Proof): *5 Full Steps*—Common; *6 Full Steps*—Common.

1972

Circulation-Strike Mintage: 202,036,000

1972 • Market Values • Circulation Strikes

MS-60	MS-63	MS-64	MS-64FS	MS-65	MS-65FS	MS-66	MS-66FS	MS-67	MS-67FS
$0.10	$0.25	$0.50	$7.	$1.	$25.	—	$175.	—	—

Availability (Certified Populations) • Circulation Strikes

<MS-60	MS-60	MS-61	MS-62	MS-63	MS-64	MS-65	MS-66	MS-67	MS-68	MS-69	MS-70
2	0	0	4	22	94	94	37	23	3	0	

Key to Collecting: Many minted, making a coin that is just right easy for you to find. *Walter Breen's Complete Encyclopedia of U.S. and Colonial Coins* (1988) describes some minor obverse variations for this year.
Step-Detail Availability (MS-65 and Higher): *5 Full Steps*—1 in 5; *6 Full Steps*—Scarce.

1972-D

Circulation-Strike Mintage: 351,694,600

1972-D • Market Values • Circulation Strikes

MS-60	MS-63	MS-64	MS-64FS	MS-65	MS-65FS	MS-66	MS-66FS	MS-67	MS-67FS
$0.10	$0.25	$0.50	$7.	$1.	$25.	—	$175.	—	—

Availability (Certified Populations) • Circulation Strikes

<MS-60	MS-60	MS-61	MS-62	MS-63	MS-64	MS-65	MS-66	MS-67	MS-68	MS-69	MS-70
10	3	2	8	19	97	100	49	3	0	0	

Key to Collecting: Common enough. Many places to look to find well-stepped coins. Usually with great eye appeal.
Step-Detail Availability (MS-65 and Higher): *5 Full Steps*—1 in 10; *6 Full Steps*—Very scarce.

1972-S

Proof Mintage: 3,260,996

1972-S • Market Values • Proof Strikes

PF-60	PF-63	PF-64	PF-65	PF-66	PF-67	PF-68
$0.50	$1.	$2.	$3.	$5.	$10.	$28.

Availability (Certified Populations) • Proof Strikes

< PF-60	PF-60	PF-61	PF-62	PF-63	PF-64	PF-65	PF-66	PF-67	PF-68	PF-69	PF-70
0	0	0	0	0	18	34	93	298	532	141	

Key to Collecting: No challenge to find. Nice to have.
Step-Detail Availability (Proof): *5 Full Steps*—Common; *6 Full Steps*—Common.

1973

Circulation-Strike Mintage: 384,396,000

1973 • Market Values • Circulation Strikes

MS-60	MS-63	MS-64	MS-64FS	MS-65	MS-65FS	MS-66	MS-66FS	MS-67	MS-67FS
$0.10	$0.25	$0.50	$6.	$1.	$15.	—	$70.	—	—

Availability (Certified Populations) • Circulation Strikes

<MS-60	MS-60	MS-61	MS-62	MS-63	MS-64	MS-65	MS-66	MS-67	MS-68	MS-69	MS-70
1	1	0	4	30	152	98	80	4	0	0	

Key to Collecting: Most high-grade coins have great eye appeal and decent strike.
Step-Detail Availability (MS-65 and Higher): *5 Full Steps*—1 in 3; *6 Full Steps*—Scarce.

1973-D

Circulation-Strike Mintage: 261,405,400

1973-D • Market Values • Circulation Strikes

MS-60	MS-63	MS-64	MS-64FS	MS-65	MS-65FS	MS-66	MS-66FS	MS-67	MS-67FS
$0.10	$0.25	$0.50	$6.	$1.	$11.	—	$70.	—	—

Availability (Certified Populations) • Circulation Strikes

<MS-60	MS-60	MS-61	MS-62	MS-63	MS-64	MS-65	MS-66	MS-67	MS-68	MS-69	MS-70
4	2	0	4	11	120	201	134	10	0	0	

Key to Collecting: Most high-grade coins have great eye appeal and decent strike.
Step-Detail Availability (MS-65 and Higher): *5 Full Steps*—1 in 3; *6 Full Steps*—Scarce.

1973-S

Proof Mintage: 2,760,339

1973-S • Market Values • Proof Strikes

PF-60	PF-63	PF-64	PF-65	PF-66	PF-67	PF-68
$0.50	$1.00	$1.50	$2.	$5.	$10.	$25.

Availability (Certified Populations) • Proof Strikes

< PF-60	PF-60	PF-61	PF-62	PF-63	PF-64	PF-65	PF-66	PF-67	PF-68	PF-69	PF-70
0	0	0	0	0	11	15	48	125	156	1,203	

Key to Collecting: Nice eye appeal and everything else.
Step-Detail Availability (Proof): *5 Full Steps*—Common; *6 Full Steps*—Common.

1974

Circulation-Strike Mintage: 601,752,000

1974 • Market Values • Circulation Strikes

MS-60	MS-63	MS-64	MS-64FS	MS-65	MS-65FS	MS-66	MS-66FS	MS-67	MS-67FS
$0.10	$0.25	$0.50	$60.	$1.	$350.	—	$900.	—	—

Availability (Certified Populations) • Circulation Strikes

<MS-60	MS-60	MS-61	MS-62	MS-63	MS-64	MS-65	MS-66	MS-67	MS-68	MS-69	MS-70
4	1	0	2	14	68	81	31	0	0	0	

Key to Collecting: Usually with nice eye appeal. Sharply detailed coins are in the minority, but with hundreds of millions minted, not to worry.
Step-Detail Availability (MS-65 and Higher): *5 Full Steps*—1 in 10; *6 Full Steps*—Very scarce.

1974-D

Circulation-Strike Mintage: 277,373,000

1974-D • Market Values • Circulation Strikes

MS-60	MS-63	MS-64	MS-64FS	MS-65	MS-65FS	MS-66	MS-66FS	MS-67	MS-67FS
$0.10	$0.25	$0.50	$8.00	$1.	$40.	—	$150.	—	—

Availability (Certified Populations) • Circulation Strikes

<MS-60	MS-60	MS-61	MS-62	MS-63	MS-64	MS-65	MS-66	MS-67	MS-68	MS-69	MS-70
2	0	0	7	16	87	129	49	6	0	0	

Key to Collecting: Usually with nice eye appeal. Again, sharply detailed coins are elusive percentage-wise, but on an absolute basis they are not hard to find.
Step-Detail Availability (MS-65 and Higher): *5 Full Steps*—1 in 10; *6 Full Steps*—Very scarce.

1974-S

Proof Mintage: 2,612,568

1974-S • Market Values • Proof Strikes

PF-60	PF-63	PF-64	PF-65	PF-66	PF-67	PF-68
$0.50	$1.00	$1.50	$2.	$5.	$10.	$20.

Availability (Certified Populations) • Proof Strikes

< PF-60	PF-60	PF-61	PF-62	PF-63	PF-64	PF-65	PF-66	PF-67	PF-68	PF-69	PF-70
0	0	0	0	3	4	12	41	105	171	1,626	

Key to Collecting: Usually very nice.
Step-Detail Availability (Proof): *5 Full Steps*—Common; *6 Full Steps*—Common.

1975

Circulation-Strike Mintage: 181,772,000

1975 • Market Values • Circulation Strikes

MS-60	MS-63	MS-64	MS-64FS	MS-65	MS-65FS	MS-66	MS-66FS	MS-67	MS-67FS
$0.10	$0.50	$0.75	$7.	$1.	$60.	—	$550.	—	—

Availability (Certified Populations) • Circulation Strikes

<MS-60	MS-60	MS-61	MS-62	MS-63	MS-64	MS-65	MS-66	MS-67	MS-68	MS-69	MS-70
1	0	1	2	11	85	115	45	3	0	0	

Key to Collecting: Common, inexpensive issue that usually is very attractive. If you have a friendly neighborhood dealer who has a stock of rolls, visit him/her, look through the rolls, buy some of the sharply step details coins from this era, and before you leave, make a courtesy purchase of a few books or supplies, in addition to these inexpensive coins.
Step-Detail Availability (MS-65 and Higher): *5 Full Steps*—1 in 30; *6 Full Steps*— Very scarce.

1975-D

Circulation-Strike Mintage: 401,875,300

1975 • Market Values • Circulation Strikes

MS-60	MS-63	MS-64	MS-64FS	MS-65	MS-65FS	MS-66	MS-66FS	MS-67	MS-67FS
$0.10	$0.25	$0.50	$6.00	$1.	$9.	—	$50.	—	—

Availability (Certified Populations) • Circulation Strikes

<MS-60	MS-60	MS-61	MS-62	MS-63	MS-64	MS-65	MS-66	MS-67	MS-68	MS-69	MS-70
4	1	0	2	10	83	132	32	2	0	0	

Key to Collecting: Same comment as preceding entry.
Step-Detail Availability (MS-65 and Higher): *5 Full Steps*—1 in 30; *6 Full Steps*— Very scarce.

1975-S

Proof Mintage: 2,845,450

1975-S • Market Values • Proof Strikes

PF-60	PF-63	PF-64	PF-65	PF-66	PF-67	PF-68
$0.50	$1.00	$1.50	$2.	—	—	—

Availability (Certified Populations) • Proof Strikes

< PF-60	PF-60	PF-61	PF-62	PF-63	PF-64	PF-65	PF-66	PF-67	PF-68	PF-69	PF-70
0	0	0	0	0	4	10	22	136	309	2,709	

Key to Collecting: Nearly all are very nice.
Step-Detail Availability (Proof): *5 Full Steps*—Common • *6 Full Steps*—Common.

1976

Circulation-Strike Mintage: 367,124,000

1976 • Market Values • Circulation Strikes

MS-60	MS-63	MS-64	MS-64FS	MS-65	MS-65FS	MS-66	MS-66FS	MS-67	MS-67FS
$0.25	$0.50	$0.75	$65.	$1.	$275.	—	$600.	—	—

Availability (Certified Populations) • Circulation Strikes

<MS-60	MS-60	MS-61	MS-62	MS-63	MS-64	MS-65	MS-66	MS-67	MS-68	MS-69	MS-70
4	1	1	9	16	82	68	20	2	0	0	

Key to Collecting: Common, but with a quality problem. Eye appeal varies. An unexpected roadblock rises in the step department.
Step-Detail Availability (MS-65 and Higher): *5 Full Steps*—1 in 1,000; *6 Full Steps*—Very rare.

1976-D

Circulation-Strike Mintage: 563,964,147

1976-D • Market Values • Circulation Strikes

MS-60	MS-63	MS-64	MS-64FS	MS-65	MS-65FS	MS-66	MS-66FS	MS-67	MS-67FS
$0.25	$0.50	$0.75	$6.	$1.	$30.	—	$250.	—	—

Availability (Certified Populations) • Circulation Strikes

<MS-60	MS-60	MS-61	MS-62	MS-63	MS-64	MS-65	MS-66	MS-67	MS-68	MS-69	MS-70
9	3	0	1	22	110	147	46	1	0	0	

Key to Collecting: Plentiful, although finding ones with sharp steps will take some looking.
Step-Detail Availability (MS-65 and Higher): *5 Full Steps*—1 in 100; *6 Full Steps*—Rare.

1976-S

Proof Mintage: 4,149,730

1976-S • Market Values • Proof Strikes

PF-60	PF-63	PF-64	PF-65	PF-66	PF-67	PF-68
$0.50	$1.00	$1.50	$2.	—	—	—

Availability (Certified Populations) • Proof Strikes

< PF-60	PF-60	PF-61	PF-62	PF-63	PF-64	PF-65	PF-66	PF-67	PF-68	PF-69	PF-70
0	0	0	0	0	10	9	32	289	266	80	

Key to Collecting: Usually attractive. Bicentennial year coin, but Thomas Jefferson was not invited to the numismatic commemoration thereof.
Step-Detail Availability (Proof): *5 Full Steps*—Common *6 Full Steps*—Common.

1977

Circulation-Strike Mintage: 585,376,000

1977 • Market Values • Circulation Strikes

MS-60	MS-63	MS-64	MS-64FS	MS-65	MS-65FS	MS-66	MS-66FS	MS-67	MS-67FS
$0.10	$0.25	$0.50	$90.	$1.	$200.	—	$875.	—	—

Availability (Certified Populations) • Circulation Strikes

<MS-60	MS-60	MS-61	MS-62	MS-63	MS-64	MS-65	MS-66	MS-67	MS-68	MS-69	MS-70
2	2	0	5	28	67	54	30	5	0	0	

Key to Collecting: Many appealing gems exist, but many less than beautiful coins are around as well. Be selective. Steps will be a challenge. Obverse modification used, with slight strengthening of hair details and other minor touches. Reverse modification introduced this year and continued into 1982.

Step-Detail Availability (MS-65 and Higher): *5 Full Steps*—1 in 200; *6 Full Steps*—Very rare.

1977-D

Circulation-Strike Mintage: 297,313,422

1977-D • Market Values • Circulation Strikes

MS-60	MS-63	MS-64	MS-64FS	MS-65	MS-65FS	MS-66	MS-66FS	MS-67	MS-67FS
$0.25	$0.50	$0.75	$8.	$1.	$20.	—	$115.	—	—

Availability (Certified Populations) • Circulation Strikes

<MS-60	MS-60	MS-61	MS-62	MS-63	MS-64	MS-65	MS-66	MS-67	MS-68	MS-69	MS-70
6	0	0	4	13	108	123	43	3	0	0	

Key to Collecting: Nearly always with good luster and eye appeal.
Step-Detail Availability (MS-65 and Higher): *5 Full Steps*—1 in 10; *6 Full Steps*—Very scarce.

1977-S

Proof Mintage: 3,251,152

1977-S • Market Values • Proof Strikes

PF-60	PF-63	PF-64	PF-65	PF-66	PF-67	PF-68
$0.50	$1.00	$1.50	$2.	—	—	—

Availability (Certified Populations) • Proof Strikes

< PF-60	PF-60	PF-61	PF-62	PF-63	PF-64	PF-65	PF-66	PF-67	PF-68	PF-69	PF-70
0	0	0	0	0	3	10	33	86	235	2,974	7

Key to Collecting: Attractive, in keeping with other Proofs of this era.
Step-Detail Availability (Proof): *5 Full Steps*—Common; *6 Full Steps*—Common.

1978

Circulation-Strike Mintage: 391,308,000

1978 • Market Values • Circulation Strikes

MS-60	MS-63	MS-64	MS-64FS	MS-65	MS-65FS	MS-66	MS-66FS	MS-67	MS-67FS
$0.10	$0.25	$0.50	$50.	$0.75	$200.	—	$300.	—	—

Availability (Certified Populations) • Circulation Strikes

<MS-60	MS-60	MS-61	MS-62	MS-63	MS-64	MS-65	MS-66	MS-67	MS-68	MS-69	MS-70
5	0	1	4	33	90	46	26	18	0	0	

Key to Collecting: Common and inexpensive, unless you are looking for a six-stepper. Even then it might be inexpensive if you look around casually. Coin shops and shows are usually the best place to do this, mail order being more of a hassle for cheap coins.
Step-Detail Availability (MS-65 and Higher): *5 Full Steps*—1 in 30; *6 Full Steps*—Extremely rare.

1978-D

Circulation-Strike Mintage: 313,092,780

1978-D • Market Values • Circulation Strikes

MS-60	MS-63	MS-64	MS-64FS	MS-65	MS-65FS	MS-66	MS-66FS	MS-67	MS-67FS
$0.10	$0.25	$0.50	$7.00	$0.75	$20.	—	$100.	—	—

Availability (Certified Populations) • Circulation Strikes

<MS-60	MS-60	MS-61	MS-62	MS-63	MS-64	MS-65	MS-66	MS-67	MS-68	MS-69	MS-70
2	0	0	4	17	83	139	65	3	0	0	

Key to Collecting: Nearly always very nice.
Step-Detail Availability (MS-65 and Higher): *5 Full Steps*—1 in 10; *6 Full Steps*—Very scarce.

1978-S

Proof Mintage: 3,127,781

1978-S • Market Values • Proof Strikes

PF-60	PF-63	PF-64	PF-65	PF-66	PF-67	PF-68
$0.50	$1.00	$1.50	$2.	—	—	—

Availability (Certified Populations) • Proof Strikes

< PF-60	PF-60	PF-61	PF-62	PF-63	PF-64	PF-65	PF-66	PF-67	PF-68	PF-69	PF-70
0	0	0	0	1	2	10	23	74	207	3,525	31

Key to Collecting: Quality is the byword, common to all Proofs of this era.
Step-Detail Availability (Proof): *5 Full Steps*—Common; *6 Full Steps*—Common.

1979

Circulation-Strike Mintage: 463,188,000

1979 • Market Values • Circulation Strikes

MS-60	MS-63	MS-64	MS-64FS	MS-65	MS-65FS	MS-66	MS-66FS	MS-67	MS-67FS
$0.10	$0.25	$0.50	$85.	$0.75	$450.	—	$900.	—	—

Availability (Certified Populations) • Circulation Strikes

<MS-60	MS-60	MS-61	MS-62	MS-63	MS-64	MS-65	MS-66	MS-67	MS-68	MS-69	MS-70
6	1	0	6	21	73	49	21	4	0	0	

Key to Collecting: Usually very nice. Steps offer a challenge.
Step-Detail Availability (MS-65 and Higher): *5 Full Steps*—1 in 150; *6 Full Steps*—Extremely rare or unknown.

1979-D

Circulation-Strike Mintage: 325,867,672

1979-D • Market Values • Circulation Strikes

MS-60	MS-63	MS-64	MS-64FS	MS-65	MS-65FS	MS-66	MS-66FS	MS-67	MS-67FS
$0.10	$0.25	$0.50	$7.00	$0.75	$30.	—	$110.	—	—

Availability (Certified Populations) • Circulation Strikes

<MS-60	MS-60	MS-61	MS-62	MS-63	MS-64	MS-65	MS-66	MS-67	MS-68	MS-69	MS-70
2	0	0	1	8	87	91	54	2	0	0	

Key to Collecting: Very common and with fine eye appeal. Step sharpness is elusive as noted below.
Step-Detail Availability (MS-65 and Higher): *5 Full Steps*—1 in 10; *6 Full Steps*—Very scarce.

1979-S

Proof Mintage: 3,677,175

1979-S • Market Values • Proof Strikes

PF-60	PF-63	PF-64	PF-66	PF-66	PF-67	PF-68
$0.50	$1.00	$1.50	$2.	—	—	—

Availability (Certified Populations) • Proof Strikes

< PF-60	PF-60	PF-61	PF-62	PF-63	PF-64	PF-65	PF-66	PF-67	PF-68	PF-69	PF-70
0	0	0	0	0	9	21	72	165	445	5,093	46

Key to Collecting: Another nice set, attractively packaged and with coins of high quality.
Two Mintmark Styles: In this year the S mintmark punch, heavy and often appearing as a blob (more or less), called "filled S," was replaced with a new punch, thin and open, "clear S." The last is scarcer. Both are widely listed, included in the Red Book.
Step-Detail Availability (Proof): *5 Full Steps*—Common; *6 Full Steps*—Common.

1980-P

Circulation-Strike Mintage: 593,004,000

1980-P • Market Values • Circulation Strikes

MS-60	MS-63	MS-64	MS-64FS	MS-65	MS-65FS	MS-66	MS-66FS	MS-67	MS-67FS
$0.10	$0.25	$0.50	$20.	$0.75	$70.	—	$400.	—	—

Availability (Certified Populations) • Circulation Strikes

<MS-60	MS-60	MS-61	MS-62	MS-63	MS-64	MS-65	MS-66	MS-67	MS-68	MS-69	MS-70
15	3	4	22	75	160	174	67	6	0	0	

Key to Collecting: Easy enough to find, but 5 Full Steps coins are in the minority. The reverse of this and other dates until the 1982 modification can have shallow details in certain die areas (see Nagengast).
Step-Detail Availability (MS-65 and Higher): *5 Full Steps*—1 in 20; *6 Full Steps*— Very rare.

1980-D

Circulation-Strike Mintage: 502,323,448

1980-D • Market Values • Circulation Strikes

MS-60	MS-63	MS-64	MS-64FS	MS-65	MS-65FS	MS-66	MS-66FS	MS-67	MS-67FS
$0.10	$0.25	$0.50	$7.00	$0.75	$12.	—	$250.	—	—

Availability (Certified Populations) • Circulation Strikes

<MS-60	MS-60	MS-61	MS-62	MS-63	MS-64	MS-65	MS-66	MS-67	MS-68	MS-69	MS-70
4	0	1	4	27	147	124	62	5	0	0	

Key to Collecting: Same story as for the preceding entry.
Step-Detail Availability (MS-65 and Higher): *5 Full Steps*—1 in 10; *6 Full Steps*— Very rare.

1980-S

Proof Mintage: 3,554,806

1980-S • Market Values • Proof Strikes

PF-60	PF-63	PF-64	PF-65	PF-66	PF-67	PF-68
$0.50	$1.00	$1.50	$2.	—	—	—

Availability (Certified Populations) • Proof Strikes

< PF-60	PF-60	PF-61	PF-62	PF-63	PF-64	PF-65	PF-66	PF-67	PF-68	PF-69	PF-70
0	0	0	0	1	2	2	21	66	375	4,493	18

Key to Collecting: Attractive as usual, and with good details.
Step-Detail Availability (Proof): *5 Full Steps*—Common; *6 Full Steps*—Common.

1981-P

Circulation-Strike Mintage: 657,504,000

1981-P • Market Values • Circulation Strikes

MS-60	MS-63	MS-64	MS-64FS	MS-65	MS-65FS	MS-66	MS-66FS	MS-67	MS-67FS
$0.10	$0.25	$0.50	$150.	$0.75	$600.	—	$2,350.	—	—

Availability (Certified Populations) • Circulation Strikes

<MS-60	MS-60	MS-61	MS-62	MS-63	MS-64	MS-65	MS-66	MS-67	MS-68	MS-69	MS-70
8	2	0	7	22	83	63	100	29	0	0	

Key to Collecting: Mint State coins are usually attractive. Steps can be a challenge, mainly due to weak details in the dies, not to the procedures of striking.
Step-Detail Availability (MS-65 and Higher): *5 Full Steps*—1 in 30; *6 Full Steps*—Unverified.

1981-D

Circulation-Strike Mintage: 364,801,843

1981-D • Market Values • Circulation Strikes

MS-60	MS-63	MS-64	MS-64FS	MS-65	MS-65FS	MS-66	MS-66FS	MS-67	MS-67FS
$0.10	$0.25	$0.50	$7.00	$0.75	$35.	—	$400.	—	—

Availability (Certified Populations) • Circulation Strikes

<MS-60	MS-60	MS-61	MS-62	MS-63	MS-64	MS-65	MS-66	MS-67	MS-68	MS-69	MS-70
0	0	0	1	15	120	152	52	3	0	0	

Key to Collecting: Same comment as for 1981-P.
Step-Detail Availability (MS-65 and Higher): *5 Full Steps*—1 in 20; *6 Full Steps*—Extremely rare.

1981-S

Proof Mintage: 4,063,083

1980-S • Market Values • Proof Strikes

PF-60	PF-63	PF-64	PF-65	PF-66	PF-67	PF-68
$0.50	$1.00	$1.50	$2.	—	—	—

Availability (Certified Populations) • Proof Strikes

< PF-60	PF-60	PF-61	PF-62	PF-63	PF-64	PF-65	PF-66	PF-67	PF-68	PF-69	PF-70
0	0	0	0	1	10	16	61	187	698	5,706	31

Key to Collecting: Attractive, as is standard for Proofs of this era.
Two Mintmark Styles: In this year the S mintmark punch, the "clear S" (see 1979-S), was replaced with a slightly different version, a bit more open. The last is scarcer. These mintmarks may be hard to differentiate, as the depth which the punch was entered into the Proof die can make a mintmark seem light (shallow depth) or heavy.
Step-Detail Availability (Proof): *5 Full Steps*—Common; *6 Full Steps*—Common.

1982-P

Circulation-Strike Mintage: 292,355,000

1982-P • Market Values • Circulation Strikes

MS-60	MS-63	MS-64	MS-64FS	MS-65	MS-65FS	MS-66	MS-66FS	MS-67	MS-67FS
$1.00	$2.50	$4.	$110.	$6.	$200.	—	$300.	—	—

Availability (Certified Populations) • Circulation Strikes

<MS-60	MS-60	MS-61	MS-62	MS-63	MS-64	MS-65	MS-66	MS-67	MS-68	MS-69	MS-70
7	0	2	4	17	50	113	49	2	0	0	

Key to Collecting: This was a transitional year, and sharpness varies, as indicated below. The master hubs and dies had become quite worn by this time. The obverse was modified slightly, with lettering farther from the rim. See Breen's 1988 *Encyclopedia* for extended comment about the obverse. The reverse changes involved sharpening and seemed to occur about May 1982, with Dwight Stuckey being the first to report them, in absence of any information given out by the Mint.

REVERSE OF 1977

Step-Detail Availability (MS-65 and Higher): *5 Full Steps*—1 in 50; *6 Full Steps*— Extremely rare.

REVERSE OF 1982

Step-Detail Availability (MS-65 and Higher): *5 Full Steps*—1 in 5; *6 Full Steps*— Scarce.

1982-D

Circulation-Strike Mintage: 373,726,544

1982-D • Market Values • Circulation Strikes

MS-60	MS-63	MS-64	MS-64FS	MS-65	MS-65FS	MS-66	MS-66FS	MS-67	MS-67FS
$0.75	$2.00	$2.50	$50.	$3.	$65.	—	$475.	—	—

Availability (Certified Populations) • Circulation Strikes

<MS-60	MS-60	MS-61	MS-62	MS-63	MS-64	MS-65	MS-66	MS-67	MS-68	MS-69	MS-70
1	0	1	3	12	66	67	57	1	0	0	

Key to Collecting: Transitional year. The reverse differences are not dramatic, and the varieties are mainly interesting to specialists. Gems are plentiful. Sharp steps are a challenge.

REVERSE OF 1977

Step-Detail Availability (MS-65 and Higher): *5 Full Steps*—1 in 30; *6 Full Steps*— Very rare.

REVERSE OF 1982

Step-Detail Availability (MS-65 and Higher): *5 Full Steps*—1 in 5; *6 Full Steps*—Rare.

1982-S

Proof Mintage: 3,857,479

1982-S • Market Values • Proof Strikes

PF-60	PF-63	PF-64	PF-65	PF-66	PF-67	PF-68
$0.50	$1.	$2.	$3.	—	—	—

Availability (Certified Populations) • Proof Strikes

< PF-60	PF-60	PF-61	PF-62	PF-63	PF-64	PF-65	PF-66	PF-67	PF-68	PF-69	PF-70
0	0	0	0	0	1	8	16	58	118	1,853	7

Key to Collecting: Most Proofs are very attractive. As with other nickels of this year there are two reverse varieties, with the Reverse of 1982 being the most often seen. These differences are not widely listed, resulting in limited demand for them.

REVERSE OF 1977
Step-Detail Availability (Proof): *5 Full Steps*—Available; *6 Full Steps*—Available.

REVERSE OF 1982
Step-Detail Availability (Proof): *5 Full Steps*—Available; *6 Full Steps*—Common.

1983-P

Circulation-Strike Mintage: 561,615,000

1983-P • Market Values • Circulation Strikes

MS-60	MS-63	MS-64	MS-64FS	MS-65	MS-65FS	MS-66	MS-66FS	MS-67	MS-67FS
$0.50	$1.50	$3.	$40.	$4.	$375.	—	$2,000.	—	—

Availability (Certified Populations) • Circulation Strikes

<MS-60	MS-60	MS-61	MS-62	MS-63	MS-64	MS-65	MS-66	MS-67	MS-68	MS-69	MS-70
11	1	0	5	12	25	38	15	0	0	0	

Key to Collecting: Attractive coins are the rule among Mint State pieces, but steps are a problem, as nearly always.
Step-Detail Availability (MS-65 and Higher): *5 Full Steps*—1 in 20; *6 Full Steps*—Very rare.

1983-D

Circulation-Strike Mintage: 536,726,276

1983-D • Market Values • Circulation Strikes

MS-60	MS-63	MS-64	MS-64FS	MS-65	MS-65FS	MS-66	MS-66FS	MS-67	MS-67FS
$0.50	$1.00	$2.00	$40.00	$2.50	$140.	—	$700.	—	—

Availability (Certified Populations) • Circulation Strikes

<MS-60	MS-60	MS-61	MS-62	MS-63	MS-64	MS-65	MS-66	MS-67	MS-68	MS-69	MS-70
1	0	0	0	4	33	75	31	0	0	0	

Key to Collecting: Same comment as preceding. As these step problems occurred in recent times it is small wonder that some dedicated numismatists did not arrange trips to the mints, usually easy enough to do, and query the press operators on the subject. Who knows, perhaps some 6 Full Steps coins could have been struck on the spot!
Step-Detail Availability (MS-65 and Higher): *5 Full Steps*—1 in 20; *6 Full Steps*—Very rare.

1983-S

Proof Mintage: 3,279,126

1983-S • Market Values • Proof Strikes

PF-60	PF-63	PF-64	PF-65	PF-66	PF-67	PF-68
$1.	$1.	$2.	$3.	—	—	—

Availability (Certified Populations) • Proof Strikes

< PF-60	PF-60	PF-61	PF-62	PF-63	PF-64	PF-65	PF-66	PF-67	PF-68	PF-69	PF-70
0	0	0	0	0	2	6	14	53	115	1,902	7

Key to Collecting: Gems are the rule as are sharp steps.
Step-Detail Availability (Proof): *5 Full Steps*—Scarce; *6 Full Steps*—Standard.

1984-P

Circulation-Strike Mintage: 746,769,000

1984-P • Market Values • Circulation Strikes

MS-60	MS-63	MS-64	MS-64FS	MS-65	MS-65FS	MS-66	MS-66FS	MS-67	MS-67FS
$0.50	$1.00	$1.50	$7.	$2.	$55.	—	$70.	—	—

Availability (Certified Populations) • Circulation Strikes

<MS-60	MS-60	MS-61	MS-62	MS-63	MS-64	MS-65	MS-66	MS-67	MS-68	MS-69	MS-70
5	1	1	10	23	124	105	63	2	0	0	

Key to Collecting: Mint State coins are nearly always attractive.
Step-Detail Availability (MS-65 and Higher): *5 Full Steps*—1 in 30; *6 Full Steps*—Rare.

1984-D

Circulation-Strike Mintage: 517,675,146

1984-D • Market Values • Circulation Strikes

MS-60	MS-63	MS-64	MS-64FS	MS-65	MS-65FS	MS-66	MS-66FS	MS-67	MS-67FS
$0.10	$0.25	$0.50	$6.00	$0.75	$50.	—	$200.	—	—

Availability (Certified Populations) • Circulation Strikes

<MS-60	MS-60	MS-61	MS-62	MS-63	MS-64	MS-65	MS-66	MS-67	MS-68	MS-69	MS-70
6	2	0	4	15	95	91	39	1	0	0	

Key to Collecting: Same story. During this era ANA Summer Seminar students visited the Denver Mint each year, but no one thought to zero in on nickel striking. Such emphasis did not arise until later times.
Step-Detail Availability (MS-65 and Higher): *5 Full Steps*—1 in 30; *6 Full Steps*—Rare.

1984-S

Proof Mintage: 3,065,110

1984-S • Market Values • Proof Strikes

PF-60	PF-63	PF-64	PF-65	PF-66	PF-67	PF-68
$1.	$2.	$3.	$4.	—	—	—

Availability (Certified Populations) • Proof Strikes

< PF-60	PF-60	PF-61	PF-62	PF-63	PF-64	PF-65	PF-66	PF-67	PF-68	PF-69	PF-70
0	0	0	0	0	0	3	7	31	117	1,783	8

Key to Collecting: Beautiful, as expected. Good work.
Step-Detail Availability (Proof): *5 Full Steps*—Scarce; *6 Full Steps*—Standard.

1985-P

Circulation-Strike Mintage: 647,114,962

1985-P • Market Values • Circulation Strikes

MS-60	MS-63	MS-64	MS-64FS	MS-65	MS-65FS	MS-66	MS-66FS	MS-67	MS-67FS
$0.25	$0.50	$0.75	$6.	$1.	$50.	—	$425.	—	—

Availability (Certified Populations) • Circulation Strikes

<MS-60	MS-60	MS-61	MS-62	MS-63	MS-64	MS-65	MS-66	MS-67	MS-68	MS-69	MS-70
5	1	2	5	19	82	92	29	3	0	0	

Key to Collecting: Same story, but steps are a challenge.
Step-Detail Availability (MS-65 and Higher): *5 Full Steps*—1 in 40; *6 Full Steps*—Rare.

1985-D

Circulation-Strike Mintage: 459,747,446

1985-D • Market Values • Circulation Strikes

MS-60	MS-63	MS-64	MS-64FS	MS-65	MS-65FS	MS-66	MS-66FS	MS-67	MS-67FS
$0.25	$0.50	$0.75	$7.	$1.	$50.	—	$500.	—	—

Availability (Certified Populations) • Circulation Strikes

<MS-60	MS-60	MS-61	MS-62	MS-63	MS-64	MS-65	MS-66	MS-67	MS-68	MS-69	MS-70
0	0	0	1	19	63	90	27	1	0	0	

Key to Collecting: Ditto, including about the steps.
Step-Detail Availability (MS-65 and Higher): *5 Full Steps*—1 in 40; *6 Full Steps*—Rare.

1985-S

Proof Mintage: 3,362,821

1985-S • Market Values • Proof Strikes

PF-60	PF-63	PF-64	PF-65	PF-66	PF-67	PF-68
$1.	$1.	$2.	$3.	—	—	—

Availability (Certified Populations) • Proof Strikes

< PF-60	PF-60	PF-61	PF-62	PF-63	PF-64	PF-65	PF-66	PF-67	PF-68	PF-69	PF-70
0	0	0	0	0	3	1	10	26	115	2,015	17

Key to Collecting: Beginning in 1985 the S mintmark on Proof coins was added to the hub and master dies, and all have the same placement.
Step-Detail Availability (Proof): *5 Full Steps*—Scarce; *6 Full Steps*—Standard.

1986-P

Circulation-Strike Mintage: 536,883,483

1986-P • Market Values • Circulation Strikes

MS-60	MS-63	MS-64	MS-64FS	MS-65	MS-65FS	MS-66	MS-66FS	MS-67	MS-67FS
$0.25	$0.50	$0.75	$8.	$1.	$65.	—	$150.	—	—

Availability (Certified Populations) • Circulation Strikes

<MS-60	MS-60	MS-61	MS-62	MS-63	MS-64	MS-65	MS-66	MS-67	MS-68	MS-69	MS-70
2	0	0	0	9	65	67	49	4	0	0	

Key to Collecting: Attractive as a rule, but steps are a challenge.
Step-Detail Availability (MS-65 and Higher): *5 Full Steps*—1 in 40; *6 Full Steps*—Rare.

1986-D

Circulation-Strike Mintage: 361,819,140

1986-D • Market Values • Circulation Strikes

MS-60	MS-63	MS-64	MS-64FS	MS-65	MS-65FS	MS-66	MS-66FS	MS-67	MS-67FS
$0.50	$1.00	$1.50	$7.	$2.	$50.	—	$250.	—	—

Availability (Certified Populations) • Circulation Strikes

<MS-60	MS-60	MS-61	MS-62	MS-63	MS-64	MS-65	MS-66	MS-67	MS-68	MS-69	MS-70
2	0	0	4	17	101	61	21	3	0	0	

Key to Collecting: Same as the foregoing.
Step-Detail Availability (MS-65 and Higher): *5 Full Steps*—1 in 40; *6 Full Steps*—Rare.

1986-S

Proof Mintage: 3,010,497

1986-S • Market Values • Proof Strikes

PF-60	PF-63	PF-64	PF-65	PF-66	PF-67	PF-68
$1.	$3.	$5.	$7.	—	—	—

Availability (Certified Populations) • Proof Strikes

< PF-60	PF-60	PF-61	PF-62	PF-63	PF-64	PF-65	PF-66	PF-67	PF-68	PF-69	PF-70
0	0	0	0	0	1	4	10	27	99	2,030	4

Key to Collecting: Lovely to look at and to own.
Step-Detail Availability (Proof): *5 Full Steps*—Scarce; *6 Full Steps*—Standard.

1987-P

Circulation-Strike Mintage: 371,499,481

1987-P • Market Values • Circulation Strikes

MS-60	MS-63	MS-64	MS-64FS	MS-65	MS-65FS	MS-66	MS-66FS	MS-67	MS-67FS
$0.10	$0.25	$0.50	$6.00	$0.75	$8.	—	$20.	—	$500.

Availability (Certified Populations) • Circulation Strikes

<MS-60	MS-60	MS-61	MS-62	MS-63	MS-64	MS-65	MS-66	MS-67	MS-68	MS-69	MS-70
2	1	0	2	9	118	252	19	29	0	0	

Key to Collecting: Common. In this year the details were strengthened in the hubs, with Jefferson's hair and Monticello being made slightly sharper, this obverse hub continuing in use until 1991, the reverse after that time. Five Full Steps and 6 Full Steps coins are readily available as there are so many coins from which to choose.
Step-Detail Availability (MS-65 and Higher): *5 Full Steps*—1 in 2; *6 Full Steps*—Rare.

1987-D

Circulation-Strike Mintage: 410,590,604

1987-D • Market Values • Circulation Strikes

MS-60	MS-63	MS-64	MS-64FS	MS-65	MS-65FS	MS-66	MS-66FS	MS-67	MS-67FS
$0.10	$0.25	$0.50	$7.00	$0.75	$8.	—	$100.	—	—

Availability (Certified Populations) • Circulation Strikes

<MS-60	MS-60	MS-61	MS-62	MS-63	MS-64	MS-65	MS-66	MS-67	MS-68	MS-69	MS-70
4	0	0	3	26	168	189	99	12	0	0	

Key to Collecting: Common. In this year the details were strengthened in the hubs (see 1987-P listing). Five Full Steps and 6 Full Steps coins are readily available.
Step-Detail Availability (MS-65 and Higher): *5 Full Steps*—1 in 2; *6 Full Steps*—Rare.

1987-S

Proof Mintage: 4,227,728

1987-S • Market Values • Proof Strikes

PF-60	PF-63	PF-64	PF-65	PF-66	PF-67	PF-68
$1.	$1.	$2.	$3.	—	—	—

Availability (Certified Populations) • Proof Strikes

< PF-60	PF-60	PF-61	PF-62	PF-63	PF-64	PF-65	PF-66	PF-67	PF-68	PF-69	PF-70
1	1	0	0	0	0	4	10	32	115	2,002	9

Key to Collecting: Always appealing. In this year the details were strengthened in the hubs (see 1987-P listing). Five Full Steps and 6 Full Steps coins are readily available.
Step-Detail Availability (Proof): *5 Full Steps*—Scarce; *6 Full Steps*—Standard.

1988-P

Circulation-Strike Mintage: 771,360,000

1988-P • Market Values • Circulation Strikes

MS-60	MS-63	MS-64	MS-64FS	MS-65	MS-65FS	MS-66	MS-66FS	MS-67	MS-67FS
$0.10	$0.25	$0.50	$6.00	$0.75	$20.	—	$60.	—	—

Availability (Certified Populations) • Circulation Strikes

<MS-60	MS-60	MS-61	MS-62	MS-63	MS-64	MS-65	MS-66	MS-67	MS-68	MS-69	MS-70
4	1	0	4	18	81	86	67	6	0	0	

Key to Collecting: Gems are common.
Step-Detail Availability (MS-65 and Higher): *5 Full Steps*—1 in 3; *6 Full Steps*—Rare.

1988-D

Circulation-Strike Mintage: 663,771,652

1988-D • Market Values • Circulation Strikes

MS-60	MS-63	MS-64	MS-64FS	MS-65	MS-65FS	MS-66	MS-66FS	MS-67	MS-67FS
$0.10	$0.25	$0.50	$6.00	$0.75	$25.	—	$90.	—	—

Availability (Certified Populations) • Circulation Strikes

<MS-60	MS-60	MS-61	MS-62	MS-63	MS-64	MS-65	MS-66	MS-67	MS-68	MS-69	MS-70
3	0	1	3	11	85	112	60	4	0	0	

Key to Collecting: Common.
Step-Detail Availability (MS-65 and Higher): *5 Full Steps*—1 in 3; *6 Full Steps*—Rare.

1988-S

Proof Mintage: 3,262,948

1988-S • Market Values • Proof Strikes

PF-60	PF-63	PF-64	PF-65	PF-66	PF-67	PF-68
$2.	$3.	$4.	$5.	—	—	—

Availability (Certified Populations) • Proof Strikes

< PF-60	PF-60	PF-61	PF-62	PF-63	PF-64	PF-65	PF-66	PF-67	PF-68	PF-69	PF-70
0	0	0	0	0	1	2	7	25	89	1,473	22

Key to Collecting: Again, beautiful.
Step-Detail Availability (Proof): *5 Full Steps*—Scarce; *6 Full Steps*—Standard.

1989-P

Circulation-Strike Mintage: 898,812,000

1989-P • Market Values • Circulation Strikes

MS-60	MS-63	MS-64	MS-64FS	MS-65	MS-65FS	MS-66	MS-66FS	MS-67	MS-67FS
$0.10	$0.25	$0.50	$6.00	$0.75	$15.	—	$60.	—	—

Availability (Certified Populations) • Circulation Strikes

<MS-60	MS-60	MS-61	MS-62	MS-63	MS-64	MS-65	MS-66	MS-67	MS-68	MS-69	MS-70
3	1	1	5	14	84	142	127	21	1	0	

Key to Collecting: Common. Not much of a challenge with the steps, either.
Step-Detail Availability (MS-65 and Higher): *5 Full Steps*—1 in 5; *6 Full Steps*—Very scarce.

1989-D

Circulation-Strike Mintage: 570,842,474

1989-D • Market Values • Circulation Strikes

MS-60	MS-63	MS-64	MS-64FS	MS-65	MS-65FS	MS-66	MS-66FS	MS-67	MS-67FS
$0.10	$0.25	$0.50	$6.00	$0.75	$50.	—	$200.	—	—

Availability (Certified Populations) • Circulation Strikes

<MS-60	MS-60	MS-61	MS-62	MS-63	MS-64	MS-65	MS-66	MS-67	MS-68	MS-69	MS-70
2	0	0	2	24	84	73	35	0	0	0	

Key to Collecting: Ditto.
Step-Detail Availability (MS-65 and Higher): *5 Full Steps*—1 in 5; *6 Full Steps*—Very scarce.

1989-S

Proof Mintage: 3,220,194

1989-S • Market Values • Proof Strikes

PF-60	PF-63	PF-64	PF-65	PF-66	PF-67	PF-68
$1.	$2.	$3.	$4.	—	—	—

Availability (Certified Populations) • Proof Strikes

< PF-60	PF-60	PF-61	PF-62	PF-63	PF-64	PF-65	PF-66	PF-67	PF-68	PF-69	PF-70
0	0	0	0	0	1	1	4	19	81	1,765	59

Key to Collecting: Sharp and beautiful.
Step-Detail Availability (Proof): *5 Full Steps*—Scarce; *6 Full Steps*—Standard.

1990-P

Circulation-Strike Mintage: 661,636,000

1990-P • Market Values • Circulation Strikes

MS-60	MS-63	MS-64	MS-64FS	MS-65	MS-65FS	MS-66	MS-66FS	MS-67	MS-67FS
$0.10	$0.25	$0.50	$7.00	$0.75	$6.	—	$40.	—	—

Availability (Certified Populations) • Circulation Strikes

<MS-60	MS-60	MS-61	MS-62	MS-63	MS-64	MS-65	MS-66	MS-67	MS-68	MS-69	MS-70
2	1	0	3	12	52	108	94	7	0	0	0

Key to Collecting: Easy enough to find. "Scarce" step definition is in relation to the whole population. On an absolute basis, many exist.
Step-Detail Availability (MS-65 and Higher): *5 Full Steps*—1 in 5; *6 Full Steps*—Scarce (small percentage).

1990-D

Circulation-Strike Mintage: 663,938,503

1990-D • Market Values • Circulation Strikes

MS-60	MS-63	MS-64	MS-64FS	MS-65	MS-65FS	MS-66	MS-66FS	MS-67	MS-67FS
$0.10	$0.25	$0.50	$7.00	$0.75	$20.	—	$500.	—	—

Availability (Certified Populations) • Circulation Strikes

<MS-60	MS-60	MS-61	MS-62	MS-63	MS-64	MS-65	MS-66	MS-67	MS-68	MS-69	MS-70
1	1	0	3	34	126	86	20	1	0	0	0

Key to Collecting: Common. Building a nice set of sharply detailed coins of the later years is an excellent prelude to investigating the earlier issues. What a change from the 1960s.

Step-Detail Availability (MS-65 and Higher): *5 Full Steps*—1 in 5; *6 Full Steps*—Scarce (small percentage).

1990-S

Proof Mintage: 3,299,559

1990-S • Market Values • Proof Strikes

PF-60	PF-63	PF-64	PF-65	PF-66	PF-67	PF-68
$1.	$2.	$3.	$4.	—	—	—

Availability (Certified Populations) • Proof Strikes

< PF-60	PF-60	PF-61	PF-62	PF-63	PF-64	PF-65	PF-66	PF-67	PF-68	PF-69	PF-70
0	0	0	0	1	0	0	10	25	74	2,710	75

Key to Collecting: Another great Proof production.

Step-Detail Availability (Proof): *5 Full Steps*—Scarce; *6 Full Steps*—Standard.

1991-P

Circulation-Strike Mintage: 614,104,000

1991-P • Market Values • Circulation Strikes

MS-60	MS-63	MS-64	MS-64FS	MS-65	MS-65FS	MS-66	MS-66FS	MS-67	MS-67FS
$0.10	$0.25	$0.50	$15.00	$0.75	$35.	—	$150.	—	—

Availability (Certified Populations) • Circulation Strikes

<MS-60	MS-60	MS-61	MS-62	MS-63	MS-64	MS-65	MS-66	MS-67	MS-68	MS-69	MS-70
2	2	0	4	12	50	62	38	0	0	0	

Key to Collecting: Common. In this year Jefferson's hair details were strengthened in the obverse hub, which was used through 1992.

Step-Detail Availability (MS-65 and Higher): *5 Full Steps*—1 in 2; *6 Full Steps*—Common.

1991-D

Circulation-Strike Mintage: 436,496,678

1991-D • Market Values • Circulation Strikes

MS-60	MS-63	MS-64	MS-64FS	MS-65	MS-65FS	MS-66	MS-66FS	MS-67	MS-67FS
$0.10	$0.25	$0.50	$9.00	$0.75	$15.	—	$300.	—	—

Availability (Certified Populations) • Circulation Strikes

<MS-60	MS-60	MS-61	MS-62	MS-63	MS-64	MS-65	MS-66	MS-67	MS-68	MS-69	MS-70
0	0	0	5	18	75	86	33	1	0	0	

Key to Collecting: Common. In this year Jefferson's hair details were strengthened in the obverse hub, which was used through 1992.
Step-Detail Availability (MS-65 and Higher): *5 Full Steps*—1 in 2; *6 Full Steps*—Common.

1991-S

Proof Mintage: 2,867,787

1991-S • Market Values • Proof Strikes

PF-60	PF-63	PF-64	PF-65	PF-66	PF-67	PF-68
$1.	$3.	$4.	$5.	—	—	—

Availability (Certified Populations) • Proof Strikes

< PF-60	PF-60	PF-61	PF-62	PF-63	PF-64	PF-65	PF-66	PF-67	PF-68	PF-69	PF-70
0	0	0	0	1	0	2	6	16	50	2,079	75

Key to Collecting: In this year Jefferson's hair details were strengthened in the obverse hub, which was used through 1992.
Step-Detail Availability (Proof): *5 Full Steps*—Scarce; *6 Full Steps*—Standard.

1992-P

Circulation-Strike Mintage: 399,552,000

1992-P • Market Values • Circulation Strikes

MS-60	MS-63	MS-64	MS-64FS	MS-65	MS-65FS	MS-66	MS-66FS	MS-67	MS-67FS
$0.50	$1.50	$2.00	$7.00	$2.50	$15.	—	$50.	—	—

Availability (Certified Populations) • Circulation Strikes

< MS-60	MS-60	MS-61	MS-62	MS-63	MS-64	MS-65	MS-66	MS-67	MS-68	MS-69	MS-70
0	0	0	1	9	58	90	108	4	0	0	0

Key to Collecting: Common.
Step-Detail Availability (MS-65 and Higher): *5 Full Steps*—1 in 2; *6 Full Steps*—Common.

1992-D

Circulation-Strike Mintage: 450,565,113

1992-D • Market Values • Circulation Strikes

MS-60	MS-63	MS-64	MS-64FS	MS-65	MS-65FS	MS-66	MS-66FS	MS-67	MS-67FS
$0.10	$0.25	$0.50	$6.00	$0.75	$12.	—	$125.	—	—

Availability (Certified Populations) • Circulation Strikes

< MS-60	MS-60	MS-61	MS-62	MS-63	MS-64	MS-65	MS-66	MS-67	MS-68	MS-69	MS-70
4	1	0	2	13	59	110	45	2	0	0	0

Key to Collecting: Common.
Step-Detail Availability (MS-65 and Higher): *5 Full Steps*—1 in 2; *6 Full Steps*—Common.

1992-S

Proof Mintage: 4,176,560

1992-S • Market Values • Proof Strikes

PF-60	PF-63	PF-64	PF-65	PF-66	PF-67	PF-68
$1.	$2.	$3.	$4.	—	—	—

Availability (Certified Populations) • Proof Strikes

< PF-60	PF-60	PF-61	PF-62	PF-63	PF-64	PF-65	PF-66	PF-67	PF-68	PF-69	PF-70
0	0	0	0	1	0	4	7	29	114	3,691	110

Key to Collecting: Nice, as always.
Step-Detail Availability (Proof): *5 Full Steps*—Scarce; *6 Full Steps*—Standard.

1993-P

Circulation-Strike Mintage: 412,076,000

1993-P • Market Values • Circulation Strikes

MS-60	MS-63	MS-64	MS-64FS	MS-65	MS-65FS	MS-66	MS-66FS	MS-67	MS-67FS
$0.10	$0.25	$0.50	$6.00	$0.75	$20.	—	$100.	—	—

Availability (Certified Populations) • Circulation Strikes

< MS-60	MS-60	MS-61	MS-62	MS-63	MS-64	MS-65	MS-66	MS-67	MS-68	MS-69	MS-70
2	1	0	3	14	66	85	88	11	0	0	0

Key to Collecting: Common. In this year Jefferson's hair details were strengthened again (last done in 1991) in the obverse hub.
Step-Detail Availability (MS-65 and Higher): *5 Full Steps*—1 in 2; *6 Full Steps*—Common.

1993-D

Circulation-Strike Mintage: 406,084,135

1993-D • Market Values • Circulation Strikes

MS-60	MS-63	MS-64	MS-64FS	MS-65	MS-65FS	MS-66	MS-66FS	MS-67	MS-67FS
$0.10	$0.25	$0.50	$6.00	$0.75	$6.	—	$20.	—	$450.

Availability (Certified Populations) • Circulation Strikes

< MS-60	MS-60	MS-61	MS-62	MS-63	MS-64	MS-65	MS-66	MS-67	MS-68	MS-69	MS-70
1	0	0	0	19	95	176	167	16	0	0	0

Key to Collecting: Common. In this year Jefferson's hair details were strengthened again (last done in 1991) in the obverse hub.
Step-Detail Availability (MS-65 and Higher): *5 Full Steps*—1 in 2; *6 Full Steps*—Common.

1993-S

Proof Mintage: 3,394,792

1993-S • Market Values • Proof Strikes

PF-60	PF-63	PF-64	PF-65	PF-66	PF-67	PF-68
$1.	$2.	$3.	$4.	—	—	—

Availability (Certified Populations) • Proof Strikes

< PF-60	PF-60	PF-61	PF-62	PF-63	PF-64	PF-65	PF-66	PF-67	PF-68	PF-69	PF-70
0	0	0	0	0	1	2	1	30	103	3,181	137

Key to Collecting: Nice, as expected. In this year Jefferson's hair details were strengthened again (last done in 1991) in the obverse hub.
Step-Detail Availability (Proof): *5 Full Steps*—Scarce; *6 Full Steps*—Standard.

1994-P

Circulation-Strike Mintage: 722,160,000
Matte-Finish Mintage: 167,703

1994-P • Market Values • Circulation Strikes and Matte-Finish Strikes[a]

MS-60	MS-63	MS-64	MS-64FS	MS-65	MS-65FS	MS-66	MS-66FS	MS-67	MS-67FS
$0.10	$0.25	$0.50	$6.00	$0.75	$7.	—	$50.	—	—
$40.	$60.	$80.	[b]	100.00	[b]	—	[b]	—	[b]

Availability (Certified Populations) • Circulation Strikes and Matte-Finish Strikes[a]

< MS-60	MS-60	MS-61	MS-62	MS-63	MS-64	MS-65	MS-66	MS-67	MS-68	MS-69	MS-70
1	0	0	4	17	70	69	63	3	1	0	0
0	0	0	0	2	4	9	10	45	200	772	7

[a] Circulation strikes, red ■ Matte-finish strikes, green ■
[b] According to Full Step–valuations contributor Mark Hooten, nearly all have 6 Full Steps, and the major grading services differ on whether to distinguish FS coins as such. Hence, pricing data across grading services are not comparable, and FS values are difficult to estimate. The reader is cautioned that, at higher grades, prices for FS coins of this year can vary dramatically among the major grading services, so comparison shopping is the order of the day.

Key to Collecting: Common. This year the Mint was innovative in its marketing, and among its purchase options was a 1993 Thomas Jefferson commemorative dollar (250th anniversary of his birth) packaged with a $2 bill (of which about 5% are star notes[5]) and a Jefferson nickel, the last with a "special Uncirculated" or "Matte Proof" finish, depending on what you want to call it.

Matte Finish: Special Matte Finish nickels, designated as Mint State but closely resembling Proofs, were included in certain packaging options for the *1993* Thomas Jefferson commemorative dollar (such being sold in 1994). The sales for the nickels totaled 167,703 pieces.

Step-Detail Availability (MS-65 and Higher): *5 Full Steps*—1 in 2; *6 Full Steps*—Common.

Step-Detail Availability (Special Matte Finish): *5 Full Steps*—Available; *6 Full Steps*—Common.

1994-D

Circulation-Strike Mintage: 715,762,110

1994-D • Market Values • Circulation Strikes

MS-60	MS-63	MS-64	MS-64FS	MS-65	MS-65FS	MS-66	MS-66FS	MS-67	MS-67FS
$0.10	$0.25	$0.50	$9.00	$0.75	$9.	—	$100.	—	—

Availability (Certified Populations) • Circulation Strikes

< MS-60	MS-60	MS-61	MS-62	MS-63	MS-64	MS-65	MS-66	MS-67	MS-68	MS-69	MS-70
1	0	1	4	17	70	86	40	2	0	0	0

Key to Collecting: Common.

Step-Detail Availability (MS-65 and Higher): *5 Full Steps*—1 in 2; *6 Full Steps*—Common.

1994-S

Proof Mintage: 3,269,923

1994-S • Market Values • Proof Strikes

PF-60	PF-63	PF-64	PF-65	PF-66	PF-67	PF-68
$1.	$2.	$3.	$4.	—	—	—

Availability (Certified Populations) • Proof Strikes

< PF-60	PF-60	PF-61	PF-62	PF-63	PF-64	PF-65	PF-66	PF-67	PF-68	PF-69	PF-70
0	0	0	0	0	1	2	9	20	90	3,216	96

Key to Collecting: Attractive, sharply detailed.

Step-Detail Availability (Proof): *5 Full Steps*—Scarce; *6 Full Steps*—Standard.

1995-P

Circulation-Strike Mintage: 774,156,000

1995-P • Market Values • Circulation Strikes

MS-60	MS-63	MS-64	MS-64FS	MS-65	MS-65FS	MS-66	MS-66FS	MS-67	MS-67FS
$0.10	$0.25	$0.50	$6.00	$0.75	$20.	—	$85.	—	—

Availability (Certified Populations) • Circulation Strikes

< MS-60	MS-60	MS-61	MS-62	MS-63	MS-64	MS-65	MS-66	MS-67	MS-68	MS-69	MS-70
2	0	0	3	14	47	82	52	6	0	0	0

Key to Collecting: Common.
Step-Detail Availability (MS-65 and Higher): *5 Full Steps*—1 in 2; *6 Full Steps*—Common.

1995-D

Circulation-Strike Mintage: 888,112,000

1995-D • Market Values • Circulation Strikes

MS-60	MS-63	MS-64	MS-64FS	MS-65	MS-65FS	MS-66	MS-66FS	MS-67	MS-67FS
$0.25	$0.50	$0.75	$6.	$1.	$15.	—	$120.	—	$1,500.

Availability (Certified Populations) • Circulation Strikes

< MS-60	MS-60	MS-61	MS-62	MS-63	MS-64	MS-65	MS-66	MS-67	MS-68	MS-69	MS-70
5	0	0	5	15	74	110	45	6	0	0	0

Key to Collecting: Common.
Step-Detail Availability (MS-65 and Higher): *5 Full Steps*—1 in 2; *6 Full Steps*—Common.

1995-S

Proof Mintage: 2,797,481

1995-S • Market Values • Proof Strikes

PF-60	PF-63	PF-64	PF-65	PF-66	PF-67	PF-68
$1.	$3.	$4.	$5.	—	—	—

Availability (Certified Populations) • Proof Strikes

< PF-60	PF-60	PF-61	PF-62	PF-63	PF-64	PF-65	PF-66	PF-67	PF-68	PF-69	PF-70
0	0	0	0	1	3	0	4	24	92	2,603	101

Key to Collecting: Another nice Proof.
Step-Detail Availability (Proof): *5 Full Steps*—Scarce; *6 Full Steps*—Standard.

1996-P

Circulation-Strike Mintage: 829,332,000

1996-P • Market Values • Circulation Strikes

MS-60	MS-63	MS-64	MS-64FS	MS-65	MS-65FS	MS-66	MS-66FS	MS-67	MS-67FS
$0.10	$0.25	$0.50	$6.00	$0.75	$15.	—	$25.	—	$500.

Availability (Certified Populations) • Circulation Strikes

< MS-60	MS-60	MS-61	MS-62	MS-63	MS-64	MS-65	MS-66	MS-67	MS-68	MS-69	MS-70
1	1	0	2	19	58	75	175	27	2	0	0

Key to Collecting: Common.
Step-Detail Availability (MS-65 and Higher): *5 Full Steps*—1 in 2; *6 Full Steps*—Common.

1996-D

Circulation-Strike Mintage: 817,736,000

1996-D • Market Values • Circulation Strikes

MS-60	MS-63	MS-64	MS-64FS	MS-65	MS-65FS	MS-66	MS-66FS	MS-67	MS-67FS
$0.10	$0.25	$0.50	$7.00	$0.75	$15.	—	$20.	—	$200.

Availability (Certified Populations) • Circulation Strikes

< MS-60	MS-60	MS-61	MS-62	MS-63	MS-64	MS-65	MS-66	MS-67	MS-68	MS-69	MS-70
5	1	0	1	18	117	136	211	25	0	0	0

Key to Collecting: Common.
Step-Detail Availability (MS-65 and Higher): *5 Full Steps*—1 in 2; *6 Full Steps*—Common.

1996-S

Proof Mintage: 2,525,265

1996-S • Market Values • Proof Strikes

PF-60	PF-63	PF-64	PF-65	PF-66	PF-67	PF-68
$1.00	$2.00	$2.50	$3.	—	—	—

Availability (Certified Populations) • Proof Strikes

< PF-60	PF-60	PF-61	PF-62	PF-63	PF-64	PF-65	PF-66	PF-67	PF-68	PF-69	PF-70
0	0	0	0	0	0	2	5	18	70	2,964	124

Key to Collecting: Nice.
Step-Detail Availability (Proof): *5 Full Steps*—Scarce; *6 Full Steps*—Standard.

1997-P

Circulation-Strike Mintage: 470,972,000
Matte-Finish Mintage: 25,000

1997-P • Market Values • Circulation Strikes and Matte-Finish Strikes[a]

MS-60	MS-63	MS-64	MS-64FS	MS-65	MS-65FS	MS-66	MS-66FS	MS-67	MS-67FS
$0.25	$0.50	$0.75	$6.00	$1.00	$20.	—	$250.	—	$1,750.
MS-60	MS-63	MS-64	MS-64FS	MS-65	MS-65FS	MS-66	MS-66FS	MS-67	MS-67FS
$150.	$200.	$225.	b	$250.	b	—	b	—	b

Availability (Certified Populations) • Circulation Strikes and Matte-Finish Strikes[a]

< MS-60	MS-60	MS-61	MS-62	MS-63	MS-64	MS-65	MS-66	MS-67	MS-68	MS-69	MS-70
3	0	0	7	11	56	48	29	8	0	0	0
< MS-60	MS-60	MS-61	MS-62	MS-63	MS-64	MS-65	MS-66	MS-67	MS-68	MS-69	MS-70
0	0	0	1	2	3	1	—	7	52	598	76

[a] Circulation strikes, red ▇   Matte-finish strikes, green ▇

[b] According to Full Step–valuations contributor Mark Hooten, nearly all have 6 Full Steps, and the major grading services differ on whether to distinguish FS coins as such. Hence, pricing data across grading services are not comparable, and FS values are difficult to estimate. The reader is cautioned that, at higher grades, prices for FS coins of this year can vary dramatically among the major grading services, so comparison shopping is the order of the day.

Key to Collecting: Common. Following an idea tried in 1994, in 1997 the Mint packaged a special finish Jefferson nickel with a new Botanic Garden commemorative dollar and a $1 note. The nickel had a "special Uncirculated" or "Matte Proof" finish, depending on what you want to call it. These are scarce today.

Matte Finish: Special Matte Finish nickels, designated as Mint State but closely resembling Proofs, were made for inclusion in certain packaging with the 1997 Botanic Gardens commemorative coins. Just 25,000 were sold.

Step-Detail Availability (MS-65 and Higher): *5 Full Steps—1 in 2; 6 Full Steps—* Common.

Step-Detail Availability (Special Satin Finish): *5 Full Steps—Available; 6 Full Steps—* Common.

1997-D

Circulation-Strike Mintage: 466,640,000

1997-D • Market Values • Circulation Strikes

MS-60	MS-63	MS-64	MS-64FS	MS-65	MS-65FS	MS-66	MS-66FS	MS-67	MS-67FS
$0.25	$0.50	$1.00	$8.00	$1.50	$40.	$2.	$150.	—	—

Availability (Certified Populations) • Circulation Strikes

< MS-60	MS-60	MS-61	MS-62	MS-63	MS-64	MS-65	MS-66	MS-67	MS-68	MS-69	MS-70
2	0	0	1	8	73	45	32	2	0	0	

Key to Collecting: Common.
Step-Detail Availability (MS-65 and Higher): *5 Full Steps—1 in 2; 6 Full Steps—* Common.

1997-S

Proof Mintage: 2,796,678

1997-S • Market Values • Proof Strikes

PF-60	PF-63	PF-64	PF-65	PF-66	PF-67	PF-68
$0.50	$1.	$2.	$3.	—	—	—

Availability (Certified Populations) • Proof Strikes

< PF-60	PF-60	PF-61	PF-62	PF-63	PF-64	PF-65	PF-66	PF-67	PF-68	PF-69	PF-70
0	0	0	0	1	0	3	1	17	101	2,611	185

Key to Collecting: Gem is the rule.
Step-Detail Availability (Proof): *5 Full Steps*—Scarce; *6 Full Steps*—Standard.

1998-P

Circulation-Strike Mintage: 688,272,000

1998-P • Market Values • Circulation Strikes

MS-60	MS-63	MS-64	MS-64FS	MS-65	MS-65FS	MS-66	MS-66FS	MS-67	MS-67FS
$0.10	$0.25	$0.50	$9.00	$0.75	$20.		$65.	—	—

Availability (Certified Populations) • Circulation Strikes

< MS-60	MS-60	MS-61	MS-62	MS-63	MS-64	MS-65	MS-66	MS-67	MS-68	MS-69	MS-70
1	1	2	10	29	79	80	40	5	0	0	

Key to Collecting: Common.
Step-Detail Availability (MS-65 and Higher): *5 Full Steps*—1 in 2; *6 Full Steps*—Common.

1998-D

Circulation-Strike Mintage: 635,360,000

1998-D • Market Values • Circulation Strikes

MS-60	MS-63	MS-64	MS-64FS	MS-65	MS-65FS	MS-66	MS-66FS	MS-67	MS-67FS
$0.10	$0.25	$0.50	$6.00	$0.75	$25.	—	$250.	—	—

Availability (Certified Populations) • Circulation Strikes

< MS-60	MS-60	MS-61	MS-62	MS-63	MS-64	MS-65	MS-66	MS-67	MS-68	MS-69	MS-70
5	0	0	3	29	74	35	13	0	0	0	

Key to Collecting: Common.
Step-Detail Availability (MS-65 and Higher): *5 Full Steps*—1 in 2; *6 Full Steps*—Common.

1998-S

Proof Mintage: 2,086,507

1998-S • Market Values • Proof Strikes

PF-60	PF-63	PF-64	PF-65	PF-66	PF-67	PF-68
$0.50	$1.	$2.	$3.	—	—	—

Availability (Certified Populations) • Proof Strikes

< PF-60	PF-60	PF-61	PF-62	PF-63	PF-64	PF-65	PF-66	PF-67	PF-68	PF-69	PF-70
0	0	0	0	0	0	3	10	17	113	3,190	270

Key to Collecting: Beautiful. It is somewhat strange that Proof production figures seem to be in the same general range over a long period of years.

Step-Detail Availability (Proof): *5 Full Steps*—Scarce • *6 Full Steps*—Standard.

1999-P

Circulation-Strike Mintage: 1,212,000,000

1999-P • Market Values • Circulation Strikes

MS-60	MS-63	MS-64	MS-64FS	MS-65	MS-65FS	MS-66	MS-66FS	MS-67	MS-67FS
$0.10	$0.25	$0.50	$6.00	$0.75	$30.	—	$40.	—	$425.

Availability (Certified Populations) • Circulation Strikes

< MS-60	MS-60	MS-61	MS-62	MS-63	MS-64	MS-65	MS-66	MS-67	MS-68	MS-69	MS-70
24	4	3	21	60	131	150	160	15	1	0	0

Key to Collecting: Common.

Step-Detail Availability (MS-65 and Higher): *5 Full Steps*—1 in 2; *6 Full Steps*—Common.

1999-D

Circulation-Strike Mintage: 1,066,720,000

1999-D • Market Values • Circulation Strikes

MS-60	MS-63	MS-64	MS-64FS	MS-65	MS-65FS	MS-66	MS-66FS	MS-67	MS-67FS
$0.10	$0.25	$0.50	$6.00	$0.75	$100.	—	$130.	—	—

Availability (Certified Populations) • Circulation Strikes

< MS-60	MS-60	MS-61	MS-62	MS-63	MS-64	MS-65	MS-66	MS-67	MS-68	MS-69	MS-70
20	2	0	15	22	84	91	83	3	0	0	0

Key to Collecting: Common.

Step-Detail Availability (MS-65 and Higher): *5 Full Steps*—1 in 2; *6 Full Steps*—Common.

1999-S

Proof Mintage: 3,347,966

1999-S • Market Values • Proof Strikes

PF-60	PF-63	PF-64	PF-65	PF-66	PF-67	PF-68
$1.	$2.	$3.	$4.	—	—	—

Availability (Certified Populations) • Proof Strikes

< PF-60	PF-60	PF-61	PF-62	PF-63	PF-64	PF-65	PF-66	PF-67	PF-68	PF-69	PF-70
0	0	0	0	0	5	0	6	32	157	5,824	325

Key to Collecting: High quality as usual.
Step-Detail Availability (Proof): *5 Full Steps*—Scarce; *6 Full Steps*—Standard.

2000-P

Circulation-Strike Mintage: 846,240,000

2000-P • Market Values • Circulation Strikes

MS-60	MS-63	MS-64	MS-64FS	MS-65	MS-65FS	MS-66	MS-66FS	MS-67	MS-67FS
$0.10	$0.25	$0.50	$6.00	$0.75	$10.	—	$20.	—	$550.

Availability (Certified Populations) • Circulation Strikes

< MS-60	MS-60	MS-61	MS-62	MS-63	MS-64	MS-65	MS-66	MS-67	MS-68	MS-69	MS-70
1	1	3	28	76	81	148	17	1	0	0	0

Key to Collecting: Common.
Step-Detail Availability (MS-65 and Higher): *5 Full Steps*—1 in 2; *6 Full Steps*—Common.

2000-D

Circulation-Strike Mintage: 1,509,520,000

2000-D • Market Values • Circulation Strikes

MS-60	MS-63	MS-64	MS-64FS	MS-65	MS-65FS	MS-66	MS-66FS	MS-67	MS-67FS
$0.10	$0.25	$0.50	$9.00	$0.75	$7.	—	$80.	—	$700.

Availability (Certified Populations) • Circulation Strikes

< MS-60	MS-60	MS-61	MS-62	MS-63	MS-64	MS-65	MS-66	MS-67	MS-68	MS-69	MS-70
3	0	1	3	13	85	100	108	15	0	0	0

Key to Collecting: Common. Especially large mintage.
Step-Detail Availability (MS-65 and Higher): *5 Full Steps*—1 in 2; *6 Full Steps*—Common.

2000-S

Proof Mintage: 4,047,993

2000-S • Market Values • Proof Strikes

PF-60	PF-63	PF-64	PF-65	PF-66	PF-67	PF-68
$0.50	$1.	$2.	$3.	—	—	—

Availability (Certified Populations) • Proof Strikes

< PF-60	PF-60	PF-61	PF-62	PF-63	PF-64	PF-65	PF-66	PF-67	PF-68	PF-69	PF-70
0	0	1	0	0	2	1	11	54	237	6,210	393

Key to Collecting: Attractive as usual.
Step-Detail Availability (Proof): *5 Full Steps*—Scarce; *6 Full Steps*—Standard.

2001-P

Circulation-Strike Mintage: 675,704,000

2001-P • Market Values • Circulation Strikes

MS-60	MS-63	MS-64	MS-64FS	MS-65	MS-65FS	MS-66	MS-66FS	MS-67	MS-67FS
$0.10	$0.25	$0.50	$6.00	$0.75	$9.	—	$15.	—	$50.

Availability (Certified Populations) • Circulation Strikes

< MS-60	MS-60	MS-61	MS-62	MS-63	MS-64	MS-65	MS-66	MS-67	MS-68	MS-69	MS-70
1	1	0	0	2	51	90	234	254	5	0	0

Key to Collecting: Common.
Step-Detail Availability (MS-65 and Higher): *5 Full Steps*—1 in 2; *6 Full Steps*—Common.

2001-D

Circulation-Strike Mintage: 627,680,000

2001-D • Market Values • Circulation Strikes

MS-60	MS-63	MS-64	MS-64FS	MS-65	MS-65FS	MS-66	MS-66FS	MS-67	MS-67FS
$0.10	$0.25	$0.50	$6.00	$0.75	$9.	—	$20.	—	$150.

Availability (Certified Populations) • Circulation Strikes

< MS-60	MS-60	MS-61	MS-62	MS-63	MS-64	MS-65	MS-66	MS-67	MS-68	MS-69	MS-70
3	0	2	8	7	55	103	129	43	1	0	0

Key to Collecting: Common.
Step-Detail Availability (MS-65 and Higher): *5 Full Steps*—1 in 2; *6 Full Steps*—Common.

2001-S

Proof Mintage: 3,184,606

2001-S • Market Values • Proof Strikes

PF-60	PF-63	PF-64	PF-65	PF-66	PF-67	PF-68
$0.50	$1.	$2.	$3.	—	—	—

Availability (Certified Populations) • Proof Strikes

< PF-60	PF-60	PF-61	PF-62	PF-63	PF-64	PF-65	PF-66	PF-67	PF-68	PF-69	PF-70
0	0	0	0	0	3	1	3	20	114	4,890	467

Key to Collecting: Superb.
Step-Detail Availability (Proof): *5 Full Steps*—Scarce; *6 Full Steps*—Standard.

2002-P

Circulation-Strike Mintage: 539,280,000

2002-P • Market Values • Circulation Strikes

MS-60	MS-63	MS-64	MS-64FS	MS-65	MS-65FS	MS-66	MS-66FS	MS-67	MS-67FS
$0.10	$0.25	$0.50	$6.00	$0.75	$10.	—	$35.	—	$115.

Availability (Certified Populations) • Circulation Strikes

< MS-60	MS-60	MS-61	MS-62	MS-63	MS-64	MS-65	MS-66	MS-67	MS-68	MS-69	MS-70
0	0	0	3	10	60	142	172	51	1	0	0

Key to Collecting: Common.
Step-Detail Availability (MS-65 and Higher): *5 Full Steps*—1 in 2; *6 Full Steps*—Common.
Double-Denomination Muling: At the Philadelphia Mint a 2000-P Jefferson nickel obverse die was accidentally combined with a Lincoln cent reverse die, and coins were struck on nickel planchets.[6] None have been reported as having been released.

2002-D

2002-D • Market Values • Circulation Strikes

MS-60	MS-63	MS-64	MS-64FS	MS-65	MS-65FS	MS-66	MS-66FS	MS-67	MS-67FS
$0.10	$0.25	$0.50	$6.00	$0.75	$11.	—	$165.	—	—

Availability (Certified Populations) • Circulation Strikes

< MS-60	MS-60	MS-61	MS-62	MS-63	MS-64	MS-65	MS-66	MS-67	MS-68	MS-69	MS-70
0	0	1	5	3	77	116	31	3	0	0	0

Circulation-Strike Mintage: 691,200,000
Key to Collecting: Common.
Step-Detail Availability (MS-65 and Higher): *5 Full Steps*—1 in 2; *6 Full Steps*—Common.

2002-S

Proof Mintage: 3,211,995

2002-S • Market Values • Proof Strikes

PF-60	PF-63	PF-64	PF-65	PF-66	PF-67	PF-68
$0.50	$1.	$2.	$3.	—	—	—

Availability (Certified Populations) • Proof Strikes

< PF-60	PF-60	PF-61	PF-62	PF-63	PF-64	PF-65	PF-66	PF-67	PF-68	PF-69	PF-70
0	0	0	0	0	2	2	1	17	91	5,297	226

Key to Collecting: Beautiful, as expected. A collection of S-mint Proofs, inexpensive, can be an attraction in itself.

Step-Detail Availability (Proof): *5 Full Steps*—Scarce; *6 Full Steps*—Standard.

2003-P

Circulation-Strike Mintage: 441,840,000

2003-P • Market Values • Circulation Strikes

MS-60	MS-63	MS-64	MS-64FS	MS-65	MS-65FS	MS-66	MS-66FS	MS-67	MS-67FS
$0.10	$0.25	$0.50	$4.00	$0.75	$6.	—	$12.	—	$90.

Availability (Certified Populations) • Circulation Strikes

< MS-60	MS-60	MS-61	MS-62	MS-63	MS-64	MS-65	MS-66	MS-67	MS-68	MS-69	MS-70
2	1	0	7	12	87	177	280	69	6	0	0

Key to Collecting: Common.

Step-Detail Availability (MS-65 and Higher): *5 Full Steps*—1 in 2; *6 Full Steps*—Common.

2003-D

Circulation-Strike Mintage: 383,040,000

2003-D • Market Values • Circulation Strikes

MS-60	MS-63	MS-64	MS-64FS	MS-65	MS-65FS	MS-66	MS-66FS	MS-67	MS-67FS
$0.10	$0.25	$0.50	$6.00	$0.75	$50.	—	$150.	—	—

Availability (Certified Populations) • Circulation Strikes

< MS-60	MS-60	MS-61	MS-62	MS-63	MS-64	MS-65	MS-66	MS-67	MS-68	MS-69	MS-70
1	0	1	8	43	90	153	42	3	0	0	0

Key to Collecting: Common. Although 6 Full Steps nickels may be common on an absolute basis in view of the total mintage, it still takes some searching find them. Darrell Crane advertised in the *Portico* (July–August 2003): "2003-D MS-65+ [6 Full Steps]. Just searched a box of 50 rolls. The majority of these coins are very heavily nicked with the obverse showing the most damage. Of the 2,000 nickels I saved about 20. These coins are high grade, virtually nick-free obverse and reverse (no large nicks), nice eye appeal." • A reminder: Many obverse nicks on modern nickels are from areas of the original planchet not fully struck up, not from contact by the finished coin.

Step-Detail Availability (MS-65 and Higher): *5 Full Steps*—1 in 2; *6 Full Steps*—Common.

2003-S

Proof Mintage: 3,298,439

2003-S • Market Values • Proof Strikes

PF-60	PF-63	PF-64	PF-65	PF-66	PF-67	PF-68
$0.50	$1.	$2.	$3.	—	—	—

Availability (Certified Populations) • Proof Strikes

< PF-60	PF-60	PF-61	PF-62	PF-63	PF-64	PF-65	PF-66	PF-67	PF-68	PF-69	PF-70
0	0	0	0	0	0	0	4	9	42	9,555	941

Key to Collecting: Attractive.
Step-Detail Availability (Proof): *5 Full Steps*—Scarce; *6 Full Steps*—Standard.

2004-P PEACE MEDAL

Circulation-Strike Mintage: 361,440,000

2004-P Peace Medal • Market Values • Circulation Strikes

MS-60	MS-63	MS-64	MS-65	MS-66	MS-67
$0.10	$0.25	$0.50	$0.75	—	—

Availability (Certified Populations) • Circulation Strikes

< MS-60	MS-60	MS-61	MS-62	MS-63	MS-64	MS-65	MS-66	MS-67	MS-68	MS-69	MS-70
2	0	1	6	62	254	329	189	60	5	0	0

2004-D PEACE MEDAL

Circulation-Strike Mintage: 372,000,000

2004-D Peace Medal • Market Values • Circulation Strikes

MS-60	MS-63	MS-64	MS-65	MS-66	MS-67
$0.10	$0.25	$0.50	$0.75	—	—

Availability (Certified Populations) • Circulation Strikes

< MS-60	MS-60	MS-61	MS-62	MS-63	MS-64	MS-65	MS-66	MS-67	MS-68	MS-69	MS-70
2	0	0	0	15	122	319	556	230	25	0	0

2004-S PEACE MEDAL

Proof Mintage: 2,992,069

2004-S Peace Medal • Market Values • Proof Strikes

PF-60	PF-63	PF-64	PF-65	PF-66	PF-67	PF-68
$2.	$3.	$4.	$5.	—	—	—

Availability (Certified Populations) • Proof Strikes

< PF-60	PF-60	PF-61	PF-62	PF-63	PF-64	PF-65	PF-66	PF-67	PF-68	PF-69	PF-70
0	0	0	0	0	0	1	4	11	89	15,883	1,355

2004-P KEELBOAT

Circulation-Strike Mintage: 366,720,000

2004-P Keelboat • Market Values • Circulation Strikes

MS-60	MS-63	MS-64	MS-65	MS-66	MS-67
$0.10	$0.25	$0.50	$0.75	—	—

Availability (Certified Populations) • Circulation Strikes

< MS-60	MS-60	MS-61	MS-62	MS-63	MS-64	MS-65	MS-66	MS-67	MS-68	MS-69	MS-70
0	0	2	3	25	101	86	196	187	26	0	0

2004-D KEELBOAT

Circulation-Strike Mintage: 344,880,000

2004-D Keelboat • Market Values • Circulation Strikes

MS-60	MS-63	MS-64	MS-65	MS-66	MS-67
$0.10	$0.25	$0.50	$0.75	—	—

Availability (Certified Populations) • Circulation Strikes

< MS-60	MS-60	MS-61	MS-62	MS-63	MS-64	MS-65	MS-66	MS-67	MS-68	MS-69	MS-70
0	1	0	1	7	66	92	261	271	14	0	0

2004-S KEELBOAT

Proof Mintage: 2,992,069

2004-S Keelboat • Market Values • Proof Strikes

PF-60	PF-63	PF-64	PF-65	PF-66	PF-67	PF-68
$2.	$3.	$4.	$5.	—	—	—

Availability (Certified Populations) • Proof Strikes

< PF-60	PF-60	PF-61	PF-62	PF-63	PF-64	PF-65	PF-66	PF-67	PF-68	PF-69	PF-70
0	0	0	0	0	0	0	4	15	89	15,815	1,302

2005-P BISON

Circulation-Strike Mintage: 448,320,000

2005-P Bison• Market Values • Circulation Strikes

MS-60	MS-63	MS-64	MS-65	MS-66	MS-67
$0.10	$0.25	$0.50	$0.75	—	—

Availability (Certified Populations) • Circulation Strikes

< MS-60	MS-60	MS-61	MS-62	MS-63	MS-64	MS-65	MS-66	MS-67	MS-68	MS-69	MS-70
1	1	0	12	71	178	248	83	2	0	2	0

2005-D BISON

Circulation-Strike Mintage: 487,680,000

2005-D Bison • Market Values • Circulation Strikes

MS-60	MS-63	MS-64	MS-65	MS-66	MS-67
$0.10	$0.25	$0.50	$0.75	—	—

Availability (Certified Populations) • Circulation Strikes

< MS-60	MS-60	MS-61	MS-62	MS-63	MS-64	MS-65	MS-66	MS-67	MS-68	MS-69	MS-70
0	14	0	11	49	213	343	155	8	0	0	0

2005-S BISON

Proof Mintage: 3,273,000

2005-S Bison • Market Values • Proof Strikes

PF-60	PF-63	PF-64	PF-65	PF-66	PF-67	PF-68
$2.	$3.	$4.	$5.	—	—	—

Availability (Certified Populations) • Proof Strikes

< PF-60	PF-60	PF-61	PF-62	PF-63	PF-64	PF-65	PF-66	PF-67	PF-68	PF-69	PF-70
0	0	0	0	0	2	3	5	16	92	23,115	2,542

2005-P OCEAN IN VIEW

Circulation-Strike Mintage: 411,120,000

2005-P Ocean in View • Market Values • Circulation Strikes

MS-60	MS-63	MS-64	MS-65	MS-66	MS-67
$0.10	$0.25	$0.50	$0.75	—	—

Availability (Certified Populations) • Circulation Strikes

< MS-60	MS-60	MS-61	MS-62	MS-63	MS-64	MS-65	MS-66	MS-67	MS-68	MS-69	MS-70
1	2	2	1	19	36	112	6	13	0	0	0

2005-D OCEAN IN VIEW

Circulation-Strike Mintage: 394,080,000

2005-D Ocean in View • Market Values • Circulation Strikes

MS-60	MS-63	MS-64	MS-65	MS-66	MS-67
$0.10	$0.25	$0.50	$0.75	—	—

Availability (Certified Populations) • Circulation Strikes

< MS-60	MS-60	MS-61	MS-62	MS-63	MS-64	MS-65	MS-66	MS-67	MS-68	MS-69	MS-70
0	0	0	2	10	17	161	17	3	0	0	0

2005-S OCEAN IN VIEW

Proof Mintage: 3,273,000

2005-S Ocean in View • Market Values • Proof Strikes

PF-60	PF-63	PF-64	PF-65	PF-66	PF-67	PF-68
$2.	$3.	$4.	$5.	—	—	—

Availability (Certified Populations) • Proof Strikes

< PF-60	PF-60	PF-61	PF-62	PF-63	PF-64	PF-65	PF-66	PF-67	PF-68	PF-69	PF-70
0	0	0	0	0	0	2	6	10	65	21,524	2,684

2006-P

2006-P • Market Values • Circulation Strikes

MS-60	MS-63	MS-64	MS-65	MS-66	MS-67
$0.10	$0.25	$0.50	$0.75	—	—

Availability (Certified Populations) • Circulation Strikes

< MS-60	MS-60	MS-61	MS-62	MS-63	MS-64	MS-65	MS-66	MS-67	MS-68	MS-69	MS-70
0	0	0	0	0	1	4	9	0	0	0	0

2006-D

2006-D • Market Values • Circulation Strikes

MS-60	MS-63	MS-64	MS-65	MS-66	MS-67
$0.10	$0.25	$0.50	$0.75	—	—

Availability (Certified Populations) • Circulation Strikes

< MS-60	MS-60	MS-61	MS-62	MS-63	MS-64	MS-65	MS-66	MS-67	MS-68	MS-69	MS-70
0	0	0	0	0	7	12	36	8	0	0	0

2006-S

2006-S • Market Values • Proof Strikes

PF-60	PF-63	PF-64	PF-65	PF-66	PF-67	PF-68
$2.	$3.	$4.	$5.	—	—	—

Availability (Certified Populations) • Proof Strikes

< PF-60	PF-60	PF-61	PF-62	PF-63	PF-64	PF-65	PF-66	PF-67	PF-68	PF-69	PF-70
0	0	0	0	0	0	0	0	0	686	371	

Appendix A
Chronology of the
Nickel Five-Cent Piece

The following chronology lists events central to the production and numismatic aspects of nickel five-cent pieces from 1913 to date.

1912: James Earle Fraser prepares models for what would become the new nickel design of 1913.

1913: Indian Head / Buffalo nickels are made for circulation, first with the Type I design showing the bison on a raised mound, then with Type II showing the bison on level ground.

1914: Some 1913 obverse dies are overdated to read 1914/3.

1916: Matte Proofs are made for the last time. Proof production would resume in 1936, but with a different finish. LIBERTY is made bolder and some minor details of the design are also modified.

1931: Only 1,200,000 1931-S nickels are made. Despite the ongoing Depression, the issue becomes an investment favorite. Dealer Barney Bluestone of Syracuse, New York, features a previously unknown 1918/7-D overdate in an auction catalog.

1934: The *Standard Catalogue of U.S. Coins* is launched. Seventeen editions are published from 1934 through 1957. The book is an instant success, and in the 1930s helps spur a passion for coin collecting. Popular albums and folders issued during the decade would stimulate a great demand for scarce date and mintmark varieties.

1936: Proof Buffalo nickels are struck for the first time since 1916. Early Proofs of 1936 have the satin finish; later ones are of the brilliant, or mirror, style.

1938: Indian Head / Buffalo nickels are made for the last time, and only at the Denver Mint. The first overmintmark, 1938-D/S is produced. Felix O. Schlag, a Chicago sculptor, wins a competition in which 390 entrants submitted ideas for a new nickel design. The Jefferson nickel is born.

1942: The Act of March 27 provides for an alloy of 35% silver, 56% copper, and 9% manganese to be used for the nickel five-cent piece. These Nickels are recognizable by their large mintmarks (including P for Philadelphia) above the dome of Monticello. Use of this alloy continues through 1945.

1946: Use of the earlier alloy of 75% copper and 25% nickel resumes.

1950: Only 2,630,000 nickels are made at the Denver Mint. Use of this alloy continues through 1945. This is the smallest mintage in the Jefferson series to date. A fierce speculation arises, and most pieces are retrieved from banks and other repositories. Proof sets of five coins, including the Jefferson nickel, are made for the first time since 1942.

1955: The government announces the permanent closing of the San Francisco Mint. Its last issue was the 1954-S. In 1968, however, the Mint would reopen and resume producing coins, including nickels, bearing the S mintmark.

1960: Several factors, including publicity surrounding the "rare" 1960 Small Date Lincoln cent and the April launching of *Coin World*, the first weekly numismatic publication, ignite a coin investment boom. The 1950-D nickel becomes the single most sought-after investment coin. The boom lasts until 1964 before collapsing.

1964: Proof sets are made for the last time until 1968, at which time production would shift from Philadelphia to San Francisco. The use of silver is discontinued in larger denomination coins. Although the change does not affect the current composition of five-cent pieces, some time later when silver would rise in value, many nickels of 1942 to 1945 would be melted down for their silver content.

1965: Special Mint Sets (SMS) are first made at the San Francisco Mint. These coins bear no mintmarks and have a finish that closely resembles Proofs. Special Mint Sets would also be made in 1966 and 1967.

1966: The initials FS for Felix O. Schlag, the designer of the Jefferson nickel, are added to the obverse.

1968: The San Francisco Mint begins producing Proof sets. Proofs from this year forward would bear S mintmarks.

1971: The S mintmark is unintentionally omitted from one Proof die. The estimated 1,655 San Francisco Proofs made without the mintmark are considered a rarity.

1994: Matte Finish 1994-P nickels are made for inclusion in certain packaging with the 1993 Thomas Jefferson commemorative dollar being sold in 1994.

1997: Matte Finish 1997-P nickels are made for inclusion in certain packaging with the 1997 Botanic Gardens commemorative coins.

2004: The Westward Journey series of Jefferson nickels commences. Two different reverse designs are used: the Keelboat and the Indian Peace Medal.

2005: The Westward Journey series continues. A new Jefferson portrait obverse design and new Bison and Ocean in View reverse motifs are launched.

2006: The Jefferson portrait is modified again, and the Monticello design on the reverse is slightly restyled.

Appendix B
Nickel Mint Errors

To err is human, but when the humans at the Mint make mistakes, collectors become energized. So many billions of nickels have been made over such a long period of time, and at various mints, that mistakes abound. Pieces are struck on planchets intended for dimes or cents, some are off center to various degrees, others are double struck, and on and on. . . .

With the advent of new coining machinery in recent years, the number of Mint-error coins has dropped dramatically. Moreover, the so-called riddler machine catches most of the few mistakes that are made. On occasion though, a dramatic error slips into circulation and is found by some lucky bank teller or collector.

Mint errors are enthusiastically collected. I can only touch upon them lightly here, through the courtesy of Fred Weinberg, a long-time Buffalo nickel specialist who is often called upon to give opinions and perform authentications.[1] The selections below are representative pieces from a very wide field; the information has been adapted from comments made by Weinberg. As very few Mint errors are the same, valuations are apt to vary in actual transactions. The Combined Organizations of Numismatic Error Collectors of America (CONECA) publishes *Errorscope*, and provides a forum for those interested in this specialty.

Buffalo nickel, date not visible, struck on a silver dime planchet. AU-58 (PCGS). Estimated value: $50,000. An extremely rare and beautiful coin, this "silver Buffalo" is one of only three pieces reported to date. It was found in an original roll of 1937-S Buffalo nickels in the early 1970s. The Buffalo nickel series is an extremely popular field. Errors and off-center coins, clips, and off-metals are eagerly collected when available. There are about three dozen Buffaloes on cent planchets, hundreds of off-center strikes, and fewer than ten double strikes known.

1936 Buffalo nickel struck 15% off-center. MS-63 (PCGS). Estimated value: $1,250. Interestingly, 1920 and 1936 are the most common dates for off-center Buffalo nickels, while there are no off-center pieces known in the high-mintage 1937-D or 1938-D issues. Most other dates and mintmarks from 1913 on are known, including some of the rarer varieties. There is one deep die cap reverse Buffalo nickel (reverse die was used as the "hammer" die for this series) known, and is considered one of the kings of Buffalo nickel errors.

Undated Buffalo nickel, 100% split planchet, reverse only. Mint State. Estimated value: $75. If the metal used to create planchet strips is not mixed properly, the planchets can literally split apart upon striking or after the coins have reached circulation. This is the reverse half only of a circulated Buffalo nickel. It weighs slightly over 35 grains, whereas a normal nickel would weigh 77 grains.

1942-S nickel struck on a silver dime planchet. AU-58 (PCGS). Estimated value: $3,250. Nickels made during the World War II (1942–1945) contained 35% silver, but here is a wartime nickel struck on a 90% silver dime planchet. Because of the smaller diameter of the dime, and the fact that the nickel date is on the outer edge, many off-metal nickels on cent or dime planchets do not show the date. There are probably 15 to 20 known Jefferson nickels struck on steel planchets intended for the 1943 cents. These have the unusual look of a "steel nickel" and are quite popular.

1943-S silver-content wartime nickel with a 6% (by weight) planchet clip. Mint State. Estimated value: $40. Clipped planchets are considered common, and most are worth under $10, except for exceptionally large clips or scarce dates. All are popular with numismatists.

1968-S nickel struck on bronze cent planchet. MS-64 (PCGS). Estimated value: $750. Although Jefferson nickels struck on cent planchets are common, those from San Francisco are much scarcer than from any other mint. A 2001 sale of an unclaimed safe deposit box in California made known over 300 mint errors of all types and denominations. The stash had concealed some rare or unknown dates of nickels struck on cent planchets, including 1968-S, 1969-S, and 1970-S. Some of these curiosities, including a two-tailed Washington quarter, are presumed to have been "struck at midnight," so to speak, at the San Francisco Mint!

1996 nickel, multiply struck and indented. MS-64 (PCGS). Estimated value: $175. This dramatic looking nickel was struck once as a regular nickel, and was then struck at least two more times with a blank planchet covering 98% of the obverse of the original strike.

Undated nickel, 24% clipped and struck 40% off center. MS-61 (PCGS). Estimated value: $150. Known as a "combo" error, this Jefferson nickel from the 1960s or 1970s was struck 40% off-center on a planchet that is missing almost 25% of the metal (by weight) due to a clipped blank planchet.

1998 nickels, a mated *pair*. Both are MS-65 (PCGS). Estimated value: $750. Very scarce and always popular, this pair of Jefferson nickels illustrates what happens when a second coin or blank overlaps a coin sitting in the collar just before it is struck. Note the brockage (incused design) on coin #1 from the off-center second strike of coin #2. There are probably 12 to 15 such sets known, and most are dated in the 1990s.

Undated nickel struck 60% off center on a cent planchet. MS-67 Red (NGC). Estimated value: $3,750. Another "combo" error, this beautiful full flaming red nickel was struck 60% off-center on a copper-coated zinc planchet. It is probably from 1998 or 1999, and is the finest among four or five known examples.

Undated nickel struck 65% off center on a dime planchet. MS-66 (PCGS). Estimated value: $2,300. Similar in concept to the piece described above, this Jefferson nickel is struck more than half off-center on a clad dime planchet. Any off-metal strike is considered scarce, and combination off-metal and off-center examples are especially so.

1979-S Proof nickel, struck through thread on obverse. Estimated value: $150. A thread was on the die surface. Proof errors involving double or off center striking are very rare and valuable, but "struck-through" items caused by debris on the die are seen occasionally and are more available.

1995 nickel, struck on the edge and also 40% off center. Mint State. Estimated value: $450. An extremely rare type of error, this coin was struck with the planchet literally standing up on the blank edge, opposite the date. It received a small amount of the Monticello design on the edge of the coin, and was then struck 40% off center. The planchet is buckled from the first edge strike. Remnants of an unidentifiable portion of the obverse die are visible on the edge area where Jefferson's mouth should be.

APPENDIX C
PATTERN BUFFALO NICKELS

INTRODUCTION

The following is based upon the ninth edition of J. Hewitt Judd's *United States Pattern Coins*, to which refer for additional information.

PATTERNS OF 1913

The pattern nickel five-cent pieces of 1913 are variations on the Indian Head / Buffalo (bison) design created by James Earle Fraser. Most of these involved tweaking the basic motif. In addition to struck patterns, a number of electrotypes exist (but are not listed here).

Judd-1950—*Obverse:* Head of Indian facing right, date 1913 (with flat-top 3) on shoulder. LIBERTY at border in front of face. *Reverse:* Bison or "buffalo" standing on mound facing left. UNITED STATES OF AMERICA above at border, E / PLURIBUS / UNUM beneath to the right in small letters. FIVE CENTS on mound below. • Seventeen were struck on January 13, 1913. Two are in the Smithsonian Institution, six were melted, and the other nine are held privately. • Nickel alloy • Low Rarity-7

Judd-1951—*Obverse:* Similar to preceding, but with round-top 3 and with raised rims distant from devices. *Reverse:* Similar to preceding, but with some minor differences in details, particularly in the lower areas. Four were struck on oversize planchets to see what the design would look like if moved farther in from the rim, as requested by the Hobbs Manufacturing Co., which was developing a coin-detecting device for use in vending machines. The large planchets allowed the use of regular dies, thus saving the expense of cutting new hubs and dies.[2] Two are in the Smithsonian Institution, one was melted, and the fourth went to Secretary of the Treasury Franklin MacVeagh. • Nickel alloy • Rarity-8

Judd-1954—Regular Indian Head / Buffalo 1913 Type II dies, but in a copper alloy. Owned by Eric P. Newman, who acquired it from the Colonel E.H.R. Green estate along with the five 1913 Liberty Head nickels. • Copper alloy • Unique

APOCRYPHA AND CURIOSA RELATED TO PATTERN NICKELS

The varieties listed below are of private manufacture as described, but are of interest in connection with the nickel series.

1938 "pattern" of the Schlag design—In 2003, the Gallery Mint in Eureka Springs, Arkansas, created new dies to reproduce Felix O. Schlag's 1938 designs, except with different lettering. These were made in Proof and satin finishes to the announced quantities of 1,938 each, and were sold through the Full Step Nickel Club and elsewhere.

1965 "pattern" Martha Washington design—In 1965, the Mint created dies for "tokens" matching the diameter of currently circulating coins so that various metal alloys and substitutes, particularly for the silver denominations, could be tested in the private sector. On the obverse, the dies, designed by Edward Groves, depict a right profile portrait of Martha Washington, the date 1759, and the inscription MARTHA / WASHINGTON. The reverse shows a corner view of Mount Vernon, the inscription HOME OF THE WASHINGTON FAMILY around the border, and the words MOUNT VERNON below the building. In August 2004, Lot 899 of the Superior Galleries' sale offered a "Martha Washington nickel," which was the diameter of a nickel and struck in an alloy resembling that used for the nickel five-cent piece. In March 2005, American Numismatic Rarities auctioned this same coin. Saul Teichman suggests that this piece was struck in the 1980s to test the Schuler coin press. No change in design or composition of the nickel five-cent piece was contemplated at that time.

NOTES

Chapter 1

1. *A Guide Book of Shield and Liberty Head Nickels* (Atlanta, GA, Whitman Publishing, 2006) contains a four-part series of galleries, each illustrating nickel-using machines and businesses.

Chapter 2

1. Certain of the minting, grading, and other information is similar to that in *A Guide Book of Shield and Liberty Head Nickels*, here with different illustrations and with adaptations to suit the Buffalo and Jefferson series.

Chapter 3

1. Communication, July 30, 2005.

Chapter 4

1. For extensive correspondence, Treasury commentary, etc., beyond the scope of what is given here, refer to the introductory material in *The Complete Guide to Buffalo Nickels* (David W. Lange, 2002).
2. As quoted by Michael Wescott in *The United States Nickel Five-Cent Piece: A Date-by-Date Analysis and History*, 1991, pp. 87–88. I picked up the Black Diamond story and repeated it, this before acquiring the Van Ryzin study (a gift from the author in 2005). Future writing on the subject will be different!
3. Roger W. Burdette, communication to the author, December 10, 2005; information from National Archives data.
4. Lange, *Complete Guide to Buffalo Nickels*, p. 13.
5. Wescott, *Nickel Five-Cent Piece*, p. 97.
6. *Twisted Tails: Sifted Fact, Fantasy and Fiction From U.S. Coin History*, 1995, p. 41.
7. A different chief from Two *Moons* (see Roger W. Burdette, *Renaissance of American Coinage, 1908–1913*, manuscript copy), the incorrect usage being popular in numismatic texts.
8. See Van Ryzin, *Twisted Tails*, pp. 34 and 222. It is not known where this Fraser comment first appeared.
9. *The Numismatist*, March 1913.
10. Letter provided by Roger W. Burdette from the National Archives.
11. Letter furnished by Roger W. Burdette, part of his research in the National Archives for the book *Renaissance of American Coinage, 1909–1913*.
12. *The Numismatist*, August 1934, under news of that club.
13. As quoted by Wescott, *Nickel Five-Cent Piece*, p. 101.
14. Mrs. Fraser, letter of April 17, 1964, as quoted by Wescott, *Nickel Five-Cent Piece*, p. 94.
15. Letter copy to the author by Roger W. Burdette. Much detailed information about 20th-century designs will be included in books already issued or now being prepared by Burdette.
16. *Walter Breen's Complete Encyclopedia of U.S. and Colonial Coins*, 1988, p. 257.
17. *The Complete Guide to Buffalo Nickels*, p. 17.
18. The correct location should have been stated as the Central Park Zoo, not the New York Zoological Garden (popularly known as the Bronx Zoo).

Chapter 5

1. The wording of these notes is from the *Official ANA Grading Standards for United States Coins* (sixth edition), and may differ slightly from the present text.
2. Correspondence, 2004, and Ron Pope's survey results from checking thousands of coins.
3. "Abe Kosoff Remembers," *Coin World*, December 13, 1967.
4. Communication to the author, May 2005.
5. Oscar G. Schilke to the author, circa 1962.

Chapter 6

1. The Complete Guide to Buffalo Nickels, p. 17.
2. Ibid.
3. J.P. Martin, "ANA Authentication Bureau, Authenticating the 1918/7-D Nickel," *The Numismatist*, January 1997.
4. In *The Numismatist*, November 1992, in the article "No Worse for Wear," David W. Lange described these pieces as being "special," but stopped short of calling them Proofs. At present in American numismatics, the term *specimen* has no universally agreed-upon definition.
5. R.W. Julian, cited by Lange, *Complete Guide to Buffalo Nickels*.

Chapter 7

1. Most 1938 citations are from Don Taxay, *U.S. Mint and Coinage*, 1966.
2. Hollywood *Citizen News* as quoted by Taxay, *U.S. Mint and Coinage*.
3. Wescott, *Nickel Five-Cent Piece*, p. 130.
4. File received by the author from the National Archives, July 29, 2004. With partner J.A. Casaletta, Rotundo operated the Modern Studio, photographers at 675 Bleecker Street, Utica, New York.
5. H.H. Amason, *Sculpture by Houdon: A Loan Exhibition* (Worcester, MA, 1964), p. 104, as cited by Cornelius Vermeule in *Numismatic Art in America, Aesthetics of the United States Coinage*, 1971, pp. 206–207.
6. This transcript was furnished to me by *Coin World*'s Margo Russell, who attended the Schlag presentation, and was used in my *United States Three-Cent and Five-Cent Pieces*, 1985. The text or a version of it appeared earlier under the title "Felix Schlag Captures Audience During Forum," *Coin World*, September 2, 1964. It is used here by later permission (2005). A similar transcript was published in *The Numismatist*, January 1965.
7. R.W. Julian, "Interest in Jefferson Nickels Revitalized," *Numismatic News*, May 18, 2004.
8. Certain information concerning design modifications is from Bernard Nagengast, correspondence with the author, various dates; from his books and studies submitted for use in the present text; and from his article "Jefferson Nickel Design Changes," *Coin World*, February 28, 1979. Other information is specifically attributed in notes.
9. Mark A. Benvenuto, "The War Nickel: Metal Saver or Morale Booster?" *The Numismatist*, March 2000.
10. *The Numismatist*, February 1966, p. 165.
11. Certain information concerning this and the keelboat-design nickel is from a series of articles by Paul Gilkes in *Coin World*, 2004, and contributions by various authors in *Numismatic News*. Coverage by these two publications has been continuous.
12. Information sources include R.W. Julian, *Medals of the United States Mint: The First Century 1892*, 1977, p. 33.
13. *Numismatic News*, August 3, 2004, "Keelboat Nickel Release Planned."
14. See Bowers, *A Guide Book of Washington and State Quarter Dollars*, 2006, for extensive details of the designs and critiques of them.
15. Paul Gilkes, "Designers at Mint: AIP Designers to Have Initials on Coins, Medals They Design," *Coin World*, February 29, 2004.
16. Paul Gilkes, "Fore Years at Mint: Former Mint Director Reflects on Her Four Years Serving Collectors, Public," *Coin World*, September 5, 2005.
17. Paul Gilkes, "Mint Sells 25 Million Bison 5¢" and "New Bison 5¢ Debuts," *Coin World*, March 21, 2005. The accounts covered the launch ceremony and the first four days of sales.
18. From the Lewis and Clark Journals as quoted by *Smithsonian*, November 2005.
19. "New Nickel" announcement, CNN, February 23, 2005.

Chapter 8

1. The wording of these notes is from the *Official ANA Grading Standards* and may differ slightly from the present text.
2. "NGC Adds to Nickels," *Numismatic News*, February 17, 2004.

Chapter 9

1. Reported by Bob Salawasser and published in *Coin World*, May 11, 1983, p. 82.
2. Also see the monograph "The Counterfeit 1944 Jefferson Nickel," by Dwight H. Stuckey.
3. *COINage*, August 1973, covered the presentation ceremony.
4. Mark Powell, "Top 10 Rarest Full Step Nickels," *The Portico* (January–February 2005).
5. Dave Andreas, "Step by Step," *The Portico* (July–August 2003).
6. "Mint Made, Caught Additional Mules," *Coin World* (November 3, 2003).

Appendix C

1. Fred Weinberg to the author, January 2005. Photographs by Douglas Plasencia of American Numismatic Rarities.
2. Roger W. Burdette, Renaissance of American Coinage, 1908–1913, manuscript copy.

SELECTED BIBLIOGRAPHY

Altman, Charles I. "History of the United States Nickel Five-Cent Piece," *The Numismatist*, January 1949.

ANACS Domestic Population Report. Austin, TX: Various issues.

Annual Report of the Director of the Mint, Various years, especially 1912 to date.

Benvenuto, Mark A. "The War Nickel: Metal Saver or Morale Booster?" *The Numismatist*, March 2000.

Bonser, Don. "The Collector's Edge: Buffalo Nickel Die Varieties," *The Numismatist*, November 1991.

Bowers, Q. David. *The History of United States Coinage as Illustrated by the Garrett Collection*. Los Angeles, CA: Bowers and Ruddy Galleries, 1979; later printings by Bowers and Merena Galleries, Inc., Wolfeboro, NH.

———. *Abe Kosoff: Dean of Numismatics*. Wolfeboro, NH: Bowers and Ruddy Galleries, 1985.

———. *United States Three-Cent and Five-Cent Pieces*. Wolfeboro, NH: Bowers and Ruddy Galleries, 2005.

Breen, Walter H. *Walter Breen's Encyclopedia of U.S. and Colonial Proof Coins, 1792–1977*. Albertson, New York: FCI Press, 1977; updated, Wolfeboro, NH: Bowers and Merena Galleries, forthcoming.

———. *Walter Breen's Complete Encyclopedia of U.S. and Colonial Coins*. New York: Doubleday, Inc., new edition forthcoming.

Bressett, Kenneth E., and Q. David Bowers. *The Official American Numismatic Association Grading Standards for United States Coins*. 6th ed. Atlanta, GA: Whitman Publishing, LLC, 2005.

Burdette, Roger W. *Renaissance of American Coinage 1909–1915* (manuscript scheduled for publication in 2006; includes a detailed examination of the origin, design, and original production of the 1913 nickel by Fraser).

Certified Coin Dealer Newsletter, Torrance, California, 2000 to date.

Coin Dealer Newsletter, Torrance, California, 1963 to date.

Coin World Almanac. Sidney, OH: Coin World, 2000.

Coin World, Sidney, OH: Amos Press, 1960 to date.

Doty, Richard. *America's Money, America's Story*. Iola, WI: Krause Publications, 1998.

Fivaz, Bill, and J.T. Stanton. *The Cherrypickers' Guide to Rare Die Varieties*, 4th ed., vol. 1. Savannah, GA: Stanton Books & Supplies, Inc., 2000.

Flynn, Kevin, and John Wexler. *Over Mintmarks and Hot Repunched Mintmarks*. Brooklyn, NY: Brooklyn Galleries Coins & Stamps, Inc., 2003.

A Guide Book of United States Coins. Racine, WI: Western Publishing Co.; Atlanta, GA: Whitman Publishing, LLC, various modern editions.

Judd, J. Hewitt, M.D. *United States Pattern, Experimental and Trial Pieces*. 8th ed. Atlanta, GA: Whitman Publishing, LLC, 2003.

———. *United States Pattern Coins*. 9th ed. Atlanta, GA: Whitman Publishing, LLC, 2005.

Kosoff, Abe. "Abe Kosoff Remembers" column in *Coin World*, various issues.

Lange, David W. "Grading Buffalo Nickels," *The Numismatist*, September 1996.

———. "Grading Jefferson Nickels," *The Numismatist*, April 1997.

———. *The Complete Guide to Buffalo Nickels*, Virginia Beach, VA, 2000. (Basic foundational reference for this specialty.)

Martin, J.P. "ANA Authentication Bureau: Authenticating the 1918/7-D Nickel," *The Numismatist*, January 1997.

Nagengast, Bernard. "Jefferson Nickel Design Changes," *Coin World*, February 28, 1979.

———. *The Jefferson Nickel Analyst*. 2nd ed. Sidney, OH, 2002. (Basic foundational reference for this specialty.)

Numismatic Guaranty Corporation of America Census Report. Sarasota, FL: Numismatic Guaranty Corporation of America, various issues.

Numismatic News. Iola, WI: Krause Publications, 1952 to date.

Numismatist, The. The American Numismatic Association. Colorado Springs, CO (and other addresses), 1888 to date.

PCGS Population Report. Newport Beach, CA. Professional Coin Grading Service, Various issues.

Portico, The. Journal of the Full Step Nickel Club, Burbank, CA, Darrell Crane, editor. Various issues.

Pollock, Andrew W. *United States Pattern Coins and Related Pieces*. Wolfeboro, NH: Bowers and Merena Galleries, 1994.

Ratzman, Leonard J. "The Buffalo Nickel, A 50-Year-Old Mystery," *Whitman Numismatic Journal*, May–June 1964.

Raymond, Wayte. *Standard Catalogue of United States Coins and Paper Money* (titles vary). Scott Stamp & Coin Co. (and others): New York, 1934 to 1957 editions.

Sanders, Mitch. "Houdon and U.S. Coin Design," *The Numismatist*, March 2000.

Stride, H.G. *Nickel for Coinage*. London: Hutchinson & Co., Ltd., 1964

Taxay, Don. *U.S. Mint and Coinage*. New York City, NY: Arco Publishing, 1966.

———. *The Comprehensive Catalogue and Encyclopedia of United States Coins*. New York: Scott Publications, 1970.

Treasury Department, United States Mint, *et al. Annual Report of the Director of the Mint*. 1912 onward.

Van Ryzin, Robert R. *Twisted Tails: Sifted Fact, Fantasy and Fiction from U.S. Coin History*. Iola, WI: Krause Publications, 1995.

Vermeule, Cornelius. *Numismatic Art in America*. Cambridge, MA: Belknap Press, Harvard, 1971.

Wescott, Michael. *The United States Nickel Five-Cent Piece: A Date-by-Date Analysis and History*. Wolfeboro, NH: Bowers and Merena Galleries, 1991.

Wexler, John A., and Brian A. Ribar. *The Best of the Jefferson Nickel Doubled Die Varieties*. 2nd edition. Brooklyn, NY: Brooklyn Galleries Coins & Stamps, Inc., 2002.

Wexler, John A., Ron Pope, and Kevin Flynn. *Treasure Hunting Buffalo Nickels*. Savannah, GA: Stanton Printing & Publishing, 1999.

Wiles, James. *The Jefferson Nickel RPM Book: An Attribution and Pricing Guide*. Savannah, GA: Stanton Printing & Publishing, 2002.

INDEX

Danek, Charles, 154
denticle, defined, 1
Denver Mint, 17, 18
design competitions
    for 2005 issues, 153–158
    to replace Buffalo design, 127–129
Details System, 59–60, 60–61
dies
    anvil, 13
    doubled, 77, 168
    hammer, 13
    hub, 167–168
    making, 8–10
    preparation of Indian Head / Buffalo, 42
    Proof, 15
    relapped, 77–78
    spacing of, 14, 174–175
    tired, 67, 175
    working, 8

electrotype, 9
errors, Mint. *See appendix B*
Everhard, Don, 154, 158
Extremely Fine (EF) grade, defined
    for Indian Head / Buffalo nickels, 54
    for Jefferson nickels, 164
eye appeal, 67
    for Indian Head / Buffalo nickels, 69–70
    for Jefferson nickels, 179

field populations, methodology for estimating, iv
fin, 14
"Fine" grade, defined
    for Indian Head / Buffalo nickels, 55
    for Jefferson nickels, 165
Fitzgerald, Joe, 154, 157, 159
Franki, Jamie N., 155, 158, 159
Fraser, James Earle, x, 31–33, 259
Fraser, Laura Gardin, 34
Full Details (FD), 22–23, 59–60
    rarity of Buffalo nickels with, 61–66
    reason for scarcity of, 12–13
    See also Details System; Full Steps (FS)
Fullingim, Sharon, 157
Full Steps (FS), 24, 166–167, 169–170
    defined, 144
    values for 5 vs. 6, 181
    See also Full Details (FD); partial steps

Gamble, Susan, 157, 158
gambling machines, 5, 6, 7
"Good" grade, defined
    for Indian Head / Buffalo nickels, 55
    for Jefferson nickels, 165
grades, numerical, 27–30
    for Indian Head / Buffalo nickels, 68–69
    for Jefferson nickels, 178–179
    in transition, 56–57